THE UNFINISHED WAR IN AFGHANISTAN

2001-2014

THE UNFINISHED WAR IN AFGHANISTAN 2001-2014

Vishal Chandra

idsa
INSTITUTE FOR DEFENCE STUDIES & ANALYSES
NEW DELHI

PENTAGON PRESS

The Unfinished War in Afghanistan: 2001-2014
By Vishal Chandra

First Published in 2015

ISBN 978-81-8274-762-3

Published by
PENTAGON PRESS
206, Peacock Lane, Shahpur Jat,
New Delhi-110049
Phones: 011-64706243, 26491568
Telefax: 011-26490600
email: rajan@pentagonpress.in
website: www.pentagonpress.in

Branch:
Prime Arcade
Office #11
1154 Saifee Street
Opp. M.G.Road, Camp
Pune-411001
Email: pentagonpresspune@gmail.com

In association with
Institute for Defence Studies and Analyses
No. 1, Development Enclave,
New Delhi-110010
Phone: +91-11-26717983
Website: www.idsa.in

Printed at Avantika Printers Private Limited.

Dedicated
to
Buddhas of Bamiyan

*BUDDHA,**

Listen to my voice,
That rolls, reflects and echoes in the sad and broken valleys of your land,

Buddha,
Listen to my voice, as I murmur your pain that is closely woven into mine,

Buddha,
Listen to my tale of senseless and insane destruction of a civilization,

Buddha,
Bear with me, as I tell you the tales of terror, fear and horror of your land,
As I tell you the saga of helpless Afghans,
As I mourn the tragedy of your destruction, and the fall of a great nation,

Buddha,
Your ruins and my head both did not crunch the thirst of barbarians,
How ridiculous that your silent, peaceful existence and my spark of ideas and logic,
Posed a deadly threat to THEIR hollow, poisonous existence!

Buddha,
Your ashes and my beheaded body,
Went unnoticed and forgotten,
Just like the death of thousands before you and after me,
In the precious land, sadly ruled by ignorant unruly.

Buddha,
Your place is empty,
Like an eye drawn from its socket,
When my mother went blind,
As she sobbed herself to sleep each night with the vision of my beheaded body.

Buddha,
Your destruction will always remind mankind of the suffering,
Of women beaten, men beheaded, and children imprisoned.

Buddha,
Though your tenacious statue is no more,
We can declare with pride, honour, and glory,
That Buddha suffered alongside his people to ensure,
The world witnessed and will remember forever the agony of the Afghan nation.

Buddha,
I know that You wanted to be no more because of intolerable savagery,
That You longed for ending the endless pain that you felt in your nation,

---

* Lina Rozbih-Haidari, "The Fallen Buddha Statues in Bamiyan," *Diplomatic Courier*, March 03, 2012.

Buddha,
They tell us You intended to fall in the land of lunies,
Not as a gesture of surrender and submission,
But as a rebellious voice of voiceless,

Against,

Oppression,
Tyranny,
Injustice,
Cruelty,
Ignorance,

And SHAME!

—Lina Rozbih-Haidari
Afghan journalist & poet

Contents

Foreword

Political stability in Afghanistan is critical to regional peace. Unfortunately, the efforts of the international community to bring peace to Afghanistan have not succeeded so far. For more than a decade, the US-led international forces have been fighting a resurgent Taliban without much success. In fact, the Taliban appear to go from strength to strength, while the international forces are withdrawing from Afghanistan trying to convince themselves that they are going to leave at a time when Afghanistan has become a much better place than when they came in.

The truth remains that the new Afghanistan that they have ushered in is not established enough to survive on its own. The 'unfinished war', which the title of the book alludes to, is threatening to engulf Afghanistan as the international forces are leaving the country. The reconciliation processes being attempted at various levels to persuade the Taliban to join the process have failed, and the latter are perhaps waiting in patience to retake Kabul by all means and put an end to the Afghan experiment with democracy.

Against this backdrop, the book attempts a wholesome analysis of the processes that led to a new experiment with representative system in Afghanistan, the successes and failures of the Afghan Government, the nature of internal politics, the role of the warlords, the re-emergence of the Taliban, the capabilities as well as the constraints of the Afghan National Security Forces (ANSF), the limits of the reconciliation efforts, the post-withdrawal commitments of the international community, and the role of the regional countries in Afghanistan. The conclusions drawn in the book by the author are far from optimistic. They are informed by a realistic assessment of the ground situation and indicate that Afghanistan is poised for greater socio-political turmoil in the coming years.

The author, Vishal Chandra, has consulted a variety of primary and secondary source materials, research papers, books and reports, and has undertaken field trips to Afghanistan, to ascertain the views from the ground and enrich his study. The study was subjected to anonymous review by acknowledged experts and revised as per the suggestions offered by them. At its present shape, it provides a useful overview of the evolving situation in Afghanistan. It critiques the Western engagement in Afghanistan as fragile and points to the confusion and bewilderment that characterise it. Its prognosis of ethnic polarisation and protracted war based on the author's perception of re-emergence of old patterns of conflict in the country may be disturbing, but worth a read for anybody seeking to understand the Afghan maze. As an Indian scholar, he has analysed the Indian engagement in the process of Afghan reconstruction, possible options for India in the post-withdrawal phase; and has recommended that India must take a long-term view and stay engaged in Afghanistan, even in the worst case scenario.

I hope the book will be appreciated by the strategic community in India and abroad, and add to the emerging literature on the subject.

Dr. Arvind Gupta
Director General
Institute for Defence Studies & Analyses
New Delhi

Acknowledgements

This book comes exactly at the end of my decade long research on Afghanistan at the Institute for Defence Studies and Analyses (IDSA) in New Delhi. It is by no means a culmination of my research on Afghanistan; rather, it is part of my constant and a continuing endeavour to understand some of the perceptibly most intricate and inescapable socio-political realities of the Afghan conflict. Studying Afghanistan, its evolution and development through the cross-currents of history, formation and transformation of its complex social and political identities, the various nuances of its ever dynamic politics, has not been a mere professional pursuit for me. All these years, it has been something much more, something I almost lived with. Yet, I feel I have a long way to go before I could really fathom the depth of what could be regarded as the defining core of what we simply refer to as Afghan (-istan). My interest and curiosity has only grown with time. This book arguably still has several gaps and shortcomings which I ardently seek to address and compensate in my future research and publications on Afghanistan.

In pursuance of this book, I received support, guidance and motivation from various people. This book would not have been possible without the support and encouragement of Dr. Arvind Gupta, the Director General of IDSA, and Brig. (Retd.) Rumel Dahiya, the Deputy Director General. I am particularly thankful to my senior colleague Dr. Ashok Kumar Behuria (Coordinator of the South Asia Centre, to which I belong), for patiently perusing through the draft of the book and offering his critical inputs in a very independent manner. Here, I also wish to express my gratitude to the anonymous reviewers for offering their valuable inputs on the preliminary draft of the book.

In retrospect, I particularly wish to acknowledge Mr. K. Santhanam, former Director General IDSA, for encouraging and valuing specialised research on Afghanistan. My sincere gratitude also goes to former Deputy Directors Cmde. (Retd.) C. Uday Bhaskar and particularly Ambassador Virendra Gupta, whose holistic and dynamic approach gave an entirely new direction to our research on South Asia by initiating the Neighbourhood Studies Programme, with active provision for field visits. Having spent a decade with IDSA, I humbly wish to remember and thank all my former and current colleagues, who have in their own ways contributed to my research endeavours.

I am particularly indebted to my Institute for facilitating my field visits, which gave me an invaluable opportunity to have a first hand view of the amazing diversity and plurality in Afghan life and thinking. My interaction with countless Afghans, a cross-section of Afghan people from diverse walks of life, during my visits to the country and especially in the provinces, has over the years helped me in understanding the unique political and diverse cultural setting of Afghan life. There are several names from Afghanistan that crowds and rushes across my mind when it comes to acknowledging their contribution in enhancing my personal understanding of the Afghan situation. Though it is not possible to individually acknowledge each of them here; nevertheless, I remain indebted to them for all their assistance and particularly for sharing their personal views and perceptions. Similarly, interaction with several internationally acclaimed scholars on the subject at numerous conferences and academic platforms that I attended, from Singapore to Stockholm and Tashkent to Istanbul, has also contributed to my overall understanding of the concerns and perceptions about Afghanistan, both at the regional and wider international levels.

I am also indebted to the teaching faculty and staff at the Centre for Russian and Central Asian Studies at the School of International Studies in Jawaharlal Nehru University (JNU), New Delhi, especially Prof. Shams-ud Din, Late (Prof.) Shashikant Jha, and Prof. Devendra Kaushik, for initiating me into the realm of area studies. My special thanks to Associate Professors Dr Sanjay Kumar Pandey and Dr Bhaswati Sarkar for their encouragement during my early days of research at JNU. I must also mention the JNU Central Library, where I did some of my first readings on Afghanistan as a university researcher.

During the writing of this book, I greatly benefited from the wonderful library at IDSA. The staff at IDSA Library has been extremely supportive and provided me with relevant study materials as and when needed. In fact, I must thank the entire administrative staff at IDSA led by Assistant Director Ms. Hemlata Lohani, including those who have left or have completed their services. My sincere thanks to Col. (Retd.) Ravi Sikri, Ms. Ameeta Narang, Mr. Ramesh Kumar Arora, Mr. I.P. Singh, Mr. R.C. Sharma, Ms. Sebi Jolly, Ms. Aparna Krishna, Ms. Suman Chhabra, Mr. Pushkar Pathak, Ms. Sindhu Joshi, Mr. Mukesh Dabas, Late (Mr.) B.M. Mathew, Mr. Ashutosh Mishra, Ms. Rashmi Thomas, Ms. Jatinder Kaur, Ms. Sudesh Bhatia, Ms. Gowri Bhaskar, Mr. Bhookan Singh, Mr. Yogesh Bharadwaj, Mr. Pitambar Dutt, Ms. Kamlesh Verma, Late (Mr.) Dharam Pal Sharma, Mr. Rajkumar Tripathi, Mr. Pardeep Negi, Mr. Sanjeev Kumar, Ms. Deepika Sharma, Mr. Virender Singh Rawat, Mr. Santosh Kumar, Mr. Surender

Jagariya, Mr. Ramesh Chand, Mr. Babu Lal, Mr. Mukesh Jha, Mr. Manohar Lal, Mr. Dharajeet, Mr. Rohit Sharma, Mr. Raj Kiran and others.

The biggest strength in the journey of this book came from my wife, Lovely my ultimate companion. She gave me great strength in times of great despair, and showed wonderful understanding and patience when it came to taking care of various responsibilities which should have been mine. As a proud father of two little daughters – Varenya and Araadhya – I with great admiration acknowledge their quiet contribution in the completion and publication of this book. They have been my constant companion in the journey of this book. Perhaps, the greatest of all my acknowledgements here goes to my ever loving parents - *Amma* and *Papa* – for their kindest blessings and boundless affection. I am ever grateful to them for making me worth this life. I also wish to acknowledge the contribution of my brother and his family, particularly Kartikey, my nephew.

I would also like to thank my colleague in the publication division, Mr. Vivek Kaushik, who ensured timely refereeing and copy-editing of the manuscript of this book; and Mr. Vivek Dhankar, G.I.S. Technical Officer at IDSA, for helping me with maps for this book. Last but not the least, I wish to place my special thanks to the publisher, the Pentagon Press, for bringing out this book in a thorough professional manner.

I present my first book to the interested readers with a hope that it would contribute to the ongoing debate and discourse on the future of a country, which at once seems so familiar and yet remains so unknown. This book, which comes at a time when Afghanistan is again at a critical juncture of history and future, hope and despair, is admittedly a work in progress. Several sections of this book have been drawn from my earlier publications on Afghanistan; and, an attempt has been made here to put together the past and present course of primarily key internal dimensions of the Afghan conflict and war, beginning with the end of the Taliban regime in December 2001, in a broader future perspective.

Any lapse in the accuracy of factual details or error in attribution is inadvertent, unintentional, and humbly mine.

New Delhi **Vishal Chandra**

Abbreviations

AAF	Afghan Air Force
AEA	Afghanistan Electoral Alliance
AEPA	Afghanistan Eastern People's Alliance
Af-Pak	Afghanistan-Pakistan
AGT	Afghanistan Green Trend
AIA	Afghan Interim Authority/Administration
AIHRC	Afghanistan Independent Human Rights Commission
AISA	Afghanistan Investment Support Agency
AIT	Advanced Individual Training
ALP	Afghan Local Police
AMF	Afghan Military Force
AN	Afghanistan Naween
ANA	Afghan National Army
ANAA	Association of National Amity of Afghanistan
ANAAC	Afghan National Army Air Corps
ANAOA	Afghan National Army Officer Academy
ANATC	Afghan National Army Training Command
ANDS	Afghanistan National Development Strategy
ANP	Afghan National Police
ANSF	Afghan National Security Forces
APEC	Asia-Pacific Economic Cooperation
APPF	Afghan Public Protection Force
APRP	Afghan Peace & Reintegration Programme
ARSIC	Afghan Regional Security Integration Command
ARTF	Afghan Reconstruction Trust Fund
ASFF	Afghan Security Forces Fund

ATA	Afghan Transitional Authority/Administration
BAG	Budget Activity Group
BSA	Bilateral Security Agreement
CARs	Central Asian Republics
CASA	Central Asia-South Asia
CCAP	Coordination Council of Arab People
CCTV	China Central Television
CDU	Christian Democratic Union
CENTCOM	Central Command
CFC-A	Combined Forces Command-Afghanistan
CGSC	Command and General Staff College
CIA	Central Intelligence Agency
CJTF	Combined Joint Task Force
CLJ	Constitutional Loya Jirga
CNPC	China National Petroleum Corporation
CPC	Communist Party of China
CPD	Combat Plans Division
CRI	China Radio International
CSTC-A	Combined Security Transition Command-Afghanistan
CSTO	Collective Security Treaty Organisation
CTWG	Counter Terrorism Working Group
DDR	Disarmament, Demobilisation & Reintegration
DEA	Drug Enforcement Administration (United States of America)
DIA	Defence Intelligence Agency
DIAG	Disarmament of Illegal Armed Groups
ECC	Electoral Complaints Commission
ELJ	Emergency Loya Jirga
ETIM	East Turkistan Islamic Movement
ETT	Embedded Liaison Team
FATA	Federally Administered Tribal Area
FDCS	Federal Drug Control Service
FDI	Foreign Direct Investment
FSKN	Federal Drug Control Service (Russian Federation)
GAO	Government Accountability Office
HPC	High Peace Council
IEC	Independent Election Commission
IED	Improvised Explosive Device
IJC	ISAF Joint Command

IMU	Islamic Movement of Uzbekistan (now Islamic Movement of Turkistan)
IPP	Islamic People's Party
IRGC	Islamic Revolutionary Guards Corps
IRNA	Islamic Republic News Agency
ISAF	International Security Assistance Force
ISI	Inter-Services Intelligence
ISIS	Islamic State of Iraq and Syria
IUAM	Islamic Union of Afghan Mujahideen
JEMB	Joint Electoral Management Body
JTM	Jabha-e Tafahom-e Melli
JUI	Jamiat-ul Ulema-e Islam
KMTC	Kabul Military Training Centre
LAS	Light Air Support
MANPADS	Man-Portable Air Defence Systems
MAT	Military Advisory Team
MCIT	Ministry of Communications and Information Technology
MMA	Muttahida Majlis-e Amal
MoD	Ministry of Defence
MoU	Memorandum of Understanding
NA	Northern Alliance
NATO	North Atlantic Treaty Organisation
NCA	National Coalition of Afghanistan
NCO	Non Commissioned Officer
NCPJ	National Consultative Peace Jirga
NDN	Northern Distribution Network
NDS	National Directorate of Security
NFA	National Front of Afghanistan (Jabha-e Milli)
NFP	National Front Party
NMA	National Movement of Afghanistan
NMAA	National Military Academy of Afghanistan
NRC	NATO-Russia Council
NTM-A	NATO Training Mission-Afghanistan
NWFP	North West Frontier Province (renamed as Khyber Pukhtunkhwa)
OCC	Operation Coordination Centre
OEF	Operation Enduring Freedom
OIC	Organisation of Islamic Cooperation (formerly Organisation of the Islamic Conference)

OMC-A	Office of Military Cooperation-Afghanistan
OMLT	Operational and Mentoring Liaison Team
OSC-A	Office of Security Cooperation-Afghanistan
OSCE	Organisation for Security and Co-operation in Europe
PAT	Police Advisory Team
PBAS	Programme Budget Accounting System
PDPA	People's Democratic Party of Afghanistan
PRC	People's Republic of China
PRT	Provincial Reconstruction Team
PTS	Programme Takhim-e Solh
RCAC	Regional Corps Advisory Command
RECCA	Regional Economic Cooperation Conference on Afghanistan
RFE/RL	Radio Free Europe/Radio Liberty
SAARC	South Asian Association for Regional Cooperation
SAG	Sub budget Activity Group
SCO	Shanghai Cooperation Organisation
SDPs	Small Development Projects
SNTV	Single Non-Transferable Voting
SoFA	Status of Force Agreement
SPA	Strategic Partnership Agreement
TAPI	Turkmenistan, Afghanistan, Pakistan and India
TNSM	Tahrik-e Nifaz Shariat-e Muhammadi
TTP	Tehrik-e Taliban Pakistan
UK	United Kingdom
UN	United Nations
UNAMA	United Nations Assistance Mission in Afghanistan
UNDP	United Nations Development Programme
UNHCR	United Nations High Commissioner of Refugees
UNODC	United Nations Office on Drugs & Crime
UNSC	United Nations Security Council
US	United States
USAID	US Agency for International Development
USSR	Union of Soviet Socialist Republics
WMD	Weapon of Mass Destruction
ZTE	Zhong Xing Telecommunication Equipment Company Limited

List of Tables and Maps

(A) Tables

(B) Maps

Map 1: Afghanistan and its Immediate Neighbours

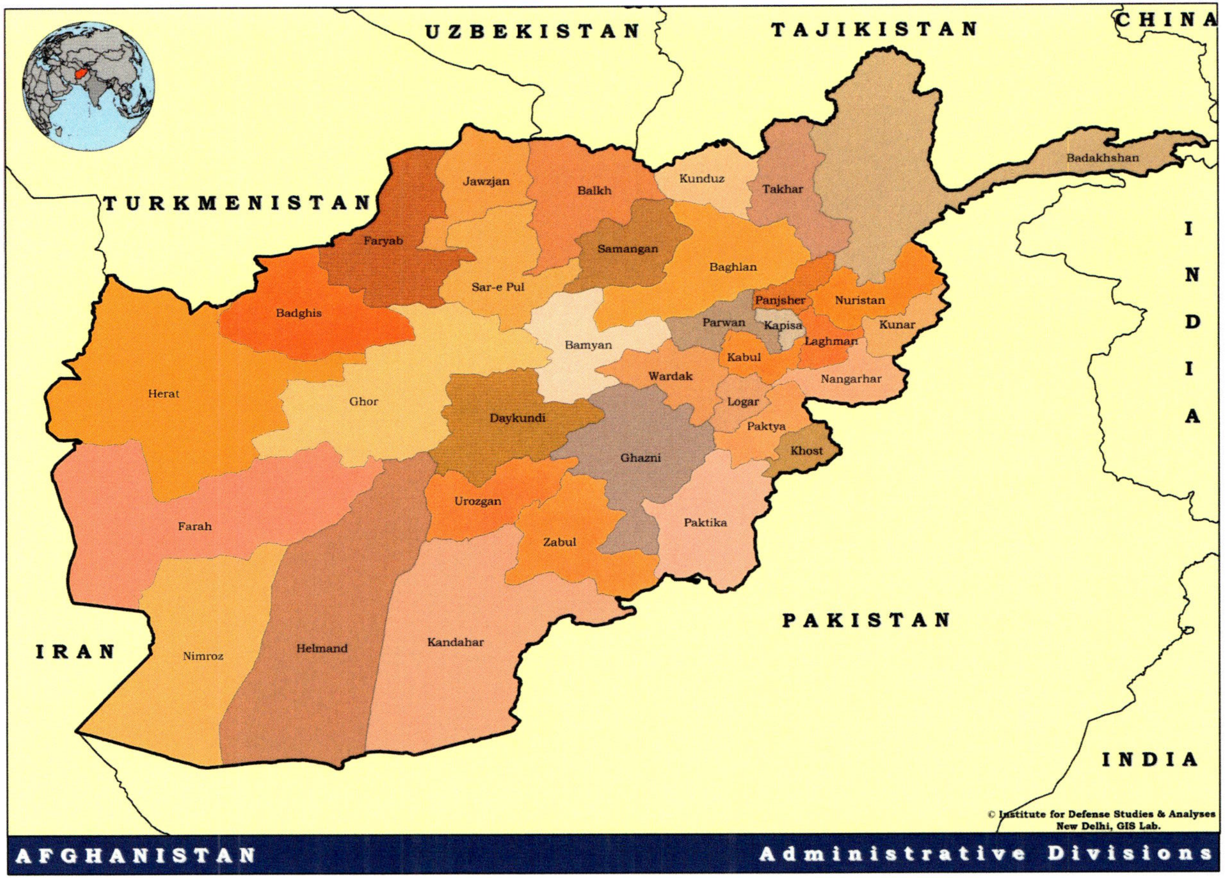

Courtesy: *GIS Lab, Institute for Defence Studies and Analyses, New Delhi*

Afghanistan: Key Socio-Economic Indicators

Total Area	652,230 sq km
Land Boundaries	5,529 km Pakistan 2,430 km, Tajikistan 1,206 km, Iran 936 km, Turkmenistan 744 km, Uzbekistan 137 km, China 76 km
Natural Resources	Natural gas, petroleum, coal, copper, chromite, talc, barites, sulphur, lead, zinc, iron ore, salt, precious and semiprecious stones
Land Use	Arable land: 11.95 % Permanent crops: 0.18% Other: 87.87% (2011)
Ethnic Groups	Pashtun 42% Tajik 27% Hazara 9% Uzbek 9% Aimak 4% Turkmen 3% Baloch 2% Other 4%
Languages	50% Afghan Persian or Dari (official) 35% Pashto (official) 11% Turkic languages (primarily Uzbek and Turkmen) 04% 30 minor languages (primarily Balochi and Pashai) Much bilingualism, but Dari functions as the lingua franca
Religions	Sunni Muslim 80%, Shia Muslim 19%, other 1%
Population	31,822,848 (July 2014 est.)

Age Structure	0-14 years: 42% (male 6,793,832/female 6,579,388) 15-24 years: 22.2% (male 3,600,264/female 3,464,781) 25-54 years: 29.4% (male 4,771,323/female 4,586,963) 55-64 years: 2.5% (male 603,197/female 622,539) 65 years and over: 2.5% (male 371,753/female 428,808) (2014 est.)
Population Growth Rate	2.29% (2014 est.)
Urbanization	Urban population: 23.5% of total population (2011) Rate of urbanization: 4.41% annual rate of change (2010-15 est.)
Sex Ratio	At birth: 1.05 male(s)/female 0-14 years: 1.03 male(s)/female 15-24 years: 1.04 male(s)/female 25-54 years: 1.04 male(s)/female 55-64 years: 1.03 male(s)/female 65 years and over: 0.87 male(s)/female Total population: 1.03 male(s)/female (2014 est.)
Life Expectancy at Birth	Total population: 50.49 years Male: 49.17 years Female: 51.88 years (2014 est.)
Total Fertility Rate	5.43 children born/woman (2014 est.)
Health Expenditures	09.6% of GDP (2011)
Physicians Density	0.19 physicians/1,000 population (2010)
Hospital Bed Density	0.4 beds/1,000 population (2010)
Drinking Water Source	Urban: 85.4% of population Rural: 53% of population Total: 60.6% of population
ECONOMY	
GDP Real Growth Rate	03.1% (2013 est.) 12.5% (2012 est.) 06.1% (2011 est.)
GDP-Per Capita (PPP)	$1,100 (2013 est.) $1,100 (2012 est.) $1,000 (2011 est.)

GDP-Composition, by Sector of Origin	Agriculture: 20% Industry: 25.6% Services: 54.4%
Agriculture Products	Opium, wheat, fruits, nuts; wool, mutton, sheepskins, lambskins
Industries	Small-scale production of bricks, textiles, soap, furniture, shoes, fertilizer, apparel, food-products, non-alcoholic beverages, mineral water, cement; hand woven carpets; natural gas, coal, copper.
Labour Force	7.512 million (2012 est.)
Labour Force-By Occupation	Agriculture: 78.6% Industry: 05.7% Services: 15.7% (FY08/09 est.)
Unemployment Rate	35% (2008 est.) 40% (2005 est.)
Population Below Poverty Line	36% (FY08/09)
Budget	Revenues: $2.333 billion Expenditures: $4.122 billion (2012 est.)
Taxes & Other Revenues	11.3% of GDP (2012 est.)
Inflation Rate (Consumer Prices)	6.8% (2012 est.) 5.7% (2011 est.)
Exports	$376 million (2012 est.) $388.5 million (2011 est.)
Exports-Commodities	Opium, fruits and nuts, handwoven carpets, wool, cotton, hides and pelts, precious and semi-precious gems.
Export Partners	Pakistan 32.2%, India 27%, Tajikistan 8.5%, US 06.2% (2012)
Imports	$06.39 billion (2012 est.) $05.154 billion (2011 est.)
Imports-Commodities	Machinery and other capital goods, food, textiles, petroleum products
Imports – Partners	Pakistan 24.3%, US 18%, Russia 8.7%, India 5.8%, China 5.6%, Germany 4.4% (2012)
Reserves of Foreign Exchange & Gold	$5.983 billion (31 December 2012 est.) $5.268 billion (31 December 2011 est.)
Debt External	$1.28 billion (FY10/11) $2.7 billion (FY08/09)

ENERGY	
Electricity	
Production	986.1 million kWh (2010 est.)
Consumption	2.489 billion kWh (2010 est.)
Imports	1.572 billion kWh (2010 est.)
Installed Generating Capacity	489,100 kW (2010 est.)
From Fossil Fuels	23.5% of total installed capacity (2010 est.)
From Hydroelectric Plants	76.5% of total installed capacity (2010 est.)
From Other Renewable Sources	0% of total installed capacity (2010 est.)
Crude Oil	
Production	1,950 bbl/day (2012 est.)
Exports	0 bbl/day (2010 est.)
Imports	0 bbl/day (2010 est.)
Proved Reserves	NA bbl (1 January 2013 est.)
Refined Petroleum Products	
Production	0 bbl/day (2010 est.)
Consumption	4,229 bbl/day (2011 est.)
Exports	0 bbl/day (2010 est.)
Imports	36,250 bbl/day (2010 est.)
Natural Gas	
Production	140 million cu m (2011 est.)
Consumption	140 million cu m (2010 est.)
Exports	0 cu m (2011 est.)
Imports	0 cu m (2011 est.)
Proved Reserves	49.55 billion cu m (1 January 2013 est.)

COMMUNICATION	
Telephones	
Main Lines	13,500 (2012)
Mobile Cellular	18 million (2012)
Broadcast Media	State-owned broadcaster, Radio Television Afghanistan (RTA), operates a series of radio and television stations in Kabul and the provinces; an estimated 150 private radio stations, 50 TV stations, and about a dozen international broadcasters are available (2007)
Internet Hosts	223 (2012)
Internet Users	1 million (2009)

TRANSPORTATION	
Airports	Total: 52 (2013) With Paved Runways: 23 With Unpaved Runways: 29
Heliports	09 (2013)
Roadways	42,150 km Paved: 12,350 km Unpaved: 29,800 km (2006)
Waterways	1,200 km; (chiefly Amu Darya, which handles vessels up to 500 DWT) (2011)

Source: *Afghanistan—The World Factbook*, Central Intelligence Agency, March 31, 2014, at https://www.cia.gov/library/publications/the-world-factbook/geos/af.html

Introduction

Afghanistan is awaiting another major transition as the US and NATO-led forces drawdown, if not completely withdraw, before ending their longest ever combat mission in December 2014. This has almost coincided with the third round of presidential and parliamentary elections, which are considered as critical for sustaining and consolidating whatever little or more has been achieved since the overthrow of the Taliban regime in 2001. The process of security transition from the Western to the Afghan forces is stated to be "irreversible." Since 2009-10, the Western coalition has been busy revisiting its priorities and formulating an exit strategy almost on an annual basis. Meanwhile, Taliban and its various allies with support from within Pakistan continue to expand their operations beyond their traditional strongholds inside Afghanistan, making the war unsustainable and unviable for the West.

This book is a modest effort to contribute to the ongoing debate on the likely future of Afghanistan as the largest ever coalition of Western forces, after more than a decade of extended deployment, prepares to retreat into history. At the larger geo-political level, more than the Taliban and its various foreign affiliates, it is the Pakistani military and intelligence which has been positioning for a grand bargain in anticipation of a supposedly post-West scenario in Afghanistan. One is inevitably reminded of the Pakistani role in the aftermath of the Geneva Accords of 1988 as former Afghan President Mohammad Najibullah unsuccessfully struggled to put together a national unity government before stepping down in April 1992. The evolving security and political scenario as the Western forces drawdown suggests that elections alone would not help bring stability and order to Afghanistan. The next dispensation in Kabul, irrespective of its composition, is most likely to be confronted with a host of old and familiar challenges to its legitimacy and survival.

Though it is still early to be conclusively dismissive of the future Western role in the region, the continuing lack of clarity in their policy objectives and approaches could prove fatal and counter productive in the coming years. The killing of al Qaeda chief, Osama bin Laden, by the American commandoes deep inside Pakistan has failed to reinvigorate the Western commitment or transform their over all approach towards the war against extremism and terrorism. It was not long ago when in 2009 American President Barack Obama had described it as a "war of necessity." However, as the West continues to retreat, the spectre of security and political vacuum in large parts of Afghanistan and possible brinkmanship in regional complex is once again raising familiar concerns and challenges. It is hard not to believe that the country could be moving towards another round of socio-political chaos and anarchy. The post-2014 Afghanistan may not casually relapse into a state of total civil war, but at the same time it is logically impossible to think of a stable and peaceful Afghanistan in the near future.

An attempt has been made in this book to examine key political developments within Afghanistan over the last one decade in response to, or as a result of, the largest ever US-led Western military and political intervention. Perhaps, much more is still to come in a war that could aptly be termed as the last big war of the twentieth and first big war of the twenty-first century. The emerging social and political narratives are unmistakably old and echo a mix of articulation from 1960s onwards when, in response to growing aspirations of an expanding educated urban class, Afghanistan first experimented with limited parliamentary democracy; and thereafter, nationalists, communists and Islamists jostled for social and political space in 1970s, which soon degenerated into an externally sponsored violent armed conflict in 1980s; and until late 1990s when Taliban declared the establishment of an emirate. The multiplicity and diversity of narratives and perceptions, and successive failure of several political transitions to build a sustainable internal balance of power based on changed social and political realities, has turned Afghanistan into a complex entity that defies established theoretical formulations and explanations.

In view of growing uncertainty about the future course of politics and conflict within Afghanistan, the idea behind this book is to look into the politics of the past decade to be able to assess the probable future trends of what is clearly an unfinished war. The ultimate objective of the study therefore is to examine the continuing as well as newly emerging patterns of the Afghan politics, and try to identify the likely determinants or driving factors of the Afghan war beyond 2014. This book is a macro-level study, broadly focussing on key internal dimensions of the Afghan politics and war since 2001; and, it does not intend to scrutinise any particular development or issue to its finest details.

The continuum in the Afghan war has been remarkable. More than three-decade old Afghan war has twice been punctuated by failed interventions of big powers, every time leaving the country further destabilised, polarised and vulnerable to a highly competitive domestic and regional power play. Oblivious of the fundamental shifts in the international order, especially the collapse of the Soviet Union and the end of the Cold War era, if not its politics, the conflict in Afghanistan continued through the 1990s. The tragic events of 9/11, and the subsequent US invasion of Afghanistan in October 2001, pulled a largely forgotten and internationally abandoned war back into the global spotlight. It remains to be seen if Afghanistan will be abandoned again until a revived or a fresh round of external/international intervention is forced upon the country.

The decade-long US-led Western intervention, investment and engagement have failed in transforming the conflict dynamics in the Af-Pak region. Today, whatever little progress has been made in terms of rebuilding Afghan state institutions and its capacities is threatened by a new round of instability and uncertainty. As the US and NATO decide to remain partly or minimally engaged until 2024, and as Pakistan-sponsored and armed militant Afghan groups once again threaten to plunge the country into deeper chaos and anarchy, it is understood that the Afghan war is still in for a long haul. Amidst rising uncertainty, Afghanistan is surging towards a yet another major transition even as old and familiar patterns of violence and socio-political divide in its over three-decade old conflict re-appear. Prospects of yet another superpower being humbled on the Afghan soil often appear real and inevitable unless the West is willing to take a comprehensive and a decisive view of the various key dimensions, particularly the external ones, to the Afghan conflict.

The study covers the period beginning with the establishment of the first post-Taliban administration in December 2001 to the ongoing security and political transition in 2014. Though the US and some European NATO member-states have entered into strategic partnerships with Kabul, assuring Afghanistan of their continued support well beyond 2014, it is not clear what exactly the nature of Western role and presence will be or how effective it will be in years to come.

The book is thematically divided into eight chapters, each looking into significant developments in the internal politics of Afghanistan since the overthrow of the Taliban regime in late 2001. The findings of each chapter, treated as possible pointers to perhaps what awaits Afghanistan, is summarised in the last chapter.

The first chapter, *New Order, Old Politics,* deals with the establishment of the post-Taliban political order that flowed from the first Bonn Conference, the result of an agreement among disparate Afghan groups sans the Taliban and Hezb-e Islami in December 2001. The composition of the interim and transitional administrations between December 2001 and October 2004, and political competition among its constituents, confirmed the return of the old factional politics to Afghanistan. The West-sponsored Bonn Process, for various reasons, largely failed in putting the institution building process on a solid footing. In fact, it exposed Kabul once again to a range of regressive forces. Some of the old political tendencies of the 1990s soon began weighing upon the nascent post-Taliban political process. Though a relatively peaceful period, the new political system re-institutionalised and legitimised the role of the exiled old factional commanders and their militia. The process though to some extent succeeded in civilianising the role of various factional and militia commanders, it at the same time also exacerbated the identity-based political competition within the country.

The second chapter dealing with Afghanistan's *Tryst with Democracy* examines how two rounds of presidential and parliamentary elections have fared, including the drafting of a new constitution prior to it, both of which brought out the growing thrust on centralisation of power against a deeply fragmented polity. The not so latent ethno-political fault lines had re-emerged in the run up to the *Constitutional Loya Jirga* (CLJ) as Karzai tried to strengthen his position by dividing and marginalising the groups from the north in the new power structure. However, it failed to strengthen the position of either Karzai or those of the Pashtuns, and instead added to the growing mistrust among various groups. Afghan politics became more competitive as factions from the north began re-aligning in an attempt to put up a strong opposition to Karzai.

The third chapter, *Opposition Politics & Karzai the Master Survivor*, looks at the unique position and leadership of Hamid Karzai amidst the emergence of a relatively organised political opposition. Karzai, who has been at the helm of affairs since 2001, is the longest serving head of Afghan state. He interestingly does not have a defined support base within the country. Despite criticism from foes and friends alike, he has successfully held on to his position and has tried to manage the political opposition with tact and foresight of a veteran strategist. He has thwarted the political challenge especially from the north by selectively engaging and simultaneously playing upon the divides among them. The *Jabha-e Milli* or the National Front of Afghanistan (NFA) that emerged and splintered within short span of time, brought to fore the incipient politics of decentralised local power structures against a relatively centralised presidency. As Karzai's second and constitutionally the final presidential term comes to an end in 2014, and uncertainty over the next line of leadership thereafter grows, the chapter also tries to unravel the perceptions and politics of the supposedly marginalised anti-Taliban leadership which has a critical role in shaping the post-ISAF Afghan politics.

The fourth chapter on *Taliban Back into Power Play* examines the transformation of Taliban from a rag tag force into a powerful guerrilla force. By 2005-06, Taliban had largely reconstituted itself in the frontier tribal agencies of Pakistan and vast rural tracts in bordering south-eastern areas of Afghanistan.

The role of Pakistan and the US-led war in the resurgence of the Taliban, including factors within Afghanistan, has been weaved into the narrative. The military and political tactic of the Afghan Taliban and their allies has rapidly changed and adapted to the newer challenges posed by the NATO's expanding operations in the south-eastern parts of the country. They rose from the fringes and subsequently evolved into a force to reckon with. They rapidly turned the war to their advantage by locking a largely reluctant ISAF into a protracted guerrilla warfare. Re-emergence of Taliban factor at a time when the West is seeking to cut down its engagement is raising the spectre of greater chaos and political fragmentation in years to follow.

The fifth chapter explores the *Politics of Taliban Reconciliation & Reintegration* considered critical to the Western transition process and the future of Afghanistan. It has evolved into a multi-track competitive process involving diverse entities, both Afghan and foreign, each with an agenda of their own. Unmindful of its short and long-term impact, the West continues to seek political settlement of the conflict by trying to reach out to the Taliban leadership based in Pakistan. The ambiguity about the whole process is raising suspicions among vast sections of the Afghan population. At the moment, it is apparently dividing the Afghan nation along ethnic and ideological lines, and is likely to impact on developments after 2014. The politics over the idea of reconciliation is, however, not likely to lose its appeal even as the current initiatives fail to yield any notable result. It is rather expected to be a significant aspect of the post-2014 Afghan politics.

The sixth chapter on *Quest for a National Army* deals with the evolution and position of the Afghan National Army (ANA) as Western forces drawdown. The development of ANA, along with Afghan National Police (ANP), is supposed to be a critical component of the transition and post-transition Western strategy. Despite greater commitment of resources and attention by the Western countries as part of the security transition process, doubts remain over the capability of the ANA to secure the country after 2014. The ANA still has a long way to go before it evolves into an effective national institution. It remains severely dependent on external support and will continue to for at least another decade. As the West scales down its engagement, and if the next round of political transition in Kabul fails, the survival and sustenance of the ANA would be a major challenge for the post-ISAF Afghanistan.

The seventh chapter on *The 'Other' Key Neighbours – Iran, India, China and Russia* examines the role of Afghanistan's key neighbours, other than Pakistan, which are directly impacted by instability in Afghanistan and Pakistan and could be playing significant roles in the post-transition period. Pakistan's role that remains central to the Western strategy in Afghanistan has often been over-analysed, and at times may be even over-estimated. Continuing lack of a regional approach in the US strategy, and various other regional factors, may have limited and constrained the role of Afghanistan's other neighbours but that may not remain the case for long after 2014. The potential role and response of Iran, India, China and Russia, especially in view of post-2014 uncertainty, on one hand, and the US decision to maintain a prolonged but reduced military presence in Afghanistan, on the other, has been factored into the chapter.

In the eighth and last chapter, *The Unfinished War*, an effort has been made to broadly identify the historical factors which continue to define and impact the conflict dynamics within the country, and the more immediate issues of critical concern, as Afghanistan braces for yet another major transition. Year 2014-15 could in fact be a yet another watershed in more than three-decade old Afghan war, which in all probability is far from over. Afghanistan today stands at a critical juncture of fragile hope and fatal despair as the country undergoes third round of presidential election which was held in April 2014, with the parliamentary election due sometime next year in 2015. The key question now is whether this political transition will successfully usher the country into the 'decade of transformation' (2015-24), and will the post-Karzai and post-ISAF leadership in Kabul be able to cater to the heightened aspirations as well as scepticism of the Afghan people.

The outcomes of the various overlapping processes of transition in Afghanistan, and the way various dimensions of the conflict unravels in due course, would play a decisive role in shaping the Afghan politics as well as conflict after 2014. Though the emerging patterns of violence and several conflicts within are quite familiar and parallels could easily be drawn with earlier transitions and their outcomes, it is still a complex task to fully ascertain the likely role and position of various stakeholders in the next round of political *buzkashi*. Nevertheless, Afghanistan is changing and must continue to change, for its own survival, and its own future.

"For us, Afghanistan is destroyed. It is turning to poison, and not only for us but for all others in the world. If you are a terrorist, you can have shelter here, no matter who you are. Maybe one day they (the Americans) will have to send hundreds of thousands of troops to deal with that, and if they step in, they will be stuck. We have a British grave in Afghanistan. We have a Soviet grave. And then we will have an American grave."*

—Commander Abdul Haq, The New York Times, March 1994

"Do not let them break up. Keep them there. Lock them up if you have to. We do not want this to go anywhere else. We're almost there, and this is the time to grind it out on this line. If they go off, I don't know when I'll get them all back together."**

—Colin Powell, former US Secretary of State, to his deputy, Richard Armitage, reacting to possible collapse of the Bonn Conference held in December 2001

---

* Tim Weiner, "Blowback From the Afghan Battlefield," *The New York Times*, March 13, 1994, at http://www.nytimes.com/1994/03/13/magazine/blowback-from-the-afghan-battlefield.html?pagewanted=all&src=pm

** "Interview: Colin Powell," *Frontline, Public Broadcasting Service (PBS)*, United States of America, June 07, 2002, at http://www.pbs.org/wgbh/pages/frontline/shows/campaign/interviews/powell.html

CHAPTER I

New Order, Old Politics

Afghanistan for almost a decade has been a relatively manageable chaos. But as the Western forces continue to 'drawdown' or 'withdraw', the likely course of Afghan politics and the conflict thereafter has emerged as a subject of remarkable speculation. It has generated an immense sense of anxiety and uncertainty over the political fate of Afghanistan. Prospects of a fresh round of factional conflict or may be an open civil war, interspersed with the proxy politics of regional and extra-regional powers, is not being ruled out. The current developments are very much part of the remarkable continuum in the three decade old Afghan conundrum. It remains a continuing and often a puzzling saga of conflicts within conflict and wars within war.

Afghanistan has undergone several phases of failed transition and conflict cycles particularly since the end of nearly two centuries old monarchical order in the early 1970s. The persistent instability has since brought about a major fundamental and structural transformation—social, economic, cultural and political—in Afghanistan. It has successively de-structured the old socio-political order, but has thus far failed to re-structure and establish an alternate sustainable political order within the country. In fact, none of the political transitions—be it the one attempted by Sardar Mohammad Daud in 1973, by Afghan communists in late 1970s and 80s, by the anti-Soviet resistance leadership[1] in early 1990s, or by the Taliban[2] in mid 1990s—could reach their logical conclusions. Same appears to be the case with developments after 2001. When the US invaded Afghanistan after the tragic events of 9/11, Afghanistan witnessed another major political transition with the overthrow of the Taliban regime at the end of 2001, which in turn could be under threat from a possibly another inconclusive or failed transition in 2014-15.

After more than a decade of Western intervention, prospects of post-Taliban political set up falling apart, almost as part of the continuing trend from the past, cannot be fully ruled out. West is preparing to end its combat mission exactly when Afghanistan is on the verge of a major political transition and the Haqqani-Taliban network continue to gain ground in several parts of the country. President Hamid Karzai's second and constitutionally his final term is supposed to end in 2014, and that of the Afghan Parliament in 2015. At this point of time, it is not clear in what kind of an environment the next government will be formed, and how credible and legitimate would be the electoral exercise; or how effective it would be in terms of preserving the 'post-Taliban' political system. Also, nothing definitive can be stated about the kind of political coalition that would emerge in Kabul as various groups gear up for the post-2014 scenario.

The next round of political transition could pave the way either for a new or a reordered political coalition, though again fragile, in continuation of the present one; or in a worst case scenario, another round of civil war. As various old and current actors try to recast their role in view of Western drawdown, and are likely to remain lead protagonists of the post-2014 (dis-) order, it is perhaps pertinent to re-examine their role past one decade prior to assessing their potential future role.

The nine day eventful conference held at Bonn during November 27-December 05, 2001, nearly two weeks after Taliban forces made a tactical retreat from Kabul, had sealed the fate of what was soon to be a post-Taliban Afghanistan. The crafting of what generally came to be known as the Bonn Agreement,[3] to which the select four disparate Afghan groups were made to acquiesce, defined the character of an American-led and West-sponsored 'nation-building' exercise in the country. It also clearly brought out the kind of political groups and actors that would be leading and defining the new political process. Though the ouster of the Taliban from power and the crafting of the Bonn Agreement had led to a new political process after 2001, but failed to effectively institutionalise the political transition brought about by the US invasion of Afghanistan. Another remarkable development was the return of the exiled anti-Soviet Afghan resistance leadership to power, reviving the old factional politics of the 1990s.

An Abandoned and Forgotten War

The signing of the Geneva Accords in 1988 and subsequent withdrawal of the Soviet Red Army by early 1989, had led to a quick abandonment of Afghanistan by both the US and the Soviet Union, pushing the war into near oblivion. The Mohammad Najibullah Government, which was critically dependent on Soviet support, could not withstand the sustained onslaught of the Pakistan-backed Afghan militant factions for long. His government finally collapsed in April 1992 to make way for the UN-led effort to build consensus on power-sharing among various warring Afghan groups. It marked the end of nearly a decade-long communist rule in Afghanistan and opened up a new chapter in the country's continuing civil conflict. The communist rank-and-file, civil and military, melted and merged into the factional politics of the Afghan war. The country soon plunged into an endless cycle of factional violence with various militant groups scrambling for power. By 1992-93, the Afghan state had withered away with not a single functional state institution in place.

The simultaneous emergence of five independent but landlocked Central Asian Republics (CARs) bordering northern Afghanistan, known to be floating on large reserves of hydrocarbons, initially increased the geo-strategic value of Afghanistan as a potent transit route to the ports on the Arabian Sea and the Persian Gulf. Pakistan, which was a frontline ally of the US in its anti-Soviet campaign, was also left to pursue its geo-political ambitions in Afghanistan. Pakistan's continued involvement and the emergence of an ultra-conservative and a unified Pashtun force inside Afghanistan, soon invited the attention of other neighbouring countries. It led to the regionalisation of the Afghan conflict in the latter half of 1990s.

It was not until May 1996 when the al Qaeda chief Osama bin Laden shifted his base from Sudan to eastern Afghanistan, from where he issued the *Declaration of Jihad on the Americans Occupying the Country of Two Sacred Places* i.e., Saudi Arabia, that the US began to take note of developments in Afghanistan. After Kabul fell to the Taliban in September 1996, US began re-building its intelligence on Afghanistan. But more than the rise of the Taliban and their anomalous social and religious decrees, it was the presence of Osama bin Laden and the unaccounted cache of Stinger Missiles which the US had supplied to the Afghan resistance groups in 1986-87 which was worrying the US Administration.

Though several attempts were made to build political consensus on power-sharing among major resistance factions, stability continued to elude Afghanistan owing to dissension among them. The Peshawar-based seven-party alliance of the anti-Soviet Afghan factions, the Ittehad-e-Islami Afghan Mujahideen or the Islamic Union of Afghan Mujahideen (IUAM), repeatedly failed in forming a broad-based interim government. Lack of cohesion and political consensus among disparate members of the IUAM, and Pakistan's attempt to play upon their differences, rendered all efforts for a negotiated settlement of the conflict ineffective. Attempts by Pakistan and Iran, as also by international organisations like the United Nations (UN) and the Organisation of Islamic Cooperation (OIC, formerly Organisation of the Islamic Countries), ultimately failed to make warring factions agree on any power-sharing formula.

The factional rivalry for political supremacy continued to devastate Afghanistan as the civil war entered into a new phase with the arrival of the hitherto unknown Taliban in the latter half of 1994. By 1996-97, Taliban had emerged as another remarkable actor on the embattled political stage of

Afghanistan. Their rise in the Afghan body politic was phenomenal. Initially seen as a solution to the faction-ridden Afghan polity especially in the south, they later turned into an outcast for many; often seen as a potential destabilising factor in the neighbouring countries, wary of the spill-over of their radical ideology and factional conflict within Afghanistan onto their territories. Their anomalous interpretation of Islam and the way they went about capturing power became a role model for other aspiring Islamist groups in the region, especially Central Asia. Taliban, a predominantly Pashtun and a radical Sunni Islamist movement with *Deobandi-Wahhabi* orientation, was largely sustained with Pakistan's direct military support, Saudi Arabia's financial backing, and indirectly by the US indifference. Known more for their extreme interpretation of Islam and social decrees, particularly those relating to women and minority ethnic/religious groups, the Taliban were nonetheless initially able to impart a semblance of law and order particularly in the south and eastern parts of the country. However, their uncompromising attitude towards non-Pashtuns and extreme intolerance towards Afghanistan's traditional diversity, further perpetuated the ethnic cleavages in Afghan society, and soon made them unpopular with the international community as well.

Lack of international recognition and legitimacy has since been an unsettling issue with the Taliban leadership. Their intimacy with Osama bin Laden, held responsible by the US for masterminding several terror operations, including the attacks on the World Trade Centre and Pentagon, proved fatal for them. Taliban's lack of political/national vision and governing skills was more than evident as they failed in developing critical institutions. Coupled with this, the creeping differences between the *Kandahar shura* and *Kabul shura*, with hardly any non-Pashtun representation, were also factors limiting their emergence as a pan-Afghan force.

Some analysts ascribed the hardened position of Taliban on various contentious issues to the failure of international community to engage them with tact and diplomacy. In their opinion, enforcement of penalising mechanisms like sanctions further isolated them and made it difficult for the Taliban regime to reconcile or moderate their position. According to Ahmed Rashid, "...the Taliban are also Afghans, who are masters of *bazaari* politics and economics and know a good deal when they see one. Unfortunately, thus far, no one has shown them an offer they cannot refuse."[4] If that was the case, then the Taliban too had failed to respond to the regional and international concerns with tact and skilful diplomacy. Destruction of nearly 1,500 year old giant Buddha statues in the central Bamiyan Province in March 2001 was symptomatic of the belligerence inherent in the very ideological and socio-political fundamentals of the Taliban regime. It was not meant merely as an affront to the universally acceptable norms of state governance and responsibility or a deliberately crude and decisive signalling in reaction to continuing sanctions, but was reflective of their fundamental indifference to the pluralistic past and present of the Afghan society. It clearly brought out the beginning of the al Qaedisation of the Taliban thinking. In fact, the Taliban regime proved no different from other militant Afghan factions in terms of their intensely violent and confrontational power politics, narrow or virtually no sense of governance, and exploitation of religious/sectarian and social identities as a political tool. Perhaps, this explains the notable absence of notions of comprehensive social and political reconciliation, and long-term developmental vision for the country, in the Taliban discourse.

It was apparently not due to the above reasons that the US later turned against the Taliban regime, which at one point of time even had an office in the US. It was after the US failed to negotiate the extradition of Osama bin Laden with the Taliban regime post 9/11 that it firmed up to wage war against both. However, destruction of the Taliban was *per se* not the focal point of the US-led war on terror. As the US began cobbling a 'coalition of the willing' to invade Afghanistan, efforts were on within Afghanistan to restrain the US by presenting an alternative to the Taliban regime. Attempt by Abdul Haq, a prominent anti-Soviet Pashtun militia commander from Nangarhar, to create a political alternative to the Taliban, however, failed as he was killed by the Taliban on October 25, 2001. His idea of an Afghan-led internal rebellion against the Taliban leadership also did not find enough favour and support from the West.[5] In an interview to the British daily *Evening Standard* in Peshawar on October 05, 2001, Haq had claimed:

> "Every night I meet commanders who cross the mountains in darkness to brief me. They are part of the Taliban forces, but they no longer support them. These men will join us and there are many of them. When the time is right, they and others will rise up and this Taliban government will be swept aside.....The people are starving, they are already against them. Many tribal leaders are with us, more will follow. With these pressures and the help of the international community, we will drive them out."[6]

While pleading for assistance from the West, he had warned against launching air strikes in Afghanistan. He was of the opinion:

> "The Taliban is collapsing from within – if the missiles strike, this will be delayed, even halted....I know my people. If they are bombed, they will close ranks. Don't forget the majority of the population has no access to news from outside....People don't know what the war against terrorism is about – the Taliban banned television and what news there is is censored. All they know is that when bombs fall, the Taliban will say 'The Americans are trying to kill us, we must fight.' They will fight....Afghans will always unite in the face of what they see as a foreign enemy and this will serve to strengthen the Taliban."[7]

Two days after his murder, a report in *The New York Times* stated that Abdul Haq had "entered Afghanistan with no direct support from any nation, any army or any intelligence service, as even the United States declined to back him with anything except an offer of satellite phones." Haq reportedly turned down the satellite phones offered by the CIA and British agents. The report, quoting former US National Security Advisor (NSA) Robert C. McFarlane, stated that Haq and his 19-member band "was armed with only a few rifles, a few automatic weapons, and a pistol. The plan was to meet with Pashtun leaders opposed to the Taliban and foment a rebellion." McFarlane, while rebuking his country's intelligence establishment, had lamented that, "They spend $30 billion and do not have anybody out there who speaks Dari or who understands who these players are. Everybody is bad-mouthing Abdul Haq as if they have never read a history of the Soviet war."[8]

The West apparently failed to heed to Afghan voices offering possible political alternatives to military invasion. One could debate and question Abdul Haq's over all intentions or the viability of his idea, but efforts of his kind could have ensured that there was no political vacuum in the south after the overthrow of the Taliban regime. The issue of Pashtun alienation in the post-Taliban political process too could have been addressed. The anti-Taliban Pashtun front in the south and east could have been strengthened over the next few years. Haq was part of the Assembly for Peace and National Unity of Afghanistan that was formed in Peshawar by a group of anti-Taliban Pashtun commanders under the chairmanship of Pir Sayed Ahmed Gailani, who headed a relatively moderate pro-royalist faction in the 1980s.[9] This could have led to greater Pashtun participation in the Bonn Process, thereby making the process more legitimate and credible at the pan-Afghan level. It could have in turn worked as an Afghan deterrent, especially in Pashtun areas in the south-east, to Pakistan's continuing support for the Taliban and allies. Pashtun factor to this day remains critical to the stabilisation and rebuilding of Afghanistan. In fact, Haq had been working towards building up an anti-Taliban front months before 9/11 happened. In July 2001, he had reportedly met Jamiat-e Islami Commander Ahmad Shah Masoud at Kulyab where they two had entered into a 'mutually acceptable agreement' to work together.[10] The US Administration, however, had decided to work with the Northern Alliance, and was intent on unleashing its military might on a country already bombed to pieces in the previous decades. The US wanted to strongly react to the events of 9/11, and cash on the opportunity that came along with it to make good on its geo-political ambitions. However, in the process, the US failed to rationally visualise the complex challenge of creating an effective political alternative to the Taliban leadership, especially in their strongholds in the south and east.

Initially, the strategy of the Taliban was to take on the US troops as they took to the ground. Belying their expectations, the US decided against making heavy deployment on the ground and instead opted for massive air power for dismantling the Taliban military infrastructure. As for the ground offensive, US sponsored the anti-Taliban Afghan factions, especially the United Front (also known as the Northern Alliance).[11] Probably, aware of the coming winters, the US wanted to wrap up their military operations by December 2001. This perhaps explains the US decision to work with the Northern Alliance factions, which was probably the first key point of divergence with Rawalpindi.

When the *Operation Enduring Freedom* (OEF) was launched on October 07, 2001, the Taliban were controlling most of Afghanistan (except parts of Takhar and Badakhshan Province in the northeast), with most of the older militia leaders and commanders either having sought refuge in neighbouring countries or on the run. The sole exception here was the legendary Tajik guerrilla leader, Ahmad Shah Masoud, whom neither the Soviets nor the Taliban could dislodge from his stronghold in the Panjshir Valley, until his assassination by Arab suicide bombers two days before 9/11.

The US air power combined with ground offensive by the heavily armed factions of the Northern Alliance, which Colin Powell later described as marrying off the First World Air Force with a Fourth World Force, had led to the removal of the Taliban from all the urban centres by the year end. Powell also later stated that the "Northern Alliance was really the only coherent functioning military organization that we could partner with and use as we undertook our military operations."[12] The US Army's over-reliance on air power was to remain a key component of its counter-terrorism/insurgency operations in subsequent years. The disproportionately high collateral damage caused over the years, especially in terms of Afghan lives, proved counter-productive in several ways. James Dobbins, former US President George W. Bush's first envoy to Afghanistan, while calling the US efforts in Afghanistan "grossly underfunded and undermanned," stated that the military doctrine was the first error: "The US focus on force protection and substitution of firepower for manpower creates significant collateral damage." But the faith in firepower sustained the illusion that the mission could be "quicker, cheaper, easier." It fitted with Afghanistan being relegated into a sideshow to Iraq. There was also "a generally negative appreciation of peacekeeping and nation building as components of US policy, a disinclination to learn anything from ... Bosnia and Kosovo."[13]

After a month of bombardment of Taliban positions, Kabul finally fell to the descending Tajik militia from the north. On November 13, 2001, as Mohammad Qasim Fahim and his fighters took control of the key strategic areas in Kabul despite assurances against it, Afghanistan went through yet another chaotic transition of power. As the Taliban retreated, various militia commanders quickly filled in the power vacuum and re-established themselves in their respective power bases, "leading to inherently unstable situations."[14] Afghanistan was once again parcelled out among various factions, reminiscent of the early 1990s: Muhammad Ismail Khan in western Herat Province, Uzbek Commander Abdul Rashid Dostum in north-western provinces, Tajik Commander Mohammad Qasim Fahim in the north-eastern provinces, and Hizb-e-Wahdat in the central Bamiyan Province. Some of the older Pashtun factions too were able to re-establish their control in south and south-eastern provinces. Gulbuddin Hekmatyar's Hezb-e Islami faction once backed by Pakistan and the US, soon returned from Iran and began to make its presence felt in eastern Afghanistan, particularly in and around Jalalabad. Fearing sustained Tajik hold over the city, the UN and Western mediators at Bonn insisted on deploying the UN-mandated multi-national force in Kabul and its vicinity. This was vociferously opposed by the Northern Alliance delegates during the Bonn Conference. Later, the delegates finally agreed "to withdraw all military units from Kabul and other urban centers or other areas in which the UN mandated force is deployed."[15] Kabul was to again become a centre of hectic international political engagement. As for the Taliban, they dispersed and melted into the local population, receded to the countryside, or crossed over into Pakistan. They were to soon reorganise themselves and later wage a protracted guerrilla war against the US and NATO-led troops along with Hizb-e Islami and the Haqqani faction, which continues to this day.

Recasting Old Fault Lines

Fall of the Taliban regime was as meteoric as its rise. Negotiations among four Afghan groups—the Northern Alliance, Rome Group, Cyprus Group and Peshawar Group—soon followed under the UN auspices at Bonn.[16] What the Bonn Conference (November 27-December 05, 2001) clearly brought out was the resumption of the old factional rivalry and divisions along political as well as ethnic lines. The Conference was marred by walkouts and protests by delegates of different Afghan groups alleging lack of representation and improper distribution of portfolios.

Haji Abdul Qadir, then Governor of Nangarhar Province and the senior most Pashtun member of the Northern Alliance, had walked out of the Bonn Conference on the issue of lack of Pashtun representation in the delegation. Karim Khalili, a prominent Hazara leader of the Northern Alliance, had also demanded greater representation for the Hazaras in the delegation. Similarly, the Uzbek commander, Abdul Rashid Dostum, and Abdurrab Rasul Sayyaf, a powerful Pashtun leader, both from the Northern Alliance, had expressed their strong dissatisfaction over the distribution of portfolios. Former President Burhanuddin

Rabbani, who still led the UN-recognised government of Afghanistan, had refused to attend the Bonn Conference. He demanded that the conference be held in Kabul and was opposed to the idea of stationing a multi-national peacekeeping force in Kabul. Rabbani was also not in favour of establishing interim and transitional administrations and had instead asked for direct elections to be conducted. Russia and Iran had played a significant role towards the end in convincing Rabbani to allow the Northern Alliance delegates attending the Bonn Conference to propose candidates for the interim administration.

According to James Dobbins, democracy was an afterthought for the White House. He stated that "the word 'democracy' was introduced at the insistence of the Iranian delegation."[17] Similarly, according to former Afghan Foreign Minister Abdullah Abdullah, Russia "passed on a message that the world expect[s] an agreement," and that the Northern Alliance "shouldn't expect that without an agreement [Russian] support ... can continue." Under pressure from Russia, the younger members of the Northern Alliance decided to continue to participate in the Bonn Conference with or without the support of former President Rabbani."[18] The idea was clearly to press the Afghan delegates to finalise the list of candidates for the interim administration before they leave Bonn as Tajik militia's continuing control over Kabul could have led to confrontation among factional militias.

The divisions within the Northern Alliance too, which has always been a loose *mélange* of predominantly minority ethnic factions from the north, had fully come to the fore during the Bonn Conference. It certainly goes to the credit of the US and the UN interlocutors for bringing various Afghan factions together and making them reach a compromise. The Bonn Agreement, had initially set a timeline of two-and-a-half years for accomplishing its key objective of creating democratic institutions of governance. It was a comprehensive document "determined to end the tragic conflict in Afghanistan and promote national reconciliation, lasting peace, stability and respect for human rights in the country"[19] (see Appendix 1).

The very fact that the old factional commanders were invited by the UN to prepare a roadmap for stabilising and rebuilding Afghanistan made clear would be actors in the new political set-up at Kabul. The Bonn Agreement facilitated and legitimised the role for the older resistance groups in the post-Taliban political process. The Panjshiri Tajik triumvirate of Mohammad Qasim Fahim, Mohammad Yunus Qanuni and Abdullah Abdullah, and to lesser extent the pro-Zahir Shah Rome Group, emerged as key players.[20] The changing dynamics within the Northern Alliance post-Masoud was more than evident. Apart from Uzbek and Hazara factions, Burhanuddin Rabbani too now was marginalised within the Alliance as the Panjshiri trio bagged the three 'power ministries'—Defence, Interior and Foreign—in the 29-member interim administration.

Abdullah in his interview later stated that Rabbani had sent his own list of people who should be included in the interim administration, but that list did not include his and Yunus Qanuni's name.[21] In November end, Rabbani was also reported to have secretly met Pakistan's newly appointed ISI chief, Lt. Gen. Ehsan ul Haq, in United Arab Emirates (UAE) much to the discomfiture of the Panjshiri leaders.[22] The few senior Pashtun members of the Alliance were also at variance with the Panjshiri trio on certain contentious issues, especially the role of former King Zahir Shah and Pashtun representation in the post-Taliban provisional set up.

With the possibility of Taliban elements being part of the negotiations at Bonn completely ruled out, Hamid Karzai was propelled as a central figure for the Pashtuns to rally behind. The other three key contenders were Abdul Sattar Sirat, who was heading the pro-royalist Rome Group; former President Sebghatullah Mojadeddi; and Pir Sayed Ahmad Gailani, who headed the Qadiriyah Sufi order and a pro-royalist moderate faction, the Mahaz-i-Milli Islami-ye Afghanistan (or the National Islamic Front of Afghanistan).[23] He also headed the Assembly for Peace and National Unity of Afghanistan formed by a group of Pashtun commanders as Taliban forces retreated from Kabul in November 2001. Abdul Sattar Sirat, an Uzbek, who was said to have defeated Hamid Karzai, another pro-royalist, in an internal vote to elect the leader of the interim administration, had to step aside under the US pressure to pave way for Karzai.[24] The West needed a Pashtun face for the new political set up as it struggled to put together an interim administration. Interestingly, Hamid Karzai was not a participant in the Bonn Conference and was away in Kandahar, but he reportedly addressed the delegates on the very first day of the Conference via a satellite phone.[25] As both the Northern Alliance and the US were sceptical about the role of the ageing 87 year old exiled Afghan King Zahir Shah who many believed could have served as a central unifying figure, was marginalised in a planned manner. The king was expected to head the Supreme Council for the National Unity of Afghanistan, which was initially proposed to be established along with the interim administration.[26] However, due to lack of consensus on its composition and mandate among Afghan delegates, the Supreme Council could not be formed. Zahir Shah was later declared *Baba-e Millat-e Afghanistan* or the Father of the Afghanistan Nation. With his death in July 2007, the last of the remaining vestiges of nearly 260-year old Pashtun monarchy came to a final end in Afghanistan.

In fact, one of the biggest challenges before the US was to strike a balance between the overgrown power of the Northern Alliance and the sense of alienation and under-representation among the Pashtun people. In the absence of the predominantly Pashtun Taliban and the political prospects of Zahir Shah curtailed, the challenge lay in establishing an alternate Pashtun leadership which was not only amiable to the West and its interests but was also capable of securing the support of the country's largest ethnic group for the new political process. Karzai, given his strong Pashtun lineage (Popalzai clan), moderate views, fluency in English, sophisticated mannerism, his connections with the US, expected antipathy towards the Taliban who assassinated his father in Quetta in 1999, and a relatively non-controversial image in the Afghan politics, became the obvious choice.[27] Karzai's understanding of the complex Afghan politics soon made him a central figure in the externally sponsored political process. Finally, a fragmented and squabbling post-Taliban provisional authority came into being. Though headed by a Pashtun, it had a disproportionate Panjshiri Tajik component to it (see Table 1.1).

Table 1.1: Composition of the Afghan Interim Administration (AIA) (December 22, 2001-June 2002)

Position in AIA	Name	Ethnicity/Affiliation
Chairman	Hamid Karzai	Pashtun/Rome Group
Vice Chair & Defence Minister	Mohammad Qasim Fahim	Tajik/NA
Vice Chair & Women's Affairs Minister	Sima Samar	Hazara/Rome Group
Vice Chair & Planning Minister	Mohammad Mohaqiq	Hazara/NA
Vice Chair and Water & Power Minister	Mohammad Shakar Kargar	Uzbek/NA
Vice Chair & Finance	Hedayat Amin Arsala	Pashtun/Rome Group
Foreign Affairs Minister	Abdullah Abdullah	Tajik/NA
Interior Minister	Mohammad Yunus Qanuni	Tajik/NA
Commerce Minister	Syed Mustafa Kazemi	Hazara/NA
Mines & Industries Minister	Mohammad Alem Razm	Uzbek/NA
Small Industries Minister	Aref Noorzai	Pashtun/NA
Information & Culture Minister	Sayed Makhdoom Raheen	Tajik/Rome Group
Communications Minister	Abdul Rahim	Tajik/NA
Labour & Social Welfare Minister	Mirwais Sadeq	Tajik/NA
Haj & Islamic Affairs Minister	Mohammad Hanif Balkhi	Tajik/Independent
Martyrs & Disabled Minister	Abdullah Wardak	Pashtun/NA
Education Minister	Abdul Rassoul Amin	Pashtun/Rome Group
Higher Education Minister	Sharif Faez	Tajik/NA
Public Health Minister	Suhaila Seddiqi	Pashtun/Independent
Public Works Minister	Abdul Khaliq Fazal	Pashtun/Rome Group
Rural Development Minister	Abdul Malik Anwar	Tajik/NA
Urban Development Minister	Abdul Qadir	Pashtun/NA

(*Contd.*)

Position in AIA	Name	Ethnicity/Affiliation
Reconstruction Minister	Mohammad Amin Farhang	Pashtun/Rome group
Transport Minister	Sultan Hamid Sultan	Hazara/NA
Refugees Minister	Enayatullah Nazeri	Tajik/NA
Agriculture Minister	Syed Hussain Anwari	Hazara/NA
Irrigation Minister	Mangal Hussain	Pashtun/Peshawar Group
Justice Minister	Abdul Rahim Karimi	Uzbek/NA
Civil Aviation & Tourism Minister	Abdul Rahman *(killed in February 2002; succeeded by Zalmay Rassoul in March 2002)*	Tajik/Rome Group
Border Affairs Minister	Amanullah Khan Zadran	Pashtun/Rome Group

Author's Note: This table has been drawn and compiled from various sources as no two sources give similar details. Wherever the information provided by key sources are at variance with each other, the same has been verified and further corroborated by consulting an extended range of sources in order to ensure the accuracy of information to the extent possible. Key sources of information are as: personal profiles/biographies of incumbent ministers available on Afghan Government websites, and other websites, such as *Afghanistan Online* (available at www.afghan-web.com), *Afghan Biographies* (available at www.afghan-bios.info), etc.

Under the provisions of the Bonn Agreement, the UN-recognised government of President Burhanuddin Rabbani formally handed over political power to the Hamid Karzai-led Afghan Interim Authority (AIA) on December 22, 2001 (the first day of the Afghan month of Jaddi in the year 1380). Lakhdar Brahimi, Special Representative of the UN Secretary General, in his speech on the occasion, candidly stated that though the Bonn Agreement is "far from perfect," it is still a "momentous day" for a country "physically and psychologically devastated." He added that, "Failure is not an option, because neither the people of Afghanistan nor the nations of the world will take kindly to any individual or group, wherever they may be located, and whatever their motives, that stand in the way of this singular opportunity."[28]

The AIA, constituted for a period of six months, was supposed to consist of an Interim Administration headed by a Chairman, a Special Independent Commission for the Convening of the *Emergency Loya Jirga*, and a Supreme Court. The Agreement enunciated the task of creating institutions like the judiciary, the army and the police force, constitutional commission, election commission, banking, drug enforcement directorate and an independent human rights commission. It also enshrined provisions for disarmament and demobilisation of militias, drafting of a new constitution, fighting terrorism, drugs and organised crime, repatriation and resettlement of refugees, and other related subjects. The entire process was supposed to culminate with the "establishment of a broad-based, gender-sensitive, multi-ethnic and fully representative government," elected through a free and fair exercise of electoral rights by the people of Afghanistan.[29]

However, Hamid Karzai and his Western-backers had their task cut out given the fragility of the Bonn Agreement and the fractious nature of the Afghan polity. The divide in the Afghan polity along the lines of ethnicity, tribe and language was reflected all through the nine-day negotiations in Bonn. The scramble for a greater share in the post-Taliban set-up was unmistakable. The external powers involved too tried to influence the course of events by directly or indirectly lobbying for their proxy's inclusion. Some factions had their own reservations *vis-à-vis* the Bonn Agreement, generally alleging lack of representation and partisan distribution of portfolios.

The younger and dynamic Panjshiri Tajik trio of Qanuni, Fahim and Abdullah, all of whom held senior positions in the provisional governments, were an eyesore to the older Pashtun *mujahideen* leadership. Disruptive tendencies within the Karzai-led Interim and Transitional Administrations/Authorities often came to the fore. The murder of Abdul Rahman, Minister of Civil Aviation and Tourism in the Interim Administration, at Kabul Airport in February 2002,[30] and the assassination of the newly appointed Vice President and Minister of Public Works, Abdul Qadir, in July 2002,[31] were gruesome reminders of the fragility of the post-Taliban political order. Karzai had clearly stated that the murder of Abdul Rahman was a premeditated assassination plot. He had accused the members of the Jamiat-e-Islami who were top officials in the defence, interior, intelligence and justice ministries for planning minister's murder. All the aforesaid ministries were then led and largely manned by the Panjshiri Tajiks. Rahman was among the few Tajik members of the Rome Group. Both Rahman and Qadir were also in favour of former King Zahir Shah playing a greater role in post-Taliban political set up.

In accordance with the Bonn Agreement, within six months of the inauguration of the Interim Authority in December 2001, an *Emergency Loya Jirga* (ELJ) was convened in Kabul from June 11-19, 2002. The function of the ELJ was to elect the chairman and members of the Afghan Transitional Administration (ATA) for a period of two years. The ATA was supposed to draft a new constitution and convene a *Constitutional Loya Jirga* to ratify it within eighteen months i.e., December 2003; and thereafter, in accordance with the new constitution, to hold democratic elections to elect a president and the parliament within two years i.e., June 2004. Hamid Karzai, who was again elected at the ELJ to lead the ATA, finally announced his new cabinet at the end of June 2002 (See Table 1.2).

Table 1.2: Composition of the Afghan Transitional Administration (ATA) (June 2002-October 2004)

Position in ATA	Name	Ethnicity/Affiliation	Change from Interim Administration
President	Hamid Karzai	Pashtun/Rome Group	Same
Vice President & Defence Minister	Mohammad Qasim Fahim	Tajik/NA	Same
Vice President	Hedayat Amin Arsala	Pashtun/Rome Group	Same; earlier also headed the Finance Ministry
Vice President	Karim Khalili	Hazara/NA	New Member
Vice President	Abdul Qadir	Pashtun/NA (killed on July 06, 2002)	Earlier, was Urban Development Minister
Vice President & Chairman of Constitution Commission	Neamatullah Shahrani	Uzbek/Independent	New Member; Appointed later through a presidential decree & not during the *Emergency Loya Jirga*
Special Advisor on Security Affairs	Yunus Qanuni	Tajik/NA	New Position; earlier Interior Minister
Foreign Minister	Abdullah Abdullah	Tajik/NA	Same
Finance Minister	Ashraf Ghani	Pashtun/Independent	New Member
Interior Minister	Taj Mohammad Wardak	Pashtun	New Member/Later, Vice Presidential Nominee of Yunus Qanuni in 2004 Presidential Election
	Ali Ahmed Jalali replaced Wardak in January 2003	Pashtun	New Member
Planning Minister	Mohammad Mohaqiq	Hazara/NA	Same; was earlier Vice Chair as well
Communications Minister	Masoom Stanekzai	Pashtun	New Member
Border Affairs Minister	Aref Noorzai	Pashtun/NA	Earlier, Small Industries Minister
Refugees Minister	Enayatullah Nazeri	Tajik/NA	Same

(Contd.)

Position in ATA	Name	Ethnicity/Affiliation	Change from Interim Administration
Mines Minister	Juma M. Muhammadi	Pashtun	New Member
Light Industries Minister	Mohammad Alem Razm	Uzbek/NA	Earlier, Mines & Industries Minister
Public Health Minister	Suhaila Seddiqi	Pashtun	Same
Commerce Minister	Syed Mustafa Kazemi	Hazara	Same
Agriculture Minister	Syed Hussain Anwari	Hazara/NA	Same
Justice Minister	Abdul Rahim Karimi	Uzbek/NA	Same
Information & Culture Minister	Sayed Makhdoom Raheen	Tajik/Rome Group	Same
Reconstruction Minister	Mohammad Amin Farhang	Pashtun/Rome Group	Same
Haj & Islamic Affairs Minister	Mohammad Amin Naziryar	Pashtun	New Member
Urban Affairs Minister	Yousef Pashtun (Gul Agha Sherzai took over from August 16, 2003)	Pashtun/Royalist Pashtun/Royalist	Both were new members Yousef was appointed Governor of Kandahar Province)
Public Works Minister	Abdul Qadir (killed on July 06, 2002; succeeded by Abdul Ali)	Pashtun/NA Pashtun	Earlier, Urban Development Minister New Member
Labour & Social Affairs Minister	Noor Mohammad Qarqin	Turkmen	New Member
Water & Power Minister	Mohammad Shakar Kargar	Uzbek/NA	Same; was earlier one of the five Vice Chair as well
Irrigation & Environment Minister	Ahmed Yusuf Nuristani	Pashtun	New Member; Environment added to the Ministry
Martyrs & Disabled Minister	Abdullah Wardak	Pashtun/NA	Same
Higher Education Minister	Sharif Faez	Tajik/NA	Same
Civil Aviation & Tourism Minister	Mirwais Sadeq	Tajik/NA	Earlier, Labour & Social Welfare Minister
Transport Minister	Saeed Mohammed Ali Jawad	—	New Member

Position in ATA	Name	Ethnicity/Affiliation	Change from Interim Administration
Education Minister	Mohammad Yunus Qanuni	Tajik/NA	Earlier, Interior Minister
Rural Development Minister	Mohammad Hanif Atmar	Pashtun	New Member
Women's Affair Minister	Habiba Sarobi	Hazara	New Member
Other Key Appointments			
Chief Justice of the Supreme Court	Fazl Hadi Shinwari	Pashtun/Peshawar Group	Newly Appointed
National Security Advisor	Zalmay Rassoul	Pashtun/Rome Group	Earlier, Civil Aviation Minister in Interim Administration appointed after the killing of Abdul Rehman in February 2002
Governor, Afghan Central Bank	Anwar-ul Haq Ahadi	Pashtun/Technocrat	Newly Appointed
Minister of State & Advisor on Women's Affair	Mahboba Hoqoqmal	Hazara	Newly Appointed
Permanent Representative to the UN	Ravan A.G. Farhadi (January 2002-2006)	Tajik/NA	Re-appointment Earlier, Afghan Ambassador/Permanent Representative to the UN under Rabbani Government (since April 1993) Prime Minister of NA (August 21, 1997-November 13, 2001) Prime Minister of Afghanistan (November 13-December 22, 2001)

Author's Note: This table has been drawn and compiled from various sources as no two sources give similar details. Wherever the information provided by key sources are at variance with each other, the same has been verified and further corroborated by consulting an extended range of sources in order to ensure the accuracy of information to the extent possible. Key sources of information are as: personal profiles/biographies of incumbent ministers available on Afghan Government websites, and other websites, such as, *Afghanistan Online* (available at www.afghan-web.com), *Afghan Biographies* (available at www.afghan-bios.info), etc.

The conduct and proceedings of the *Jirga*, right from the selection of participants to the way deals were negotiated for power sharing, further legitimised the role and position of the old anti-Soviet factional commanders and leaders who were chosen six months back to decide on the political roadmap for a post-Taliban Afghanistan. The country was again getting parcelled out among various militia commanders as they, on one hand, sought to consolidate their hold in their respective areas of influence and, on the other, within the West-sponsored new political set up in Kabul. Return of the old competitive factional politics soon overshadowed the institution-building process as envisaged under the Bonn Agreement. All ideas and prospects of carrying out necessary social and political reforms, critical to the rebuilding of a modern Afghan state, were purposely stymied to simply keep the process going. Of particular note was the establishment of Taliban-style Ministry for the Promotion of Virtue and Prevention of Vice in August 2002 by the newly-appointed Chief Justice, Fazl Hadi Shinwari. It came less than a year after the overthrow of the Taliban regime which was internationally condemned and targeted for its strict religious and moral policing.

Mujahideen within Local Structures

The factional politics of the old resistance leadership, institutionalised over the years, has been an abiding factor in the Afghan polity. Except for a brief interregnum during the Taliban rule, when most of them were on the run, the anti-Soviet resistance leadership has shown a strong survival instinct. Their return to the Afghan political stage, along with their whole gamut of old ideological differences and interest disparities, bears testimony to their position in the country's polity. Involvement of external powers, both regional and extra-regional, also played an important role in reinforcing the position of various *mujahideen* factions in the Afghan socio-political structure.

The ethnicity of Afghanistan, which is as diverse as its geography, has been a determining factor in Afghan polity. The overlapping distribution of various ethnic groups that make up Afghanistan, and the presence of their respective co-ethnics across the national boundaries, have often led to some of the neighbouring countries seek influence in the Afghan politics. The geo-strategic significance of Afghanistan, as a land bridge between South and Central Asia and much beyond, has since times immemorial ensured that regional and extra-regional powers have had politico-military and economic stakes in the affairs of the country. The stridently tribal-ethnic character of Afghanistan interspersed with post-monarchy power politics imparted an element of factional competition for control of power and resources in the Afghan polity. Often these tribal and ethnic factions played proxy to the Afghan agenda of their respective foreign patrons who in turn provided them with material support and solidarity in their power struggle within

Afghanistan. The proxy politics as a two-way process has since been a feature of Afghan politics.

The Afghan civil war has to be seen in the above context. To begin with, it was in reaction to the radical socio-economic modernisation policy pursued by successive communist governments during the late 1970s and 80s, which was bitterly opposed by the traditional clergy and political elite in the countryside, as pockets of opposition rose across provincial Afghanistan. The gulf between the vision and belief of the small urban elite fired by the ideals of the Soviet communism, and the large majority of traditionally conservative people in Afghanistan's vast countryside, came to the fore. It also brought out the fault lines in the Afghan state structures which have relatively been weak in the outlying provinces. Due to the absence of effective state institutions in the provinces, people in the provinces have by and large lived by traditional tribal-ethnic leadership and age-old tribal institutions and codes of conduct. The leadership of the resistance movement in different parts of Afghanistan was largely a mix of traditional clergy, radical Islamists, and the tribal heads, representing classes least likely to be benefited from the reforms and the system put in place by the communist government in Kabul. The anti-Soviet resistance which began as an indigenous local opposition to the radical reforms being carried out by Kabul, soon metamorphosed into a CIA-driven *jihad* directly aimed at rolling back the Soviet influence, with the Inter-Services Intelligence (ISI) of Pakistan providing full political and logistical support to it.

The US had realised the potential of engaging different *mujahideen* factions in building anti-Soviet resistance as their leadership was well-embedded in the tribal-ethnic structures of Afghanistan. They controlled the resources and commanded the loyalty of the people in their respective areas. The US continued to arm these factions heavily with Pakistan playing key conduit between the two. This led to the linking of various *mujahideen* factions to the US-led anti-Soviet alliance (more precisely to the US bloc). It was aptly stated by Barnett R. Rubin that:

> ...there is an interrelationship between the patronage connections in Afghanistan (which are partly based on so-called tribalism or clan relations, which themselves are not static but are constantly re-formed in various ways) and the international system. The patronage relations have become internationalised because resources are imported into the networks through global and transnational political, military, and economic networks. We should not think that Afghanistan is backward or pre-modern. No, Afghanistan is part of the process of globalisation. But it is the other side of globalisation.[32]

Afghan *mujahideen* leadership draws its authority from traditional sources and also by virtue of being in command of resources at the local level. By sharing and distributing the resources they maintain a network of patronage relations which helps in sustaining their leadership. Loyalty to the tribal or ethnic leadership by the co-ethnics is supposed to be traditionally unquestionable. In fact, ethnic-tribal loyalties and identities have often overridden the predominantly Muslim identity of the Afghan population. It is noteworthy that majority of the resistance groups remained primarily mono-ethnic and failed to become ethnically diverse, and same goes for the Taliban as well. The strong sense of ethnic identity prevalent among the Afghans thwarted all attempts by radical Islamists for a united Islamic front cutting across tribal, ethnic, linguistic and sectarian identities and loyalties. In fact, the traditional resistance parties have been more successful than the Islamist resistance parties in Afghanistan. This also led to short-term alliance politics among the competing *mujahideen* factions, which remains a determining factor in the power politics of Afghanistan to this day.

Interestingly, factional politics often based on competing identities and interests are regarded as an important element in the Afghan civil war though no proper census has ever been conducted in the country. There are no credible figures available regarding the exact demographic composition of the country. Every major group has its own projections to make and estimates to offer with regard to its numerical strength or its proportion of the total population which itself is not clearly known. This is best illustrated by a tabulation published by *Hewad*, an Afghan daily, showing ethnic composition of Afghanistan as drawn from various old sources (see Table 1.3).

However, for purpose of convenience, an updated demographic profile of the country and key socio-economic indicators have been provided at the beginning of the book. Suffice to state here that there is a strong demographic dimension to the competitive domestic politics of the country as well as the much talked about divisive proxy politics of its neighbours. The identity based politics has often helped strengthen the position of local commanders and their militia at subnational levels. The post-2001 political process too has been bedevilled with fault lines often based on socio-ethnic considerations. The electoral process at best has had limited, rather temporary, success in civilianising the roles of various militia based factions in Afghanistan, other than the armed Pashtun factions operating from Pakistan.

The destruction of central authority at Kabul during the civil war further reinforced the tribal-ethnic leadership at the local and provincial level. Even historically, provincial Afghanistan has largely remained autonomous with Kabul having nominal presence by way of institutions or governance. It has been rightly stated by Magnus and Naby that:

Table 1.3: The Ethnic Composition of Afghanistan in Different Sources (As published in Afghan daily, Hewad)

Source	Author	Publication	Ethnic Groups							
			Pashton	Tajik	Hazara	Uzbek	Baluch	Turkmen	Aimaq	Pashae
The Ethnic Composition of Afghanistan	A six year survey and research	WAK Foundation 1999 Norway	62.73	12.4	9	6		2.69	2.68	
Afghanistan	Max Clumborg	1960	60	30	3	3				
Fundamentalism Reborn? Afghanistan and the Taleban	William Maley	London 1998	62.73	12.4	9	6		2.69	2.68	
The World Geoethnology	Academic Research M. Mahjub F. Yawari	5th – Ed, 1987 Iran	60	20	5	5				
The World Population	Prof. C. I. Brok	1981 U.S.S.R	52.8	18.6	8.6	8.6		2	3	
Afghanistan	Prof. M. Ali	1955 Kabul	60	20						
The National Language of Afghanistan	Prof. Aslanov	1964 U.S.S.R	60							
Afghanistan Federation System?	M. Enam Wak	2000 Pakistan	62	12	9	6				
Afghan Mellat journal	Issue 42-43	1995 Pakistan	50	21	8	8				
History & Establishment of Afghanistan	Abdullah Ahmad Almir	1980 London – Qattar	58.7	28.7	2.7	8		2		
Ibid	Abdul Azim Walyan	1987 Iran	70	13						
Sukhan Journal	Ali Akbar Jafaryan		50	20						
Afghanistan	Louis Dupree	1973 U.S.A	46	25	6	7				
Afghanistan	World Almanac	1997 U.S.A	38	25	19	6				
The World Large Languages	McKenzei	1987 Europe	55-65							
Afghanistan	Anthony Hyman		45	23	10	8	0.6	2	5	6

Source: "The Ethnic Composition of Afghanistan in Different Sources," *Hewad*, at http://www.hewad.com/ethnic.htm

> "…the basic elements of the Afghan lifestyle depend on family relationships, multigenerational living patterns, dependence on agriculture, symbiotic living with the natural world, including domestic animals, and a sense of permanence, not of the individual but of the community. Loyalty patterns begin with family and extend to village or tribe, and then to ethnic group. The extension of loyalty to country has not achieved universal acceptance as has allegiance to Islam, which is imbedded in the community traditions rather than in the intellect or the written word."[33]

Thus, in view of the near absence of state institutions and authority in Afghanistan's vast countryside, traditional tribal institutions based on personalised networks form the repository of *mujahideen* power and authority. The ethnic and ideological divide and interest disparities among Afghanistan's various factions, enmeshed with the involvement of foreign powers, have for long fashioned the Afghan polity. The personalised nature of Afghan social structures, which manifests in every relational aspect of life, be it politics or economy, has also played a crucial role in evolving and sustaining the institution of warlordism. These personalised networks, based on loyalty to primordial identities as instrument of power, accruing out of tribal, ethnic, religious and linguistic distinctiveness of the various communities that form the Afghan ethnic mosaic, have for long resisted any outside interference and subjugation, whether from Kabul or from external powers.

Return of Old Militia Networks

Given the heavy reliance of the US on anti-Taliban militia, especially from the north, their role in the new political order was assured. Unlike the 1980s, when the US relied more on the Pakistan-backed Pashtun factions, this time around the US had to reinforce non-Pashtun factions from the north. The Afghan Military Force (AMF), which along with the 18,000 US-led coalition troops were tracking down the 'remnants' of the Taliban and the al Qaeda, comprised largely of various militia networks revived after 2001. The continued dependence of the coalition force on the AMF further complicated the task of demobilising and disarming the militia later. The disbandment of thousands of irregular armed mercenaries was critical to extending Kabul's authority to the provinces. Failure to do so soon led to the re-emergence of multiple centres of power in the country, undermining Kabul's authority from the very beginning.

Variously known as warlords, *mujahideen*, freedom fighters, ethnic or factional or militia commanders, the latest being regional strongmen, they have shown tremendous survival instinct. The changing semantics are indicative of the changing perception of the West about the expected role and status of the militia commanders. Hailed as *mujahideen* and freedom fighters at the peak of anti-

Soviet resistance in the 1980s, and referred to as warlords when they endlessly fought among themselves until displaced by the Taliban, they are now being preferably addressed as regional strongmen. Take for instance the once influential commanders from the Arsala family of Nangarhar. During the anti-Soviet *jihad*, they were dubbed as 'Resistance Royalty' but later they were referred to as 'warlords.' As the UN and the international community geared up to deal and work with various former *mujahideen* commanders for stabilising the post-Taliban Afghanistan, a more acceptable and respectable term like 'regional strongman' had to be coined and introduced. The Afghan 'warlords' were now expected to change their role, primarily from military to civilian, in the West-sponsored political process mandated by the Bonn Agreement.

To what extent the Bonn process succeeded in bringing about any qualitative change in their role will be subsequently dealt with in the chapter. Suffice to state here that shifting alliances and realignments among various factions have been the hallmark of Afghan politics. The alliance and proxy politics, and the traditional inter and intra-ethnic divide entwined with the interests of regional and extra-regional powers, continued to determine the Afghan political landscape.

The US-led war in Afghanistan was not supposed to have been a long drawn affair, which largely explains their short-term approach and a quick response strategy particularly in the initial months after the invasion. For the US, which did not have enough troops on the ground first few years, a quicker way of achieving their objectives in Afghanistan was to rely more on surgical aerial strikes and the anti-Taliban militia commanders whose power and authority rested on personalised networks and patronage connections. The synergy that was forged between the US and the old militia networks, continued to impact on the course of Afghan politics. The growing factional divide and social polarisation prevalent within and outside the new political order further came to fore when draft constitution was debated in a specially convened *Constitutional Loya Jirga* (CLJ) in December 2003. The debate that went into the finalising of the draft constitution provided a broad sweep of divergent notions about state system and distribution of power in the backdrop of prevalent identity-based power politics of the country.

Debating the New Constitution

The making of the new constitution and its subsequent ratification by the 502-member CLJ in January 2004 was a landmark event in the post-Taliban political transition. The *Jirga*, which started on December 14, 2003, and was initially slated for 10 days, went on for 22 days until draft constitution was adopted on January 04, 2004. The entire deliberation brought out the fractious nature of Afghan society and polity. The long-standing divide between Pashtun factions and the minority groups from the north, overshadowed the basic objective and spirit of the *Jirga*. There were occasions when the proceedings were almost derailed due to seemingly irreconcilable differences between the US-backed Karzai, his West-educated advisors and the Pashtun delegates on the one hand, and the Tajik and Uzbek delegates from the north on the other.

Consensus appeared to be most elusive with deadlock setting in on various crucial issues, such as, the nature of the Afghan state, the form of government, status and role of Islam, centre-province relations, question of double citizenship, status of women and minorities, human rights and the language issue. The *Jirga* struggled for a workable consensus amidst conflicting interests and competing agendas of the delegates, representing diverse factions and political voices from across Afghanistan.

In the end, much of the differences on issues of vital concern were said to be 'settled' and not 'resolved,' largely through hectic behind-the-scene negotiations, rather than debate and consensus. *Human Rights Watch* reported that the US officials had met with factional leaders, including Abdul Rashid Dostum and Abdurrab Rasul Sayyaf, to negotiate their support for the draft Constitution.[34] The involvement of the UN and US mediators in brokering deals among quarrelling factions was a known fact. Zalmay Khalilzad, the then US ambassador to Afghanistan, and Lakhdar Brahimi, the then UN special envoy, apparently played key roles in enabling the opposing factions to reach a compromise on what appeared to be irreconcilable differences between them.

It would not be wrong to say that the new Constitution was a compromise document, which tried to pacify and accommodate the interests of all political and ethnic factions. However, whatever might have been the points of disagreement over the Constitution as also the ensuing amendments, its basic content and tenor was largely retained. Overall, it was a progressive document, which enshrined a presidential form of government with a bicameral legislature - the *Meshrano Jirga* (House of Elders) and *Wolesi Jirga* (House of Commons). The 162-Article Constitution contained more than 40 changes from the original draft. Some of the important issues that provoked heated debate and finally led to amendments in the draft Constitution were:

Centralisation versus Decentralisation

The strongest opposition to a centralised presidential form of government with overriding powers over the bicameral legislature came mainly from the non-Pashtun delegates. Fearing presidential authoritarianism and marginalisation of minority ethnic groups in the new power structure, they demanded further decentralisation of presidential powers by way of giving greater power to the parliament, which would serve as a check and balance mechanism. They also called for greater devolution of power to the provinces to check any undue concentration of power at the Centre, and the resultant imbalance in the centre-province relationship. While they strongly favoured a parliamentary system with the president and prime minister sharing power, the removal of the provision for the post of a prime minister from the draft Constitution before it was released for public debate denied them this opportunity. The mainly Pashtun supporters of a strong centralised Afghan state, with president having wide powers, were opposed to the idea of a decentralised political system citing it as a necessity in the absence of political parties, critical institutional structures, and above all, to deal with factional commanders. Hamid Karzai too had made it clear that he would not stand for the presidential election if there was any marked dilution in presidential powers.

A compromise was finally reached between the opposing groups by making certain amendments in the powers of the president – making the president more accountable to the nation and the parliament. Thus, as outlined in the draft Constitution, the president would have no sweeping powers over the appointment of the attorney-general, ministers, governors, members of the Supreme Court, governor of the central bank, head of the national security directorate and other such senior positions. The president's office would have to seek prior approval of the parliament before making key appointments and also for setting national policy agendas or undertaking administrative reforms.

In an effort to broaden the scope of ethnic representation at the higher executive level, two vice-presidents were to be appointed instead of one. Also, it was left to the *Wolesi Jirga* to decide on the controversial question of whether people with dual citizenship could hold governmental positions. Accordingly, the lower house was endowed upon the right to confirm or reject the nomination of ministers with dual citizenship. Some of the members in the Karzai-led provisional government then had dual citizenship.

Status and Role of Islam

The status and role of Islam in the new Constitution and its place in the overall political system had generated lot of debate even before the *Jirga* was convened. Islamic hardliners, wary of reduced authority in the new political structure, demanded greater Islamic content in the Constitution. To allay their fears, Article 3 of the draft Constitution was amended. While it initially stated: "In Afghanistan, no law can be contrary to the sacred religion of Islam and the values of this Constitution"; but after amendment it read: "In Afghanistan, no law can be contrary to the beliefs and provisions of the sacred religion of Islam." Some analysts felt that the amended language left enough room for anomalous interpretation of Islamic tenets and traditions, which could have a significant bearing on human rights in general and the rights of women and minorities in particular.

The idea of constituting a higher council or *Diwan-e-Ali* to supervise the implementation and interpretation of the Constitution, and to oversee the activities of the government along the lines of the Guardian Council in Iran, was rejected outright. However, buckling under the pressure of the Islamic hardliners, the *Jehadi* rallying cry of the resistance, *Allah-o-Akbar*, was put into the national anthem.

Status of Women, Minorities and Human Rights

In complete contrast to the Taliban's infamous social decrees barring women from all public affairs, women's representation and participation in the *Jirga* was encouraging. Women delegates from different parts of the country, numbering about a hundred, forcefully demanded changes in the draft. Chairperson Sebghatullah Mojadeddi had to reluctantly concede to their demand for appointing at least one woman deputy chairperson of the total four. It was due to their hectic lobbying that the Constitution defined the term "Afghan citizen" as including all citizens of Afghanistan, whether man or woman, who have equal rights and duties before the law.

It was again due to their persuasion that the representation of women in the legislature was augmented. It was agreed that at least two women, instead of one as mentioned in the original draft, would be elected from each province to the *Wolesi Jirga*. This meant that women would hold at least 64 of the 250 seats in the *Wolesi Jirga*, or more than 25 per cent seats. With regard to the religious freedom of minorities, the final draft declared, with an added emphasis, that religious minorities "are free to exercise their faith" and perform their religious rites "within the limits of law." On the issue of official recognition of ethnic minorities, Article 4 of the final draft clearly identified the names of 14 ethnic groups as comprising the nation of Afghanistan.

Language Issue

The original draft declared *Pashto* to be the national language of Afghanistan. Delegates belonging to minority ethnic groups, particularly the *Farsiwan* and the Uzbeks took exception to this. They strongly demanded that their languages be given status equal to that of *Pashto*. This led to a heated debate on the issue of national language and the official status of minority languages. Under a compromise, the final draft did not mention any language as the national language. However, the national anthem, which mentions the name of all 14 ethnic groups, was to be in *Pashto*. In addition to *Pashto* and *Dari*, six additional languages – *Uzbeki, Turkmen, Baluchi, Pashai, Nuristani* and *Pamiri* – were made the third official language in regions where a majority of the population spoke them.

Such contentious issues raised at the CLJ not only highlighted the simmering discontent in Afghanistan's social and political life, but also underlined the potential causes and sources of future conflict. Also, there was certain scepticism over the way the Constitution was rushed through; there were reports about political intimidation and vote-buying, and the credentials of many of the delegates were doubtful.[35] In the absence of law-enforcement agencies and a well-organised independent judiciary, the implementation aspect of the Constitution remained questionable. Nevertheless, it did emerge as a key reference or guiding principle as Afghanistan experimented and experienced electoral politics in the following years.

NOTES

1. Generally referred to as *mujahideen* (the holy warriors) or the warlords. The United Nations (UN) prefers the term 'regional strongmen.'
2. Taliban is the Persian and Pashto plural of the Arabic word *Talib*, meaning 'seeker of (religious) knowledge.' The Arabic plural is *talaba* or *tulaba.*
3. The Bonn Agreement is formally known as 'Agreement on Provisional Arrangements in Afghanistan Pending the Re-Establishment of Permanent Governing Institutions.' Also known as the Petersburg Agreement, it was signed on December 05, 2001, the ninth day of the Bonn Conference which began on November 27, 2001.
4. Ahmed Rashid, "Afghanistan: Ending the Policy Quagmire," *Journal of International Affairs*, 54 (2), Spring 2001, p. 410.
5. For details, see Lucy Morgan Edwards, *The Afghan Solution. The Inside Story of Abdul Haq, the CIA and How Western Hubris Lost Afghanistan*, Bactria Press, London, 2011.
6. Keith Dovkants, "Rebel Chief Begs: Don't Bomb Now, Taliban Will be Gone in a Month," *Evening Standard* (London), October 05, 2001, as cited in Lucy Morgan Edwards, *The Afghan Solution. The Inside Story of Abdul Haq, the CIA and How Western Hubris Lost Afghanistan*, Bactria Press, London, 2011, pp. 2, 324-25. The book also mentions that Abdul Haq was reportedly dubbed by the Pakistan intelligence as 'Hollywood Haq.'
7. Ibid.
8. Michael R. Gordon and Tim Weiner, "A Nation Challenged: The Mission; A Frantic Call for U.S. Help Came Too Late," *The New York Times*, October 27, 2001, at http://www.nytimes.com/2001/10/27/world/a-nation-challenged-the-mission-a-frantic-call-for-us-help-came-too-late.html?pagewanted=all
9. Richard Lloyd Parry, "Anti-Taliban warlords set the rules for a new round of the Great Game," *The Independent* (UK), October 12, 2001, at http://www.afghanistannewscenter.com/news/2001/october/oct12k2001.html
10. Lucy Morgan Edwards, no. 5, p. 10.
11. Northern Alliance, a loose *melange* of ethnically and ideologically disparate, primarily non-Pashun factions from the north, evolved out of the power struggle that ensued after the Soviet withdrawal. It first came into existence in 1992 to put up a united front against the communist Najibullah Government. The key leaders of the first Northern Alliance were Uzbek Commander Abdul Rashid Dostum who had rebelled against the Najibullah Government, the Tajik leader Ahmad Shah Masoud, and the Iran-backed Afghan Shia

confederacy, Hizb-e-Wahadat-e-Islami-ye Afghanistan. By 1993, it had disintegrated due to a power contest between Masoud, Dostum and Hekmatyar. The Alliance was again resurrected in October 1996 after the fall of Kabul to the Taliban in September. It again comprised of mainly Tajik, Uzbek and Hazara factions, represented by Burhanuddin Rabbani and Ahmad Shah Masoud, Abdul Rashid Dostum and Muhammad Karim Khalili, respectively. Formally known as Jabha-ye Muttahid-e-Islami-ye Milli bara-ye Nijat-e-Afghanistan or the National Islamic United Front for the Salvation of Afghanistan, the Northern Alliance was the only organised resistance to Taliban's march northwards toward Kabul and beyond, though it failed to effectively stop the Taliban from capturing most of northern Afghanistan, including its headquarters at Mazar-e-Sharif. Henceforth, the term Northern Alliance would be used throughout the text for purpose of convenience.

12. "Interview: Colin Powell," *Frontline, Public Broadcasting Service* (PBS), June 07, 2002, at http://www.pbs.org/wgbh/pages/frontline/shows/campaign/interviews/powell.html
13. Sidney Blumenthal, "Democracy was only an afterthought," *The Guardian*, July 21, 2005, at http://www.guardian.co.uk/world/2005/jul/21/afghanistan.comment/print
14. Chris Johnson, Jolyon Leslie, *Afghanistan: The Mirage of Peace*, Zed Books, London and New York, 2004. p. 15.
15. See "Agreement on Provisional Arrangements in Afghanistan Pending the Re-Establishment of Permanent Government Institutions," *United Nations Regional Information Centre for Western Europe,* December 05, 2001, at http://www.unric.org/de/component/content/article/11-peace/26329-agreement-on-provisional-arrangements-in-afghanistan-pending-the-re-establishment-of-permanent-government-institutions
16. The four Afghan groups invited to the Bonn Conference were – the Northern Alliance (representing minority ethnic groups from the north) led by Yunus Qanuni; the Rome Group (pro-Zahir Shah Royalists) led by Abdul Sattar Sirat; the Cyprus Group (the Iranian-backed Afghan exiles) led by Humayun Jareer, son-in-law of Gulbuddin Hekmatyar of Hezb-e Islami faction; and the Peshawar Group (Peshawar-based mujahideen exiles) led by Hamid Gailani, son of Pir Sayid Ahmed Gailani, each representing varying background and political interests. Mustafa Zahir, grandson of King Zahir Shah, was the only member from the former royal family participating in the Conference.
17. Sidney Blumenthal, "Democracy was only an afterthought," *The Guardian*, July 21, 2005, at http://www.guardian.co.uk/world/2005/jul/21/afghanistan.comment/print
18. "Filling the Vacuum: The Bonn Conference," *Public Broadcasting Service (PBS)*, at http://www.pbs.org/wgbh/pages/frontline/shows/campaign/withus/cbonn.html
19. Agreement on Provisional Arrangements, no. 15.
20. In the 29-member Afghan Interim Administration, there were 18 ministers from the Northern Alliance, 8 from the Rome Group, 1 from the Peshawar Group and 2 independent ministers, excluding Chairman Hamid Karzai. As for the ethnic composition of the AIA, there were 11 Tajik, 10 Pashtun, 5 Hazara and 3 Uzbek ministers. Chairman Hamid Karzai was a Pashtun from the Rome Group. For the list of members of the AIA, see Text of the Bonn Agreement, at http://www.un.org/News/dh/latest/afghan/afghan-agree.htm
21. See "Interview: Dr. Abdullah," *Public Broadcasting Service (PBS)*, April 05, 2002, at http://www.pbs.org/wgbh/pages/frontline/shows/campaign/interviews/abdullah.html
22. Rory McCarthy and Ewen MacAskill, "King's aide is favourite to be next leader," *The Guardian*, December 03, 2001, at http://www.guardian.co.uk/world/2001/dec/03/afghanistan.ewenmacaskill1
23. Of the four contenders, three were pro-royalist and had supported the return of King Zahir Shah from exile at different points of time. Pir Gailani was married to a granddaughter of King Habibullah Khan (1901-19).

24. Sirat, an Uzbek from Samangan, is an Islamic theologian. He held several ministerial positions including Ministry of Justice under former King Zahir Shah. During the king's exile beginning 1973, he served as his advisor. He was also the presidential candidate in the October 2004 election. He is also brother-in-law to Yunus Qanuni. For more about Sirat, see Amanullah Nasrat, "Dr Abdul Satar Sirat: Royalist Promotes Unity," *Institute for War & Peace Reporting (IWPR)*, ARR Issue 139, September 01, 2006, at http://iwpr.net/report-news/dr-abdul-satar-sirat-royalist-promotes-unity
25. Vaiju Naravane, "Great Expectations," *Frontline*, 18 (25), December 08 - 21, 2001, at http://www.frontlineonnet.com/fl1825/18251250.htm
26. See "Press Briefing by Prof. Abdul Sattar Sirat, Head of the Rome Group Delegation, and Other Members of the Delegation," *United Nations Regional Information Centre for Western Europe,* November 29, 2001, at http://www.unric.org/de/frieden-und-sicherheit/26336
27. Hamid Karzai was also the deputy foreign minister in the first government established by the resistance leadership after the collapse of Najibullah regime in 1992. His father Abdul Ahad Karzai was the Deputy Speaker of the first Afghan Parliament established in 1960s during King Zahir Shah's reign. He was killed by the Taliban in August 1999 in Quetta in Pakistan. Karzai's grandfather, Khair Mohammad Khan, had served in the 1919 war for independence and was Deputy Speaker of the Afghan Senate under King Amanullah Khan.
28. "Statement By Lakhdar Brahmi, Special Representative of the Secretary-General for Afghanistan," *United Nations*, December 22, 2001, at http://www.un.org/News/dh/latest/lakhdar.htm
29. Agreement on Provisional Arrangements, no. 15.
30. Abdul Rahman had earlier worked with Ahmad Shah Masoud and was a founder member of the Shura-e Nazar. Later, the two fell out and Rahman joined the pro-Zahir Shah Rome Group. His wife, Foruzan Fana, had fought the 2009 presidential election.
31. Known as Haji Abdul Qadir, he came from the influential Pashtun Arsala family of Nangarhar Province with a long history of having served under successive Afghan kings. He was the elder brother of anti-Soviet Commander Abdul Haq who was killed by the Taliban in October 2001. His father was an engineer and was associated with the US-funded Helmand river valley project in the 1950s and 1960s. His great grandfather was the foreign minister of Afghanistan under King Sher Ali Khan (1863-79). Qadir was earlier affiliated with Hezb-e Islami (Yunus Khalis) and was governor of Nangarhar during the *mujahideen* government (1992-96). It is said that as provincial governor he had welcomed Osama bin Laden in 1996 when the latter shifted his base from Sudan to eastern Afghanistan. However, he had to soon leave the country after Taliban came to power. He later joined the Northern Alliance upon his return in 1999 when his son Abdul Zahir Qadir who was under Taliban detention had escaped along with commander Ismael Khan of Herat. Qadir was vice-chairman of the Northern Alliance delegation to the Bonn Conference (November 27-December 05, 2001). After the defeat of the Taliban, he had formed the Eastern Shura in Nangarhar along with prominent local commanders, Hazrat Ali and Haji Zaman. Qadir was initially reluctant to take up position in the central administration and wanted to return to Jalalabad of which he was earlier the governor. At the time of his assassination, he was expected to take over as Interior Minister in the newly formed Transitional Authority. His son Zahir Qadir became the first deputy speaker of *Wolesi Jirga* (the lower house) in Afghan Parliament. Another son, Jamal Qadir, was the chairman of the provincial council of Nangarhar Province.
32. Barnett R. Rubin, "(Re) Building Afghanistan: The Folly of Stateless Democracy," *Current History*, April 2004, p. 166.
33. Ralph H. Magnus and Eden Naby, *Afghanistan. Mullah, Marx and Mujahid*, HarperCollins, New Delhi, 1998, pp. 18-19.

34. See "Constitutional Process Marred by Abuses," *Human Rights Watch*, January 07, 2004, at http://www.hrw.org/english/docs/2004/01/07/afghan6914.htm
35. The 502 delegates attending the *Jirga* were divided into ten committees, each comprising about 50 members, to discuss various sets of articles. There were many former resistance leaders, commanders and religious figures participating in the *Jirga*. Burhanuddin Rabbani, Abdurrab Rasul Sayyaf, Ahmed Nabi Muhammadi (son of Maulvi Muhammad Nabi Muhammadi), Ustad Abdul Farid (former Prime Minister representing Gulbuddin Hekmatyar in 1992) and Hashmat Ghani Ahmadzai (brother of former finance minister, Ashraf Ghani Ahmadzai) headed some of the committees.

"These are the moral equivalent of America's founding fathers."

—Former US President Ronald Reagan referring to a delegation of anti-Soviet Afghan resistance leaders visiting White House in 1985.

CHAPTER II

Tryst with Democracy

With the new constitution ratified by the *Constitutional Loya Jirga* (CLJ) in January 2004, attention turned towards Afghanistan's first democratic elections. Afghanistan's emergence as a democracy was one of the key achievements of the Bonn Process that concluded with the successful completion of the first round of presidential and parliamentary elections in 2004-05. Afghanistan has since been a democracy. Five years later, the second round of presidential and parliamentary elections were held in 2009-10. With the US and its NATO allies transferring the security responsibilities to an ill-prepared Afghan army and police, doubts are being expressed about the survival of the post-Taliban political system and the constitution. The efficacy of the third round of presidential and parliamentary elections, particularly in terms of strengthening the inclusive political process in the country as the Western coalition ends its combat mission in December 2014, too is clouded with uncertainty. The strength of nascent democracy in Afghanistan is being clearly put to test. How indispensable or dispensable is the current political system and the constitution for various stakeholders in the Afghan politics, would largely determine the future of democracy in the country.

The old socio-political fault lines, enmeshed with divergent interests of various internal and external forces involved, however, continue to grow. Whether the country's decade-long tryst with democracy is about to be over as the Western troops drawdown or is it likely to survive, remains to be seen. Though prospects of a new and rather more chaotic political arrangement emerging after 2014-15 cannot be ruled out, the impact of a decade long democratisation process on the younger generation of Afghans too cannot be ignored. A notable section of Afghan society may have actually benefited in terms of political and social empowerment from an elective and inclusive political system.

The outcome of the previous two rounds of national elections though noted largely for the continuing influence of the old political elements and their divisive politics, but at the same time it also created opportunities and space for civilianising their roles in the new order. More importantly, and perhaps for the first time since 1973, the political transitions were largely peaceful and relatively sustainable. The elections were able to channelise the old factional divides and competing interests into a manageable chaos. Compared to the extremely violent conflict of the 1990s, Afghanistan in the first decade of the post-Taliban phase has experienced relative peace and development in most parts of the country.

A country which had been at war for three decades and with hardly any functional state institution in place, could not have transformed into a stable thriving democracy in a short span of time. Progress was bound to be gradual, fragmented, restricted and strained by severe challenges from within and without. It would be absolutely unfair to judge whatever progress Afghanistan has made in the last one decade on the basis of established benchmarks and standardised parameters of measuring success. However, as the West scales down its engagement and anxiety over the future of the country grows, an assessment of the decade long electoral politics and its varying impact on upcoming political developments is critical to understanding the transition and post-transition challenges.

The First Election (2004-05)

Given the fragility of the post-Taliban political process and the delicate position of Hamid Karzai, West was keen on holding the first presidential election as early as possible.[1] There was an urgent need to legitimise and stabilise Karzai's position in the new political structure, lest more alternative candidates or political opposition emerges, further fragmenting the potential share of vote. Already 17 candidates, apart from Karzai, were in the fray. With different factions of the Northern Alliance fielding their own candidates, it would have been increasingly difficult for Karzai to consolidate his support among the minority ethnic groups, who together formed a substantial chunk of the Afghan population. His limited authority, absence of local support base, and dependency on the West, stood in stark contrast to those of factional commanders and leaders, particularly from the former Northern Alliance, in the fray.

Interestingly, Karzai commenced his presidential election campaign in July 2004 by calling the private militias as the biggest threat to Afghanistan, greater than the Taliban insurgency.[2] On December 09, 2004, two days after his inauguration as an elected President, he declared *Jihad* against drugs during a national counter-narcotics conference in Kabul, calling it a national disgrace.[3] Perhaps, Karzai's forceful assertion against the overarching influence of factional commanders and the growing drug menace carried the trappings of a failing war on terror in Afghanistan.

Another important issue at stake was the credibility of the Bonn Process. The UN had already declared that it would prefer an 'imperfect' election in Afghanistan, rather than let the Bonn Process be questioned or wrecked.[4] In the circumstances, it was felt that an early presidential election would help reinforce Karzai's political legitimacy as well as the credibility of the West-sponsored Bonn Process in the eyes of the Afghans as well as the international community. It was also felt that a democratically elected government in Kabul would keep international donors and investors engaged in Afghanistan.

Some Afghan leaders, including number of presidential candidates, however, contended that the elections were being hastily arranged as there were still many logistical issues waiting to be addressed. The timing of the October 2004 election was also seen in the light of the US presidential elections which were due next month in November. There was a perception that the Afghan presidential election was more a part of the Bush Administration's electoral agenda. However, Karzai's supporters strongly felt that for a long time to come there would not be a perfect time or conditions for elections in a country devastated by decades of civil strife. It was argued that however flawed the election might be, it would still strengthen Kabul's position and accord it the necessary political legitimacy to deal with the challenges of state-building.

Much of the argument against the October 2004 presidential election was based on the worsening security situation across the country, lack of critical institutional structures, shortage of trained manpower and requisite funds, overarching influence of factional commanders, unfinished disarmament programme, and repatriation and rehabilitation of refugees. Among key challenges to the first elections in post-Taliban Afghanistan were:

Deteriorating Security

A year after the overthrow of the Taliban regime, deteriorating security in parts of the country had emerged as a major impediment to the ongoing process of political transition. The 18,000 US-led coalition troops faced increasing challenge from the Taliban-al Qaeda-Hekmatyar combine, who had declared *jihad* against foreign troops and the transitional government in Kabul as the US shifted its focus to Iraq. In October 2003, the then Under-Secretary General for UN Peacekeeping Operations, Jean Marie Guehenno, in a regular briefing to the Security Council, had stated: "In several border districts (near Kandahar and Paktika), the Taliban have been able to establish *de facto* control over district administration."[5] There were also reports suggesting that the Taliban were controlling eight of the 11 districts in the south-eastern Zabul Province alone.[6]

By May-June 2004, the violence, which was earlier confined to south-eastern parts of the country, had begun moving to the relatively peaceful provinces in the north. An increasingly concerted effort was being made by various militant groups, especially the Taliban and their allies, to disrupt and derail the election process. There were numerous instances of attacks on election offices and workers across the country, including in Kabul. In a gruesome incident of voter intimidation, the Taliban reportedly executed 16 Afghans for registering to vote and carrying election identity cards in Urozgan Province on August 25, 2004. On August 29, in one of the deadliest attacks in Kabul since September 2002 (when 26 civilians were killed in a car bombing), at least 12 people, including few Americans, were killed in a truck bomb blast. The attack took place close to the office of the US security contract firm, DynCorp Inc., which was responsible for providing security to Hamid Karzai, and was assisting in training the Afghan police. Taliban had also launched a leaflet campaign exhorting people against participating in the elections and threatened to kill anyone found supporting the government or the coalition troops.

Karzai's Limited Authority

Karzai's authority was precariously confined to Kabul, as rest of the country reeled under factionalism, widening ethnic tensions, increasing militant attacks, growing drug production and widespread corruption. Regional commanders often openly challenged the authority of provincial governors and other Kabul-appointees. There were cases where provincial governors had to flee for their lives in the face of violent opposition from local people or regional commanders.[7]

Due to the deteriorating security situation, especially in the southern and south-eastern provinces, and keeping in view his limited authority, Karzai began making overtures to the low and mid-level Taliban commanders and Hekmatyar's Hizb-e-Islami. As part of the changed political tactics to deal with violence, Karzai and the US invited them to participate in the election process. They had also been working on an amnesty scheme for them. In addition, realising the centrality of regional commanders in the Afghan polity, Karzai reportedly also sought their cooperation and support for his presidential candidature. This was reflective of the dominant position of the factional commanders especially in the provinces. In the absence of effective law enforcement agencies, it was getting increasingly difficult for Kabul to extend its authority to the provinces. The faltering security situation had adversely impacted on the voter registration process, as much of the southern and south-eastern provinces remained inaccessible to election officials.

Even the UN-Japan run Disarmament, Demobilisation and Rehabilitation Programme (DDR), which initially planned to demobilise and disarm an estimated 100,000 militias (the UN later reduced the figure to 50,000-60,000) across the country in two-three years, and merge them into the upcoming national army and police force, remained ineffective. The success of the DDR programme was considered as crucial for diluting the power of various militias and in de-weaponising the country. Due to the lack of trust among themselves and, collectively, in the transitional administration, most of the regional commanders openly refused to surrender their heavy weaponry or disband their militia. It is noteworthy that some of these commanders who were also ministers in the government maintained some of the largest militia in the country. Similarly, the Provincial Reconstruction Teams (PRTs) or armed units of civil-military administration, created under the provisions of the Bonn Agreement with the objective of bolstering Karzai's authority in the provinces, also failed to serve its purpose. Due to the prevailing insecurity and lack of logistics, the PRTs remained largely confined to the relatively peaceful northern and western provinces and were yet to be effective in the volatile south and south-eastern provinces.

A Reluctant NATO

The NATO, which took over the command of the International Security Assistance Force (ISAF) in August 2003 and was unanimously mandated in October the same year by the UN Security Council (UNSC) to expand its operations beyond Kabul, remained beset with severe financial and logistical shortcomings. Not many NATO countries came forward to reinforce the ISAF with fresh supplies of troops and other necessary logistics to enable it to expand its scope of operations beyond Kabul. In fact, the then NATO Secretary-General Jaap de Hoop Scheffer, on the eve of the NATO Summit at Istanbul on June 28-29, 2004, had lamented at the yawning gap between political decisions and commitment of resources for operations by the member-states. Scheffer, describing the attitude of member-states as "simply intolerable," urged them to commit the necessary resources to existing NATO operations, especially in Afghanistan.[8]

Growing Drug Menace

The spurt in Taliban attacks and revived power of the regional commanders coincided with the poppy boom in the country. Afghanistan had emerged as the world's largest opium producer, providing almost 85-90 per cent of the world's illicit opium production by 2004. The link between local militia commanders, poppy cultivators and heroin traders was abiding and ran through various power networks. Many of the commanders, who financed their militia through drug money and encouraged farmers to produce more poppy, were holding senior positions in the government. This has since been a restraining factor in eradicating poppy production in Afghanistan. Due to Karzai's and West's dependence on these militia commanders to keep the political process going, little could be done against the drug menace.

A major contradiction, thus, emerged in the US-led war with regard to counter-terrorism and counter-narcotics in Afghanistan. Even otherwise, the US-led coalition was not in a position to spare more troops and logistics to open a large-scale front against the drug menace in Afghanistan. Possible rebellion from the militia commanders and the reluctance of the Afghan farmers to give up poppy cultivation for lack of alternate livelihood, were major limiting factors. Except for the year 2001, when opium production crashed to a mere 185 tonnes from 3,276 tonnes the previous year due to a strict Taliban ban, poppy cultivation in Afghanistan has since seen a phenomenal rise.

Shortage of Funds

Apart from serious security challenges, the election officials also had to struggle against severe shortage of funds. According to the UN, Afghanistan urgently needed $101 million for conducting the elections. Of this only $70 million was pledged by the donor countries, leading to a shortfall of $31 million. The estimated immediate need was for $87 million to provide for voting screens, ballot papers and to hire and train Afghan election personnel. Similarly, at the Berlin Donors Conference held from March 31 to April 01, 2004, the international community could pledge only $8.2 billion over the next three years, far short of the $27.6 billion sought by the Karzai Government and the UN over the next seven years for rebuilding the country in their joint report called *Securing Afghanistan's Future.*[9]

Absence of Political Parties

Afghanistan went to elections without political parties. Most of the presidential candidates lacked a well-defined agenda or vision for the future of Afghanistan. They were either offshoots of some factional group or had the support of one of them. Though political parties were restrained from fighting elections, they were, however, allowed to register themselves. It is noteworthy that Article 35 of the new Constitution clearly stated that the citizens of Afghanistan have the right to form political parties provided the "organisational structure and financial sources of the party are made public;" "the party does not have military or paramilitary aims and structures," and that the "party is not affiliated to foreign political parties or sources." It further states, "Formation and functioning of a party based on ethnicity, language, Islamic school of thought (mazhab-e-fiqhi) and region shall not be permissible."[10] Now, if any one of these clauses were applied, then most of the political formations in Afghanistan would not have qualified to be registered as political parties. Interestingly, the issue has not lost its appeal and is raised even to this day.

President Elect and the First Cabinet

The October 2004 presidential election marked the end of the phase of provisional governments as envisaged in the Bonn Agreement. The final results announced in November by the Joint Electoral Management Body (JEMB) declared Hamid Karzai as the elected president of Afghanistan. Karzai secured 55.04 per cent of the total votes, distantly followed by the Tajik candidate Yunus Qanuni (16.03 per cent), Hazara candidate Mohammad Mohaqiq (11.07 per cent) and the Uzbek candidate Abdul Rashid Dostum (10.03 per cent) as second, third and fourth, respectively. The pattern of voting made it amply clear that the election was fought along the much-anticipated ethnic lines. Perhaps, Karzai also benefited from the division of votes among the non-Pashtun communities.

The dominance of the regional commanders was amplified by the fact that all the candidates who made it to the top four, except for Karzai, either commanded militia units or had the support of one or the other militia groups. It was noteworthy that Karzai in the run-up to the election had referred to the warlords as the greatest threat to Afghanistan and had promised not to work with them, if elected. However, despite all his political assertions, Karzai had a tough time in announcing his cabinet. He had to negotiate with his strongest presidential rival Yunus Qanuni, whom he had offered the post of defence minister. Qanuni refused to participate in the government and instead formed a new political party. Karzai and his backers were well aware of the fact that without reaching a compromise with minority ethnic factions, Kabul would not be able to extend its authority in the north.

On December 23, 2004, President Karzai finally announced his 27-member cabinet, which was low on the old resistance leadership and high on technically and professionally qualified people (see Table 2.1). It is evident from the table that in his first cabinet Karzai tried to strike a balance between the aspirations of the regional commanders and the requirement of qualified people to carry forward the much-needed reforms. The objective seems to be to keep the powerful militia commanders out of the Kabul power structure by offering posts either in provinces or appointing them to inconsequential or ceremonial positions in the centre. However, keeping in view the forthcoming parliamentary and local elections in September 2005, Karzai did not completely marginalise the Northern Alliance leadership, especially the Panjshiri faction. He appointed Uzbek leader Dostum as chief-of-staff to the commander-in-chief of the Afghan armed forces,[11] and granted lifetime special privileges to the leader of the Tajik militia, Mohammad Qasim Fahim, allowing him to retain his military rank of a Marshall throughout his life.[12] It was clear from the presidential election that the parliamentary elections too would also be fought along ethnic lines, with several alliances, combinations and permutations emerging.

Table 2.1: Composition of First Elected Government of Afghanistan (December 2004 to October 2009)

Cabinet Position	Name	Change from Transitional Administration	Notable Points
President	Hamid Karzai	Same Position	Pashtun/Rome Group Headed Post-Taliban Interim and Transitional Authorities earlier (December 2001-2004)
First Vice President	Ahmad Zia Masoud	New Member	Tajik/NA Brother of Ahmad Shah Masoud; former ambassador to Russia (2001-04)
Second Vice President	Karim Khalili	Same as in ATA	Hazara/Hezb-e Wahadat/NA
Senior Minister	Hedayat Amin Arsala	Vice Chair & Finance Minister in AIA & Vice President in ATA	Pashtun/Rome Group
Foreign Minister	Abdullah Abdullah Rangin Dadfar Spanta	Same as in AIA & ATA New Member; appointed in April 2006 after cabinet reshuffle	Tajik/NA Tajik Previously Senior Advisor on International Affairs to President Hamid Karzai
Defence Minister	Abdul Rahim Wardak	Deputy Defence Minister under Mohammad Qasim Fahim in ATA	Pashtun/Pro-Royalist Peshawar Group Mahaz-eMilli Islami-e Afghanistan of Pir Sayyed Ahmad Gailani
Interior Minister	Ali Ahmed Jalali (resigned in September 2005) Zarar Ahmad Moqbil September 2005-October 2008) Mohammad Hanif Atmar (October 2008-June 2010)	Same as in ATA New Member Rural Development Minister in ATA	Pashtun Former Colonel in the Afghan Army Tajik/NA Previously Deputy Interior Minister Pashtun

Finance Minister	Anwar-ul Haq Ahadi	Previously Governor of Central Bank in ATA	Pashtun/Technocrat
	Omar Zakhliwal (appointed in February 2009)	New Member	Pashtun Previously appointed as Acting Minister of Transport & Civil Aviation in November 2008
Economy Minister	Mohammad Amin Farhang (till march 2006)	Reconstruction Minister in AIA & ATA	Pashtun/Rome Group
	Mohammad Jalil Shams	New Member Previously, Deputy Minister of Water & Energy	Tajik
Justice Minister	Sarwar Danish	New Member	Hazara/Hezb-e Wahdat First Governor of newly created province of Daykundi
Education Minister	Noor Mohammad Qarqin	Labour & Social Affairs Minister in ATA; Karzai's election campaign manager	Turkmen In 2006, Qarqeen switched to Ministry of Social Affairs.
	Mohammad Hanif Atmar (May 2005 – October 2008)	Rural Development Minister in ATA	Pashtun Between 2006 and 2008, Atmar was the Education Minister before he switched to Interior Ministry in 2008. Wardak succeeded Atmar in October 2008.
	Ghulam Farooq Wardak	New Member	Pashtun/Hezb-e Islami
Higher Education Minister	Amir Shah Hasanyar (December 2004-March 2006)	New member	Hazara
	Mohammad Azam Dadfar (March 2006-January 2010)	New Member	Uzbek

(*Contd.*)

Cabinet Position	Name	Change from Transitional Administration	Notable Points
Commerce Minister	Hedayat Amin Arsala (also Senior Minister in the Cabinet)	Vice Chair & Finance Minister in AIA/Vice President in ATA	Pashtun/Rome Group
Commerce & Industry Minister *(Industry was merged into Commerce Ministry after March 2006)*	Mohammad Haidar Reza (candidature not approved by Wolesi Jirga in 2006)	New Member Appointed after March 2006 cabinet reshuffle	Previously, Deputy Foreign Minister for Administrative Affairs since 2002
	Mohammad Amin Farhang (removed in late 2008)	Reconstruction Minister in AIA & ATA	Pashtun/Rome Group
	Wahidullah Shahrani	New Member	Uzbek Son of Haj Minister Neamatullah Shahrani; previously, Deputy Minister of Finance & First Deputy Governor of Central Bank
Water & Energy Minister Newly Created Ministry	Ismail Khan	New Member	Tajik/NA Former Governor of Herat
Transport & Civil Aviation Minister	Enayatullah Qasemi	New Member (December 2004-March 2006)	Hazara
	Gul Hussain Ahmedi (appointment disapproved by Wolesi Jirga)	New Member (March 2006 - August 2006)	Former Director of Department of Cultural Affairs, Ministry of Foreign Affairs
	Neamatullah Ehsan Jawed (removed due to mismanagement of national carrier)	New Member (August 2006-March 2008)	
	Hamidullah Qaderi (removed due to corruption charges)	New Member (March 2008 - November 2008)	Pashtun
	Omar Zakhliwal (acting minister)	New Member (November 2008-February 2009)	Pashtun
	Hamidullah Farooqi	New Member (February 2009-January 2010)	Pashtun

Women's Affair Minister	Masooda Jalal (till July 2006)	New Member	Tajik
	Suraya Raheem Sabarang Candidature rejected by *Wolesi Jirga*	New Member	Tajik
	Husn Bano Ghazanfar (since August 2006)	New Member	Uzbek/Independent
Youth Affairs Minister	Amina Afzali (December 2004-06)	New Member A Newly Created Ministry	Tajik/NA
Youth & Culture Affairs Minister	Sayed Makhdoom Raheen (disapproved by *Wolesi Jirga*)	Same as in AIA & ATA	Tajik/Rome group
	Abdul Karim Khorram (since August 2006)	New member	Pashtun/Hezb-e Islami (Hekmatyar)
Haj & Islamic Affairs Minister	Neamatullah Shahrani	Vice President in ATA/Head of the Constitution Commission	Uzbek
Public Works Minister	Sohrab Ali Saffari	New Member	Hazara
Public Health Minister	Mohammad Amin Fatemi	New Member	Tajik Same position in the Rabbani Government during 1993-95.
Agriculture Minister	Obaidullah Ramin (till October 2008)	New Member	Tajik
	Mohammad Asef Rahimi	New Member	Pashtun
Mines & Industry Minister *The Ministry was bifurcated and Industry went with Commerce Ministry after March 2006*	Mir Mohammad Sediq (December 2004-March 2006)	New Member	
	Ibrahim Adel (Mines Minister only)	New Member	Tajik Previously, Deputy Mines & Industries Minister since 2005

(*Contd.*)

Cabinet Position	Name	Change from Transitional Administration	Notable Points
Communications Minister	Amirzai Sangeen	New Member	Pashtun/Technocrat
Rural Rehabilitation & Development Minister	Mohammad Hanif Atmar (December 2004-March 2006)	Same as in ATA	Pashtun
	Mohammad Ehsan Zia (since May 2006)	New Member	Pashtun
Labour & Social Affairs Minister	Syed Ekramuddin Masoomi (till March 2006)	New Member	Tajik
Martyrs & Disabled/Labour & Social Ministry merged in March 2006	Noor Mohammad Qarqin (succeeded Masoomi in March 2006	Same as in ATA Previously, the Education Minister in this cabinet	Turkmen
Border & Tribal Affairs Minister	Abdul Karim Brahui (January 2005-February 2009)	New Member	Brahui Previously, Governor of Nimroz Province
	Asadullah Khalid	New Member	Pashtun/NA Previously, Governor of Kandahar & Ghazni Province
Urban Development Minister	Yousef Pashtun	Same as in ATA	Pashtun/Royalist
Counter Narcotics Minister	Habibullah Qaderi (January 2004-July 2007)	New Member Ministry was created in December 2003	Pashtun
	Gen. Khodaidad (March 2008-June 2010)	New Member	Hazara/Ex-Army Officer Previously, Deputy Minister of Counter-narcotics
Refugees & Repatriation Minister	Azam Dadfar (December 2004-March 2006)	New Member	Uzbek
	Mohammad Akbar Akbar	New Member	Pashtun
	Abdul Karim Brahui (February 2009 -August 2010)	Previously Border & Tribal Affairs Minister	Brahui

Martyrs and Disabled Minister	Sediqa Balkhi (till March 2006) *In March 2006 cabinet reshuffle, this ministry was merged into Labour & Social Affairs Ministry under Noor Mohammad Qarqin as listed before.*	New Member	Hazara
Other Key Positions			
Chief Justice of the Supreme Court	Fazl Hadi Shinwari (till 2006)	Same as in ATA	Pashtun/Peshawar Group
National Security Advisor	Zalmay Rassoul	Same as in ATA	Pashtun/Rome Group
Governor of the Central Bank	Noorullah Delawari (2005-07) Abdul Qadir Fitrat (September 2007-11)	New Appointment (replaced Anwar ul Haq Ahadi in 2004) New Appointment	Tajik/Technocrat Tajik/Technocrat
Permanent Representative to the UN	Ravan A.G. Farhadi (January 2002-06) Zaher Tanin (since December 2006)	Same as in ATA New Appointment	Tajik/NA Tajik

Author's Note: This table has been drawn and compiled from various sources as no two sources give similar details. Wherever the information provided by key sources are at variance with each other, the same has been verified and further corroborated by consulting an extended range of sources in order to ensure the accuracy of information to the extent possible. Key sources of information are: personal profiles/biographies of incumbent ministers available on Afghan Government websites, and other websites, such as *Afghanistan Online* (www.afghan-web.com), *Afghan Biographies* (www.afghan-bios.info), etc.

Assessing the Bonn Process

With the Bonn Agreement's timeframe having ended with the first presidential election in October 2004 and parliamentary election in September 2005, the element of political uncertainty continued to shroud the future of Afghanistan. The key questions then were—did Bonn went the same way as previous agreements and accords? If not, then was it able to prompt any qualitative change in the Afghan polity since Afghanistan's identity-based power politics continued to play a significant role? The long-standing ethno-political divide though was a constant source of dissension within the Karzai-led provisional authorities; it goes to the credit of Karzai and his Western-backers that they could largely keep the diverse constituents of the provisional governments together until the announcement of the presidential candidates.

If one looks at the political equation that emerged after Hamid Karzai refused to have Qasim Fahim, his powerful Tajik defence minister, as his vice presidential running mate, one finds a repeat of the old story. With Tajiks, Uzbeks and Hazaras having announced their separate presidential candidates, the Pashtun-Northern Alliance or the Pashtun and non-Pashtun divide, as well as the divide among non-Pashtun groups, was complete. The Northern Alliance too had failed to announce a common presidential candidate. Yunus Qanuni, the former interior and education minister in the transitional administration, who enjoyed the backing of Qasim Fahim and Foreign Minister Abdullah Abdullah, secured the support of the Tajiks. He was considered as Karzai's most serious contender. Uzbek commander Dostum, Karzai's former military advisor and representative in the north, claimed the support of Uzbek and Turkmen people. Similarly, Mohammad Mohaqiq, Karzai's former planning minister who commanded several militia units, claimed Hazara support.

Hamid Karzai tried to marginalise and divide the Northern Alliance by naming late Ahmad Shah Masoud's brother, Ahmad Zia Masoud, and the prominent Hazara leader, Mohammad Karim Khalili, as his two running vice-presidential mates. Karzai could not have relied completely on his Pashtun constituency where he had a limited appeal due to Pashtun indifference to the Bonn Process and often their latent support for the Taliban. Apart from this, due to regular Taliban offensive the voter registration in predominantly Pashtun southern and south-eastern provinces had been low. Karzai's attempt to break away from the hold of powerful factional leaders and commanders from the north, particularly Tajik, further polarised the politics along ethnic lines. However, Karzai's greater political assertion won him limited appreciation of Pashtuns in general, as they remain wary of his dependence on the West. Nevertheless, Karzai's centrality in the Bonn Process remained steady. Though his position was not even remotely proportionate to the influence and resources commanded by the regional commanders, Karzai remained a crucial link to Afghanistan for the international community in years to come.

The continued dependence of the US-led coalition on the factional militias presented a major policy dilemma for Hamid Karzai too. It often proved to be a restraining factor in realising most of the provisions and objectives of the Bonn Agreement; and a hindrance to building effective institutions of governance in the country.

Militia forces of various commanders were frequently at loggerheads in parts of the country. However, West's dependence on the militia commanders re-institutionalised their position and role in the Afghan power play. The highly centralised presidential form of government as envisaged in the new Constitution also stood in sharp contrast to the current political realities in Afghanistan where provinces remained under the strong control of various factional and local commanders. This did not augur well for the ongoing political process and the overall future of Afghanistan.

The Bonn Process, which was supposed to have been an Afghan agenda guiding the course of state-building, was instead guided by the interests of the US and its allies both within and outside Afghanistan. With Bush's Iraq venture not faring well, and Osama bin Laden and Mullah Omar still elusive, holding of 'democratic' elections in Afghanistan was expected to give a boost to President Bush's image in the foreign policy domain and also reinforce the US-led war on terror. At the same time, if the canvas of the Afghan conflict is widened, its strong linkage to the larger game being played over Central Asia's vast and untapped energy resources and the politics of reconstruction cannot be missed. Nevertheless, it was still important to protect the results of the Bonn Agreement, for never before the UN and the West were involved in such a big way in re-building Afghanistan. It was an agreement which had for the first time envisaged the creation of viable institutions of governance in Afghanistan.

It was considered crucial for the future of Afghanistan that the establishment of modern political, legal, constitutional and economic institutions, congruent with the Afghan environment, is placed high in the order of priority. Elections alone could not have served the ultimate objective of establishing Afghanistan as a modern democratic state. The process failed to strengthen Kabul's position against the extra-constitutional authorities embedded in the provinces. It was clear that any stop-gap political arrangement or any short-term policy objective was not going to work in Afghanistan. Instead, sustainable approaches to state-building backed by indigenous efforts at multiple levels to resolve the various conflicts within the country were called for.

The US-sponsored Bonn Process to a large extent failed in bringing about any qualitative change in the Afghan polity. The inclusion and participation of different *mujahideen* factions led to contradictions in the central scheme of the Bonn political process, which was to build institutions of governance. Being part of the problem, the competing political agendas of the various Afghan factions were bound to come in direct conflict with the reforms and re-building aspect of the Bonn Process. The ideological divide and interest disparities among various factions, which had neither allowed them to put up a united front against the Soviets in the 1980s nor consensus over any power-sharing agreements in the past, simply resumed after the ouster of the Taliban.

The contradictions inherent in the Bonn Process were primarily due to the paradoxes in the US-led war on terror in Afghanistan. The short-term approach adopted by the Bush Administration at the beginning of the war has been the single biggest limiting factor behind the continuing political uncertainty in Afghanistan. West soon realised the limitations of its policy objectives in Afghanistan as it confronted the realities and the complexities of the Afghan politics. When the Bush Administration decided to wage a war on the Taliban and their al Qaeda allies, they had probably thought of destroying the Taliban infrastructure and apprehending Osama bin Laden and his close associates by launching surgical air strikes and swift military operations which could be wrapped up in two to three months before the harsh Afghan winter sets in.

The US did not seem to have been very keen on addressing or confronting the greater malaise that afflicted the war-torn Afghanistan. American reliance on certain *mujahideen* factions in overthrowing the Taliban, and also their inclusion in the Bonn Process, ensured that some of the most recalcitrant militia commanders remain unaccountable to the central government. The US forces have also continuously ignored their involvement in the opium trade in exchange for their help in fighting al-Qaeda and the Taliban. The fear of provoking rebellion among influential militia groups as well as losing the co-operation and support of the people in rural areas, both of which were critical to the American-led war on terror, largely restricted the counter-narcotic operations from the very beginning. The potential economic fallout of directly clamping on poppy cultivation and drug trade that kept the largely illicit economy of Afghanistan afloat too was a restraining factor. Even otherwise, the US-led coalition was not in a position to spare more troops and logistics to open a large-scale front against the drug menace in Afghanistan. The volatile security situation in Iraq, on one hand, and the reluctance of the NATO member-states to spare more troops or take to counter-terrorism, on the other, had left the US forces too stretched.

However, by 2005, there was a strong sense of realisation and resultant debate within the US establishment about the growing contradiction in its objectives in Afghanistan. Senior US officials at the time had even tried to rephrase the 'war on terror' as the 'Global Struggle against Violent Extremism.'[13] Probably, the idea was to de-emphasise the military character of the phrase by replacing 'war' with 'struggle.' It was also to widen its ideological scope at the international level and its acceptability within the US. The growing confusion within the American establishment on how to carry Afghanistan through its transition, and how to deal with the larger security threat emanating from the Afghanistan-Pakistan region, was more than apparent. Meanwhile, some of the former Taliban members had been nominated or appointed by President Karzai to the *Meshrano Jirga* (the upper house) of the new Afghan Parliament, part of his constant effort since 2003 to co-opt low and mid-level Taliban into the political process.

At the same time, the Bush Administration was also contemplating a gradual drawdown in the US presence, at least militarily, by widening the scope for the greater involvement of the European member-states of NATO. However, be it counter-insurgency or counter-narcotics, several NATO member-states and partner countries were neither willing nor prepared enough to commit adequate resources to the Afghan mission. As a result, the US failed to scale down its military presence particularly in view of the Taliban resurgence. At the level of the larger game being played over Central Asia's energy resources, the war in Afghanistan had initially and also for the first time in history provided the US with a foothold in Central Asia in the form of two bases or transit facilities, one in Karshi-Khanabad in Uzbekistan and the other at Manas in Kyrgyzstan.[14] The US interest in Afghanistan is also to be seen in the larger context of the highly competitive oil and pipeline politics over the Caspian energy resources, and a possible containment of Iran and China in the long run.

Apart from differences between the US and its European allies over the direction of the Afghan war and the role and mandate of the ISAF; severe differences with President Karzai too began to emerge on similar issues. Karzai became increasingly sceptical and critical of the Western strategy as Taliban re-appeared in villages and cities in the south and also as casualty levels due to coalition air strikes rose among the civilian population. He has since been asking the West to address the issue of safe sanctuaries that the Taliban and allies continue to enjoy in the bordering tribal areas within Pakistan.

Kabul began articulating its position in a more categorical and unambiguous manner both on the US' and Pakistan's role in the war. Perhaps, the first signs of serious differences that were to later emerge between the US and its regional allies, Pakistan and Afghanistan, and also between the two allies, had began appearing in 2005-06. At the domestic level, Karzai began facing stiff challenge from the elements of the former Northern Alliance and the old Islamists that had come to dominate the Afghan Parliament after September 2005 elections. Yunus Qanuni, the former interior minister in the provisional government, had emerged as the speaker of the elected 249-member *Wolesi Jirga* or the Lower House of the new Afghan Parliament. The protracted debate over the issue of dual citizenship of many of the cabinet members appointed by Karzai dominated the proceedings of the parliament. It is difficult to state whether it was a sign of democracy in exercise or simply a continuing manifestation of the old fault lines.

Karzai's Re-election: Chaotic Exercise

The second round of presidential and provincial council elections held on August 20, 2009, which led to the re-election of Karzai for the second-term, were relatively chaotic and marred by allegations of widespread electoral fraud and subversion of institutions relevant to the election process. According to a spokesman for the Electoral Complaints Commission (ECC), Ahmed Muslim Khuram, there were about 1,915 formal reports of fraudulent voting. Abdullah Abdullah, within a week of elections, referred to the whole exercise as "state-engineered fraud."[15] The preliminary result declared by the Independent Election Commission (IEC) was immediately contested and matter was referred to the UN-backed ECC, which conducted an enquiry into allegations of electoral fraud and subsequently ordered a partial recount of votes. The recount led to a brief standoff as Karzai's share of vote fell to less than 50 per cent from the previous 54 per cent. Abdullah Abdullah, the runner up, however, subsequently refused to take the contest to the next level, a run off with Karzai, reiterating his lack of confidence in the whole exercise. He referred to the results declared by the Commission as a "fraudulent outcome" and Karzai's re-election as "illegitimate rule for another five years."[16] Later, as per the final certified results of the presidential election issued by the IEC, President Karzai secured 49.67 per cent of the total vote, with Abdullah Abdullah in the second position (30.59 per cent), Ramazan Bashardost in the third (10.46 per cent), and Ashraf Ghani Ahmadzai in the fourth position (02.94 per cent).[17]

It is noteworthy that Karzai was far more strongly aligned with some of the militia commanders in the run up to 2009 elections than during the 2004 elections, when he had referred to them as a major threat to the future of the country. The shift in Karzai's approach could be seen within the context of growing friction between him and his Western backers which had reached a new high during the 2009 elections. In the face of persistent Western criticism and mistrust, both during and post-election years, Karzai became politically more assertive and sought to strengthen his position by further centralising the decision-making process in the coming years. In the run up to 2009 elections, he apparently had the backing of a range of old influential militia commanders, including Uzbek Commander Dostum; key Hazara commanders, such as, Karim Khalili and Mohammad Mohaqiq; Pashtun commanders, Gul Agha Sherzai and Abdurrab Rasoul Sayyaf; and Tajik commander from Herat, Ismail Khan. Interestingly, though Karzai had succeeded in effectively marginalising the Panjshiri triumvirate in the run up to and after 2004 elections, he still had to nominate Qasim Fahim as his vice presidential nominee in 2009 elections. As a result of Karzai's alignments with Uzbek, Hazara and some influential Tajik and Pashtun commanders, Abdullah Abdullah was effectively checkmated. Again, despite their overt opposition to Karzai, several factions of the Northern Alliance backed Karzai's re-election for various reasons.

The conflict between President Karzai and the parliament reached a new high as Karzai forwarded the list of his proposed cabinet members for necessary parliamentary approval. The rift between president and parliament was largely on account of alleged rigging of presidential election. Several of his cabinet nominees were disapproved and Karzai had to repeatedly nominate new members to secure the approval for his cabinet. It was not until 2012, three years into his second term, when Karzai was finally able to secure parliamentary approval for most of his cabinet nominees with few still as acting ministers (see Table 2.2 to 2.7).

Prospects of Democracy

Perhaps, democracy in typical Afghan-style was in full play in the run up to the 2009 presidential election. Though mostly based on personalised networking, deal making and consensus building through informal consultative mechanisms has long been an integral aspect of the traditional Afghan politics. It is something not alien even to some of the established democracies where often old surviving traditions are integral to local dynamics and serve as informal mechanisms to deal with complex issues of collective concern. They are often valued more than the constitutional and legal frameworks. After three decades of incessant jehadisation and militarisation sponsored from outside, one simply cannot apply Western standards to measure the success or failure of a decade-old half-hearted democratisation effort. It is neither a 'post-war' nor 'post-revolution' situation, where often politics is about bringing, rather enforcing, extensive transformation in principles of governance through planned reforms. There is no single dominant socio-economic narrative, centreing on a particular political ideology with a long-term national vision, in Afghanistan.

Table 2.2: First List of Cabinet Ministers Proposed by President Hamid Karzai (December 19, 2009)

Position	Name	Position in First Cabinet	Notable Details
President	Hamid Karzai	Incumbent	Pashtun/Rome Group
First Vice President	Mohammad Qasim Fahim	None	Tajik/Jamiat-e Islami Vice Chair/Vice President & Defence Minister in the AIA & ATA
Second Vice President	Mohammad Karim Khalili	Incumbent	Hazara/Hezb-e Wahdat Second Vice President in ATA & First Cabinet

First List of 24 Cabinet Nominees for Parliamentary Approval

Cabinet Position	Name	Position in Previous Cabinet	Notable Details	Approved/Rejected by the Afghan Parliament
Defence Minister	Abdul Rahim Wardak	Incumbent	Pashtun/Pro-Royalist Peshawar Group Earlier associated with Mahaz-e Milli Islami-e Afghanistan of Pir Sayyed Ahmad Gailani	APPROVED
Interior Minister	Mohammad Hanif Atmar *(removed in June 2010)*	Incumbent	Pashtun (former Khalqi)	APPROVED
Foreign Minister	Not Proposed	Rangin Dadfar Spanta to remain acting minister till the London Conference on January 28, 2010	—	—
Finance Minister	Omar Zakhliwal	Incumbent	Pashtun (Technocrat)	APPROVED
Economy Minister	Anwar ul Haq Ahadi	Finance Minister	Pashtun Afghan Mellat (Technocrat)	**Rejected**

Justice Minister	Sarwar Danish	Incumbent	Hazara (Hezb-e Wahdat – Khalili faction)	**Rejected**
Information & Cultural Affairs Minister	Syed Makhdoom Raheen	In the first cabinet, his appointment was disapproved by the Parliament in 2006	Tajik (Rome Group)	APPROVED
Education Minister	Ghulam Farooq Wardak	Incumbent	Pashtun (Hezb-e Islami)	APPROVED
Higher Education Minister	Obaidullah Obaid	New Member	Tajik	**Rejected**
Trade & Commerce Minister	Ghulam Mohammad Elaqi	New Member	Hazara	**Rejected**
Water & Energy Minister	Ismail Khan	Incumbent	Tajik (Northern Alliance)	**Rejected**
Civil Aviation & Transport Minister	Mohammadullah Batash	New Member	Uzbek (Northern Alliance)	**Rejected**
Women's Affairs Minister	Husn Bano Ghazanfar	Incumbent	Uzbek (Independent)	**Rejected**
Haj & Islamic Affairs Minister	Enayatullah Baligh	New Member	Pashtun (Ittehad-e Islami of Abdurrab Rasul Sayyaf); Member, National Ulema Council, and Imam of Pul-e Khishti Mosque in Kabul	**Rejected**
Public Works Minister	Mirza Hussain Abdullahi	New Member	Hazara (Hezb-e Wahdat – Mohaqiq faction)	**Rejected**
Public Health Minister	Syed Mohammad Amin Fatemi	Incumbent	Tajik (close to Jamiat-e Islami)	Rejected
Agriculture Minister	Mohammad Asef Rahimi	Incumbent	Pashtun	APPROVED
Mines Minister	Wahidullah Shahrani	Commerce Minister	Uzbek	APPROVED

(*Contd.*)

Cabinet Position	Name	Position in Previous Cabinet	Notable Details	Approved/Rejected by the Afghan Parliament
Communications Minister	Amirzai Sangeen	Incumbent	Pashtun	**Rejected**
Rural Development Minister	Wais Ahmed Barmak	New Member	Tajik (close to Jamiat-e Islami)	**Rejected**
Labour & Social Affairs Minister	Mohammad Ismail Monshi	New Member	Turkmen (Jumbish-e Melli)	**Rejected**
Border & Tribal Affairs	Sayed Hamid Gailani	New Member	Pashtun (Mahaz-e Milli); Son of Mahaz leader Pir Sayed Ahmed Gailani	**Rejected**
Reconstruction Minister	Mohammad Yousef Pashtun	Urban Development Minister	Pashtun (Royalist)	**Rejected**
Counter-narcotics Minister	Khodaidad	Incumbent	Hazara (Khalili faction); former Army officer & Khalqi	**Rejected**
Refugees Minister	Enayatullah Nazeri	Former Minister of Refugees in AIA & ATA	Tajik (Jamiat-e Islami)	**Rejected**
Ministers for New Ministries Proposed by President Karzai for Parliamentary Approval				
Martyrs & Disabled Minister	Taj Ali Saber	New Member	Pashtun	*Not Voted Upon*
Literacy Minister	Wazhma Zurmati	New Ministry Proposed by Karzai	Pashtun	*Not Voted Upon*

Result: Out of 24 ministers proposed by President Hamid Karzai on December 19, 2009, only seven were approved by the *Wolesi Jirga* or the Lower House of the Afghan Parliament in a vote on January 02, 2010.

Table 2.3: Second List of 17 Cabinet Nominees for Parliamentary Approval (January 09, 2009)

Cabinet Position	Name	Position in Previous Cabinet	Notable Details	Approved/Rejected by the Parliament
Foreign Minister	Zalmay Rassoul	Incumbent Civil Aviation Minister in AIA; National Security Advisor in ATA & First Cabinet	Pashtun/Rome Group	APPROVED
Economy Minister	Abdul Hadi Arghandiwal	New Member	Pashtun/Hezb-e Islami breakaway faction formed in 2008; served as Planning Minister in 1970s and Finance Minister in 1996	APPROVED
Justice Minister	Habibullah Ghaleb	New Member	Pashtun/Pro-King/Nejat-e Milli Chairman, Legal Consultative Board under President's office; earlier served in the same Ministry in 1970s and 1990s	APPROVED
Higher Education Minister	Mohammad Hashim Esmatullahi	New Member	Hazara; Head of the Union of Afghan Journalists	Rejected
Commerce Minister	Zahir Waheed	New Member	—	Rejected
Transport & Civil Aviation Minister	Abdul Rahim Horas	New Member	Tajik; Acting Head of the Third Political Division in Ministry of Foreign Affairs	Rejected
Women's Affairs Minister	Palwasha Hassan	New Member	Hazara	Rejected
Haj & Islamic Affairs Minister	Mohammad Yousef Neyazi	New Member	Pashtun; Advisor to Education Minister; served at the Afghan Embassy in Saudi Arabia (1996-2001)	APPROVED

(*Contd.*)

Cabinet Position	Name	Position in Previous Cabinet	Notable Details	Approved/Rejected by the Parliament
Public Works Minister	Mohammad Bashir Lali	New Member	Pashtun	Rejected
Public Health Minister	Soraya Dalil	New Member	Uzbek Worked with UNICEF	Rejected
Communications Minister	Abdul Qudus Hamidi	New Member	Uzbek; Previously, Deputy Minister of Industry & Mines	Rejected
Rural Development Minister	Jarullah Mansouri	New Member	Tajik/Jamiat-e Islami	**APPROVED**
Labour, Social Affairs, Martyrs & Disabled Minister	Amina Afzali	Youth Affairs Minister (2004-06) in the first Cabinet	Tajik/Jamiat-e Islami; former member, Afghan Independent Human Rights Commission	**APPROVED**
Border & Tribal Affairs Minister	Arsala Jamal	New Member	Pashtun/Hezb-e Islami; Was member of Karzai's re-election campaign team; Earlier, Governor of Khost (2006-08), and worked with Ministry of Rural Development	Rejected
Urban Development Minister	Sultan Hussein Hasery	New Member	—	Rejected
Counter Narcotics Minister	Zarar Ahmad Moqbil	Minister of Interior in the first cabinet (September 2005-October 2008)	Tajik/NA	**APPROVED**
Refugees Minister	Abdul Rahim	Communications Minister in the AIA	Tajik/NA	Rejected

Result: Out of 17 nominees for vacant cabinet positions, the *Wolesi Jirga* (the Lower House of Afghan Parliament) again approved only seven, making the total number of cabinet nominees thus far approved by the Parliament to 14. President Karzai, however, decided to retain 11 of the total nominees rejected (six in the first round of parliamentary vote, four in the second round, and one was never nominated) by the *Wolesi Jirga* as 'Acting Ministers.'

Table 2.4: List of Acting Ministers in the Second Cabinet (January-July 2010)

Cabinet Position	Name	Previous Position	Rejected in First/Second Round of Parliamentary Vote
Higher Education Minister	Sarwar Danish	Justice Minister Hazara/Hezb-e Wahdat-Khalili faction	First Round
Trade & Commerce Minister	Ghulam Mohammad Elaqi	New Member Hazara	First Round
Water & Energy Minister	Ismail Khan	Incumbent Tajik/NA	First Round
Transport & Civil Aviation Minister	Mohamuddullah Batash	New Member Uzbek/NA	First Round
Women's Affairs Minister	Husn Bano Ghazanfar	Incumbent Uzbek	First Round
Public Works Minister	Sohrab Ali Saffary	Incumbent Hazara	Not Nominated for Vote
Public Health Minister	Soraya Dalil	New Member Uzbek	Second Round
Communications Minister	Amirzai Sangeen	Incumbent Pashtun/Technocrat	First Round
Border & Tribal Affairs	Arsala Jamal	Pashtun/Hezb-e Islami; Member of Karzai's re-election campaign team; Former Governor of Khost (2006-08), and worked with Ministry of Rural Development	Second Round
Urban Development Minister	Sultan Hussein Hasery	Hazara New Member	Second Round
Refugees Minister	Abdul Rahim	Tajik/NA Communications Minister in AIA	Second Round

Cabinet Status: 14 of the 24 ministerial nominees approved. Remaining 11 ministries were headed by above 'Acting Ministers' until Karzai presented the third list of nominees for parliamentary approval in July 2010.

Table 2.5: Third List of Seven Cabinet Nominees for Parliamentary Approval (July 2010)

Cabinet Position	Name	Previous Position	Approved/Rejected
Higher Education Minister	Sarwar Danish	Acting Minister Hazara/Hezb-e Wahdat-Khalili faction	Rejected
Interior Minister	Bismillah Khan Mohammadi *(succeeded Hanif Atmar who was removed in June 2010)*	New Name Chief of Staff of the Afghan National Army (ANA)	**APPROVED**
Commerce Minister	Anwar ul Haq Ahadi	Pashtun Governor of Afghan Central Bank in ATA; Finance Minister in the first cabinet	**APPROVED**
Transport & Civil Aviation Minister	Daud Ali Najafi	Hazara Earlier worked with IEC	Rejected
Public Works Minister	Abdul Qadus Hamidi	Uzbek Previously, Deputy Minister of Industry & Mines	**APPROVED**
Border & Tribal Affairs Minister	Asadullah Khalid	Uzbek Previously, Deputy Minister of Industry & Mines	**APPROVED**
Refugees Minister	Jamahir Anwari	Turkmen Served at the Ministry of Public Health	**APPROVED**

Cabinet Status: With five more nominees approved in the third round of vote by the Parliament, the strength of approved cabinet ministers grew from 14 to 19. However, seven ministries – Higher Education, Water & Energy, Transport & Civil Aviation, Women's Affairs, Public Health, Communications, and Urban Development - still remained under 'Acting Ministers.' Karzai proposed the fourth list of nine nominees (including seven nominations for ministries with Acting Ministers and replacements for two previously approved ministers).

Table 2.6: Fourth List of Nine Nominees for Parliamentary Approval (February 2012)

Served at the Ministry of Public Health

Cabinet Position	Name	Previous Position	Approved/Rejected
Higher Education	Obaidullah Obaid	Earlier rejected in the first proposed list; replaced Acting Minister Sarwar Danish Tajik/Ambassador to Iran	APPROVED
Transport & Civil Aviation	Dawood Ali Najafi	Acting Minister Hazara	APPROVED
Water & Energy Minister	Ismail Khan	Acting Minister Tajik/NA	APPROVED
Women's Affairs Minister	Husn Bano Ghazanfar	Acting Minister Uzbek	APPROVED
Public Works Minister	Najeebullah Ozhan (replaces Abdul Qadus Hamidi who was earlier approved by Parliament in July 2010)	New Member Pashtun	APPROVED
Public Health Minister	Soraya Dalil	Acting Minister Uzbek	APPROVED
Communications & Technology Minister	Amirzai Sangeen	Acting Minister Pashtun	APPROVED
Urban Development Minister	Hasan Abdullahi	Hazara; Replaces Acting Minister Sultan Hussein Hasery	APPROVED
Rural Development Minister	Wais Ahmad Barmak (replaces Jarullah Mansouri whose appointment was earlier approved by the Parliament)	Tajik/considered close to Jamiat-e Islami Deputy Rural Development Minister; Earlier rejected by the Parliament in the first proposed list	APPROVED

Table 2.7: List of Cabinet Ministers of the Second Elected Government (As of early 2013)

Cabinet Position	Name (approved in which round of parliamentary voting)	Ethnicity/Political Affiliation	Previous Positions
President	Hamid Karzai	Pashtun/Rome Group	Chairman Interim and Transitional Authorities; Second Term President
First Vice President	Mohammad Qasim Fahim	Tajik/Jamiat-e Islami	Vice Chair/Vice President & Defence Minister in Interim & Transitional Authorities (December 2001-October 2004)
Second Vice President	Abdul Karim Khalili	Hazara/Hezb-e Wahdat	Vice President in the Transitional Administration and the First Cabinet
Foreign Minister	Zalmai Rasoul (second voting)	Pashtun/Rome Group	National Security Advisor (June 2002-January 2010)
Defence Minister	Abdul Rahim Wardak (first voting) *Resigned after vote of no-confidence by Parliament in August 2012.*	Pashtun/Pro-Royalist Peshawar Group; formerly member of Mahaz-eMilli Islami-e Afghanistan of Pir Sayyed Ahmad Gailani.	Deputy Defence Minister in ATA (June 2002-04) & Defence Minister in Karzai's first cabinet (December 2004-October 2009).
	Replaced by **Bismillah Khan Muhammadi**	Tajik/Jamiat-e Islami	Interior Minister from June 2010 – August 2012. Earlier, Chief of Staff of the Afghan National Army (2002-10); Deputy Defence Minister under Ahmad Shah Masoud & commander of his forces in Kapisa & Parwan.
Interior Minister	Bismillah Khan Muhammadi (third vote) *Vote of no-confidence passed by Parliament in August 2012.*	Tajik/Jamiat-e Islami	See above
	Replaced by **Mujtaba Patang** in September 2012.		Former Deputy Interior Minister; earlier security chief for Takhar Province and deputy of the Afghan Public Protection Force (APPF)
	Patang impeached by the parliament in July 2013; replaced with **Umar Daudzai** as Acting Interior Minister in September 2013		Former Afghan Ambassador to Pakistan. Earlier served as Afghan Ambassador to Iran; and President Karzai's Chief of Staff.

Finance Minister	Omar Zakhliwal (first voting)	Pashtun	Replaced Anwar-ul Haq Ahadi as Finance Minister in February 2009; earlier appointed as Acting Minister of Transport & Civil Aviation in November 2008; was President & CEO of Afghanistan Investment Support Agency (AISA) during August 2005-February 2009; also, part of Karzai's 2009 election campaign team.
Economy Minister	Abdul Hadi Arghandiwal (second voting, January 2010)	Pashtun/Hezb-e Islami break-away moderate faction formed in 2008	Served as Planning Minister in 1970s and Finance Minister in 1996
Justice Minister	Habibullah Ghaleb (second voting, January 2010)	Pashtun/Pro-King/Nejat-e Milli	Chairman, Legal Consultative Board to the President's office; earlier served in the same Ministry in 1970s and 1990s
Information & Culture Ministry	Sayed Makhdoom Raheen (first voting, January 2010)	Tajik/Rome Group	Same position in Interim & Transitional Administrations; ambassador to India; rejected by the Parliament when appointed in Karzai's first cabinet in 2006
Education Minister	Ghulam Farooq Wardak (first voting)	Pashtun/Hezb-e Islami	Same position in Karzai's first cabinet (December 2004- October 2009)
Higher Education Minister	Obaidullah Obaid (fourth voting)	Tajik/Ambassador to Iran	Earlier rejected in the first proposed list; replaced Acting Minister Sarwar Danish
Commerce & Industry Minister	Anwar ul Haq Ahady (third voting)	Pashtun	Governor of Afghan Central Bank in ATA; Finance Minister in Karzai's first cabinet
Energy & Water Minister	Mohammad Ismail Khan (fourth voting)	Tajik/Jamiat-e Islami	Same position in the first cabinet
Transport & Civil Aviation Minister	Daoud Ali Najafi (fourth voting)	Hazara	Acting Minister; earlier associated with IEC
Women's Affairs Minister	Husn Bano Ghazanfar (fourth voting)	Uzbek	Acting Minister; Same position in the first cabinet since August 2006

(Contd.)

Cabinet Position	Name (approved in which round of parliamentary voting)	Ethnicity/Political Affiliation	Previous Positions
Haj & Islamic Affairs Minister	Mohammad Yousef Neyazi (second voting)	Pashtun	Advisor to Education Minister; served at the Afghan Embassy in Saudi Arabia (1996-2001) under Rabbani Government
Public Works Minister	Najibullah Ozhan (fourth voting)	Pashtun	Replaced Abdul Qadus Hamidi who was earlier approved by Parliament in July 2010
Public Health Minister	Soraya Dalil (fourth vote)	Uzbek	Acting Minister; Worked with UNICEF; name proposed and rejected in the second round of parliamentary vote
Agriculture, Irrigation & Livestock Minister	Mohammad Asef Rahimi (first voting)	Pashtun	Appointed in the first cabinet in late 2008
Mines Minister	Wahidullah Shahrani (first voting)	Uzbek	Son of former Haj & Islamic Affairs Minister Neamatullah Shahrani; previously, Deputy Minister of Finance & First Deputy Governor of Central Bank
Communication & Information Technology Minister	Amirzai Sangin (fourth voting)	Pashtun	Acting Minister; same position in the first cabinet
Rural Rehabilitation & Development Minister	Wais Ahmad Barmak (fourth voting; replaces Jarullah Mansouri whose appointment was earlier approved by the Parliament)	Tajik/considered close to Jamiat-e Islami	Acting Minister; Deputy Rural Development Minister; Earlier rejected by the Parliament in the first proposed list
Labour, Social Affairs, Martyrs & Disabled Minister	Amina Safi Afzali (second voting)	Tajik/NA	Youth Affairs Minister in the first cabinet (December 2004-June 2006); former member, Afghan Independent Human Rights Commission (AIHRC)

Urban Development Affairs Minister	Hassan Abdullahi	Hazara	Replaces Acting Minister Sultan Hussein Hasery
Counter narcotics Minister	Zarar Ahmad Moqbil (second voting)	Tajik/NA	Interior Minister in the first cabinet (September 2005-October 2008)
Refugees & Repatriations Minister	Jamahir Anwari (third voting)	Turkmen	Director General of Pharmaceutical Affairs, Ministry of Public Health
Border & Tribal Affairs Minister	Haji Azizuddin Mohammad *(replaced Asadullah Khalid & nominated for parliamentary approval in September 2012)*	—	Earlier, served in the *mujahideen* government as Education Minister and as Deputy Prime Minister. Also, former governor of Kabul and Nangarhar and former member of the Afghan senate.

Author's Note: This table has been drawn and compiled from various sources as no two sources give similar details. Wherever the information provided by key sources are at variance with each other, the same has been verified and further corroborated by consulting an extended range of sources in order to ensure the accuracy of information to the extent possible. Key sources of information are: personal profiles/biographies of incumbent ministers available on Afghan Government websites, and other websites, such as *Afghanistan Online* (www.afghan-web.com), *Afghan Biographies* (www.afghan-bios.info), etc.

One would have to take into account the unique social and political setting of the country. Any political system or construct in the current context is bound to have a strong Afghan flavour which many a times would not conform to the known precepts of a modern Westphalian democracy. To expect modern democracy to take roots in a country that is not even remotely homogenous and has been at war for more than three decades, would be political stupidity. This is not at all to suggest that there is no space or scope for a more representative and an inclusive political order in the country. Perhaps, what is critically needed is sustained international support and patience to allow Afghanistan's nascent democratic institutions to grow and adapt to the country's social and political ethos before it starts working the other way round. This also partly explains as to why Karzai at times had to acquiesce to certain controversial legal provisions which are deemed regressive and obscurantist in nature by liberal universal standards of modern democracy.

Afghan polity is bound to be fragmented, polarised, personality-driven, and conflicting and chaotic in nature, for a long time to come. The political system established after the overthrow of the Taliban regime is far more inclusive, participatory and representational of the inherent social and political diversity of the country. The composition of the Afghan Parliament broadly reflects the current socio-political contours of the Afghan polity, with even 'former' Hezb-e Islami and Taliban elements represented. It has largely succeeded in reducing the status of the Taliban from being a 'movement' to a 'faction.' Today, Taliban is just one among various factions vying for political power and control, though outside the existing political and constitutional framework. However, ensuring their integration or participation in the national processes remain a huge challenge for both Kabul and its Western-backers.

The survival of the current political system and constitution is, therefore, critical to preventing Afghanistan from sliding into another round of civil war. In fact, the current political system based on electoral mechanism has the potential, or is rather the only viable mechanism available, to manage the chaotic polity of the country. This is where lies the significance of the presidential and parliamentary elections in 2014-15. It would also ensure that the international community remains engaged after the end of the Western combat mission in 2014. With no end to several crises afflicting the country in sight, it is all about making the Afghan chaos more 'manageable.' Perhaps, the current system and the political transition in 2014-15 provides the best chance to transform Afghanistan into a 'manageable chaos,' until a sustainable power equilibrium emerges within the country over a period of time. Absence of strong leadership and political parties at the national level also necessitates the sustenance of the current political system in order to channelise the unwieldy elements of the Afghan polity into a 'manageable chaos.' The next round of presidential and parliamentary elections are thus critical to the sustenance of democratic institutions and the constitution after the drawdown of Western troops.

The legitimacy of the next government and the credibility of the democratic system, in view of the challenges and shortcomings of the 2009 elections, would be more or less determined by the strength of the institutions critical to the electoral exercise, particularly, the election commission and the complaints committee. The significance of the 2014 exercise lie in the fact that it is supposed to elect the country's first post-ISAF government, though international support would remain a critical factor in strengthening the next leadership in Kabul. Some of the defining aspects of formation of government after 2009 elections are likely be repeated with greater vigour and in a more chaotic manner in the face of increased threat from Pakistan-backed Haqqani-Taliban combine as Western forces retreat.

If the politics of striking tactical deals favouring the Pakistan-based Taliban leadership continue to gain traction or plays a key role in determining the composition of the next government in Kabul, the tendency of political decentralisation and factionalism too would continue to grow within Afghanistan. This has direct implications for the current political system and state institutions. In fact, it may altogether endanger the survival of the current political system, leading to political vacuum and armed conflict among factions across the country.

Whatever might be the final outcome of the 2014 presidential and 2015 parliamentary elections, the role of the political opposition groups and their interaction and relationship with the presidential set up, the Taliban factor, politics of reconciliation aimed at Pakistan-based Afghan armed insurgents, and the rebuilding of the national army, would remain critical to the future course of domestic politics in Afghanistan. All four have been discussed in detail in the following chapters in keeping with the wider objective of the subject under study.

NOTES

1. Due to the deteriorating security situation and delayed voter registration, the elections were first postponed from June to September 2004, and thereafter, the Joint Electoral Management Body (JEMB) of Afghanistan decided to hold the two exercises separately - presidential election on October 09, 2004, while the parliamentary elections were postponed until September 2005. With the conclusion of the first round of elections in 2004-05, concluded the Bonn Process.
2. Marc Ricks, "Karzai Says Militias Pose Biggest Threat to Afghan Elections," *RFE/RL Afghanistan Report*, 3 (26), July 31, 2004, at http://www.rferl.org/reports/afghan-report/2004/07/26-310704.asp. Hamid Karzai, as Chairman of the Afghan Transitional

Administration, had said in an interview published in *The New York Times* in July 2004, that Afghanistan's warlord armies, not Taliban insurgents, pose the gravest risk to his country's security. See Carlotta Gall and David Rohde, "Afghan President Describes Militias as the Top Threat," *The New York Times*, Internet Edition, July 12, 2004. On July 14, 2004, Chairman Karzai vowed to crack down on private militias and issued a decree prescribing severe punishment for warlord armies who refuse to disarm, particularly those operating outside the purview of the Afghan defence ministry.

3. Golnaz Esfandiari, "Afghanistan: President Declares Holy War Against Drugs," *RFE/RL Afghanistan Report*, December 10, 2004, at http://www.rferl.org/featuresarticle/2004/12/C1731D8A-3D90-4B0C-A0AC-0E4807EF8E81.html
4. "Afghan Elections: The Great Gamble," *Briefing Paper*, Afghanistan Research and Evaluation Unit, Kabul, November 2003, p. 9.
5. See "Taleban retaking land says UN," *BBC News*, October 25, 2003, at http://news.bbc.co.uk/2/hi/south_asia/3209639.stm
6. See Kathy Gannon, "Afghanistan Unbound," *Foreign Affairs*, 83(3), May-June 2004, p. 40.
7. In April 2004, the governor of north-western Faryab Province had to flee when Uzbek commander, Abdul Rashid Dostum, captured the capital city of Maimana. Similarly, in June 2004, the governor of Ghor Province had to take refuge in neighbouring Herat when a militia commander, Abdul Salaam Khan, stormed the capital city of Chaghcharan. See "Governor Flees Afghanistan Rebels," *BBC News*, June 18, 2004, at http://news.bbc.co.uk/2/hi/south_asia/3818141.stm. In another such instance in June 2004, the alleged supporters of Dostum restrained the newly appointed governor of the northern province of Sar-e-Pul, Abdul Haq Shafaq, from taking office. He was forced to take refuge in neighbouring Mazar-e-Sharif. See "Stone-Throwing Afghans Stop Governor Taking Office," at http://paktribune.com/news/index.php?id=67739
8. Paul Adams, "NATO Boss Pleads for Afghan Focus," *BBC News*, June 19, 2004, at http://news.bbc.co.uk/2/hi/south_asia/3820979.stm. Also, see Hikmet Cetin, "The Way Forward in Afghanistan," *NATO Review*, Istanbul Summit Special, May 2004, pp. 36-37; Rick Hillier, "Great Expectations," *NATO Review*, Istanbul Summit Special, May 2004, pp. 38-39.
9. Bushra Asif, "Afghanistan: One Step Forward, Two Steps Back," *Foreign Policy In Focus*, April 04, 2004, at http://www.fpif.org/commentary/2004/0404afghanistan.html
10. See "The Constitution of Afghanistan," Unofficial Translation, p. 7, at http://www.swisspeace.org/uploads/ACSF/GeneralDocuments/final%20new%20constitution.pdf
11. Golnaz Esfandiari, "Powerful Commander Gets High-Ranking Military Post," *RFE/RL Afghanistan Report*, 4 (8) March 07, 2005, at http://www.rferl.org/reports/afghan-report/; Amin Tarzi, "Afghan President Appoints Northern Warlord as his Chief of Staff," at http://www.azadiradio.org/en/dailyreport/2005/03/02.asp
12. See "Former Defense Minister Gets Special Privileges," *RFE/RL Afghanistan Report*, 3 (46), December 30, 2004, at http://www.azadiradio.org/en/weeklyreport/2004/12/30.asp#241572
13. Tom Regan, "The 'Rebranding' of the War on Terror," *The Christian Science Monitor*, July 28, 2005, at http://csmonitor.com/2005/0728/dailyUpdate.html. Also, see Eric Schmitt and Thom Shanker, "Washington Recasts Terror War As 'Struggle,'" *International Herald Tribune*, July 27, 2005, at http://www.iht.com/articles/2005/07/26/news/terror.php
14. Later, the US was asked by Uzbekistan to leave Karshi-Khanabad (also known as K2) base in 2005. The base in Kyrgyzstan too has seen manifold increase in rent that the US pays for using the Manas airbase. Both countries are now part of what is known as the Northern Distribution network (NDN), a web of alternate supply routes running through Russia and Central Asia Republics.

15. James Rupert, "Abdullah Spurns Karzai's 'Mafia-Like' Political Deals," *Bloomberg*, August 27, 2009, at http://bloomberg.com/apps/news?pid=20601087&sid=akFFtxtifNK4
16. Avril Ormsby, "Afghanistan's Abdullah Warns of Instability after Poll," *The New York Times*, September 10, 2009, at http://www.nytimes.com/reuters/2009/09/10/world/international-us-afghanistan-britain-abdullah.html
17. "Final Certified Presidential Results," *Independent Election Commission, Islamic Republic of Afghanistan*, October 21, 2009, at http://www.iec.org.af/results_2009/leadingCandidate.html

"If this coalition between mujahedin and communists had been formed 20 years ago, Afghanistan would not have experienced the bloodshed and so much misery in the last (several) decades." *

—A resident of Nangarhar Province on the emergence of National Front of Afghanistan

---

* Ron Synovitz, "Afghanistan: New Political Bloc Unites Old Adversaries," *RFE/RL Afghanistan Report*, April 05, 2007, at http://www.rferl.org/content/article/1075718.html.

CHAPTER III*

Opposition Politics and Karzai the Master Survivor

The constant jostling for political space and influence among diverse Afghan factions, both within and outside the post-Taliban order, has been a defining feature of the Afghan politics. It has permeated the political and social life of the country to such proportions that one often wonders what exactly is keeping the country together. Lack of any convincing explanation has often inspired odd formulations, such as the one suggesting possible *de facto* division of the country or ceding parts of the country to the Pakistan-proxied Taliban, to resolve the Afghan conflict. Perhaps, what needs to be understood here is that Afghans may be a divided lot and they may remain so, but still they cannot be divided beyond a point. The centrifugal tendencies or irreconcilable perceptions considered inherent in the Afghan polity cannot be played up far too long. A strange sense of activism envelops the squabbling Afghans when confronted particularly with a far superior force from outside. It is not about unity, but about exploiting the opportunity provided by external intervention to their best advantage, even as they continue to squabble among themselves. Some might see benefit in collaborating with external forces and others might find it convenient to do just the opposite.

Despite several decades of constant conflict and deep rupture in social relations, no faction or group in the country is ever known to have raised secessionist or separatist demands. In this regard, it is worth quoting what Ahmad Shah Masoud had stated, in his probably last interview in early August 2001, in relation to the ethnic dimension to the conflict with the predominantly Pashtun Taliban: "Despite the year-long fighting in Afghanistan, ethnic differences and all the difficulties

* Some sections on opposition politics have been drawn from the author's earlier publication: Vishal Chandra, "The National Front in Afghanistan: An Exploratory Study," *Strategic Analysis*, Routledge, 33 (4), July 2009, pp. 528-540.

that plague Afghanistan, I do not think there is even a single person who would favour the disintegration or fragmentation of the country along lines of the ethnic criteria. We are all unanimous that there should be one Afghanistan."[1] Twelve years later, Mullah Omar, the Taliban chief, too in his *Eid* message issued in August 2013 had stated: "We will not allow anyone to succeed in the wicked plan for disintegration of the country or to divide our country under geographical locations and ethnicity denominations."[2] Interestingly, Masoud in his interview had also claimed that he does not intend to "seize full power," something Mullah Omar off late too had been reiterating. In his 2013 *Eid* message, he had stated: "We have already said that the Islamic Emirate does not think of monopolizing power. Rather we believe in reaching (an) understanding with the Afghans regarding an Afghan-inclusive government based on Islamic principles. Of course, the Islamic Emirate considers it its religious and national obligation to liberate the country from the occupation. When the occupation ends, reaching an understanding with the Afghans will not be a hard task because, by adhering to and having common principles and culture, the Afghans understand each other better."[3] One could say that despite decades of civil conflict and violence, and conflicting perceptions among Afghan factions about state and its authority, there has always been some kind of consensus on maintaining the territorial integrity of the country. How centralised or decentralised the state structures should be, remains one of the most contentious issues in the Afghan politics, though.

Perhaps, the shaping of the opposition politics, especially since the first presidential election in 2004, at least partly explains the continuing lure for influence or control over Kabul. It may be stated here that various interest groups in Afghanistan have sought to protect and consolidate their political, social and territorial interests by way of projecting their stakes from time to time in the national politics of the country. This was the case during the civil war as well. They often tend to see growth or decline in their local power and influence in relation to their role and influence, whether as a dominant group or part of a coalition, in determining the politics in Kabul. It is, therefore, pertinent to particularly examine the evolution and behaviour of a key opposition group, the Jabha-e-Melli Afghanistan or the National Front of Afghanistan (NFA), which had briefly emerged in response to the first presidential and parliamentary elections held in 2004-05, especially as one tries to look beyond the current ambiguity that shrouds the future of Afghanistan.

Interestingly, the NFA splintered with as much ease as it was formed and was a precursor to several opposition mini-fronts and coalitions, each acting as a counter to the other, that have emerged in the run up to the third round presidential election in 2014. The formation of the NFA was not merely a manifestation of the shifting political dynamics in the post-Taliban period; it also showed how the fragmented and factionalised polity of the country was responding to the externally-sponsored centralised political structure established after 2001.

The Front that emerged in 2007 was the first coordinated challenge to Karzai's leadership by predominantly non-Pashtun opposition groups, tactfully divided, disempowered and marginalised in the post-2004 political order. It comprised largely of elements from the former Northern Alliance, some ex-communists, and also for the first time included a member from the former royal family. Interestingly, many of the senior NFA members were either part of the Karzai-led government or were parliamentarians. At times, it was simply not clear whether the opposition was embedded within the government or it was a part of the broader political activism which was directed against President Karzai from outside. At a more nuanced level, it demonstrated how the factionalised and polarised polity of the country was responding to the centralisation of authority; to electoral democracy and constitutionalism; to parliamentary mechanisms; and, more importantly, how multiple centres of power within the country were interacting in the new set up. On the other hand, Karzai's dealing with legal opposition both from within and outside his administration, particularly his powerful allies and competitors in various provinces, bear testimony to his political and diplomatic skills.

Evolution of NFA

There was an element of ambiguity as to exactly when the Jabha-e-Melli or the NFA formally came into being. It is generally believed that it was formed either in March or early April 2007.[4] Whatever might have been the exact date of its formation, the conditions that led to its creation are still relevant. Broadly, it may be said that the emergence of NFA was a manifestation of the socio-political polarisation prevalent in the Afghan polity, reinforced from time to time by the politics of inclusion and exclusion.

It is noteworthy that since the *Emergency Loya Jirga* (ELJ) in June 2002 and the subsequent formation of the Afghan transitional administration, Karzai, with full backing of the US representatives based in Kabul, had tried to curtail the influence of the Northern Alliance on his government. He had successfully moved Interior Minister Yunus Qanuni to the Ministry of Education in July 2002. Thereafter, in the run up to the first presidential election in 2004, he removed Ismail Khan from the post of governor of Herat and also got rid of the powerful defence minister, Qasim Fahim. Qanuni had to finally resign from his ministerial position owing to differences with Karzai. He later formed his own party called Hezb-e-Afghanistan-e-Naween or the New Afghanistan Party. Another important Tajik leader, Abdullah Abdullah, was also later removed from the post of foreign minister prior to the parliamentary elections in September 2005.

Aware of his limited appeal among the Pashtuns and authority in provinces, Karzai attempted to weaken the electoral prospects of Yunus Qanuni, an ethnic Tajik, and Mohammad Mohaqqiq, an ethnic Hazara, by nominating Ahmed Zia Masoud, brother of former Tajik Commander Ahmad Shah Masoud, and Hazara leader Mohammad Karim Khalili, as his vice-presidential nominees in the 2004 presidential election. The ethnic and political divisions within the Northern Alliance were clearly visible during the first presidential elections as Tajiks, Uzbeks and Hazaras had declared their own presidential candidates.

It was noteworthy that prior to the 2004 presidential election, at a time when Karzai was easing out powerful Tajik ministers from his transitional government, he was also trying to woo the Taliban and the Hezb-e-Islami cadres to join the electoral process. Karzai's offer of amnesty to those willing to lay down their arms and accept the new Afghan Constitution, however, excluded some 100-150 senior members of both the organisations. Again in March 2005, prior to the parliamentary elections in September 2005, veteran Afghan leader Sebghatullah Mojadeddi, a Pashtun, was appointed as the head of the newly instituted peace commission or Programme Takhim-e-Solh (PTS). In May 2005, the commission extended the offer of amnesty to Mullah Omar, Gulbuddin Hekmatyar and the Taliban detainees at the Guantanamo Bay and Bagram detention centre. It was part of Karzai's ongoing effort to strengthen his position in the Afghan political structure and especially among the Pashtuns as was evident from the increased induction of Pashtuns in his government.

The National Understanding Front

Though much of the Northern Alliance leadership was either out or on the margins of the governing structure by the end of 2005, but that did not help in augmenting the position of Karzai in any substantive manner. With their presence in the government diminished, Tajik leader Yunus Qanuni on March 31, 2005 announced the formation of Jabha-ye-Tafahom-e-Melli Afghanistan or the National Understanding Front of Afghanistan (NUFA) as the main opposition group to the central government. The NUFA, comprising of 12-14 political parties, was also formed in view of the September 2005 parliamentary elections.

The Front was probably established at the behest of former Tajik and Hazara presidential candidates though it had some Pashtun representation as well. Qanuni was the chairman of the Front, with Mohammad Mohaqiq (Hazara leader and a former presidential candidate), Ahmed Shah Ahmedzai (a former Pashtun presidential candidate) and Nazia Zehra (a relatively unknown figure) as three deputy chairpersons. Like Qanuni, Mohaqiq too had been Karzai's cabinet colleague. The most notable absentee from the NUFA was former Uzbek presidential candidate, Abdul Rashid Dostum, who was then reported to be forming his own unofficial opposition alliance along with the former presidential candidate, Abdul Latif Pedram, an Ismaili Shia and a former communist leader.

According to the Afghan media, NUFA was regarded by some as a deliberate creation of the Afghan Government and its foreign backers to showcase a symbolic opposition and to paralyse the political parties comprising it. However, according to others, it was part of the disruptive politics of the former *mujahideen*.[5] The Front was widely seen as a weak *mujahideen* tactic, a negotiating instrument of the politically marginalised, to extract privileges from the government and to cause disruption in the parliament in times to come. On the whole, NUFA seems to have been a cautious effort on the part of the marginalised factional leaders to preserve and project their relevance and to keep a check on the powers of the central government in the parliament.

In the September 2005 parliamentary elections, Yunus Qanuni was elected as the speaker of the Afghan Parliament and Chairman of the lower house, the *Wolesi Jirga*. Many of the members of the Front (including Mohammad Mohaqiq) or candidates supported by it also won the elections, adding to the strength of the opposition lobby led by Qanuni within the Parliament. The optimism that prevailed during the election (2004-05) soon paled before the rising power of the Taliban (2006-07). A strong sense of dissatisfaction with the central government spread not only across the country but also among the Western-backers of Karzai. In the face of newer challenges emerging from the growing insecurity and uncertainty in the country, the marginalised and disaffected elements/entities, especially from the minority ethnic groups, once again came together in early 2007 to form the NFA, a wider and a relatively more well-coordinated opposition grouping.

Composition and Agenda of NFA

The NFA was said to be a conglomeration of about 15-18 political parties, and initially claimed backing from about 40 per cent of Afghanistan's Parliament. The Front, as has been said earlier, mainly comprised of leaders and commanders from the former Northern Alliance, and had a sprinkling of Pashtun representation in the form of former communists, a royalist, and some parliamentarians. The former Northern Alliance was represented by former president and a veteran Tajik leader, Burhanuddin Rabbani (also the Chairman of the Front); Yunus Qanuni, chairman of the lower house of parliament and former interior and education minister in Karzai's cabinet; Ahmad Zia Masoud, first vice-president; Qasim Fahim, former defence minister in Karzai's cabinet and later senior advisor to the president on security affairs; Uzbek Commander Abdul Rashid Dostum; and Mohammad Ismail Khan, former 'Amir' of Herat and later energy and water minister in Karzai's cabinet.

Among the old communist elements in the NFA were Noor-ul Haq Ulomi, former Afghan army general from the Parcham faction of the People's Democratic Party of Afghanistan (PDPA); and Sayed Muhammad Gulabzoi, former interior minister in 1980s from the Khalq faction of the PDPA. Mustafa Zahir, a grandson of late Afghan King Zahir Shah, and head of the Environmental Commission in the Afghan Government, was the lone member in the Front from the royal family, much to the consternation of Karzai. The absence of influential Hazara leaders, like Karim Khalili (then second vice-president) and Mohammad Mohaqiq, was conspicuous. Mustafa Kazemi, former commerce minister in Karzai's transitional government and a parliamentarian, was the most notable Hazara member of the Front, until he was killed during a deadly suicide bombing in the north-eastern Baghlan Province in November 2007.

Among other notable members of the NFA were Mohammad Akbari, leader of a Shia Hazara faction and a parliamentarian; Mohammad Amin Waqad, former deputy to Gulbuddin Hekmatyar; Sayed Mansoor Naderi, head of the Ismaili sect; Taj Mohammad Wardak and Shakir Karger, former ministers in Karzai's transitional government; and Fazl Karim Aimaq, former mayor of Kabul. Apart from low Hazara representation, absence of Abdurrab Rasul Sayyaf, who was among the few Pashtun commanders in the former Northern Alliance, was also notable. Karzai was to an extent able to drive a wedge in the former Northern Alliance as was evident from the absence of senior Hazara leaders and Sayyaf in the NFA. There were unconfirmed reports of Sayyaf along with some other Pashtuns trying to create a counter to the Front.[6] Another notable absentee was former Foreign Minister Abdullah.

As stated earlier, many of the members of the NFA were either parliamentarians or former ministers from the Karzai-led provisional governments. Few of them even enjoyed senior positions in the first elected government, which gave "government-cum-opposition" status to the Front. Interestingly, the NFA argued against being an opposition coalition or a bloc though its members were constantly critical of Karzai's leadership. On this issue, the NFA had asserted that evaluating the performance and policy of the Karzai Government is an "exercise in democracy" and that Front works within the ambit of the Afghan Constitution and accepts the legitimacy of the government.[7]

As for the official rationale for the formation of NFA, its Chairman, Burhanuddin Rabbani, in an interview to the *RFE/RL*, had stated: "The weakness of the government in resolving crises and the emergence of corruption are serious threats to state security. Watching this situation, a group of parties and politicians decided not to remain on the sidelines regarding solutions to national problems anymore. So they decided to create a means of cooperation by forming the United National Front and starting joint work."[8] Arguing that the NFA was formed to fill up the growing political vacuum in the country, former spokesperson Kazemi had asserted, "There has been no party able to cope with the deteriorating situation over the past five years. There are a lot of registered parties in Afghanistan, but none of them has been able to fill the gap."[9]

The core agenda of the NFA echoed issues raised by delegates from minority ethnic communities during the *Jirga* called for ratifying Afghanistan's new draft constitution (December 2003 - January 2004), and Yunus Qanuni's idea of "a loyal opposition" to the legitimate government and "rationalization and legalization of struggle."[10] The NFA's political idea and ideals basically revolved around creating more decentralised state structures based on greater sharing of power at various levels. Some of the key agenda of the NFA were:

- To replace the current presidential system with a parliamentary form of government by making required amendments in the Afghan Constitution. In this regard, it had proposed to introduce a provision for the post of prime minister.
- A greater devolution of power to the provinces. The Front proposed that the provincial governors and mayors be elected rather than selected by the president. Interestingly, the NFA has time and again denied endorsing a federal state structure and instead cited the US model in which state governors are directly elected.
- To strengthen the role of political parties. In this regard, the Front proposed change in the electoral system from the current system of single non-transferable voting (SNTV) to a proportional system.
- Greater coordination between foreign troops and Afghan security forces in order to avoid civilian casualties and minimise other forms of collateral damage.
- Official recognition of the Durand Line as the international border between Afghanistan and Pakistan.
- Need for an international conference similar to the 2001 Bonn Conference to discuss the situation in Afghanistan. The proposed conference to be held under UN auspices for national reconciliation should involve all armed and opposition groups of the country, including Taliban and Hezb-e Islami (Hekmatyar); Afghanistan's immediate neighbours, the US and NATO, Organisation of Islamic Cooperation (OIC), Russia, India and Saudi Arabia.

Note: *The above mentioned key agendas of the NFA have been collated by the author from various sources.*

In view of the strong presence of the former Northern Alliance members, the Pashtuns were suspicious of the political agenda of the NFA, especially over the idea of strengthening the position of the provincial governors. The idea of federalism was propagated earlier by some members of the Northern Alliance.

For Pashtuns, in general, accepting a federalised state structure was tantamount to accepting a *de facto* partition of the country. They would rather support the idea of a highly centralised state structure which would enable Kabul to exercise a strong control over the country, especially over vast non-Pashtun areas in the north. There was a strong and a continuing historical disconnect between the traditional Pashtun view of a strong centralised state and the advocacy for greater devolution of powers to the provinces by the minority ethnic groups.

Reactions to the Emergence of the NFA

The emergence of the NFA had elicited reactions from the entire political spectrum of Afghanistan. Most of the Afghan political observers and analysts believed that the NFA would not survive long due to the extreme diversity of its constituents (Jihadis, ex-Khalqis, ex-Parchamites, Royalist, Tajiks, Hazaras, Uzbeks, Shias and Sunnis) and the ideological contradictions flowing from it. The Front lacked a common ideology and suffered from conflicting interests of its diverse constituents. The Front was often believed to have been formed by former constituents of the Northern Alliance along with some ex-communists to legitimise their political existence in view of alleged war crimes and gross human rights violations committed by them in the past. Though they were covered under general amnesty made from time to time, nevertheless, the fear of Kabul coming under international pressure to conduct war trials in future remained. Otherwise, the only factor which was said to have brought together such diverse actors was their shared opposition to Karzai's leadership that had left many of them marginalised.

In response to the above observations, former NFA spokesperson Kazemi had argued that the diverse composition of the Front demonstrated that even former enemies could work together within a democratic framework and asserted that, "Our movement goes beyond ethnic or regional boundaries; it is a gathering of influential political figures. Unless we form these kinds of movements, the ethnic and local tensions will persist."[11] At the same time, while agreeing that "there is no guarantee that the National United Front will not break down," he stated that "even if it does collapse, we will have lost nothing—we are practicing democracy."[12]

According to former interior minister in the Karzai Government, Ali Ahmed Jalali, the NFA was an attempt on the part of various groups to consolidate their position in view of the approaching presidential and parliamentary elections in 2009-10. On the future of the Front, he was of the opinion that, "This coalition remaining united is impossible. At the moment, people are a bit disappointed in Afghanistan. Taking that disappointment into consideration, this group has gathered together to introduce themselves as a political front that will address the desires and wishes of the people in the future." The idea of a national front was immediately rejected by the purported spokesman of the Hezb-e Islami (led by Hekmatyar) as well. Referring to it as a creation of Russia, Iran and India, he questioned the legitimacy of the new front to call itself a 'national' front.[13] The Afghan justice ministry was reported to have raised questions regarding the legality of the Front as it was not a registered political party. The Karzai Government too reportedly had expressed its concerns over the involvement of external powers in the formation of the Front.

It was believed that the agenda and politics of the NFA had an external and regional dimension to it as well. A whole range of countries—Russia, Central Asian republics (especially Uzbekistan), Iran, India, Turkey and even Pakistan—were named as probable sponsors and supporters of the Front. According to a report by *Pajhwok Afghan News*, Karzai, in a press conference on his return from 14th SAARC Summit (April 03-04, 2007), had stated that some foreign embassies were behind the creation of the NFA. The report added that the Afghan foreign ministry too had learned through diplomatic sources that the NFA has the backing of a number of neighbouring countries. The report also stated that Foreign Minister Rangin Dadfar Spanta during his visit to Moscow earlier had reportedly urged the Russian Government to strengthen the hands of the Afghan Government rather than supporting the opposition parties.[14] However, the NFA consistently denied playing proxy to the interests and agendas of any foreign country. As far as the external dimension to the NFA was concerned, it remained largely in the realm of speculation.

NFA and the Taliban

On September 02, 2007, Chairman of the Front, Burhanuddin Rabbani, during a visit to Peshawar had reportedly argued that peace cannot be restored in Afghanistan until the Karzai Government includes all the anti-government factions, including the Taliban and the Hezb-e Islami leader Hekmatyar, in the ongoing peace process.[15] In March 2008, the NFA announced that it had been secretly talking to the Taliban at least since last five months as part of its efforts for national reconciliation.[16] NFA spokesperson had revealed to the *Associated Press* that Chairman Rabbani and Mohammad Qasim Fahim had been meeting "important people" from Taliban and other anti-government groups to seek reconciliation.[17] It is interesting to note here that within days of the launching of the Front, Karzai had for the first time declared that he had been talking to the Taliban.

It is difficult to say if one of the objectives of the formation of NFA, or for that matter the very idea of NFA negotiating with the Taliban, was to undermine Karzai's efforts for reconciliation with the Taliban. It is equally difficult to say if it was the other way round, i.e., Taliban using NFA to undermine Karzai's leadership. In order to make a distinction with Kabul's effort to woo the Taliban, NFA asserted that it was more flexible in its negotiations unlike government's offer for conditional talks. Rabbani stated that the Afghan problem can only be resolved by putting in place an inclusive and a formal negotiations process. Accusing Karzai of not following up his words with action, Rabbani added, "On the issue of the negotiations it is not right to take one step forward and then one step back. This work should be continued in a very organized way."[18]

Much to the displeasure of Kabul, the NFA spokesperson reportedly demanded recognition of the Taliban as a political or a military party on April 30, 2008.[19] A week later, Mustafa Zahir, proposed the establishment of a transitional government comprising Taliban, members of the present government, and other anti-government groups. Thereafter, a *Loya Jirga* should be convened by the transitional government for discussing the issue of changing the current presidential form of government to a parliamentary system.[20] It is difficult to say if at all the NFA was talking to the Taliban, and what was the level of their engagement with other anti-government groups. Later, Burhanuddin Rabbani was appointed as head of the High Peace Council (HPC) appointed by the government in 2010. After Rabbani was killed in a suicide bombing in Kabul in September 2011, his son Salahuddin Rabbani was appointed in his position six months later in April 2012.

New Turf War Begins

The NFA went into relative oblivion with Karzai's re-election in 2009. In subsequent years, the Front suffered as its diverse constituents began to review their position in anticipation of re-ordering of political structures in 2014 and thereafter. As Afghanistan approached April 2014 presidential election amidst growing uncertainty over the future of the country, several competing fronts and alliances have emerged to shape the country's first post-Karzai and post-ISAF government. Among the leading pre-election coalitions or alliances that have recently emerged are Afghanistan Electoral Alliance (AEA),[21] Association of National Amity of Afghanistan (ANAA)[22] and Afghanistan Eastern People's Alliance (AEPA).[23]

These mini-fronts/alliances are apparently opportunistic and temporary in nature. They may be fragile or unsustainable in the long run, or may have a narrow agenda or very limited objectives, yet they are a part of the Afghan political life. They often work at cross purposes and even have overlapping memberships and political agendas. They are largely the result of a growing quest among various smaller factions to reinforce their position in the national politics by forming alliances among themselves or aligning with larger factions. They have long been a characteristic feature of the competitive politics of the country, whereby various small and large factions jostle for political space and in the process seek to consolidate and reinforce their position prior to bargaining for a share in the national government. As the state structures remain weak, the next government in Kabul too would have to network with informal power structures at the sub-national level to be able to extend its nominal authority to the provinces.

The NFA and various fronts and alliances and their counter formations that have emerged would continue to rise and collapse in the coming years. These fronts and alliances are typical Afghan political experiments. The NFA, largest of all such fronts, had all the trappings of Afghanistan's ethno-political dynamics and factional power politics, often interspersed with the interests of external powers. It was a manifestation of tendencies with a long and a varied past to it. Like any other such grouping, it drew its characteristics from the socio-political space in which it originated and fought for survival within the new political order. At a more nuanced level, it was part of a continuing effort by various factions, particularly from the north, to legitimise and mainstream their position in the post-Taliban power structure and, at the same time, evolve as a potential alternative to President Karzai and his government which was coming under increasing criticism from the West.

Its legal status as a Front may have been ambiguous, but it was not illegal either. The heterogeneity of its composition was both its strength and weakness. It represented the diversity of political opposition to Karzai's leadership, but its inherent diversity at the same time had lent a strong element of uncertainty and fragility to its very existence due to the competing interests of its various constituents. In such a scenario, it was bound to be an amorphous and somewhat ambiguous entity.

Apart from factors elucidated earlier, the NFA and other smaller fronts may have also been formed in response to the growing Taliban challenge. The impetus might have come from the weak position of Kabul and the growing divide on the idea of reconciliation with the Taliban. Though the Front was not very effective in terms of unifying the opposition against President Karzai, but it was quite successful in articulating the alternative viewpoint on several issues critical to the state-building process. It was very much part of the evolving political discourse which today finds strong resonance in the political approach and agenda of leadership from the north. In fact, as expected, some of the prominent constituents of NFA are playing a significant role in shaping the outcome of the 2014 political transition.

As far as the internal dynamics of the Afghan conflict are concerned, the role and position of President Karzai particularly after his re-election in 2009, and his response strategies to several crises his presidency went through, was in many ways remarkable. The challenges before the next Afghan president would be similar to what Karzai was up against. Rather, it would be more complicated as Western forces drawdown and external aid and assistance decline. In fact, Hamid Karzai's leadership and his role in the political labyrinth of the country over the last one decade might have some key lessons to offer for the next leadership in Kabul.

Karzai the Master Survivor

Hamid Karzai has been a master survivor of Afghan politics. He has been at the helm of Afghan affairs for more than a decade. His stints, first as chairman of the interim and transitional administrations and, thereafter, as two time elected president, is a distinction of sorts in the tumultuous politics of Afghanistan. Since the overthrow of the monarchy in 1973, Karzai is probably the only Afghan head of state, and that too an elected one, to have survived so long in a country dominated by battle-hardened commanders and militia running into hundreds. Except for a brief stint as a deputy minister in the first *mujahideen* government in 1992 and later as a member of the Rome Group, he did not have much to show by way of political experience in national politics at the time of his appointment as chairman of the post-Taliban interim administration in December 2001. Though his father, Abdul Ahad Karzai, was the deputy speaker of the first Afghan Parliament in the 1960s and his grand father, Khair Mohammad Khan, was deputy speaker in the Afghan senate during King Amanullah Khan's reign, Karzai was more or less a political newcomer.

With virtually no mass support base, Karzai's decade long political sojourn has been a testimony to his craftsmanship and ability to play through the complex web of old and evolving power politics. Once derided as 'mayor of Kabul,' he had often shown the tact of a master strategist in dealing with varied challenges to his authority. Individually, and in a strict political sense, he was neither a provincial nor a national leader. His support base, if he had any, was least defined in the political maze that is Afghanistan. Perhaps, his biggest asset was his undefined local support base, politically and socially.

He successfully partnered and at the same time weakened his opponents from the north by playing upon the political divides among them. He has thus far thwarted all attempts by non-Pashtun factions to put up a united political opposition to his authority. He has dabbled in the tribal politics of Pashtun south, and has co-opted 'former' Taliban elements into local administrative structures and in the High Peace Council. However, he failed to complement his success in keeping the northern leadership divided by building support for his leadership among his co-ethnics in the south and east. The killing of his brother, Ahmed Wali Karzai, in July 2011, who was then heading the Kandahar Provincial Council, and growing Taliban influence even beyond their traditional strongholds, had substantially weakened his position in the Pashtun heartland. Interestingly, despite several limitations to his authority, he appears to be far more independent of his external sponsors than his most fearsome of opponents, be it the Taliban or the Haqqanis, who despite their increasing influence still remain strictly under the control of Pakistan's military establishment.

Once favoured in the West, Karzai in recent years has been a subject of intense criticism and jest. Again, despite near consistent attack on his credibility as a leader both from his supposed allies and enemies, he has emerged from crisis to crisis, neither gaining nor losing much in terms of his unique position in Afghan politics. A lot was said about the flip sides of his personality, including his style of functioning or non-functioning, yet he has been the most crucial link in the 13-year old Western engagement in Afghanistan. Though Karzai is now an extremely frustrating and a peculiar figure for the West and his various detractors, nevertheless, he still may have a role to play even as his presidential term comes to an end.

As the process of security transition began, Karzai had made three significant political moves that simply could not have been dismissed as mere gimmicks. They were carefully timed with the security transition process and were significant from the point of view of public posturing as negotiations over the long-term strategic partnership agreement with the US were underway. First, he extracted memorandums of understanding on two very contentious issues from the US—one on the transfer of prisons from the US control to the Afghan Government; and the other, on greater government oversight and authority over night raids and search operations particularly in rural areas by the Western forces. These developments finally paved the way for the signing of the much-awaited strategic partnership agreement between the two countries in May 2012.

Secondly, in April 2012, Karzai had appointed Salahuddin Rabbani as the new chairman of the government-appointed HPC, which is responsible for seeking political reconciliation with the Taliban. The post had been lying vacant since its first chairman, Burhanuddin Rabbani, was killed by a Taliban suicide bomber in September 2011. The appointment of Burhanuddin's son Salahuddin as his successor was a well thought out move by Karzai. The idea was not only to revive the HPC in view of the US making its own moves on the issue of reconciliation with the Taliban leadership, but also to ensure that a prominent Tajik faction too continue to have stakes in the Kabul-led initiative.

Thirdly, he had proposed that the security transition process from Western to the Afghan forces, as well as the next presidential election, could be completed in 2013, a year ahead of the 2014 deadline. The idea probably was not as much about reducing Kabul's dependence on the West as it was about projecting his relative independence from the West. But what exactly would Karzai stand to gain in terms of his own political future post-2014, remains to be seen.

Karzai also began to forcefully call for greater curtailment of air strikes by the Western forces that often lead to civilian casualties, end to night raids on Afghan homes, and limiting the role of private security contractors and firms. He made it strict pre-conditions for signing the long-term Bilateral Security Agreement (BSA) with Washington as enshrined in the May 2012 partnership agreement. The US military commanders have been reluctant to make concessions on the above issues as they were considered critical to the US military operations in Afghanistan, and more so after 2014. Questioning the Western commitment, Karzai later sought comprehensive security guarantees for Afghanistan against armed militant groups operating from Pakistan, and a long-term funding of Afghan security forces and greater control over Western military operations inside Afghanistan. The negotiations over BSA, however, were finally stalled in mid-2013 as the two countries sparred over the status of the Taliban office in Doha and Washington's attempt to open direct negotiations with the Taliban representatives there.

The lingering negotiation over the terms and conditions of the BSA once again brought to fore the complicated nature of the relationship that Karzai and the West have come to share. Karzai's repeated refusal to accede to the US pressure on the issue of BSA was very much a part of his continuing defiance of the West, which in his perception has constantly questioned and undermined his leadership over a long period of time. It was reflective of Karzai's pent up frustration over the West's failure to heed to several of his advises and opinions—be it on the issue of avoiding civilian casualties by re-strategising the war on terror or leveraging Kabul's position by bringing international aid and allocation responsibilities under its effective control—and lack of respect for his position in the face of several constraints over his role and discretion as president. The West apparently failed to take cognisance of the fragility of Karzai's own position in the Afghan context, the complex environment in which he was struggling to operate and survive, while assessing and judging his performance and leadership. But then it was not only about Karzai's personal anger and deep mistrust of the Western coalition. There was, perhaps, something more to Karzai's dilly dallying on the issue of signing the BSA.

Interestingly, despite his growing opposition and criticism of the West, Karzai never completely opposed or rejected *per se* the utility of the BSA for Afghanistan. The provision for a long-term security agreement was one of the components of the *Enduring Strategic Partnership Agreement* which Karzai had signed with the US in May 2012. The agreement clearly stated that the BSA should be concluded within one year.[24] It is important to note here that persisting differences between Kabul and Washington made BSA look as if it was the whole of the US-Afghan strategic partnership. The sense and the message that went out was if BSA was not signed, the entire partnership agreement would simply collapse. The other obligations and components of the partnership agreement, particularly regarding assistance in social and economic development of Afghanistan, were pushed aside in the process. In November 2013, Karzai had also convened a national *jirga*, which was attended by nearly 2,500 delegates from across the country, to debate and discuss the terms and conditions of the BSA. Though the *jirga* had approved the draft of the BSA, Karzai still refused to sign on the agreement and instead surprised the West with a fresh initiative for reconciliation with the Taliban. Far from taking Washington into confidence, Karzai's office had even kept the HPC out of the process.

One of the key demands, and the one most complex, later raised by Karzai was that Washington must use its leverage over Pakistan to help start direct negotiations between Kabul and the Afghan Taliban. He later stated that if Washington does not approve of his terms and conditions, then the BSA could be signed by the next president. He was well aware of the support for the BSA among the leading presidential candidates, and therefore might have been convinced that sooner or later the security agreement will anyway be signed after the 2014 election. However, this has the potential to jeopardise the post-transition Western mission in Afghanistan if June 2014 runoff election is postponed or there is a political and constitutional crisis in view of a discredited election. He apparently took the whole issue to a point where his own position on the BSA began to appear untenable, though at the same time he left the option of signing the BSA open for his successor.

For Karzai, whose second presidential term is about to end, the West is certainly not of much strategic value. Karzai's vacillating response to repeated calls for signing the BSA could be either seen as Karzai having completely given up on the West or as part of his rather last ditch effort to be treated as an equal partner being the legitimate leader of his country. It is noteworthy that as Karzai's differences with the West intensified, he began to diversify his foreign policy and has since tried to redefine Kabul's relations with neighbouring countries, which remain either opposed to the Western presence or sceptical of the Western commitment in view of its timeline driven approach towards the security transition process. Karzai has been increasingly looking for support and direct assistance from the neighbouring countries and even tried to rework his ties with Pakistan. As he was alienated by the West, Karzai, coupled with the shift in his regional diplomacy, began to further emphasise on the need for political reconciliation with Pakistan-based Afghan Taliban leadership. Perturbed by the American attempt to unilaterally engage Taliban representatives in Doha in June 2013, Karzai tried to work with the new civilian government in Pakistan in an effort to directly reach out to the Taliban leadership. In terms of timing, it suited both

Kabul and Islamabad to be at least seen as working towards a possible breakthrough in the stalemate over the Afghan reconciliation process.

Though Karzai could not have made any progress as he was fast approaching the end of his second and final presidential term, yet he decided to further gamble over the idea of reconciliation with the Taliban as part of his continuing self assertion and possibly also to undermine the relevance of the West post-2014. By trying to achieve some kind of an understanding with the Taliban leadership, Karzai could also be trying to strengthen his over all position in the Afghan polity aware of his potential role in the formation of the next government. Karzai, given his vast political network and experience in balancing divergent interests, remains quite well positioned to help break any political or constitutional deadlock. Karzai do not seem to be averse to playing a significant role in some other capacity after the new government is formed.

There is lot of public or political posturing going on with an eye on 2014 presidential election in Afghanistan and the new political coalition/arrangement that is expected to emerge in Kabul. Karzai is probably trying to use his allies and enemies alike to his advantage. This is something Afghan leaders have been quite adept at, something which comes quite naturally to them, given their long historical experience of managing powerful neighbours and vulnerability to foreign interventions. As part of a well thought out strategy for political survival, amidst competing interests of various external forces active in Afghanistan, Kabul could be trying to play the West and Pakistan against each other, and the same may be said of Rawalpindi which too could be playing up Kabul against the West.

Karzai may have stated that he would handover power immediately after the new president is elected, but at the same time he has not spelt out his future plans. Not many within Afghanistan seem to be willing to take his statements at its face value. Interestingly, Karzai does not appear to have groomed anyone as his successor from among his core group of confidantes either, fully aware of the uncertainty in view of changing political equations and alignments. He would rather wait and might keep everybody guessing about his political favourite until the end of the election process. At the moment, there is still not enough clarity about the kind of political coalition that would emerge after the presidential election.

Karzai would certainly like his political legacy to be carried forward. Given his relatively young age compared to several presidential candidates in the 2014 election, Karzai's political innings are certainly far from over. The constitution does bar him from seeking a successive third term, but definitely not from running for the fourth presidential election in 2019. It is not clear as to what kind of political transition it would be in 2014-15, or what kind of political arrangement would emerge in case elections results are widely disputed or if it turns out to be an unusually long drawn process. In any circumstances, the current government would have to continue until the process of political transition is complete. The worst case scenario would be a widespread civil strife in the absence of a recognised central authority in Kabul.

Like a seasoned politician, Karzai knows how to play different tunes to different audiences. He could be supporting the most conservative of laws in his country, and yet could be endearing to the international community with his universalistic and liberal ideas. He can go ballistic about his Western partners and yet be admiring them for their generous assistance. He had once even threatened to resign on the issue of diluting presidential powers, and on occasion had even talked of joining ranks with the Taliban. Every time pressure was brought upon him, he has been able to put his opponents on the defensive.

All calculated efforts to prop up political alternatives to Karzai have thus far failed. But then what when his second and final presidential term, as per the Afghan Constitution, comes to an end in 2014? What does it mean to his political career, his role and position thereafter? Karzai is very much a part, rather a key protagonist, of the unfolding politics in Kabul. He has been increasingly assertive and notably obstinate on certain issues generally considered as critical to the future of Afghanistan. Though it may not have helped him much in terms of shoring up his position at the domestic level, but it has certainly strengthened his constitutional authority and control over Afghanistan's international affairs.

Unless something unexpected happens, Karzai is least likely to politically fade away. He is not likely to share former President Najibullah's fate either. Perhaps, the political instability after 2014 may throw up a completely new situation and opportunities before him. In times of back door diplomacy and brokerage of deals, his political skill and experience in balancing the divergent interests of various stakeholders may assure him a role in fashioning the new political arrangement. Though Karzai might be having plans up his sleeve, he too, however, could be in for big surprises.

The next president would most probably be facing the same set of challenges and his position could be as vulnerable to known and unknown vagaries of Afghan polity as that of the incumbent leadership. Karzai, whose position and leadership remains undoubtedly unique in the Afghan setting, has survived the ups and down in his political career in his own characteristic style. His leadership, despite all allegations of lack of it, has set a certain political precedence which would be difficult for the next leadership in Kabul to simply ignore. Like Karzai, the position and influence of his successor too would broadly depend on political networking with various powerful militia commanders and manoeuvring of factional divides, and the nature and level of engagement with the West after 2014.

NOTES

1. Piotr Balcerowicz, "The Last Interview with Ahmad Shah Masood," August 2001, at http://www.orient.uw.edu.pl/balcerowicz/texts/Ahmad_Shah_Masood_en.htm
2. "Message of Felicitation of Amir-ul-Momineen on the Occasion of Eid-ul-Fitr," *Islamic Emirate of Afghanistan*, August 06, 2013, at http://shahamat-english.com/index.php/paighamoona/35234-message-of-felicitation-of-amir-ul-momineen-may-allah-protect-him-on-the-occasion-of-eid-ul-fitr
3. Ibid.
4. According to the *Pajhwok Afghan News*, the NFA was formed after several days of deliberations on March 13, 2007. See Makia Monir, "Former strongmen forms political alliance," *Pajhwok Afghan News*, March 13, 2007, at http://www.pajhwak.com/viewstory.asp?lng=eng&id=33147. Interestingly, according to the Strategic Forecasting Inc., better known as *Stratfor*, a well-known Texas-based private intelligence agency, the NFA was founded a year earlier on April 03, 2006.
5. Amin Tarzi, "Afghanistan: Opposition Alliance Receives Official Praise, Popular Doubt," *RFE/RL Afghanistan Report*, April 06, 2005, at http://www.rferl.org/featuresarticle/2005/4/1E906174-6633-4351-AE4B-0BDEFC2A6524.html
6. Naseer Ahmad Nawidy and Sheharyar Khan, "National Front: Mapping the Afghan Political Landscape," *Policy Brief No. 3*, Institute of Policy Studies, Islamabad, May 02, 2007, at http://www.ips.org.pk/policy%20brief/Policy%20Brief-3.pdf
7. Amin Tarzi, "Afghanistan: What Unites the New 'United Front'?," *RFE/RL Afghanistan Report*, May 10, 2007, at http://www.rferl.org/featuresarticle/2007/05/64ccc722-13eb-4f66-8c60-eb7785eb64bb.html
8. Golnaz Esfandiari, "Afghanistan: New Political Bloc Unites Old Adversaries," *RFE/RL Report*, April 05, 2007, at http://www.rferl.org/featuresarticle/2007/04/d0dfc5f9-e7de-4027-a98b-022e279abbe3.html
9. Hafizullah Gardesh and Sayed Yaqub Ibrahimi, "Political Alliance Creates Strange Bedfellows," *Institute of War and Peace Reporting*, March 29, 2007, at http://www.iwpr.net/index.php?apc_state=hen&s=o&o=p=arr&s=f&o=334489
10. Amin Tarzi, no. 7.
11. Hafizullah Gardesh and Sayed Yaqub Ibrahimi, no. 9.
12. Ibid.
13. Javid Hamim, "Hezb-i-Islami rejects formation of National Front," *Pajhwok Afghan News*, April 10, 2007, at http://www.pajhwak.com/viewstory.asp?lng=eng&id=34553
14. Abdul Raouf Liwal, "Formation of new alliance sparks debate," *Pajhwok Afghan News*, April 10, 2007, at http://www.pajhwak.com/viewstory.asp?lng=eng&id=34599
15. Zakir Hassnain, "Taliban's participation necessary for peace," *Daily Times*, September 03, 2007, at http://www.dailytimes.com.pk/default.asp?page=2007%5C09%5C03%5Cstory_3-9-2007_pg7_37
16. Anand Gopal, "Afghan opposition courts Taliban," *The Christian Science Monitor*, April 03, 2008, at http://www.csmonitor.com/2008/0403/p06s01-woap.html
17. M.K. Bhadrakumar, "Afghanistan moves to center stage," *Asia Times Online*, April 19, 2008, at http://www.atimes.com/atimes/South_Asia/JD19Df02.html
18. Jason Straziuso, "Afghan opposition says it's been talking to Taliban," *Associated Press*, April 16, 2008, at http://ap.google.com/article/ALeqM5i8dGftYb0s4XWdUMRdIVs3vh1CKAD902T3L05
19. "ANF for recognition of Taliban as a party," *The Frontier Post* (Peshawar), May 02, 2008, at http://www.thefrontierpost.com/News.aspx?ncat=an&nid=315

20. "Ex-Prince Wants Taliban Brought into Afghan Government," *The New York Times*, May 07, 2008, at http://www.nytimes.com/reuters/world/international-afghan-crisis.html
21. Saleha Soadat, "'Electoral Alliance' Announces Members, Intent for Presidential Election," *TOLO News*, August 30, 2013, at http://www.tolonews.com/en/election-2014/11731-qafghanistan-electoral-allianceq-officially-announced-for-presidential-vote
22. Ahmad Ramin Ayaaz, "New Coalition Endorsed by Taliban Formed for Elections," *TOLO News*, September 05, 2013, at http://tolonews.com/en/afghanistan/11815-new-coalition-endorsed-by-taliban-formed-for-elections
23. Sayed Aazem Arash, "MPs, Senators, Tribal Elders Form New Alliance," *TOLO News*, September 08, 2013, at http://www.tolonews.com/en/afghanistan/11846-mps-senators-tribal-elders-form-new-alliance
24. The BSA is supposed to supersede the *Agreement Regarding the Status of United States Military and Civilian Personnel of the U.S. Department of Defense Present in Afghanistan in Connection with Cooperative Efforts in Response to Terrorism, Humanitarian, and Civic Assistance, Military Training and Exercises, and Other Activities* (2003). See "Enduring Strategic Partnership Agreement between the United States of America and the Islamic Republic of Afghanistan," *The White House*, May 02, 2012, at http://www.whitehouse.gov/sites/default/files/2012.06.01u.s.-afghanistanspasignedtext.pdf

"Unlike other wars, Afghan wars become serious only when they are over."

—Sir Olaf Caroe, British Governor, NWFP, 1946-47

"I am considering two promises. One is the promise of God; the other is that of Bush. The promise of God is that my land is vast. If you start a journey on God's path, you can reside anywhere on this earth and will be protected....The promise of Bush is that there is no place on earth where you can hide that I cannot find you. We will see which one of these two promises is fulfilled."*

—Taliban leader Muhammad Omar, Voice of America, September 2001

---

* "Mullah Omar - in his own words," *The Guardian*, September 26, 2001, at http://www.theguardian.com/world/2001/sep/26/afghanistan.features11. The interview was originally conducted in *Pashtu* for the *Voice of America* in September 2001.

CHAPTER IV

Taliban Back into Power Play

Taliban reappeared on the political stage of Afghanistan within five years of their tactical retreat from Kabul and Kandahar at the end of 2001. By 2005-06, the campaigners of the war on terror were confronted with the serious business of guerrilla warfare, a war within war. If history is any guide, the nuances of the Afghan wars which go round in circles have always puzzled the invading armies, and have remained rather incomprehensible to the foreign military strategists.

The old and familiar historical tendencies and the socio-political dynamics in the vast and varied Pashtun tribal belt, which the US and its Western allies either failed to discern or simply overlooked, were unravelling once again. It may be said that the course of, as well as the discourse on, the Afghan war again began changing as Taliban with support from within Pakistan re-emerged from the periphery. Taliban were once again playing upon the same factors which had earlier facilitated their rise in 1994-95, mainly weak or non-existent state structures, socio-political polarisation, widespread corruption, popular discontentment, denial of justice, conflicting factional politics, etc.

As Afghanistan could be poised for another round of anarchy, which threatens to undo the achievements of the past decade, it would be interesting to examine how the contours of the Afghan war began to change from 2005-06 onwards. Battle lines have since shifted from the fringes to the heartland of Afghanistan, despite tremendous surge in American troop levels and several reviews of the military and political strategy by the Obama Administration since 2009. Today, as Taliban and their allies remain strong and resilient while Western forces drawdown and prepare to end their combat mission, the Afghan war seems to be coming full circle. The possible or likely future scenarios, though loaded with several ifs and buts, do not inspire much confidence in the post-transition objectives and strategy of the American-led Western mission which remains familiarly vague and uncertain.

War on Terror: Losing while Winning

It is apparent that *Operation Enduring Freedom* launched by the US in October 2001 had left vast spaces in the Afghan countryside, where more than eighty per cent Afghans lived, outside the scope of their military operations. Making a tactical retreat from the urban areas, Taliban fighters in the traditional Afghan-style had melted into the local population, withdrawn into the vast countryside, or crossed over into the tribal agencies in Pakistan.

With the Bush Administration opening the second front of the war on terror in Iraq in March 2003, the international attention along with the US war-machinery gradually receded from Afghanistan. It has been aptly stated by Ahmed Rashid that, "Indeed, in March 2002, just three months after the defeat of the Taliban, the United States began to withdraw its Special Forces, surveillance satellites and drones from Afghanistan to prepare for war in Iraq. Distracted by war in Iraq, Bush Administration either failed to take notice of or simply avoided acknowledging what was happening in the tribal agencies of Pakistan. It was said that by the time the Pakistan army entered South Waziristan in March 2004, the extremists were so well entrenched that 250 Pakistani soldiers were killed in the first encounters."[1] Several areas in the north-western Khyber Pakhtunkhwa Province of Pakistan have since been virtually under the control or at least the strong influence of various militant groups who at some point of time were created or nurtured by the Pakistani establishment. There were areas where there was hardly any government presence or control. The blow back of the proxy politics ardently pursued by successive regimes in Pakistan through the 1980s and 90s, and which continues to this day, now poses a major social, political and security challenge to the internal stability and progress of Pakistan itself.

The US invasion of Iraq was in complete disregard of the fact that the Taliban and the al Qaeda were still a major threat to the delicate Bonn Process. Not a single Taliban or al Qaeda leader worth the name had been apprehended by then. It is difficult not to question the motives and the objectives behind the US' war on terror in Afghanistan. Was the US really interested in establishing stability and strong democratic state-institutions in Afghanistan? Was the recipe of 'war on terror' and 'nation-building' in Afghanistan a well-conceived move? It was not long before the inherent paradoxes and conflict in the American approach and strategy were more than apparent. The objectives were too narrow and the strategy unclear and short-sighted. The American war completely failed to comprehend and factor in the various lingering issues of conflict within Afghanistan, and particularly the strong external or trans-national dimensions to it, in their over all military and political strategy.

The Iraq war apparently led to deliberate trivialisation of potential threat to the nascent government in Kabul both from the Taliban, whose entire leadership was protected and exiled in Pakistan, and the various Afghan militia groups and factions competing for political space in the new order, in the Western thinking and discourse. Former British Defence Secretary John Reid's remarks during his visit to Afghanistan in April 2006, merely three months before NATO troops had moved into southern Afghanistan in June-July, showed that NATO had no plans for counter-insurgency operations. Drawing a clear distinction between the US and the British mission in Afghanistan, he reportedly argued that the US mission was to "go and chase and kill the terrorists who did so much to destroy the twin towers in that terrible attack," while the task of British forces was to "help and protect" the Afghan reconstruction. Clearly stating that the British mission is "primarily reconstruction"' and "not counterterrorism," he claimed, "We would be perfectly happy to leave in three years and without firing one shot because our job is to protect the reconstruction."[2] The next British Defence Secretary, Des Browne, was reported to have stated in July 2006 that, "Neither the Taliban, nor the range of illegally armed groups, currently pose a threat to the long-term stability of Afghanistan."[3]

The above remarks assume certain significance in view of the fact that Britain has been the US' closest of the European allies. It raises a key question as to whether counter-insurgency and counter-terrorism or even counter-narcotics was at all part of NATO's Afghan mission when it took over the command of the ISAF in 2003. Counterinsurgency was either initially not part of NATO's agenda in Afghanistan or there was a lack of workable consensus on the role and mandate of the ISAF, primarily between the US and the European countries. The inability of certain constituents of the ISAF to lead a systematic counter-insurgency campaign against the Taliban and other anti-government groups remained a major issue of difference between the US and most of the European member states of NATO. Interestingly, the British, the Canadians, and the Dutch were the only ones to provide troops for counter-insurgency operations in support of the US-led coalition force, while a majority of the NATO troops remained stationed in relatively peaceful parts of the country. Over the years, these countries have successfully resisted any pressure—both from the US and from within NATO—to spare their troops for counter-insurgency operations in the south and east. However, on the issue of training and mentoring of the ANSF, NATO has been relatively far more supportive of the US-led efforts.

NATO's lack of preparedness and confusion over the rules of engagement in turn led to gaps in the assessment made by its commanders and the political leadership. The NATO officials, similar to their US counterparts, too would often deliberately trivialise the potential threat to Kabul's authority from the Taliban. Just months before the ISAF moved into southern Afghanistan, General James Jones, then NATO Supreme Allied Commander Europe, had asserted in

March 2006, that "the Taliban and al Qaeda are not in a position to where they can restart an insurgency of any size and major scope."[4] Whereas, General Michael D. Maples, Director of the US Defence Intelligence Agency (DIA), had observed in March 2006 that, "Despite significant progress on the political front, the Taliban-dominated insurgency remains a capable and resilient threat.... We judge that the insurgency appears emboldened by perceived tactical successes and will be active this spring."[5]

Later, in 2007-08, as Taliban insurgency gained further momentum, the rift between the US and its NATO allies over the Afghan mission too came to the fore. On October 22, 2007, then US Defence Secretary Robert Gates had observed that it was difficult to believe that NATO "whose members have over two million soldiers, sailors, marines and airmen cannot find the modest additional resources that have been committed for Afghanistan."[6] In an interview to the *Los Angeles Times* in January 2008, Gates again blamed NATO forces of being incapable for counter insurgency which led to the rise in violence during the year. He stated, "I'm worried we're deploying [military advisors] that are not properly trained and I'm worried we have some military forces that don't know how to do counterinsurgency operations. Most of the European forces, NATO forces, are not trained in counterinsurgency; they were trained for the Fulda Gap."[7] Again, in February 2008, while making an assessment of the situation in Afghanistan before the US Senate Armed Services Committee, Gates had alluded to the possibility of NATO "evolving into a two-tiered alliance" with "some allies willing to fight and die to protect people's security, and others who are not." In his opinion, such a situation "puts a cloud over the future of the alliance if this is to endure and perhaps get even worse."[8]

Taliban No More on the Fringe

Away from the international gaze, the Taliban got a window of opportunity to regroup and revive its tribal and Islamist networks across the Durand Line. At the same time, they kept up the pressure on the sparsely distributed US-led coalition force in southern and eastern Afghanistan by making regular guerrilla offensive against them. Pakistan too saw an opportunity to regain its influence by largely reverting to its pre 9/11 policy of directly supporting the Taliban. Pakistan also wanted the battle lines of Afghan Taliban to move deeper inside Afghanistan as it grappled with Islamist militancy in its own tribal region.

With Afghan Taliban making a comeback, Pakistan's role too came under international scrutiny. In February 2007, the then US commander in Afghanistan, David Barno, had stated: "some significant change took place in 2005 that re-energised the Taliban movement and ultimately delivered this 'new Taliban' which we see today...since mid-2005, Pakistan has also re-calculated its position *vis-à-*

vis Afghanistan in light of concerns for a diminished and less aggressive US presence in the nation that lies in Pakistan's backyard."[9] In March 2007, it was reported in *Asia Times Online* that the Pakistani establishment has struck a deal with a prominent Afghan Taliban commander, Mullah Dadullah, to extend its influence to south-western Afghanistan and to enable the Taliban to make further push towards Kabul. According to the report, Mullah Dadullah "will be Pakistan's strongman in a corridor running from the Afghan provinces of Zabul, Urozgan, Kandahar and Helmand across the border into Pakistan's Balochistan province."[10] The objective of creating such a corridor was to ensure a regular flow of recruits, weapons and other logistics to the Taliban fighters from the Pakistani territories.

Though the security situation was deteriorating in general across southern Afghanistan, of particular note was the growing Taliban presence in the strategically significant southern Helmand Province. The initiative taken by British commanders to pacify the local Taliban in Musa Qala District by signing a pact with them in October 2006, had already faltered. In March 2007, then provincial governor, Assadullah Wafa, had reported the presence of, besides the local Taliban, some 700 guerrillas comprising Arab, Uzbek, Chechen, Tajik and Pakistani militants led by Abdullah Mehsud from North Waziristan.[11] Apart from Musa Qala, several other districts in the province had either fallen or were on the verge of falling under Taliban control. Taliban have also since tried to strengthen their position in various provinces surrounding Kabul. In fact, since late 2007, Taliban have been regularly carrying out well-coordinated attacks inside the capital city of Kabul.

According to another report published in October 2007, an estimated 20,000 fully trained recruits were said to be ready to cross over into Afghanistan through at least sixteen entry points along the Durand Line. The main entry points were Noshki (in Balochistan province), Ghulam Khan (North Waziristan), Angur Ada (South Waziristan), Shawal (North Waziristan), and Chitral and Bajuar agencies. The recruits were supposed to join the guerrillas fighting in the south-eastern provinces of Ghazni, Khost, Gardez, Paktia and Paktika.[12] Taliban have since come a long way. It is interesting to note that in August 2005, then leader of the opposition in Pakistan's national assembly and the Secretary-General of MMA, Maulana Fazl-ur Rehman, while reacting to the Musharraf Government's decision to shut down certain madrassas and expel foreign students and militants, had stated: "We will have to openly tell the world whether we want to support jihadis or crack down on them. We can't afford to be hypocritical anymore. The rulers (of Pakistan) are not only trying to deceive the United States and the West, but also hoodwinking the entire nation." He added, "We ask the rulers to reveal the identity of the people being transported to Afghanistan from Waziristan via Kaali Sarak in private vehicles, to reveal who is supervising their trouble-free entry into

Afghanistan, and reasons for their infiltrations." Rehman also challenged the Pakistan Government to reveal the "identities of the men being moved from Waziristan to militant camps in Mansehra."[13]

However, there were various dimensions to the Taliban resurgence, some of which have been broadly discussed below:

Issue of Pashtun alienation and competing leadership

The Bonn Process had brought into its fold set of old factional players, mainly non-Pashtun, which was said to have led to a sense of alienation among the Pashtuns, the dominant ethnic group of Afghanistan. The fact that the Bonn Process was sponsored by the West, that it was too Kabul-centric and had a predominantly Panjshiri Tajik component, had made Pashtuns largely sceptical about the whole political process as well as the leadership of Hamid Karzai. Though Karzai had a prominent Pashtun background, but due to his continuing dependence on the West and the influence of the Tajiks in his government, he failed to cobble enough support among his fellow Pashtuns. With most of the prominent Pashtun leaders particularly former King Zahir Shah either sidelined or eliminated by the Taliban like Abdul Haq, the Bonn Process attempted to project Karzai as an alternative Pashtun leader. This was to have a long-term implication for the Afghan politics which has had a strong tribal-ethnic component to it.

The West-sponsored leadership of Hamid Karzai stood in stark contrast to the predominantly Pashtun Taliban leadership at the intra-Pashtun level, particularly in the vast rural expanse in the south and east. At the inter-ethnic level too, Karzai at the time was no match to the powerful minority ethnic leaders with mass support base in their respective strongholds. Despite Karzai's political assertions against powerful *mujahideen* leaders from time to time, authority and power for various reasons continued to elude him. In such circumstances, it would not be wrong to say that Pashtuns by and large might have been looking at the Taliban as the sole organised Pashtun force in the highly competitive factional politics of Afghanistan.

Apart from this, it has been relatively easier for the conservative rural Pashtun communities to identify themselves with the Taliban who had earlier brought a semblance of order and security in the countryside, rather than an urbane Pashtun leader with no cadre-based organisation or militia to support him. Here, it would be worth-mentioning that the Taliban leadership had its roots among the tribal Pashtun *mujahideen* who had fought against the Soviet-backed Kabul regime in the 1980s. Mullah Omar and other senior Taliban leaders had been members of Mohammad Nabi Mohammadi's Harakat-e Inqelabi-e Islami.[14] Some were also from Mohammad Yunus Khalis's Hizb-e Islami. The rural background of most of the top Taliban leadership certainly gave them an edge over the Kabul-based Western-educated professionals and technocrats with no following among the Afghan people. The reported dissatisfaction among the Pashtuns with the Karzai Government on account of worsening security, slow pace of reconstruction and rehabilitation, endemic corruption among the government officials, and the threat of anti-narcotic operations, was exploited by the Taliban to their advantage. Although President Karzai was a central figure in the internationally-backed political process, and was a strong link between Kabul and the West, his position in the complex power structures of Afghanistan has been delicate if not under constant threat.

Rise of Jalal-ud Din Haqqani and the Arabs within Taliban

Apart from the above factors, it is noteworthy that sections of Pashtun commanders from the 1980s had in the past shown a tendency of cooperating with the Taliban as a matter of political expediency. The commonality of objectives and the overlapping areas of influence have at times led to certain powerful Pashtun *mujahideen* leaders to lend their support to the Taliban. Gulbuddin Hekmatyar and Jalal-ud Din Haqqani, two of the most radical Pashtun Islamists, later proved to be an asset to the Taliban. As Taliban pushed harder into the Afghan heartland, prospect of disgruntled sections of Pashtun population joining the Taliban rank increased. It would be useful to refer to what Qari Ahmadullah, former Taliban intelligence chief, while urging the opponents to join the Taliban, had stated, "We will forget the past problems with those people who join us, because now it is the question of our religion and country."[15] Taliban as a matter of propaganda and to garner support among the Afghan people have since tried to blend their strict Islamist agenda with patriotic and nationalistic appeals from time to time.

It may be surmised that the elevation of Haqqani in the Taliban military structure shows that the former *mujahideen* commander with decades of military experience was being mainstreamed in the Taliban military organisation. It appears that the Taliban as part of an effort to broaden their recruitment base had started giving space to non-Talib fighters as well. Gulbuddin Hekmatyar along with his Hizb-e Islami guerrillas was the first to reach an understanding with the Taliban after his return from exile in Iran in 2002. But at the same time, Taliban had failed in enlisting support of various other Pashtun commanders who either preferred to remain independent or cautiously sided with the new political set up in Kabul.

In the context of an increased Arab/al Qaeda role in the resurrection of the Taliban, the rise of Jalal-ud Din Haqqani as a top Taliban commander in 2006 assumes significance. Haqqani was also known for his proximity to the CIA, ISI and especially the Saudi intelligence in the 1980s. He had also come in close contact with Osama bin Laden during the late 1980s when the latter started funding pro-Arab radical Pashtun Islamists like him and Hekmatyar and Sayyaf. During the anti-Soviet *jihad* in the 1980s, Haqqani was known for managing the Arab Jihadi/Wahhabi volunteers coming to Afghanistan. Though Haqqani had joined the Taliban movement way back in 1995, he continued to run his training camps for al Qaeda in Afghanistan. In fact, Taliban links with the Arab fighters go back to the same period. Syed Saleem Shahzad, a Pakistani journalist, in one of his several writings on Taliban had reported that Mullah Omar had deputed some Taliban fighters under one Mullah Mehmood Haq Yar, supposedly an expert in guerrilla and urban warfare, to fight along with Ansar-ul Islam militants in northern Iraq before 2001. After the US invasion of Iraq in 2003, Mullah Mehmood Haq Yar returned to Afghanistan sometime before the first presidential election in October 2004, and presented the following blue print based on his Iraqi experience for reinvigorating the Taliban activity across Afghanistan:

- Recruit highly trained Arab fighters and give them a lead role, as in the jihad against the Soviets.
- Arab fighters are particularly adept at developing improvised weapons. During the US invasion, for example, Arab fighters were able to turn unexploded cluster bombs into effective improvised weapons. Such tactics will be adopted to the full.
- Arab fighters, especially those fluent in Pashtu, will be spread in key Afghan cities, such as Jalalabad, Khost, Kunar, Logar, Herat and Kabul, where they will infiltrate the population and administrations and spread the Taliban word.
- Once these few hundred Arab fighters, along with Afghan counterparts, establish themselves, they will target US forces in their region.
- The movement of US forces is already restricted because of their commitment to providing security for the October 9 presidential elections. But if they do conduct operations, two things will happen: the election process will become vulnerable as resources will be stretched, and the militants will carry out limited retaliation against US-led forces that venture out against them.[16]

However, after the ouster of the Taliban, Kabul and the US, as part of limited reconciliation and to engineer a split among the Taliban rank-and-file, had offered truce to Haqqani. He was reportedly even offered premiership in Hamid Karzai's provisional government which he refused.[17] Subsequently, it is said that it was due to the failure of the two central Taliban commanders, Mullah Akhtar Osmani and Mullah Dadullah, during the 2004 and 2005 spring offensives that Haqqani was given the lead role. It is noteworthy that prior to 2001, Haqqani never figured among the key commanders of the Taliban. During the Taliban rule, he had held the relatively low profile ministry for border affairs.

The Arab component in the resurgent Taliban too increased as guerrilla offensive gained momentum to widen the theatre of conflict. The replication of techniques employed by the Iraqi militants by the Taliban in Afghanistan bore an unmistakable imprint of the Arab/al Qaeda militants. Funds provided by al Qaeda and the immensely profitable drug trade continued to finance the Taliban movement. There were also reports that various Arab entities, including the banned *Al-Rasheed* and *Al-Akhtar Trust* and various other such organisations, apart from rich and influential Pakistani traders, too had resumed the funding for the Taliban.[18] Arab militants who had been active in the region since the days of the anti-Soviet *jihad* are known to have established a vast network of finances and are well-embedded in the region. They have developed ties with the Pakistani Islamist organisations, and also among the Pashtun tribes through matrimonial alliances. They have played a significant role in linking Taliban with the international Islamist networks.

However, at the same time, one cannot rule out the possibility of differences on matters of policy and approach between the Taliban and the predominantly Arab elements from al Qaeda. Given their respective geographical bases and overall agenda, the possibility of political and ideological friction between sections of Taliban and the al Qaeda elements remain. Taliban is primarily a Pashtun organisation which is more localised in terms of its spread and political agenda, whereas al Qaeda is essentially an Arab organisation with a global agenda and trans-national network. However, given the fact that there was growing anti-Americanism in Pakistan's tribal frontier and in Iraq, Taliban and al Qaeda have had enough reasons to stay together. The al Qaeda also wanted to keep the US troops tied down and make the war on terror implausible by expanding theatres of conflict within Afghanistan. Despite eliminating Osama bin Laden in May 2011, al Qaeda in the US' own assessment is still active and capable enough to carry out targeted attacks against its interests. Afghan provinces bordering Pakistan, particularly Kunar and Nuristan, are known to have a strong presence of al Qaeda fighters. Taliban, on the other hand, also needed funds and allies to sustain their war against the Western forces in Afghanistan.

A media savvy Taliban

Unlike before, Taliban leaders were quick to reach out to the media after their ouster in 2001. The objective was not only to show to their friends and foe that the movement was alive, but also to secure more recruits for the fledgling Taliban force through a concerted propaganda. Taliban officials and commanders had been frequently issuing statements through emails, faxes, satellite phones and purported audio tapes since early 2003. Some commanders like Mullah Dadullah even granted interviews on TV channels particularly the Pakistani, and Arab news channels like *Al Jazeera*. His offer to give a recorded interview to the *BBC* in March 2003 was the first by a Taliban leader since December 2001. Similarly, some other Taliban commanders like Akhtar Osmani were also known to have given interviews from time to time. Prior to them, Mullah Omar himself had reportedly given an interview to the *Voice of America* and *BBC Pashto* over satellite phone in September and November 2001 respectively. In April 2005, there were reports referring to the revival of the Taliban era mobile radio station, *Shariat Zhagh* or the "Voice of Shariat."[19]

The Taliban have also been distributing pamphlets and night letters or *Shabname*, basically a *mujahideen* tactic of reaching out to the Afghan people during the anti-Soviet war. Recruitment DVDs inspiring youths to join the movement are said to be easily available all along and across the Durand Line, including in Balochistan. There have also been reports of Taliban having come out with a bimonthly newsletter called *Masone* or 'Appearance.'[20] Last couple of years they have also gone online with such well maintained websites as *shahamat* and *alemarah* which regularly issues updates on attacks against Western and Afghan forces and statements on key occasions from their leadership. Taliban and their sympathisers are also believed to be active on social networking sites as part of their information and propaganda warfare.[21]

Gaining Strategic Depth in Pakistan

Whether Pakistan was ever or will ever be able to have a strategic depth within Afghanistan or not, the Afghan Taliban have definitely found a vast space and a supporting populace in Pakistan's tribal agencies to fall back upon every time they come under military pressure from the Western coalition force. Pakistan's failure to deal or subdue the armed tribal militias in its north-western region has gone a long way in exposing the weaknesses inherent in Pakistan's federal structures and its enforcement mechanisms. For decades, militant *lashkars* and Islamists of all hues have been present in the region. In fact, the tenuous hold of the Pakistan State over the region had emboldened particularly the Tehrik-e Taliban Pakistan or the Pakistani Taliban and Lashkar-e Islam to leverage their position in several parts of FATA and Khyber Pakhtunkhwa.

The Talibanisation of the politics and society in Pakistan has been phenomenal. The establishment of the Taliban style *Amr-bil-maroof wa Nahi-anil-munkar* (Prevention of Vice and Promotion of Virtue) in the Dir region and in the Tirah Valley of Khyber Agency,[22] and the Hisba Bill issue[23] in parts of Khyber Pukhtunkhwa, were instances of the growing hold of the Islamists at the expense of waning government institutions and authority in Pakistan's tribal agencies. In fact, Pakistani Taliban or pro-Taliban Pakistani militant groups are said to be virtually controlling certain areas in the Waziristan region, carrying out public executions and running private prisons. They are said to have purged the region of pro-government officials and tribal *lashkars*, including the *maliks* and the traditional clergy, who have since centuries administered the tribal regions which otherwise have never been under the purview of Pakistani constitution and legal codes. The Pakistani Taliban and some other such groups were also reported to have announced the establishment of Islamic Emirates in tribal areas of Khyber Pakhtunkhwa.

Though it is difficult to say to what extent linkages with the wider Islamist network have reduced the dependence of Afghan Taliban on the Pakistani State, the pro-Taliban Islamists including political parties active in Punjab and Khyber Pukhtunkhwa have certainly broadened the constituency of Afghan Taliban within Pakistan. Here it is noteworthy that different factions of Pakistan's Jamiat-ul-Ulema-e-Islam (JUI) party, which have had ties with the Afghan Taliban since the early 1990s, had a role in convincing Islamabad to shift its support/patronage from Hekmatyar's Hezb-e Islami to the emerging Taliban movement in 1994. The pro-Taliban JUI was earlier a key constituent of the coalition government formed in Balochistan after 2002.[24] Quetta and Chaman in Balochistan have since been a safe haven for the exiled Afghan Taliban leaders and commanders. Again, it was the banned Pakistani extremist outfit, Tehrik-e-Nifaz Shariah Muhammadi (TNSM), which had sent thousands of its volunteers to reinforce the fledgling Taliban force in the wake of the US invasion in October 2001. Growing violence in and around Dir Valley during 2007-09 and later in Swat had necessitated strong action by Pakistan Army. Though Pakistani officials insisted that the organisation has been largely decimated, various pro-Taliban Islamist militant groups have since made a strong comeback in parts of the country. The security scenario in the region has alternated between Taliban struggling to assume a more autonomous character and Rawalpindi trying to keep them under its strict control.

It appears that the first signs of a serious strain between the Afghan Taliban and its Pakistani mentors appeared in the aftermath of the 9/11 when the US began to pressurise Pakistan to use its leverage with the Taliban for the extradition of Osama bin Laden. After a lot of high drama too well-known to be repeated here, Pakistan had to briefly disassociate itself from the Afghan Taliban in the interest of its relations with the US. This might have convinced the Afghan Taliban that Pakistan could not be a patron-partner of all seasons.

In fact, the argument that 'moderate' Taliban could be included in the provisional government at Kabul was vehemently opposed by none other than

Mullah Omar himself. This was in direct opposition to Pakistan's constant refrain that 'moderate' Taliban have to be part of the Bonn Process. The successive American administrations and the Afghan Government too, however, have since been trying to wean away the middle and lower ranking cadre of the Taliban, though without much success. It is worth recalling that on being asked for his views on 'moderate' Taliban, Mullah Omar had earlier candidly stated that, "There is no such thing in the Taleban. All Taleban are moderate. There are two things: extremism (Ifraat, or doing something to excess) and conservatism (Tafreet, or doing something insufficiently). So in that sense, we are all moderates—taking the middle path."[25] However, the possibility of differences within the Taliban leadership and the cadre on the issue cannot be ruled out. There were reports that a small number of frontline Taliban commanders had split from the Taliban and formed Jaish-e Muslimeen in October 2004. However, it appears that by mid-2005 most of them had reconciled back with the Taliban leadership.

Since then, sections of Afghan Taliban have definitely been seeking a greater engagement with the wider Islamist network of the al Qaeda and pro-Taliban Pakistani Islamist groups. Both trans-national Islamist networks and the radical Pashtun Islamist commanders like Haqqani and Hekmatyar have made a common cause with the Taliban in their effort to rid Afghanistan of the Western forces and establish a purely Islamist regime in Kabul though there is no consensus among them on what kind of Islamic system should Afghanistan have.

It may be said that the term 'Taliban' has come to acquire a more generic connotation as various kinds of grouping are functioning under its banner. Taliban apparently underwent a certain transformation as it collated its resources and widened its network in the frontier tribal agencies of Pakistan. As mentioned earlier, leaders with decades of military experience, particularly Jalal-ud Din Haqqani, Saifullah Mansoor,[26] Mullah Dadullah Akhund and Gulbuddin Hekmatyar, were at the forefront in rejuvenating the war tactics of the Taliban. The well-coordinated guerrilla operations by the Taliban left both the US and NATO-led force grappling for an effective counter-strategy. Taliban and allies have effectively used suicide and car bombings and roadside attacks to inflict heavy casualty among the Western and Afghan troops. In recent years, most of the casualties among the American troops have been caused by the IEDs which are now being extensively used against the Afghan army leading the military operations.

It is apparent that the Taliban have been able to establish some kind of a military-administrative structure, though not highly centralised. It was reported that in 2003 Taliban had formed a 10-member Leadership Council and various military and political shuras.[27] Senior Taliban leaders or commanders have probably been appointed for coordinating guerrilla operations in different parts of eastern and southern Afghanistan. For instance, Hekmatyar, who is said to have his offices in the Pakistani city of Peshawar and in Bajaur region, has been coordinating the operations against the US forces in the eastern provinces of Kapisa, Kunar, Laghman, Nangahar and Nuristan. Similarly, the Haqqani faction operated from Miram Shah in North Waziristan, from where they have been leading guerrilla operations mainly in the provinces of Khost, Logar, Paktia and Paktika.[28] Commander Anwar Panghaz had been taking care of the guerrillas operating in the provinces around Kabul—Parwan, Kapisa, Wardak, and Logar. Similarly, Taliban commanders like Mullah Dadullah, Akhtar Osmani and Abdur Razzaq were put under the over-all command of Mullah Baradar who was then responsible for the southern provinces. Many of these Taliban commanders were subsequently killed in NATO operations during 2006-07 and Mullah Baradar was 'arrested' in a supposedly joint US-Pakistan operation in the Pakistani city of Karachi in early 2010.

In fact, as the anti-US sentiments increased in the region, both Afghan and Pakistani Taliban found more forces willing to fight under their banner. It would not be wrong to say that the growing strength of the Taliban was inversely proportional to the growing local sentiments against the Western intervention in the region. Given the influence of the Taliban among the pro-Taliban religious political parties and militant groups in large parts of Khyber Pakhtunkhwa and Balochistan, Taliban have apparently acquired a dynamics of their own within Pakistan. Keeping in view the sensitivity of the historically contentious Durand Line, and the ongoing insurgency in its bordering provinces, Pakistan would want Taliban and other such armed militant groups to take battle lines away from its borders to the Afghan heartland. At another level, Pakistan also continues to seek influence in the Afghan politics, and thus retain its utility for the US, by sustaining its support to the Haqqani-Taliban combine.

Changing Face of the Afghan War

Initially, it was said that the US forces are fighting the 'remnants' of the Taliban. However, by 2005-06, one finds that the 'remnants' had transformed into a 'resurgent' force. According to a report released in June 2006 by former US Army General, Barry R. McCaffrey, "the Taliban operated in small units three years ago; last year, they grew to company-sized units of 100-plus men; and for this year's summer fighting season they are maneuvering in 400-strong battalion-sized units." He added, the Taliban now have "excellent weapons" and "new field equipment" and "new IED (improvised explosive device) technology and commercial communications. They appear to have received excellent tactical, camouflage and marksmanship training" and "they are very aggressive and smart in their tactics."[29] Perhaps, the Afghan reality had begun to puzzle the Western forces of various shades operating in parts of Afghanistan. Senior Western military officials, particularly from NATO, have been making statements highlighting the anomalies in the security assessments. From 2005-06 onwards suicide bombings and roadside attacks against the ISAF, which had just expanded its operations to the south and east of the country, saw a phenomenal rise. Of particular note was the assessment of Afghan situation by the British Commander of the NATO-led ISAF. Describing the situation in Afghanistan as "close to anarchy," Gen. David Richards on July 21, 2006 referred to the "the lack of unity between different agencies." He described "poorly regulated private security companies" as unethical and "all too ready to discharge firearms." He also warned that due to continuing logistical shortcomings the Western forces are "running out of time" in terms of fulfilling the expectations of the Afghan people.[30] The growing disparity in the assessments by Western military commanders and their political leadership, who continue to project a relatively optimistic picture about the war against the Taliban, has since been a constant feature.

Initially, Taliban were known to have a rag tag force which were disorganised and lacked capability to mount any serious attack. However, Taliban and their allies were quick to regroup and launch attacks against the nascent Afghan government and the US and NATO-led forces with impunity. Using centuries old Afghan guerrilla tactics, Taliban have effectively turned the war to their own advantage. Historically, Afghanistan's guerrilla warfare has been known for making wars costly and implausible, rather incomprehensible, for invading armies by tactfully exploiting their geo-strategic location, changing alliances and shifting loyalties, weaving myths around resistance leadership, invoking tribal networks and historical memories. The myths perpetuated around the *Amir ul Momineen* Mullah Omar and the Hizb-e Islami leader Hekmatyar have proved effective in their propaganda war. Making maximum use of the mountainous terrain, they even took their guerrilla attacks and suicide bombings to the fortified bases of the US and NATO forces in southern and eastern Afghanistan. President Bush's claim in 2002 that, "We're tough, we're strong, they're well-equipped. We have a good strategy. We are showing the world we know how to fight a guerrilla war with conventional means" looked completely out of place as years passed by.[31]

The displacement of the Taliban from their urban strongholds had led many in the West to believe that the Taliban have successfully been destroyed and that they would be soon eliminated. It was aptly remarked by Paul Rogers later that, "By the end of 2001, it looked as though the war in Afghanistan was over. Senior politicians in Washington were happy to talk of victory, but military opinion was much more cautious, not least because fighting continued in parts of the country and there had been an almost complete inability to kill or capture the Taliban or Al Qaeda leadership."[32]

However, by 2006, one finds that the Taliban were looking up. Instead, one could easily discern the rapidly shifting battle lines. The battle which was so far largely confined along the Durand Line was now closing in on the urban centres of southern Afghanistan. In fact, they were trying hard to consolidate their hold and influence in the Pashtun-dominant areas as logistically deficient and ill-prepared NATO troops warily trickled into southern Afghanistan in 2006. Today, large swathes of area in southern and eastern parts of the country are under the strong or direct control of the Taliban who have set up parallel administration despite claims of success by Western political leadership from time to time. As the Afghan army began to lead operations beginning 2012-13, the Haqqani-Taliban network along with various Pakistani and other foreign militant groups has been trying to capture areas particularly in southern provinces of Helmand and Kandahar; provinces close to Kabul such as Ghazni, Logar and Nangarhar; and even in the relatively peaceful provinces in the north, such as Badakhshan and Kunduz. The Afghan National Army, which is currently fighting pitched battles against the Taliban and their allies in almost dozen provinces across the country, is said to be finding it increasingly difficult to hold on to some of the key urban areas and highways in the south.

The successive military offensives launched by the Western forces earlier probably led to decentralisation of the Taliban command structures which quite inadvertently worked to the advantage of the Taliban. It helped small but highly mobile Taliban guerrilla units to continue with their disruptive operations at various levels and at the same time helped establish pockets of resistance particularly in southern and eastern parts of the country. Taliban thereafter began adapting to the newer challenges much faster as the ISAF expanded its operations to the southern and eastern provinces beginning in 2006. The then Taliban spokesperson, Abdul Latif Hakimi, reportedly stated in early 2005 that the Taliban are changing their tactics. Apart from guerrilla attacks, they would also be deploying suicide bombers to target government officials, foreign aid workers and Western forces, and infiltrate the Afghan security structures as well. The idea was to prepare for a cheaper and a "longer-term war of attrition" against Afghan Government and the Western forces.[33] With the Obama Administration announcing military surges in 2009-10, Taliban responded by effectively deploying roadside and suicide attacks against the Western forces. Soon roadside attacks emerged as a major cause of casualty among the Western and Afghan government forces. Similarly, as the West tried to rapidly rebuild and reinforce Afghanistan's indigenous security structures and institutions, Taliban and their sympathisers infiltrated the Afghan army and police which led to a sudden rise in attacks against Western military mentors and instructors.

Western Mission Going Nowhere

Afghanistan is once again threatened with chaos and anarchy as West decides to drawdown troops and end its combat mission by December 2014. West has largely failed over the years in adapting to the changing security situation on the ground. While acknowledging the weaknesses in his government, President Karzai had remarked back in June 2006 that, "...for two years, I have systematically, consistently and on a daily basis warned the international community of what was developing in Afghanistan and of the need for a change of approach in this regard."[34] President Bush was not likely to heed to this, as Kabul was making a clear case for taking 'war on terror' inside Pakistan. Karzai's demand for re-strategising of war on terror later found its way in the conditions laid out by him for signing the Bilateral Security Agreement (BSA) with Washington.

As the Taliban stood resurrected, one was puzzled about the US plans to drawdown forces and transfer security responsibilities to the Afghan forces which were still not prepared to take full responsibility for the security of the country. Even today, the US approach is precluding the Afghan realities. From recalcitrant militia commanders to drug lords to anti-Kabul forces within Pakistan, all have remained mostly outside the direct purview of the US military operations. It remains focussed on al Qaeda elements active in areas along and across the Durand Line. It is quite clear that the war on terror has since beginning been limited to destroying the al Qaeda network in Pakistan and Afghanistan. The chasm between the broad objectives of state building and the narrow agenda of the war on terror has long been a major shortcoming with the Western mission in Afghanistan.

Perhaps, yet another round of power contest is in the making in Afghanistan. As the Taliban try to shift battle lines closer to Kabul, and seek out a better deal in the power politics of post-2014 Afghanistan, the contours of the Afghan war are rapidly changing. The response of the loosely aligned anti-Taliban forces remain uncertain. Given the competing agendas of its diverse constituents, it would be important to see how former anti-Taliban coalition partners fare in the 2014 presidential election and respond to the post-transition challenges in years to come.

The role and response of the West remains exceedingly crucial in the changing scenario. The ongoing US military operation against al Qaeda and their affiliate groups along and across the Durand Line, which so far has been backed by the ISAF, has not been completely ineffective. But the key question here is for how long can West sponsor Afghanistan? Keeping in view the fact that Afghanistan is decades away from security and stability, are the US and its NATO allies prepared for a long haul in Afghanistan? Both the US and the NATO-led ISAF have already moved several thousands of their troops out of Afghanistan. More than 33,000 of the total 100,000 American troops have already withdrawn since 2011.

Another 10,000 were slated for withdrawal by early 2014 with most of the remaining pulling out by end of the year. The BSA too is still to come through, though Karzai had reportedly offered bases to the US forces after 2014. This is conditional to US providing security and economic assistance until Afghanistan is relatively self-sufficient. Thus, despite the US signing a strategic partnership agreement with Kabul and its stated commitment to remain engaged till 2024, the Afghan people remain largely sceptical about the effectiveness of the Western role and presence in the post-transition years.

A vast section of Afghan people today are perturbed by the possibility of Western disengagement after 2014 though both the candidates in the presidential run-off, Abdullah and Ashraf Ghani, have promised to sign BSA in their election campaigns. In fact, there is a sense of betrayal as the West retreats and the position of Kabul remains vulnerable. President Karzai's earlier proposals to raise local lashkars to counter the increasing influence of the Pakistan-backed militant guerrillas in parts of the country, and to create a separate Department of Vice and Virtue, were apparently part of Kabul's effort to consolidate and strengthen its position for two reasons: First, to reduce its dependence on the West as its forces retreated and the commitment of donor countries remained largely suspect; and second, to counter the religious credentials of the Taliban and their growing influence and appeal among the conservative Pashtun rural population. President Karzai was well aware of the fact that time could be running out for him as well as Kabul.

Ironically, the US approach has constantly failed to grasp the Afghan realities and the need to address or confront the greater malaise that continues to afflict the war-torn country. Such issues of critical importance as building effective state institutions, curbing the ever-growing drug menace, or cutting off support to the anti-Kabul forces operating from across the Durand Line, have largely been left unaddressed. Consequently, Afghanistan remains unstable and vulnerable as was the case after the Soviet withdrawal in 1988-89 and particularly after the collapse of the Najibullah Government in 1992. It is thus imperative to the success of the US mission and sustenance of the current political system in the country that the West and regional countries with stakes in Afghan stability, continue to strengthen the position of Kabul *vis-à-vis* the Haqqani-Taliban combine as well as recalcitrant forces embedded in parts of the country. This is all the more critical to the survival of the first post-ISAF government which will take over as soon as the final results of the June 2014 presidential runoff election are declared. Otherwise, the whole idea of ushering in a 'decade of transformation' in Afghanistan after 2014 would remain an elusive idea.

NOTES

1. Ahmed Rashid, "He's Welcome In Pakistan," *The Washington Post*, February 26, 2006, at http://www.washingtonpost.com/wp-dyn/content/article/2006/02/24/AR2006022401639_pf.html
2. "UK Troops 'to Target Terrorists,"' *BBC News*, April 24, 2006, at http://news.bbc.co.uk/2/hi/uk_news/politics/4935532.stm
3. Brendan Carlin, "Browne in row over 'no-threat' Taliban," *The Daily Telegraph* (London), July 20, 2006, at http://www.telegraph.co.uk/news/worldnews/asia/afghanistan/1524407/Browne-in-row-over-no-threat-Taliban.html
4. "NATO Commander Downplays Afghan Insurgency Threat," *Daily Times*, March 08, 2006, at http://www.dailytimes.com.pk/default.asp?page=2006\03\08\story_8-3-2006_pg4_17
5. Walter Pincus, "Growing Threat Seen in Afghan Insurgency," *The Washington Post*, March 01, 2006, at http://www.washingtonpost.com/wp-dyn/content/article/2006/02/28/AR2006022800874.html
6. Robert Burns, "Gates Prods NATO States on Deployments to Afghanistan," *The Washington Post*, October 23, 2007, at http://www.washingtonpost.com/wp-dyn/content/article/2007/10/22/AR2007102202371.html
7. Peter Spiegel, "Gates Faults NATO Force in Southern Afghanistan," *The Los Angeles Times*, January 16, 2008, at http://www.latimes.com/news/local/la-fg-usafghan16jan16,0,174967,full.story?coll=la-home-center
8. Ann Scott Tyson and Josh White, "Gates Hits NATO Allies' Role in Afghanistan," *The Washington Post*, February 07, 2008, at http://www.washingtonpost.com/wp-dyn/content/article/2008/02/06/AR2008020604690.html
9. Lalit K. Jha, "Taliban More Powerful than Before: Ex-US General," *Pajhwok Afghan News*, February 18, 2007, at http://www.pajhwak.com/viewstory.asp?lng=eng&id=32001
10. Syed Saleem Shahzad, "Pakistan Makes a Deal with the Taliban," *Asia Times Online*, March 01, 2007, at http://www.atimes.com/atimes/South_Asia/IC01Df03.html
11. Abdul Samad Rohani and Habiburahman Ibrahimi, "Helmand on Verge of Becoming Terror Center: Governor," *Pajhwok Afghan News*, March 06, 2007, at http://www.pajhwak.com/viewstory.asp?lng=eng&id=32824. Also see Abdul Samad Rohani, "700 al-Qaeda terrorists enter Helmand," February 11, 2007, at http://www.pajhwak.com/viewstory.asp?lng=eng&id= 31702
12. Syed Saleem Shahzad, "Taliban Poised for a Big Push," *Asia Times Online*, October 05, 2007, at http://www.atimes.com/atimes/South_Asia/IJ05Df01.html
13. "Government trying to hoodwink US: Fazl," *Daily Times*, August 08, 2005, at http://archives.dailytimes.com.pk/main/08-Aug-2005/government-trying-to-hoodwink-us-fazl
14. Harakat-e Inqelabi-e Islami, considered as a relatively moderate traditionalist group by certain scholars, was one of the earliest Pashtun *mujahideen* groups who fought against the Soviets in the 1980s. It enjoyed support among Pashtuns in Kandahar, Helmand, Urozgan, Ghazni, Paktika, and Wardak. This group gradually lost its support base to the breakaway faction of Hizb-e Islami led by Gulbuddin Hekmatyar by the late 1980s, and finally to the Taliban by 1996. Its main leader Mohammed Nabi Mohamadi died in Pakistan in the late 1990s.
15. Ahmed Rashid, "Urgent need for new leaders in Kabul," *The Daily Telegraph*, October 17, 2001, at http://www.telegraph.co.uk/news/main.jhtml;jsessionid=TDRJW34FG3XPJQFIQMGCFFWAVCBQUIV0?xml=/news/2001/10/17/wafg17.xml
16. Syed Saleem Shahzad, "Osama adds weight to Afghan resistance," *Asia Times Online*, September 11, 2004, at http://atimes.com/atimes/Central_Asia/FI11Ag01.html

17. Syed Saleem Shahzad, "Through the eyes of the Taliban," *Asia Times Online*, May 05, 2004, at http://www.atimes.com/atimes/Central_Asia/FE05Ag02.html
18. Scott Baldauf and Owais Tohid, "Where Taliban go to find warm beds and recruits," *The Christian Science Monitor*, December 11, 2003, at http://www.csmonitor.com/2003/1211/p01s04-wosc.html
19. A. Jamali, "Afghans again Hear Taliban on the Airwaves," *Eurasia Daily Monitor*, 2 (83), April 28, 2005, at http://www.jamestown.org/programs/edm/single/?tx_ttnews%5Btt_news%5D=30312&tx_ttnews%5BbackPid%5D=176&no_cache=1#.UevVM9LI2gw
20. Jalal Ghazi, "Arab Media Reports: Taliban Are Back," *AlterNet*, March 03, 2005, at http://www.alternet.org/story/21401
21. Charley Keyes, "Twitter war with the Taliban," *CNN*, October 26, 2011, at http://security.blogs.cnn.com/2011/10/26/4835/?hpt=wo_bn1
22. The Amr-bil-maroof wa Nahi-anil-munkar was established in late 2003 in the Bara Tehsil in the Tirah Valley of the Khyber Agency by one Haji Namdar Afridi who is said to have spent 12 years in Saudi Arabia. However, since mid-2004 the movement has faced opposition from some tribes in the region due to its rigid ways of religious enforcement.
23. For further details on Hisba Bill issue, see Farhatullah Babar, "Talibanising Pakistan," *The Nation*, July 12, 2005, at http://www.nation.com.pk/daily/july-2005/12/columns2.php; Sarmad Bashir, "Politics behind Hasba," *The Nation*, July 12, 2005, at http://www.nation.com.pk/daily/july-2005/12/columns3.php; and Anwar Syed, "Enforcing the Shariat," *Dawn*, August 29, 2004, at http://www.dawn.com/2004/08/29/op.htm
24. It may be noted that the Afghan Deputy Interior Minister Abdul Malik Siddiqi had specifically accused Pakistan-based Lashkar-e-Taiba and Jamiat-ul Ulema-e-Islam of aiding the Taliban guerrillas in capturing the Garmser town in Helmand Province on July 16, 2006. See "Soldiers Reclaim Afghan Town From Taliban," *The New York Times*, July 19, 2006, at http://www.nytimes.com/aponline/world/AP-Afghanistan.html
25. Mullah Omar was interviewed by BBC Pashto service through a Taliban intermediary over a satellite phone. See "Interview with Mullah Omar – transcript," *BBC News, South Asia*, November 15, 2001, at http://news.bbc.co.uk/2/hi/south_asia/1657368.stm
26. Saifullah Mansoor is the son of Nasrullah Mansoor, who was a leading anti-Soviet Afghan guerrilla commander in the 1980s, and was influential in and around Gardez region.
27. For details, see "The Afghan Taliban's Top Leaders," *The Long War Journal*, February 23, 2010, at http://www.longwarjournal.org/archives/2010/02/the_talibans_top_lea.php
28. Robert D. Kaplan, "The Taliban's Silent Partner," *The New York Times*, July 20, 2006, at http://www.nytimes.com/2006/07/20/opinion/20kaplan.html
29. Arnaud De Borchgrave, "Middle Ages on comeback trail?," *United Press International*, June 29, 2006, http://www.upi.com/InternationalIntelligence/view.php?StoryID=20060629-092541-7764r
30. Richard Norton-Taylor, "Afghanistan close to anarchy, warns general," *The Guardian*, July 21, 2006, at http://www.guardian.co.uk/afghanistan/story/0,,1826303,00.html
31. See "President Bush Holds Press Conference," *The White House*, March 13, 2002, at http://www.whitehouse.gov/news/releases/2002/03/20020313-8.html
32. Paul Rogers, *A War on Terror. Afghanistan and After*, Pluto Press, London, 2004, p. 55.
33. Bill Roggio, "Desperate Taliban," *The Long War Journal*, April 20, 2005, at http://www.longwarjournal.org/archives/2005/04/desperate_talib.php
34. Alastair Leitheadm, "Frustrated Karzai toughens stance," *BBC*, June 22, 2006, at http://news.bbc.co.uk/2/hi/south_asia/5107816.stm

You may have the watches, but we have the time.

—Taliban on Western intervention in Afghanistan

CHAPTER V

Politics of Taliban Reconciliation and Reintegration

The subject assumes significance in view of the politics revolving around the issue of negotiating peace, especially with the Afghan Taliban, as the West plans to withdraw bulk of its troops by the end of 2014. The process is considered critical to the Western drawdown strategy and the future of post-transition Afghanistan. However, both the US and the Afghan Government-led reconciliation efforts seem to be going nowhere as the Afghan Taliban continue to publicly rebuff all offers for a negotiated settlement of conflict. Taliban and its various allies have instead been strengthening their position in anticipation of a post-West scenario. The US/NATO decision to end the combat mission by December 2014 has added to the growing political uncertainty, and has reduced the idea of political reconciliation to tactical deal-making with militant Afghan groups for short-term gains. Though often regarded as flawed, ill-timed, regressive, wobbly, dangerous and unworkable, the idea of reconciliation with the Afghan Taliban has nevertheless come to dominate the discourse on the Afghan war and is likely to retain its appeal well beyond 2014.

Despite several years of effort, the supposedly Kabul-led peace process (or the Kabul Process) comprising two key elements—reconciliation (aimed at the top Afghan Taliban leadership based in Pakistan) and reintegration (aimed at low and mid level Taliban guerrilla fighters)—largely remain at a preliminary stage in terms of its conceptualisation, implementation and institutionalisation. It is not clear as to what exactly would reconciliation with the Taliban leadership mean—ceding control over parts of the country to the Taliban or crafting a new power sharing agreement at the national level? Who is interested in a negotiated political settlement of the Afghan crisis; on what terms and conditions and, finally, at whose expense and at what cost? To what extent is the Taliban leadership willing to accommodate others' interests and, more importantly, are they at all in a position to directly negotiate with Kabul? These are critical issues of far reaching consequences for the future of Afghanistan and the region. Though the idea of reintegrating the Taliban is as old as the war on terror, it is very recently that the discourse on the issue of reconciliation with the senior Taliban leadership based in Pakistan has acquired increased focus and traction, as has the ambiguity and confusion shrouding the various initiatives taken with regard to it.

Growing Ambiguity

When it comes to reaching out to the Taliban leadership based inside Pakistan, nothing can be stated with any certainty. Though there are various channels at work, it is not clear as to who exactly is talking to whom and what exactly are the objectives of these talks? Those until few years back were dubbed as 'enemies of Afghanistan' are now being sought after for 'reconciliation.' Are Taliban 'brothers' as President Karzai would sometime refer to them or are they the 'enemies of Afghanistan'? How 'national' is this so-called 'reconciliation' process, and what exactly would the 'reconciliation' with the Taliban mean? Would it come at the expense of gains made last one decade? Is it about 'reconciliation' or is it merely about striking 'deals' with the Taliban, and Taliban as a whole or with sections of the Taliban or certain Taliban individuals? Is Pakistan, a key source of instability and war in Afghanistan, a 'brother' or an 'enemy'? Furthermore, why would the Taliban leaders negotiate if the West is pulling out troops and if the government in Kabul in their perception is not expected to survive for long thereafter?

At a more sociological and ideological level, the incompatibility of the Taliban ideology with the inherent religious and social diversity of the Afghan nation has long been an issue of serious concern. Taliban have so far not shown any flexibility or moderation in their ideological beliefs and political objectives. Will they regard Shias (who comprise a sizeable minority, nearly 19 per cent of the population) as Muslims; and are they going to allow people to practice their religion and follow their social norms as per their own traditions and beliefs? Will they give up on their demand for an 'emirate' and accept 'democracy'? There can be no straight answers to several of such queries even as efforts to reach out to the Taliban leadership continue. According to Waheed Mojda, a Kabul-based political analyst and former Taliban foreign ministry official:

> This is not the Taliban of Emirate times. It is a new, updated generation. They are more educated, and they don't punish people for having CDs or cassettes. The old Taliban wanted to bring sharia, security and unity to Afghanistan. The new Taliban has much broader goals — to drive foreign forces out of the country and the Muslim world.[1]

From the developmental point of view too, Taliban do not have much to offer in terms of rebuilding the Afghan economy and state structures. Related to it is the future of the current political system in Afghanistan and the nature of Afghan state—whether a unitary and a highly centralised state or a relatively decentralised state with a more federal political structure would suit the current social and political landscape of Afghanistan. This presents Kabul with two major challenges: (i) How to mainstream the process of political reconciliation with the Taliban within the current political and constitutional framework with its emphasis on inclusive approaches and mechanisms to the state-building process, and (ii) How to lead and control the reconciliation process given the role and involvement of various powerful entities in the politics of the region. Though the reconciliation process was supposed to have been an Afghan-led and owned process, but that certainly has never been the case. The Afghan perception about the current reconciliation process is obviously diverse and divided in view of a range of historical, political and ideological factors. The divide between the Pashtuns and non-Pashtuns or between north and south, on how to deal with the Taliban is palpable. However, at the same time, it would be wrong to assume that there is complete consensus among the Pashtun communities in the south on ways and means of reconciling with the Taliban. The degree of support among the Pashtun may vary from tribe to tribe and region to region depending on the nature of their relation with Kabul and the intra-Pashtun dynamics. In the south, if there was not any organised resistance to the Taliban, there was also no particular emphasis on Kabul reconciling with the Taliban at the expense of the ongoing state-building process.

The support or opposition to the idea of reconciliation with the Taliban among the country's various factions depend on broadly three factors: (i) perception about Afghan Government's capacity and capabilities to cope with the challenges of transition (ii) Taliban intentions and their ultimate ideological and political objectives, and (iii) whether the return of the Taliban jeopardises or strengthens their own position in the post-ISAF scenario. In a way, the politics of reconciliation is part of the larger power politics being played out in the country since 1990s. Several attempts have been made since the Soviet withdrawal in 1989 to bring competing Afghan factions together, including the Taliban and the United Front (or the Northern Alliance) in the late 1990s, but without any success. Apart from external interference, the inability of Afghan leadership to come to terms with the changing social and political realities has also made the post-2001 political process apparently more fragile and vulnerable from within.

The old power structures, elites and institutions, completely altered or destroyed during and after the war in the 1980s, have long been replaced. Perhaps, Afghanistan has yet to reconcile with the transformation brought about by decades of war which led to the emergence of multiple political networks and power-brokers at several levels with almost no ability to provide national leadership and governance.

Absence of a functional Afghan state for decades together has reinforced identity politics and factional interests at the sub-national level, inhibiting the emergence of strong institutions and leadership at the national level.

Talking of reconciliation with an externally-sponsored and a predominantly Pashtun militant grouping at a time when the Western forces are drawing down, is bound to evoke a sense of political and social insecurity and possible marginalisation among other Afghan groupings. At the same time, a key challenge before the next president in Kabul would be how to deal with the Haqqani-Taliban network which continues to expand and strengthen its hold in several provinces across the country. It would be interesting to see how the reconciliation process would proceed as the new government takes over and as Western forces end their combat mission in December 2014. The prospect of Quetta Shura completely renouncing its ties with al Qaeda and its various Pakistani affiliates and subsequently embracing democracy remains as remote as ever, though.

Making of the Idea

The idea of a negotiated political settlement of the Afghan conflict is as old as the Afghan war. Soon after the Soviet invasion in December 1979, the communist government in Kabul, the People's Democratic Party of Afghanistan (the PDPA) under Babrak Karmal, began engaging the various anti-Soviet *mujahideen* leaders and commanders. In November 1985, President Karmal had put forward a ten-point action programme in this regard.[2] President Mohammad Najibullah's National Reconciliation Policy of December 1986 further tried to address the issue. They were part of the initial efforts to bring about political reconciliation between Kabul and the various externally-sponsored Afghan resistance groups fighting against the Soviet Army and successive communist governments. After the Soviet withdrawal in 1988-89 and the collapse of the Najibullah Government in April 1992, larger efforts were initiated to bring various warring factions together—the UN five-point peace plan of 1991, the Peshawar Accord of April 1992, the Islamabad Accord of March 1993, and the Nangarhar Shura initiatives of 1993 and June 1995. Even after the fall of Kabul to the Pakistan-backed Taliban, unsuccessful attempts were made 1998 onwards to bring about a political understanding between the United Front (also referred to as the Northern Alliance) and the Taliban regime. The Six-plus-Two grouping comprising Afghanistan's six neighbours and the US and Russia under the UN aegis, and the subsequent Tashkent Declaration of July 1999, could also be added to the long list of failed attempts.

Perhaps, Najibullah's reconciliation policy was the only one which was all-encompassing and national in its scope and approach. It was far more comprehensive and inclusive as compared to other initiatives which were afflicted with factional considerations and politics of exclusion. Taliban regime's non-inclusive ideological and socio-political moorings, and Pakistan's proxy politics, has since been a major challenge to the idea of national reconciliation in Afghanistan.

After the US launched *Operation Enduring Freedom* (OEF) on October 07, 2001 and prior to the Bonn Conference that began on November 27, 2001, some efforts were made at the local Afghan level to create a political alternative to the Taliban leadership. Abdul Haq's failed idea of an Afghan-led internal rebellion against the Taliban leadership has already been discussed in the first chapter. In October 2001, Pir Ahmed Gailani was heading a group of Afghan leaders, the Assembly for Peace and National Unity of Afghanistan, which was even trying to win over moderate elements in the Taliban.[3] However, as discussed in the first chapter, it failed to win support among the Western countries and finally the idea died down with the convening of the Bonn Conference in November-December 2001.

There were reports suggesting that Hamid Karzai, selected at the Bonn Conference to lead the post-Taliban interim administration, was willing to offer amnesty to the Taliban at the time of fall of Kandahar in December 2001, provided they renounce violence and lay down arms. However, due to the pressure from the then US Defence Secretary Donald Rumsfeld, the proposed amnesty did not materialise and the Taliban fighters successfully crossed over into Pakistan's tribal areas. Rumsfeld reportedly had warned Kabul against making any such deal with the Taliban and had threatened to withdraw its support from the Afghan interim administration. He had categorically stated, "To the extent that our goals are frustrated and opposed, we would prefer to work with other people."[4]

Former Taliban ambassador to Islamabad, Mullah Abdul Salam Zaeef, in his autobiography published in 2010, had stated "The door was wide open for talks and negotiations; there was a way that would have spared many lives. But America was sure that it would win the war easily....America rushed into a vengeful and hasty decision to wage war, invading the defenseless territory of Afghanistan. It was a mistake. They should have sought a way towards peace and negotiation instead."[5] The complete absence of the elements from the vanquished force was later regarded by several analysts as a key flaw in the post-Taliban political process. Perhaps, the second opportunity for Kabul to work out a political understanding with the Taliban came in 2002-03. This time even the Taliban commanders and leaders were seeking protection and security guarantees from the Afghan Government and the international forces. Both Kabul and its international partners, however, failed to create viable mechanisms for bringing them into the political process.[6]

Thereafter, in 2002, Pakistan had proposed the inclusion of 'moderate

Taliban,' reportedly under Jalal-ud din Haqqani, into the new political set up.[7] According to Syed Saleem Shahzad, "two types of Taliban have left their leader Mullah Omar to join with Kabul: first, those organized by Pakistan's Inter-Services Intelligence (ISI) in Peshawar soon after the fall of the Taliban in 2001 and, second, those who were arrested in Afghanistan and subsequently cultivated. Except for a few, all are mullahs."[8] The 'moderate Taliban' organised by the Pakistani intelligence for inclusion in the Bonn process was under the name *Jamiat-ul Furqan* or *Jamiat-ul Khudamul Koran*.[9] However, the very idea of reconciliation with 'moderate Taliban' was consistently rejected and seen with great distrust until the Obama Administration decided in 2009 to explore prospects of opening negotiations with the "non-ideologically committed" elements within the Taliban.

As the US turned to Iraq in March 2003, and as sense of alienation set in among the Pashtuns in view of strong presence of Northern Alliance in the interim and transitional governments, Karzai formally offered amnesty to the Taliban and Hezb-e Islami fighters, excluding 100-150 top members of both, in the run up to the first presidential election in 2004. He thereafter issued a presidential decree in May 2005 to initiate *Programme Tahkim-e Sulh* (PTS) and appointed a veteran Afghan leader and former president, Sebghatullah Mojadeddi, as its Chairman.[10] Mojadeddi later went a step ahead and offered amnesty even to the top leadership of the Taliban and Hezb-e Islami. The programme almost ended by 2008-09 due to lack of clear cut mandate, administrative capacity, international and regional support, and financial resources.

Meanwhile, Pakistan had been trying to negotiate peace deals with its own Taliban, the Tehrik-e Taliban Pakistan (TTP) or the Pakistani Taliban. Pakistan's then military government under General Pervez Musharraf finally entered into a pact with pro-Taliban tribal elders in its North Waziristan region in September 2006 (see Appendix II). The British Minister of State for Foreign and Commonwealth Affairs, Kim Howells, visiting Islamabad within days of the signing of the North Waziristan Pact, had suggested that it could be "a good example for Afghanistan."[11] The very next month, in October 2006, the British NATO commanders negotiated a deal with the local Taliban commanders in the Musa Qala District of the southern Helmand Province of Afghanistan. Within months, the Taliban guerrillas violated the pact and captured the Musa Qala District in February 2007. Both Kabul and the US were severely critical of the British tactic as it did not have the approval of both. Such initiatives by foreign entities were opposed and resisted by the Afghan Government as it undermined its own efforts to reach out to the Taliban. However, Kabul has not been averse to the mediatory role of certain foreign powers, especially Saudi Arabia, so long as it had its consent and participation.

The very next month in March 2007, in an interview to the German daily,

Der Speigel, Karzai for the first time expressed his willingness to 'embrace' Mullah Omar and Hekmatyar for peace and stability in his country. However, he added that, "it is the Afghan people who should decide on the atrocities committed (by the Taliban) against the Afghan people."[12] The growing inability of the Western forces (especially the NATO-led force) to deal with the resurgent Taliban, and rising civilian casualties in counter-insurgency operations, further convinced Kabul of the need to weaken the Taliban through offers of amnesty and political incentives. In May 2007, the *Meshrano Jirga* (the upper house of the Afghan Parliament) reportedly passed a bill asking the government to open talks with the Taliban.[13] Former senior Taliban officials based in Kabul like Mullah Wakil Ahmed Muttawakil and Mullah Zaeef also called on the government to initiate talks with the Taliban.[14] By 2008, Mullah Zaeef along with Abdul Qayum Karzai, brother of President Karzai and an influential figure from Kandahar, and Maulvi Abdul Hadi Shinwari (former Taliban chief justice) and Arsala Rahmani (a former Taliban and Member of Parliament) began to be seen as potential intermediaries between Kabul and the Pakistan-based Afghan Taliban leadership.

In fact, 2007 onwards, a surge in reconciliation initiatives by diverse entities could be noted. The politics of reconciliation began evolving into a competitive multi-track process activated at various levels, often posing a direct challenge to the authority of Kabul. In April 2008, the National Front of Afghanistan or the Jabha-e Milli, comprising of some senior leaders of the former Northern Alliance, religious figures from the minority ethnic groups, and some ex-communists, claimed that they had been negotiating with the Taliban.[15] The spokesperson of the front is reported to have even asked for the recognition of the Taliban as a political or a military party.[16]

Meanwhile, despite the collapse of the October 2006 Musa Qala pact, British intelligence agents continued to negotiate with the Taliban in Helmand as was reported by *The Daily Telegraph* in December 2007.[17] In January 2008, Karzai retorted that Helmand "was one part of the country" which "suffered after the arrival of the British forces" for until then his government had been 'fully in charge' of the province.[18] He also appointed former Taliban governor of Urozgan Province as the chief of the Musa Qala District. The very next month in February 2008, the newly appointed governor of Helmand Province, Gulab Mangal, proposed to initiate negotiations with "second and third-tier Taliban" at the behest of the central government.[19] In the same month, strongly disapproving of the unilateral British initiatives, Karzai expelled a European Union official and former advisor to the British high commission in Islamabad, Michael Semple, for allegedly negotiating with the Taliban.[20] Interestingly, the German online daily *Netzeitung* reported that German Defence Minister Franz Josef Jung during a meeting on May 14, 2007 with his EU counterparts at Brussels had expressed his strong objection to the US military tactics in Afghanistan, which often lead to heavy civilian casualties.[21]

Though, negotiating with the Taliban was not part of NATO's official policy and political mandate, individual member-states with troops on the ground had adopted their own strategies to deal with the Taliban in their respective areas of operation. The British tactic of negotiating while not completely taking the military pressure off the Taliban militants contributed to the NATO's discourse and strategy in times to come. There were reports of Canadian and Dutch commanders too trying to negotiate with the local Taliban.[22] Talking to the Taliban came to be regarded by the European countries as a way forward in its search for a non-military solution to an otherwise seemingly endless conflict. Given their differing rules of engagement and varying perceptions of the US-led war on terror, most of the European countries stood for a negotiated political settlement of the Afghan conflict, though the Bush Administration remain opposed to the idea of negotiating with the Taliban.

The idea of reconciliation received a major boost when the US Administration under Barack Obama, in a major departure from the policy of the Bush Administration, announced in its *White Paper* on new US policy towards Afghanistan and Pakistan, released in March 2009, that "the war in Afghanistan cannot be won without convincing non-ideologically committed insurgents to lay down their arms, reject al Qaeda, and accept the Afghan Constitution." These later became three pre-conditions for political negotiations with the Taliban. The same was endorsed and adopted during the International Conference on Afghanistan at London in January 2010. The *White Paper* completely ruled out any reconciliation with hardcore Taliban elements with links to al Qaeda and cautioned that "practical integration must not become a mechanism for instituting medieval social policies that give up the quest for gender equality and human rights." The *White Paper* suggested that "we can help this process along by exploiting differences among the insurgents to divide the Taliban's true believers from less committed fighters," and for the first time emphasised that the process must be "Afghan-led"[23] (see Appendix III). Interestingly, Obama ordered another review of the Af-Pak strategy in September 2009 to bring the Afghan war "to a successful conclusion." The revised Af-Pak strategy released on December 01, 2009 too categorically came out in support of "efforts by the Afghan government to open the door to those Taliban who abandon violence and respect the human rights of their fellow citizens."[24] The American turn around has to be seen in the context of the time frame given in the revised strategy for withdrawal of coalition troops from Afghanistan beginning mid-2011.

In March 2009, when President Obama had initially referred to the prospects of reaching out to reconcilable Taliban elements in an interview to *The New York*

Times, the purported Taliban spokesperson had dismissed it as "illogical" and said that it "does not require any response or reaction". He had asserted that "the Taliban are united, have one leader, one aim, one policy" and wondered as to "why the US is talking about moderate Taliban" and "if it means those who are not fighting and are sitting in their homes, then talking to them is meaningless. This really is surprising the Taliban."[25] In April 2009, Siraj-ud Din Haqqani, son of senior Taliban commander Jalal-ud Din Haqqani, too had categorically denied the presence of 'moderates' in the Taliban rank-and-file. He rhetorically stated that the Taliban are the ones "living in the mountains, spending sleepless nights and eating dried bread, but struggling to liberate their homeland from occupation forces" and not the ones who have renounced *jihad* and are leading a luxurious life.[26]

The Taliban would often appeal to the Afghan factions to sink their internal differences and unite against the foreign occupation as part of its counter-propaganda. They have projected themselves as both nationalists and Islamists, and tried to play upon the differences in perceptions and approaches to the Afghan war. In 2009, on the eighth anniversary of the US invasion of Afghanistan, Taliban had issued a statement that this:

> ...is not a war between democracy and the so-called terrorism but rather a war between the western colonialism and the freedom-loving nationalist and Islamist forces.... We announce to all the world, our aim is obtainment of independence and establishment of an Islamic system. We did not have any agenda to harm other countries including Europe nor do we have such agenda today.[27]

The very next year during the London Conference on Afghanistan in January 2010, President Karzai in his address proposed the establishment of a *National Council for Peace, Reconciliation and Reintegration*, to be followed by a *Grand Peace Jirga* in Kabul the same year. Karzai's proposal was endorsed in the Communiqué issued and $140 was immediately committed to the *Peace and Reintegration Trust Fund* for the year 2010. As agreed during the London Conference, a three-day *National Consultative Peace Jirga* (NCPJ) was convened in Kabul from June 02-04, 2010. Chaired by former President Sebghatullah Mojadeddi, the Jirga, which comprised of 1,600 delegates from various sections of Afghan polity, endorsed Karzai's proposed peace and reintegration plans in its resolution. It also called for the establishment of the HPC to take the Afghan-led peace process forward to the provincial and district levels as well. The Council was finally established in September 2010 with Burhanuddin Rabbani as its chairman. The 70-member Council comprised of former Taliban elements,[28] religious figures, tribal elders, few civil society activists, eminent citizens, etc (see Table 5.1).

Table 5.1: Composition of the High Peace Council (HPC)*

Sl.No.	Name of the Member	Ethnicity/Political Affiliation	Previous Positions/Background
1	Burhanuddin Rabbani, CHAIRMAN (Killed on September 20, 2011 in Kabul)	Tajik/Jamiat-e Islami	Former President (1992-2001)
	Salahuddin Rabbani (Appointed as Chairman in April 2012)	Tajik/leader of Jamiat-e Islami	Former Afghan Ambassador to Turkey; Son of previous Chairman Rabbani; Acting Chairman of Jamiat-e Islami
2	Sebghatullah Mojadeddi *(refuses to join the HPC)*	Pashtun/Jabha-e Nejat-e Milli	Former President of Afghanistan/Founded Jabha-e Milli which was part of Peshawar Seven/Chairman, *Constitutional Loya Jirga & Programme Takhim-e Solh* (PTS) initiated in 2004-05
3	Pir Sayed Ahmed Gailani	Pashtun/Mahaz-e Milli	Pir of Qadiriyah Sufi order; Founder of Mahaz-e Milli-e Islami-e Afghanistan, a moderate pro-Royalist faction which was part of Peshawar Seven.
4	Ayatollah Sheikh Muhammad Asif Mohseni	Shia/Harkat-e Islami	A Shia Cleric and Founder of Harkat-e Islami-e Afghanistan; close to Jamiat-e Islami.
5	Abdurrab Rasoul Sayyaf	Pashtun/Ittehad-e Islami	Leader of pro-Arab Ittehad-e Islami which was part of Peshawar Seven/Later joined NA to oppose the Taliban/Founded Islamic Dawah Organisation of Afghanistan in 2005 as a political party.
6	Haji Muhammad Mohaqiq	Hazara/Hezb-e Wahdat	Hezb-e Wahdat commander/Member of the Northern Alliance/Vice President in Interim & Planning Minister in Transitional Administration/Presidential candidate in October 2004 elections
7	Syed Noorullah Sadat	Uzbek/Junbish-e Milli	Leader of Commander Dostum's party, Junbish-e Milli

*The first list, released at the time of appointment of HPC in September 2010, had 68 names. Two to three more names were added later. See, "List of members of the High Council for Peace is Announced", *Government Media & Information Centre*, Islamic Republic of Afghanistan, September 28, 2010, at http://www.gmic.gov.af/english/index.php?option=com_content&view=article&id=103:list-of-members-of-the-high-council-for-peace-is-announced&catid=38:news&Itemid=87. The list was also published by *Hewad*, an Afghan newspaper, and *Pajhwok Afghan News*. See, Abdul Qadir Siddiqui, "Peace Council Members Named", September 29, 2010, at http://www.pajhwok.com/en/2010/09/29/peace-council-members-named. The social and political background of the members has been collated from various sources by the aurthor.

(Contd.)

Sl.No.	Name of the Member	Ethnicity/Political Affiliation	Previous Positions
8	Syed Mansoor Naderi	Ismaili Shia	Leader of minority Ismaili sect in Afghanistan/former Governor of Baghlan in late 1980s
9	Haji Suleiman Yari	Hazara	Was member of Afghan Parliament in 1960s/ Minister in Rabbani Government during 1992-95/Twice nominated by President Karzai to *Meshrano Jirga* (the Upper House) in 2005 & 2010
10	Muhammad Ismail Khan	Tajik/Jamiat-e Islami	Water & Energy Minister in Karzai's first & second cabinet/NA commander/former Governor of Herat Province
11	Ghulam Farooq Wardak *Chairman, International Relations Committee*	Pashtun	Former Hezb-e Islami/Educations Minister in Karzai's first & second cabinet
12	Neamatullah Shahrani	Uzbek	Chairman of the Constitutional Commmission/Haj & Islamic Affairs Minister in Karzai's first cabinet
13	Arsala Rahmani Daulat (***shot dead in Kabul on May 13, 2012***) *Chairman, Political Prisoners Affairs Committee*	Pashtun FORMER TALIBAN	Former deputy leader of Harkat-e Inqalab-e Islami of Mohammad Nabi Mohammadi/Education Minister in the Rabbani Government/Taliban Deputy Minister for Higher Education; Defected from the Taliban in 2005; Member of *Meshrano Jirga* (Upper House) in the first & second parliament; Deputy leader of the revived group Jamiat-e Khuddam ul Furqan; De-listed in July 2011 from the original UN sanctions list of 1999 along with 13 other Taliban members/Headed the Sub Committee on Prisoner's Release in HPC
14	Maulvi Pir Muhammad Rohani	Pashtun FORMER TALIBAN	Headed Kabul University during the Taliban regime/exiled in Miram Shah until 2005 when he was appointed head of the Supreme Court's administrative affairs department.
15	Haji Muhammad Naeem Kochi	Kuchi (nomads) FORMER TALIBAN	Tribal leader/Governor of Bamiyan and Tribal Affairs Minister in the Taliban Regime/Released from Guantanamo Bay Detention in September 2004
16	Haji Din Muhammad	Tajik FORMER TALIBAN	Former Taliban Planning Minister/Released from Guantanamo Bay Detention Camp in 2007

(*Contd.*)

Sl.No.	Name of the Member	Ethnicity/Political Affiliation	Previous Positions
17	Mullah Taj Muhammad Mujahid	Tajik	Close to Abdurrab Rassoul Sayyaf/former Jamiat-e Islami commander
18	Maulvi Muhammad Shah Adili	Tajik	A prominent cleric from Balkh Province/Head of Asadia Madrasa and Balkh Ulema Council
19	Haji Fazal Karim Aimaq	Aimaq/Northern Alliance	First post-Taliban mayor of Kabul (2002)/Member of first *Wolesi Jirga* (2005-10) from Kunduz/close to Ahmad Shah Masoud's family/Joined the newly formed Jabha-e Milli or the National Front led by Burhanuddin Rabbani in 2007.
20	Maulvi Qayamuddin Kashaf *Spokesperson of the Council*	Pashtun/former Ittehad-e Islami	Former Chairman of the Afghan Ulema Council/Information & Culture Minister in the Rabbani Government/Former member of Ittehad-e Islami of Sayyaf
21	Maulvi Mohiuddin Baloch	—	Member of the Afghan Ulema Council/Appointed by President Karzai as head of the team investigating the case of alleged burning of Quran at Bagram Base in February 2011/Former Governor of Farah/Advisor on Religious Affairs to the Afghan President.
22	Maulvi Shafiullah Shafi	Pashtun	Influential tribal leader from Nuristan/Headed the Education Department in Nuristan
23	Arif Khan Noorzai[29]	Pashtun/NA	A close confidante of President Karzai, he was Minister of Small Industries in Interim Administration & Border & Tribal Affairs in Transitional Administration/powerful Noorzai tribal leader from Kandahar/elected to the Parliament in 2005 parliamentary elections/first deputy speaker of the Afghan Parliament/member of Ittehad-e Islami in 1980s/later joined Northern Alliance in opposition to the Taliban
24	Abdul Mahmood Daqiq	Tajik/Jamiat-e Islami	Former Attorney General of Afghanistan/Chief Prosecutor in the Executive Committee of *Constitutional Loya Jirga*
25	Maulvi Ataullah Ludin *Deputy Chairman*	Pashtun/Hezb-e Islami	Former Member of Parliament from Nangarhar
26	Anwar Khan Ishaqzai	Pashtun	Tribal leader from Helmand/former Hezb-e Islami

27	Mamur Hassan Takhari	Uzbek	Member of the Jirga Commission/Chief of Jihadi Council in Takhar Province/Was affilated to Hezb-e Islami of Hekmatvar prior to joining the United Front under Ahmad Shah Masoud
28	Maulvi Abdul Hakim Mujahid *Deputy Chairman*	FORMER TALIBAN	Former Taliban envoy for United Nations/Member of the revivied group Jamiat-e Khuddam ul Furqan since 2005
29	Asadullah Wafa *Deputy Chairman*	Pashtun	Advisor on Tribal Affairs to the President/Former Governor of Paktia (2004-05), Kunar (2005-06) and Helmand (2006-08).
30	Maulvi Khudaidad	Pashtun	Head of the Herat Ulema Council
31	Qazi Muhammad Amin Waqad *Chairman, Publicity & Public Information Committee*	Pashtun/former Hezb-e Islami	Former Deputy to Gulbuddin Hekmatyar/Vice Presidential nominee of Abdul Sattar Sirat who was a presidential candidate in 2004 elections/Joined Jabha-e Milli or National Front led by Rabbani in 2007/Communications Minister in Rabbani Government in early 1990s
32	Habibullah Fawzi	Pashtun FORMER TALIBAN	Former diplomat to the Taliban embassy in Saudi Arabia; Defected from the Taliban in 2005; revived Khuddam ul Furqan; De-listed in July 2011 from the original UN sanctions list of 1999.
33	Muhammad Akbari	Hazara/Hezb-e Wahdat	A prominent Shia Hazara leader/Twice elected as Member of Parliament from Bamiyan/First Deputy Leader of Hezb-e Wahdat under Abdul Mazari
34	Abdul Hadi Arghandiwal	Pashtun/Hezb-e Islami	Economy Minister in Karzai's second cabinet/Supported Karzai's candidacy for second term President in 2009/Leads a supposedly breakaway 'moderate' faction of Hezb-e Islami formed in 2008/ Served as Planning Minister earlier in 1978 and Finance Minister in 1996
35	Maulvi Shahzada Shahid (Called Osama bin Laden a 'martyr' in February 2014)	Pashtun/Hezb-e Islami	Head of the provincial courts in Kunar (2003-05)/Twice elected as member of parliament from Kunar in 2005 & 2010/member of the counter-narcotics committee/Joined group of legislators called 'Reformists' in 2010/Appointed by Karzai in February 2012 as head of the delegation investigating reports of civilian casualties in Kunar due to ISAF operations.

(Contd.)

Sl.No.	Name of the Member	Ethnicity/Political Affiliation	Previous Positions
36	Muhammad Ismail Qasimyar *Advisor on International Relations/Affairs*	Qizilbash	Senior negotiator of the Council/Expert in Constitutional Law/ Chairman of the Special Independent Commission for the Convening of the *Emergency Loya Jirga* appointed in January 2002/Chairman of the *Emergency Loya Jirga* in June 2002/Vice Presidential nominee of Syed Ishaq Gilani in the 2004 presidential election. Former Supreme Court Justice during President Daoud's regime/ Member of the Secretariat of the 1976 *Loya Jirga* called to ratify the new constitution/ Member of the 1964 *Loya Jirga* called by Zahir Shah to ratify the new constitution.
37	Amir Muhammad Agha	Pashtun FORMER TALIBAN	Former Taliban commander/Leading power broker in the strategically important Arghandab Valley in northern Kandahar/ Reportedly father-in-law of Taliban leader Mullah Muhammad Omar/A former Guantanamo Bay Detainee/formerly, member of Sayyaf's Ittehad-e Islami, and prior to that, Mohammadi's Harkat-e Inqalab-e Islami.
38	Faqir Muhammad Khan	Pashtun FORMER TALIBAN	Former Taliban Deputy Minister; De-listed in July 2011 from the original UN sanctions list of 1999.
39	Muhammad Yusuf Waezi	Hazara/Hezb-e Wahdat	Manager of Hezb-e Wahdat-e Islami
40	Abdul Ghani Khan Tokhi	Pashtun FORMER TALIBAN	Former Taliban commander from Zabul
41	Sher Muhammad Akhunzada	Pashtun	A power tribal leader from northern Helmand/Former Governor of Helmand (2001-05)
42	Haji Amanullah Otmanzai	Pashtun FORMER TALIBAN	Former Taliban commander from Kunduz
43	Abdul Wahid Baghrani	Pashtun FORMER TALIBAN	Also known as *Rais-da Baghran* or the chief of Baghran in north Helmand/Influential leader of Alizai tribe from Khalozai sub-tribe in Baghran/A high level Taliban commander who accepted

			President Karzai's amnesty offer of May 2005/Opposed to al Qaeda's growing influence over the Taliban/Carried Mullah Omar's message for surrender of Kandahar to Karzai in December 2001/ According to *Wikileaks*, he was Deputy Defence Secretary in the Taliban Government/Member of the Jamiat-e Islami before he joined the Taliban in 1995.
44	Khalifa Qazal Ayyaq	Turkmen	A spiritual figure of the Naqshbandia sufi order from Faryab Province
45	Maulvi Qalamuddin	Pashtun FORMER TALIBAN	Former Taliban Deputy Minister for the Promotion of Virtue and Prevention of Vice/Lost the 2005 parliamentary elections/ Captured in April 2003 and released in September 2004.
46	Ibrahim Spinzada	Pashtun	First Deputy Chairman of the National Security Council/Acting Chief of NDS for about a month after the removal of Amrullah Saleh in June 2010/Former Deputy Director of NDS/Reported to be the brother-in-law of President Karzai/Led the Afghan delegation to Guantanamo Bay in March 2012 to negotiate the release and transfer of five senior Taliban members to Qatar.
47	Haji Moosa Khan Hotak	Pashtun/Harkat-e Inqalab FORMER TALIBAN	Former Taliban Deputy PlanningMinister/Joined DDR Programme in Wardak in 2004/Briefly detained by the US at Bagram Detention Centre/Elected to the Parliament in 2005/ Member of the Parliamentary Committee on Internal Security/ De-listed from the UN Sanctions List in January 2010/Led the Afghan Public Protection Force (APPF) since 2009/Member of Harkat-e Inqalab before joining Taliban & now head of the same group.
48	Maulvi Mohammad Usman Salikzada *Member of the Conflict Resolution Committee*	Uzbek/ Hezb-e Saadat-e Melli	Advisor on Religious Affairs to the Afghan President/ Former leader of Harakat-e Inqilab-e Islami from Sar-e Pul Province/Head of the break away faction Hezb-e Saadat-e Melli wa Islami/ Governor of Balkh Province during the *mujahideen* regime.
49	Abdul Hameed Mubarez	Pashtun	Editor of Anis News Agency/President of Afghan National Journalist Union/Former Deputy Minister of Information & Culture (January 2002-December 2004)/Head of the NGO called Afghan Strategic Centre/Former Director of official Bakhtar News Agency

(*Contd.*)

Sl.No.	Name of the Member	Ethnicity/Political Affiliation	Previous Positions
50	Siddiq Ahmad Osmani	Tajik/Hezb-e Jamhuri	Elected as Member of Parliament from Parwan Province in 2005 & 2010/Member of supposedly pro-Karzai 'Reformist' group within the Parliament/Chairman of the Parliamentary Committee on Economic Affairs/First Secretary of *Meshrano Jirga* in 2005 Parliament/ Former Governor of Parwan/Brother of Counter Narcotics Minister & Former Interior Minister Zarar Ahmad Moqbil.
51	Haji Kamal ud din Maududi	Tajik	Former commander of Hezb-e Islami from Ghor Province/Held positions in the Ghor provincial administration/*Jirga* representative from Ghor.
52	Aminuddin Muzafari *Secretary of HPC*	Independent	Indirectly elected to the *Meshrano Jirga* (Upper House) in 2005 from Parwan/Elected in December 2005 as Secretary of the *Meshrano Jirga*
53	Syed Muhammad Amin Tariq	Tajik/Jamiat-e Islami	Former Governor of Badakhshan/Appointed as Advisor to the Interior Ministry in 2003
54	Baz Muhammad Khan Zurmati	Pashtun/Ittehad-e Islami	Appointed as Member of *Meshrano Jirga* by Karzai in February 2011
55	Abdul Khaliq Hussaini	Pashai/Independent	Indirectly elected to the *Meshrano Jirga* in 2005/Member of Pashai Central Assembly/Former Member of Independent Election Commission (IEC)
56	Haji Muhammad Daud Zahidyar	Gujar/Independent	Head of the Gujar tribes of Afghanistan
57	Muhammad Hashim Faulad	Pashtun/Afghan Mellat (Anwar-ul Haq Ahady)	Twice elected as Member of Parliament from Nangarhar in 2005 & 2010/Member of the Parliamentary Committee on national economy/Appointed by President Karzai as Member of Independent Election Commission (IEC) in January 2012/Was associated with the Afghan Information Office in Peshawar during 1980 -1995/Was publication in-charge for the Afghan Development Association/Was also Manager of the Magazine called *Pormokhtag*

58	Maulvi Jora Akhund	Turkmen	Turkmen representative/ Part of the HPC delegation to Pakistan and Turkey/Suggested Ashgabat as a possible venue for talks with the Taliban in 2011.
59	Haji Sherin Khan Noorzai	Pashtun	From the Nawzad District of Helmand.
60	Haji Fazal Karim Fazal	Pashtun	Founder President of Shamshad TV and Executive Director of Organisation for Mine clearance and Afghan Rehabilitation (OMAR) founded in 1990
61	Syeedur Rehman Haqqani	Pashtun FORMER TALIBAN	Former Taliban Deputy Minister of Mines & Industry; De-listed in July 2011 from the original UN sanctions list of 1999
62	Azizullah Din Mohammad *Advisor & Chairman, Contact Committee*	Pashtun	Former Governor of Nangarhar Province (2002-04) & Kabul Province (2005-09)/Brother of Commander Abdul Haq who was killed by the Taliban in October 2001 and former Vice President Abdul Qadir who was killed in July 2002/former member of Hezb-e Islami (Yunus Khalis)
Women Members (8)			
63	Sara Surkhabi	Uzbek	Twice nominated by President Karzai as member of the *Meshrano Jirga* in 2005 and 2010/Former Director of Women's Affairs Department in Faryab Province
64	Jamila Hamidi	—	—
65	Hawa Alam Nuristani	Pashtun/Journalist	Elected to the *Wolesi Jirga* from Nuristan in 2005/Member of Parliamentary Committee on International Affairs in 2005/ Member of Afghan Women Network in 2004/earlier worked with the Ministry of Women's Affairs & Radio Television Afghanistan (RTA).

(*Contd.*)

Sl.No.	Name of the Member	Ethnicity/Political Affiliation	Previous Positions
66	Najia Ziwari *Deputy Chairman & Secretary*	Hezb-e-Mahaz Milli Islami	Elected to the *Wolesi Jirga* from Paktika in 2010/Member of Parliamentary Commission on Religious & Cultural Affairs/ Advisor to Country Director, UN Women Afghanistan
67	Siddiqa Balkhi	Hazara	Twice nominated by President Karzai to the *Meshrano Jirga* in 2005 & 2010/Minister for Martyrs and Disabled (December 2004 - March 2006) in Karza's First Elected Cabinet.
68	Gulhar Jalal	Pashtun	Elected to the *Wolesi Jirga* from Kunar in 2005 & Appointed to the *Meshrano Jirga* in 2010/Member of the Parliamentary Commission on Widows, Gender Issues & Civil Society/Was earlier Member of the Parliamentary Commission on Martyrs and Disabled in 2005.
69	Gulalai Noor Safi	Hezb-e-Mahaz Milli Islami	Gynaecologist/Twice Elected to the *Wolesi Jirga* in 2005 & 2010/ Member of the Parliamentary Commission on Health Affairs.
70	Qamar Khostai	Pashtun	Twice appointed to the *Meshrano Jirga* in 2005 & 2010.

Note: The source of information given earlier in the footnote from which this list has been drawn does not mention the name of Syeedur Rehman Haqqani, another former Taliban Deputy Minister; but other sources suggest that along with other three former Taliban members who were later de-listed from the UN sanctions list in July 2011, he too was appointed by President Karzai to the HPC in September 2010.

The Afghanistan Peace & Reintegration Programme (APRP) was also launched and soon offices were opened in provinces to wean away low and mid-level Taliban commanders. A UNDP supported programme and funded by Denmark, Germany, Italy and Japan, the APRP is yet to prove effective in the Taliban-influenced and controlled southern and eastern areas of the country.

The HPC, however, suffered a major setback a year later in September 2011 when its chairman Rabbani was killed by a suicide bomber. Karzai has since made efforts to revive and further mainstream the HPC by appointing Rabbani's son Salahuddin who was ambassador to Turkey and is also acting leader of Jamiat-e Islami, a major grouping from north. The HPC has so far been reportedly involved in some exploratory talks with purported Taliban representatives and mediators. The HPC, an Afghan-led effort, is also competing to create its own space in the multi-track reconciliation initiative that involves a range of external actors.

Meanwhile, some Taliban members were de-listed by the UN in 2011, and more were likely to depending on the progress of the peace process. Several rounds of meetings were later reported to have been held in 2011 between Western interlocutors and purported Taliban representatives, first in Germany and later in Dubai as well as in Japan. Nothing substantive reportedly emerged as the identity of a key Taliban interlocutor was revealed to the media. Tayyab Agha, supposed to be a close confidante of Taliban chief Omar, was said to be representing the Taliban in these talks. In January 2012, reports of more meetings came in with Taliban agreeing to open a 'diplomatic office' in Qatar.[30] In return, the US was supposed to release five Taliban detainees from Guantanamo Bay detention centre. It was decided that the released Taliban members would be shifted to Qatar and would be allowed to stay along with their family members. However, in the aftermath of reported burning of copies of Quran in Bagram base by the ISAF personnel in March 2012, the Taliban pulled out of the talks. In fact, all along they have denied negotiating for political reconciliation. Their stance was that they are negotiating for the release of Taliban prisoners in exchange of the lone American soldier held in their captivity.

Interestingly, in November 2012, the HPC came out with its own roadmap for the peace process by 2015. Termed as *Roadmap 2015*, the document envisions that, "By 2015, Taliban, Hezb-e-Islami and other groups will have given up armed opposition, transformed from military entities into political groups, and are actively participating in the country's political and constitutional processes, including national elections." It further envisions that, "Afghanistan's political system remains inclusive, democratic and equitable, where all political actors co-exist and promote their political goals and aspirations peacefully under the Constitution." The document assumes that by 2015 the "NATO/ISAF forces will have departed from Afghanistan, leaving the ANSF as the only legitimate armed forces" in the country.

The *Roadmap 2015* upheld the so-called "red lines" laid out during the January 2010 London Conference in Afghanistan and was later endorsed in the two *Loya Jirga* held in July and November 2011, for opening direct negotiations with the Taliban leadership. The section on 'Principles Governing the Peace Process' in the document, clearly stated:

> "Any outcome of the peace process must respect the Afghan Constitution and must not jeopardize the rights and freedom that the citizens of Afghanistan, both men and women, enjoy under the Constitution. As part of the negotiated outcome, the Taliban and other armed opposition groups must cut ties with Al Qaeda and other terrorist groups, and verifiable renounce violence. Negotiating parties must strive for an outcome that is acceptable to the Afghan people, and that serves the genuine national interests of Afghanistan as a sovereign, Islamic country."

The *Roadmap*, consisting of a five-step process with each step comprising a set of specific goals and a timeline,[31] however, failed to make any headway as relations between Afghanistan and Pakistan was marred by cross-border shelling and frequent skirmishes along the Durand Line in the coming months. Attempts to organise a joint *jirga*, bringing together Afghan and Pakistani clerics to denounce violent extremism and suicide bombing, too failed to take off due to differences over inviting Taliban representatives. The HPC and various initiatives from Kabul were going nowhere. Though Pakistan 'released' several low level Afghan Taliban commanders and fighters thereafter, it has so far not been of much value to the whole process. In several cases, either the whereabouts of the Taliban elements released by Pakistan from time to time were simply not known or they were reported to have subsequently rejoined the Taliban guerrilla units.

The 'release' of Mullah Baradar, former deputy and second in command to Mullah Omar, in September 2013, however, could be regarded as a tactical move by the Pakistani establishment keeping in view the growing political uncertainty within Afghanistan. The timing of his 'release' which came immediately after the collapse of the Doha talks in mid-2013 over the status of the Taliban office there, and as Kabul and Washington continued to spar over the terms and conditions of a long-term Bilateral Security Agreement, suggests that the objective probably was to simply maintain the façade of cooperation with the Karzai regime. It was not clear if Mullah Baradar, who had been in Pakistani captivity since 2010, still enjoyed the confidence of Mullah Omar. Pakistan apparently had effectively rendered his role and position redundant. Quetta Shura was most unlikely to repose its trust and confidence in him.

Key Challenges

(i) Lack of Clarity

The first issue is of the genuineness of the very process of reconciliation. Is there a reconciliation process at all in Afghanistan, and can it be regarded as a national process? What Kabul and the US are perhaps looking for are *deals* with the Taliban leadership for their own respective purposes. The West would like to have a deal with the Taliban to ensure a reasonably peaceful withdrawal of the ISAF, and for Kabul it's about ensuring the survival of the currently inclusive political system beyond 2014. The idea could also be to make the Afghan situation more manageable and sufferable as both the US and the NATO seek to maintain minimal military presence in support of the Afghan army for at least a decade after the end of combat mission in 2014.

Would striking tactical deals with the Taliban lead to reconciliation—political and social—among the country's various factions? Would it help bridge the north-south or the social divides in the country? There is already lot of scepticism about this process among large sections of Afghan population. It is not clear as to what exactly is being negotiated? What is being offered to the Taliban, and to what extent Taliban leadership is willing to accommodate Kabul's interests? And, most importantly, who is talking to whom and who leads the reconciliation process? The involvement of diverse stakeholders in the politics of reconciliation has provided Taliban and their patrons across the Durand Line the space and scope to manipulate the whole process to their advantage.

It has thus evolved into a multi-track process with no sole negotiating authority. Much before the transition process was formalised, the European thinking on exploring non-military options had led to a surge in opening channels of communication with the Taliban at various levels. With Obama Administration agreeing in 2009 to exploring prospects of reconciliation, and Karzai pushing for direct talks with Taliban leadership based inside Pakistan, the idea has since gained greater traction and backing. Despite several initiatives, it is still not clear as to which section of the Taliban both Kabul and the Western negotiators claim to be talking to. What are the terms and conditions of these talks and what are the negotiables and non-negotiables? Lack of clarity about the whole process has raised suspicions largely among Afghanistan's ethnic minorities who have suffered from series of high profile assassinations and violent attacks carried out by the Taliban-Haqqani network in the north in recent years.

(ii) Taliban Unwillingness

Another important issue is to what extent Taliban and their patrons are interested in a negotiated settlement of the conflict. Why the Taliban should be talking to Kabul as the Western mission withers and their forces are exiting. They could simply be buying time and would rather wait out the Western drawdown. But that does not seem to be the case as Taliban keep up their guerrilla offensive and adapt to the changing scenario by shifting their targets and areas of operation. The strategy obviously is to harass and inflict maximum casualty among the Western forces even as they drawdown. The killing of Burhanuddin Rabbani, chairman of the HPC, could also have been due to the growing differences within the Taliban leadership and Pakistan's military establishment on the issue of talking to Kabul. In May 2012, another senior member of the HPC, Arsala Rahmani, also a former Taliban minister, was killed in Kabul. The provincial peace council members too have been targeted. For instance, Mohammad Hashim Munib, who headed the Kunar provincial peace council and was also a member of the national ulema council, was killed in a suicide attack in April 2012; and Malim Shahwali, who headed the Helmand provincial peace council, was killed in April 2013. A section within the Taliban may be willing to open negotiations with Kabul or the US, but Rawalpindi or pro-al Qaeda hardliners within the Taliban-Haqqani network are most unlikely to relent.

Mullah Baradar, was arrested in Karachi by Pakistani authorities in January 2010 for reportedly trying to negotiate with the Afghan Government.[32] Kabul has since been asking Pakistan for the release of Mullah Baradar who belongs to the same Popalzai tribe as President Karzai but belongs to the same Urozgan Province as Mullah Omar. It is not however clear how his release would have helped in bringing about political reconciliation between Taliban and Kabul. Earlier, in November 2010, it was reported that a shopkeeper from Quetta, masquerading as a senior Taliban commander, Akhtar Mansour, who had replaced Mullah Baradar, twice met with Afghan officials in Kabul as part of a Taliban delegation visiting from Pakistan.[33] The British-led effort to arrange a direct meeting between Afghan Government and purported Taliban representatives exposed the difficulty in verifying the identity of Taliban interlocutors and the seriousness of Pakistan on the issue. In early April 2012, it was reported that Mohammad Ismail, chief of the Taliban military council, has been detained by Pakistan for reportedly conducting "unauthorised negotiations" with members of the HPC during his visit to Dubai.[34]

Though the prospects of growing friction within the Taliban leadership and with Rawalpindi on the issue of talking to the US or Kabul cannot be completely ruled out, the Afghan Taliban leadership to this day remains in a denial mode and still inaccessible. Even if there are differences, the issue is whether Pakistan would ever allow Taliban leadership a free hand to negotiate on its own terms and conditions. At a broader level, the hardliners within the movement with links to a range of Sunni Islamist groups, both Pakistani and Arab, have a definite upper hand and are most unlikely to relent in the given circumstances. Reports pertaining to Kabul negotiating with the Taliban are regarded by the latter as part of a strategy to create confusion and rifts within its rank-and-file. They have so far been resolutely demanding complete withdrawal of Western forces as a pre-condition for any negotiations. Similarly, the Taliban have throughout rejected the idea of categorising them as 'Moderate' or 'Hardcore,' 'Good' or 'Bad,' and have always viewed it as part of a Western propaganda to create divisions within its cadre. In fact, there has been a notable consistency in their public articulation on this issue.

As early as November 2001, reacting to the idea of 'moderate Taliban,' Mullah Omar had asserted that "there is no such thing in the Taleban" and that "all Taleban are moderate." He also held that, "There are two things: extremism ("ifraat", or doing something to excess) and conservatism ("tafreet", or doing something insufficiently). So in that sense, we are all moderates—taking the middle path."[35] Taliban have not only held on to their position even as Western troop levels in Afghanistan crossed the 100,000 mark, they have also intensified and improvised on their counter offensive warfare and propaganda machinery. They have successfully raised the cost of the war for the West fully aware of their own limitations and disadvantages *vis-à-vis* the Western coalition. Making them have stakes in the peace process has thus been a big challenge for Kabul. Here it is important to factor in possible rifts between the Pakistani establishment and the Taliban, especially the Taliban perception of the US-Pakistan relations and their own experiences with Pakistan in the immediate aftermath of 9/11. In this context, it is worth quoting what Mullah Zaeef, former Taliban ambassador to Islamabad, had stated in his autobiography:

> Pakistan, which plays a key role in Asia, is so famous for treachery that it is said they can get milk from a bull. They have two tongues in one mouth, and two faces on one head so they can speak everybody's language; they use everybody, deceive everybody. They deceive the Arabs under the guise of Islamic nuclear power, saying that they are defending Islam and Islamic countries. They milk America and Europe in the alliance against terrorism, and they have been deceiving Pakistani and other Muslims around the world in the name of the Kashmiri jihad. But behind the curtain, they have been betraying everyone.
>
> Their Islam and their jihad were to destroy their neighbouring Islamic country together with the infidels. They handed over their airports to the Americans so they could kill Muslims and destroy an Islamic country. Their loyalty to the Arabs is so great that they sold diplomats, journalists and mujahedeen for dollars. Like animals. God knows whether they will ever use their nuclear bomb to defend Muslims and Islam. They might use their weapons—as they have used everything else—against Muslims.[36]

Notwithstanding Zaeef's above observations, it may be stated that the Afghan Taliban and the Pakistani state are not as such unified by any ideological affinity. The Afghan Taliban are in many ways an extension of Pakistani geo-politics, a leverage and a bargaining chip in Islamabad's quest for influence inside Afghanistan. It is part of Pakistan's divisive strategy not to allow the re-emergence of a strong Afghan state. It is noteworthy that even the Taliban regime had not recognised the Durand Line as legitimate international border between Afghanistan and Pakistan (see Map 2).

Afghan Taliban have effectively combined their version of radical Islamism with Pashtun nationalism, and are quite adept at using tribal-historical myths as means of legitimising their supposed 'jihad' against 'foreign occupation.' Whether the Afghan Taliban have provided Islamabad with a 'strategic depth' inside Afghanistan or not, they have certainly acquired a strategic rear support inside Pakistan. The Taliban tactics since 2004-05 have been extremely adaptive, manipulative and opportunistic. The Pakistani establishment has explicitly failed to take cognisance of the historical fact that Afghan insurgents are qualitatively adept at using their foes and friends alike as part of their game-changing strategy. This very well explains as to why the Afghan Taliban despite their supposed anti-Americanism and anti-Westernism have conspicuously avoided articulating their view on the long-held strategic ties between Islamabad and Washington.

(iii) Risky Transition

By December 2014, the US and NATO-led force are supposed to fully transfer security responsibilities to the Afghan army, which remains critically dependent on Western assistance and support for all practical purposes. This obviously gives rise to a pertinent question—transition to what? The transition process has charged up the politics within as well as across the border in Pakistan's tribal areas. Despite rapidly deteriorating security situation and grave doubts being expressed about the capability of the Afghan forces to take on the Pakistan-backed Haqqani-Taliban guerrillas, the West is going ahead with its transition plans unmindful of its short and long-term consequences for regional and international security. As prospects of political chaos and systematic violence grow, the sustenance of the Afghan army and police is emerging as a serious issue of concern.

The Haqqani-Taliban network and their patrons both within and outside Pakistani establishment are gearing up to fill in the likely security and political vacuum in Kabul after 2014. At the moment, the transition process clearly seems to be working to the advantage of the forces opposed to the current political order in Kabul. The Taliban-Haqqani network is likely to continue their offensive with vigour and rancour reminiscent of the 1990s. This would invariably further weaken Kabul's position and even endanger the survival of the current democratic set up if the US-Afghan Bilateral Security Agreement does not come through or

Map 2: The Durand Line

Courtesey: GIS Lab, Institute for Defence Studies and Analyses, New Delhi.

simply falls apart in the coming years. With it, the latest round of reconciliation initiatives too would come to an end; and, perhaps, a new round of politics of reconciliation would emerge as part of an effort to establish a new political order in Kabul.

Simply striking deals with the Taliban while the West draws down its engagement may lead to the reversal of gains made last one decade in terms of initiating a democratic process and building state institutions. It is also pertinent to take into account potential implications of making deals with the Taliban on evolving state structures, especially the army and the judiciary; foreign policy; educational and various other capacity building programmes. A perpetual issue lurking in the backdrop of all developments taking place is the ultimate intentions of the hardcore Taliban elements and their external support mechanisms. Are they at all interested in ending the conflict through negotiations? Have they reconciled to the social, religious and political diversity of Afghanistan? As for the Taliban guerrillas, it is not known if they would ever agree to lay down their arms or be integrated into the Afghan national army and police. Another important issue is to what extent are Afghans willing to accept a Pakistan-mediated or brokered power-sharing deal with the Taliban. Neither Pakistan nor the US is a neutral player, and even so-called neutral entities are not in a position to mediate on behalf of the warring groups.

(iv) Politics of power devolution

Three decades of war had virtually destroyed all state institutions in the country. The authority of Afghan state was systematically eroded and denuded as part of the super power rivalry and the proxy politics during 1980s and 90s. It completely destroyed the internal balance of power, the centre-province relations, and centuries-old social and political equilibrium of the Afghan polity. Kabul has since changed hands several times with political transitions attempted from time to time leading to chaos and loss of authority. The country was parcelled out among various commanders and their patrons, which came at the expense of a centralised national authority in Kabul. The emergence of extra-constitutional parallel power structures and their mutually exclusive competing agendas have since defined the political landscape of the country.

During the debate over the draft constitution in 2003-04, the differing perceptions about the nature of Afghan state and division of power had come to the fore. While Pashtun delegates to the *Constitutional Loya Jirga* (December 2003-January 2004) were largely in favour of a strongly centralised presidential system, the delegates from minority ethnic groups were arguing for a more federalised political set up. Some had even called for the creation of the post of prime minister and devolution of greater powers to the parliament and provincial authorities. Their views and perceptions about the new political order were also influenced by their experience of a highly centralised Taliban regime. Should there be a scenario where Kabul would be expected to share power with the Taliban elements, the anti-Taliban groups would like to protect their political interests and social identity by consolidating their authority and influence in their respective areas of influence.

The growing rush for reconciliation with the Taliban has brought back fears of political alienation and anomalous social-religious *diktats* among Afghan groups/factions that had opposed and fought against the Taliban. There is no doubt that the Taliban continue to pursue their agenda of establishing an *emirate* and have not shown any sense of political and social accommodation thus far. A hasty cooption of the Taliban elements in the power structure may lead to substantive changes in the character of the current constitution, further radicalisation of judiciary, and intense friction within the central government and also between the centre and some of the provinces. Given the prevalent fears over possible subversion of state structures by the Taliban, the mainly non-Pashtun groups may push and bargain for a more federalised political system to preserve their authority and identity post-2014.

Future Prospect

In the given situation, a carefully tailored negotiation strategy could at best serve a limited tactical purpose and that too in the short-term only. It is least likely to pave way for a long-term national reconciliation in Afghanistan. Prospects of defection or division within the Taliban are ruled out unless West decides to remain strategically involved in the Pakistan-Afghanistan region for many more years. Negotiating with the Taliban, while pulling out forces, is not likely to yield any concrete result. It would instead work to the advantage of Taliban hardliners and the Pakistani military establishment. Both would simply be buying time given their perception that the West is left with no option but to retreat. Unless there is some clarity about the objectives and the nature and level of future US engagement in the region, prospects of even tactical reconciliation would remain bleak. Kabul does not have the institutional capacity to bear with the challenges and potential adverse consequences of sharing power with a much stronger opponent. Worse, if one were to go by the 2014 time line, both US and Kabul do not have enough time at hand to pursue a sustained result-oriented dialogue with the Taliban and their patrons.

Following questions are critical to the assessment of the current reconciliation process in its current shape and form: (i) Are Taliban willing for a negotiated political settlement? (ii) Does the government in Kabul have the institutional capacity/capability to survive the challenges of sharing power with a much stronger opponent? (iii) Is the current reconciliation process unifying or dividing the country? (iv) Would it strengthen or weaken the political process that began after 2001 and help revive a functional modern Afghan state? (v) Would it help build a sustainable internal balance of power whereby various Afghan factions, while reconciling to each other's political space and rights would work towards a unified Afghan state? (vi) Finally, who would ensure that parties to the power sharing agreement stick to the terms and conditions of the agreement? Where are the enforcement mechanisms?

The answers to the above questions may be too well-known to be elaborated here, but they are germane to the future of Afghanistan. None of the parties involved in the negotiations are actually positioned for the reconciliation processes. Bringing armed Afghan militant groups into the state-building process will remain a key challenge for the next government too after 2014 as the Taliban continue to stand for an *emirate* and thus far have not evinced any interest in the democratic political system. There is no indication from the Taliban as to under what kind of political arrangement would they be willing to share power with Kabul.

In the evolving Afghan (dis-)order, the so-called reconciliation process would remain a wishful thinking unless it develops into a transparent and a genuinely national intra-Afghan process. The politics of exclusion as far as negotiations with the Taliban are concerned has complicated the whole issue. At the same time, involvement of too many actors with diverse agendas may spoil even limited prospects of temporary deals or ceasefires in times to come. With the US-led mission drawing down, where is the need for Pakistan's military establishment to renounce what it perceives as its assets and leverages within Afghanistan or even *vis-à-vis* the US.

Given the social-ethnic rupture in the Afghan polity, reconciliation at social levels is as much desirable as at the political level. Intra-Afghan negotiations at multiple levels and within a broad national framework would bring credibility to the process and lower suspicions among vast sections of the country. A bottom-up approach could be far more effective in terms of strengthening and sustaining the very process of negotiations. However, a key question here is whether Kabul has enough time and resources at hand to pursue a comprehensive nation-wide reconciliation process as the West continues to drawdown its troop levels. Pursuing negotiations with the Taliban, unmindful of its short and long-term implications, is more likely to weaken Kabul and eventually push Afghanistan towards greater chaos and anarchy.

In the new Afghan disorder, politics in the name of reconciliation would however continue to be part of the old and new power play both within Afghanistan and at the regional level. Interestingly, the idea of reconciliation is not likely to lose its appeal even as Afghanistan descends into chaos and anarchy. The logic that political transition after 2014 would not be sustainable if the

Pakistan-based and backed Afghan militant groups are completely kept out simply cannot be ignored. It seems that the current reconciliation and reintegration process has a limited purpose, and is not meant to resolve the Afghan conflict. In fact, the politics of reconciliation is becoming increasingly competitive as number of entities involved, both Afghan and foreign, have grown over the years. Apart from the US and other Western entities, host of regional actors—Saudi Arabia, Iran, Qatar, Turkey and the UAE—too are involved, or at least project themselves as involved, in mediating either between Kabul and the Taliban leadership or between Pakistan and Afghanistan.

At the moment, it is difficult to foresee prospects for any genuine national reconciliation process, supposed to be more comprehensive and inclusive in its scope, in the near-term. The current reconciliation process is likely to remain bedevilled with politics of inclusion and exclusion. Striking deals with sections of Taliban for short-term gains may not necessarily lead to national reconciliation. The current process has thus far failed to evolve into an intra-Afghan affair or an indigenous nation-building exercise. In the current circumstances, it is difficult to state if deals with the Taliban would at all weaken the armed opposition to the government or help avert a full scale civil war.

Both Kabul and the West are currently not in a position to lay down terms and conditions. As Kabul and Washington decide on a long-term bilateral security agreement which would define the nature of US presence and assistance beyond 2014, the Taliban and allies are more likely to raise their offensive against government and the residual American forces. In years to come, prospects of defection or split in the Taliban would to great extent depend on the effectiveness of US strategy towards Pakistan and Afghanistan and the strength of the future Afghan Government. Taliban elements willing to share power might also demand a completely new political arrangement or major revisions to the constitution. Under such circumstances, the anti-Taliban groups too would demand a more decentralised/federalised political set up to secure their own position and interests in the new set up. This has greater chances of further exacerbating the factional politics and ethno-political divide within the country.

Perhaps in future there might be a stronger case for a direct intra-Afghan dialogue involving Taliban and various Pashtun and non-Pashtun groups with UN and regional countries facilitating the process. Until then, a key challenge would be to avoid possible political vacuum in Kabul or chaos in case the 2014 elections fails to throw up a credible leadership or the electoral process itself is jeopardised by insecurity and lack of credibility.

In coming times, it is also difficult to say as to what extent the Pakistani establishment would be willing to work with the Americans in negotiating deals with the Taliban. The US' *aid-and-raid* approach to make Pakistan move against the extremist groups has not worked thus far and is least likely to work as the West turns its attention away from the region. Pakistan also is least likely to undergo any substantive structural transformation either, which basically means its political agenda in Afghanistan may remain largely unaltered.

With the Obama Administration explicitly stating that the Afghan mission is not an open-ended affair, one wonders where is the need for Pakistan to give up its existing or prospective leverages within Afghanistan. For the emboldened pro-Taliban elements within the Pakistani establishment, it is time to extract maximum concession and aid from the West, and to create conditions for a grand bargain with the US on the Afghan issue. As for Kabul, it has been under increasing pressure to reconcile with sections of Taliban in view of the West's exit strategy from Afghanistan. However, unless Pakistan gives up its Cold War-era policy of sponsoring and using a wide range of radical religious militant outfits to advance its perceived regional agenda, Kabul's reconciliation initiatives will continue to be rebuffed by the Taliban. Therefore, the reintegration element aimed at common fighters is more likely to yield results than the reconciliation component of the process. It will be far easier for Kabul to make its way up through the tribal networks than through Rawalpindi or Islamabad.

A top-down approach emphasising on direct negotiations is not likely to work in the current and in the long-term scenario partly since the top insurgent leadership is hostage to the Pakistani establishment and partly because of their conviction that they can wait out the West and thereby the Karzai Government. This raises a fundamental question: To what extent the Taliban leadership and the Pakistani establishment are willing for a negotiated political settlement. Even if there is a section in the Taliban leadership that feels that its time to open negotiations with Kabul, Rawalpindi will continue to rein in and scotch their efforts. The Pakistan Army is not likely to concede on this issue until it is assured of a central role in redefining the power structure in Afghanistan. Interestingly, former Taliban finance minister and head of Taliban political council, Mutasim Agha Jan, who has been based in Turkey for sometime now, in his interview to *Tolo News* in June 2013 had clearly alluded to divisions among moderate and extremist elements within the Taliban on the issue of national reconciliation. However, his initiatives have so far not yielded any concrete result. In his opinion, the Taliban office established in Doha in 2013 was supposedly dominated by the Taliban hardliners and had no representation from the relatively moderate section of the Taliban.[37]

The reconciliation process is thus likely to be more fragmented and chaotic as factional power politics intensifies. There is a perception that the Taliban and allies are going to gain in influence and control as the West reduces its presence and as flow of international aid to the Afghan government dries up. Needless to say that a weaker Kabul hardly holds any incentive for the anti-government armed groups to at all negotiate and certainly not on Kabul's terms and conditions.

In fact, without Western support, it would be impossible for Kabul to carry out even its reintegration programme aimed at low/middle level fighters at district levels in an effective and sustained manner. It may be safely concluded that all efforts for reintegration and reconciliation are bound to exacerbate the socio-political and ideological divides unless Afghan state structures and institutions are reasonably strengthened to face up to the rising power of the Taliban and allies. Collapse of central authority or absence of a viable political alternative after 2014 would further degrade the so-called reconciliation process into a coalition building exercise involving disparate armed Afghan factions ever distrustful of each other, reminiscent of the failed politics of power-sharing during 1991-92. Perhaps, a top-down political approach to reconciliation may not be as feasible since warring parties to the conflict are not positioned for national reconciliation, whereas a bottom-up social approach would require sustained efforts at multiple levels and immense patience, both of which are apparently short.

The peace process in Afghanistan at a broader level could also be regarded as a war of ideas and propaganda: neo-Islam versus traditional Islam; and the complex challenge of managing increasingly diverse perceptions of state, society and religion at a more local level. Though the likelihood of West remaining engaged in the region seems to be growing, it remains doubtful if the post-2001 political process in Afghanistan and thereby the Kabul-led peace process could be regarded as irreversible. Kabul will thus have to gamble its way through the current power politics and try to sustain itself, even if it means pursuing a perilous peace process.

As of now, the old patterns of the Afghan war, which is in its fourth decade, are clearly re-emerging. It has been a long war, and a continuing war of ideas and ideologies, a battle of minds and violent power shifts. Afghanistan has since been searching for a common ground or a middle path to re-establish a semblance of limited stability and progress. If the 2014 transition fails, Afghanistan would have to go through yet another round of chaos and anarchy until a relatively sustainable socio-political equilibrium emerges within the country. The politics of peace and reconciliation, even as it collapses and revives, still has a long way to go before it offers a viable way forward.

NOTES

1. Pamela Constable, "A Modernized Taliban Thrives in Afghanistan," *The Washington Post*, September 20, 2008, at http://articles.washingtonpost.com/2008-09-20/world/36866540_1_taliban-islamic-emirate-taliban-insurgency-foreign-aid-workers

2. Heela Najibullah, "Afghan Attempts at Peace and Reconciliation 1986 and 2010: A Comparison," *Delhi Policy Group*, 2011, pp. 8-9.
3. Richard Lloyd Parry, "Anti-Taliban warlords set the rules for a new round of the Great Game," *The Independent* (UK), October 12, 2001, at http://www.afghanistannews center.com/news/2001/october/oct12k2001.html
4. Patrick Cockburn and Andrew Buncombe, "The Taliban rule is finished says Karzai as Kandahar Falls," *The Independent*, December 07, 2001, at http://www.independent.co.uk/ news/world/asia/the-taliban-rule-is-finished-says-karzai-as-kandahar-falls-619314.html.
5. Alex Strick van Linschoten and Felix Kuehn (eds.), *Abdul Salam Zaeef - My Life with the Taliban*, Hachette India, 2010, p. 239.
6. This came to the notice of the author during his interaction with a former minister of the Afghan Transitional Administration in June 2010. The former minister claimed that nearly 85-90 per cent of the Taliban fighters were willing to join the peace process.
7. Syed Saleem Shahzad, "Taliban's New Commander Ready for a Fight," *Asia Times Online*, March 20, 2006, at http://www.atimes.com/atimes/South_Asia/HE20Df02.html. Also, see Jalal-ud Din Haqqani, *Public Broadcasting Service (PBS)*, at http://www.pbs.org/wgbh/ pages/frontline/taliban/militants/haqqani.html.
8. Syed Saleem Shahzad, "Revival of the Taliban," *Asia Times Online*, April 09, 2005, at http://www.atimes.com/atimes/Central_Asia/GD09Ag01.html
9. Ibid. The group did not include any senior ranking Taliban member. It mostly included some junior level Taliban ministers, provincial officials and mullahs.
10. PTS had 12 provincial offices - Kabul, Kandahar, Herat, Paktia, Kunduz, Nangarhar, Kunar, Khost, Zabul, Helmand, Urozgan and Farah. PTS claimed that nearly 7,000 militants joined the process and assisted in the release of about 800 prisoners detained without charge. See the official website of PTS, at http://www.pts.af/index.php?page=en_ Accomplishments.
11. "Senior British Diplomat: Pakistan Not a 'Source of Terrorism,'" *International Herald Tribune*, September 08, 2006, at http://www.iht.com/articles/ap/2006/09/08/asia/ AS_GEN_Pakistan_Britain.php
12. "Afghanistan Open to Dialogue with Militants," *Der Spiegel*, March 06, 2007, at http:/ /www.spiegel.de/international/0,1518,469876,00.html
13. "Afghan Bill Calls for Talks with Taliban," *The New York Times*, May 09, 2007, at http:/ /www.nytimes.com/aponline/world/AP-Afghan-Taliban-Talks.html
14. "Afghan Papers See Taleban as Possible Talks Partner," *Sabawoon Online*, February 16, 2007, at http://www.sabawoon.com/news/miniheadlines.asp?dismode=article&artid=35569
15. Anand Gopal, "Afghan Opposition Courts Taliban," *The Christian Science Monitor*, April 03, 2008, at http://www.csmonitor.com/2008/0403/p06s01-woap.html.
16. "AUNF for Recognition of Taliban as a Party," *The Frontier Post*, May 02, 2008, at http:/ /www.thefrontierpost.com/News.aspx?ncat=an&nid=315
17. Thomas Harding and Tom Coghlan, "Britain in Secret Talks with the Taliban," *The Daily Telegraph*, December 27, 2007, at http://www.telegraph.co.uk/news/uknews/1573687/ Britain-in-secret-talks-with-the-Taliban.html
18. David Charter, Anthony Loyd and Richard Beeston, "The British have made matters worse, says Afghan President," *The Times* (London), January 25, 2008, at http:// www.timesonline.co.uk/tol/news/world/asia/article3248318.ece
19. "New Helmand Governor Confirms Desire for Talks with Taliban," *RFE/RL*, March 01, 2008, at http://www.rferl.org/content/article/1079672.html
20. Henry McDonald, "We Can Persuade Taliban to be Peaceful – Expelled EU Man," *The Guardian*, February 16, 2008, at http://www.guardian.co.uk/world/2008/feb/16/ afghanistan.terrorism

21. "Berlin bashes US Afghan policy," *Pak Tribune*, May 17, 2007, at http://paktribune.com/news/index.shtml?178410
22. Graeme Smith, "Canada Reaches Out to Taliban," *The Globe and Mail*, May 01, 2008, at http://www.theglobeandmail.com/servlet/story/LAC.20080501.AFGHAN01/TPStory/TPInternational/Asia/
23. See "White Paper of the Interagency Policy Group's Report on U.S. Policy toward Afghanistan and Pakistan," *The White House*, March 27, 2009, at http://www.whitehouse.gov/assets/documents/afghanistan_pakistan_white_paper_final.pdf
24. "Remarks by the President in Address to the Nation on the Way Forward in Afghanistan and Pakistan," *The White House*, December 01, 2009, at http://www.whitehouse.gov/the-press-office/remarks-president-address-nation-way-forward-afghanistan-and-pakistan
25. "Taliban Say Obama's Call on Moderates 'Illogical,'" *The New York Times*, March 10, 2009, at http://www.nytimes.com/reuters/2009/03/10/world/international-us-afghan-taliban-obama.html.
26. "No moderates in Taliban ranks: Haqqani," *The News*, April 17, 2009, at http://thenews.jang.com.pk/top_story_detail.asp?Id=21576
27. "Statement of the Islamic Emirate of Afghanistan on the occasion of the Eighth Anniversary of the American Attack on Afghanistan," *Alemarah*, October 07, 2009, at http://www.alemarah.info/english/index.php?option=com_content&view=article&id=301:statement-of-the-islamic-emirate-of-afghanistan-on-the-occasion-of-the-eighth-anniversary-of-the-american-attack-on-afghanistan&catid=5:statement
28. The absence of key senior Kabul-based former Taliban leaders, such as Abdul Salam Zaeef, former Taliban ambassador to Pakistan, and Wakil Ahmad Muttawakil, former Taliban foreign minister, from the Grand Peace Jirga and Kabul Conference in 2010 and, more importantly, the Afghan High Peace Council, was notable.
29. A sister of Arif Khan Noorzai was married into the Karzai family in 2002. His sister's marriage with Ahmed Wali Karzai, younger half-brother of President Hamid Karzai, who in 2005 was elected as Chairman of the Kandahar Provincial Council, brought the Karzais and Noorzais together. Ahmed Wali Karzai was reportedly shot dead by one of his own bodyguards in July 2011.
30. The Taliban representatives supposed to be involved in negotiations are Tayyab Agha, Abbas Stanakzai and Shahabuddin Delawari. All three are said to have already moved to Doha from Pakistan in late 2010.
31. The documents talks of strengthening an "Afghan-led and Afghan-owned" peace process; securing the "collaboration of Pakistan" and support of other regional countries; HPC's expectations from Pakistan; trilateral and bilateral mechanisms involving Afghanistan, Pakistan and the US to take the peace process forward; need for confidence buiding measures; proposes Saudi Arabia as the venue of talks with verifiable Taliban representatives; enlisting support of Saudi Arabia and Turkey in broadening the peace process; de-listing by the UN of Taliban members identified for negotiations; ceasefire between Afghan Government and the Taliban and other armed groups; modalities for transformation of Taliban and other armed groups into a political group; long-term security guarantees for the Taliban; and, measures to ensure the implementations of the agreements reached. See "Peace Process Roadmap to 2015," *High Peace Council, Islamic Republic of Afghanistan*, November 2012, at http://www.foreignpolicy.com/files/121213_Peace_Process_Roadmap_to_2015.pdf
32. Dexter Filkins, "Pakistanis Tell of Motive in Taliban Leader's Arrest," *The New York Times*, August 22, 2010, at http://www.nytimes.com/2010/08/23/world/asia/23taliban.html?pagewanted=all. Mullah Baradar was reportedly replaced by Mullah Abdul Qayyum Zakir, a former Guantanamo detainee believed to be in his mid-30s.

33. Joshua Partlow, "Negotiator for Taliban was an impostor, Afghan officials say," *The Washington Post*, November 23, 2010, at http://www.washingtonpost.com/wp-dyn/content/article/2010/11/23/AR2010112300075.html
34. Praveen Swami, "Taliban military chief held after secret talks with Afghan envoys," *The Hindu*, April 16, 2012, at http://www.thehindu.com/news/international/article3318142.ece
35. "Interview with Mullah Omar–Transcript," *BBC*, November 15, 2001, at http://news.bbc.co.uk/2/hi/south_asia/1657368.stm
36. Alex Strick van Linschoten and Felix Kuehn, no. 5, pp. 234-35.
37. "TOLOnews Exclusive: Mutasem Agha Jan Interview Transcript," *TOLO News*, June 2013, at http://www.tolonews.com/TOLOnews_photo/Mutasem_Agha_Jan.pdf

"We can help train an army, we can help equip an army, we can help build facilities for the army, but only the Afghan people can breathe a soul into that army."*

—*Lt. Gen. Karl Eikenberry, former Commanding General, CFC-Afghanistan, January 2007*

"It cannot be predicted what the security situation will be like in 2014. But considering the current security situation…Afghanistan will need a security force numbering more than 400,000 to transition power in 2014."**

—*Gen. Zaher Azimi, Afghan Defence Ministry Spokesman, January 2011*

---

* Samuel Chan, "Sentinels of Afghan Democracy: The Afghan National Army," *Military Review*, January-February 2009, p. 25.

** "Afghanistan short of troops to take over security," *Gulf News*, January 14, 2011, at http://gulfnews.com/afghanistan-short-of-troops-to-take-over-security-1.746061.

CHAPTER VI

Quest for a National Army

The phased transition of security responsibilities from the NATO-led ISAF to the ANSF, and simultaneous withdrawal of the US and NATO-led troops, as agreed upon during the NATO's Lisbon Summit in November 2010, has been underway since July 2011. The security transition process is stated to be 'irreversible,' even as the Haqqani-Taliban network with support from Pakistan's military establishment continues to push deeper into the Afghan heartland. Nearly 33,000 US troops are stated to have withdrawn so far, 10,000 in 2011 and 23,000 in September 2012, bringing the current US troop levels down to the pre-2009 level i.e., about 68,000. Another 34,000 are to be withdrawn by February 2014. The strength of the post-transition American deployment is expected to be around 10,000 troops pending Kabul agreeing to the terms and conditions of the proposed Bilateral Security Agreement (BSA). Meanwhile, the fifth and final phase of the security transition was announced in June 2013, which means the ANSF has formally taken over security responsibilities almost across the country.

According to the declaration of the NATO Summit at Chicago in May 2012, "The pace and the size of a gradual managed force reduction from the ANSF surge peak to a sustainable level will be conditions-based and decided by the Government of the Islamic Republic of Afghanistan in consultation with the International Community. The preliminary model for a future total ANSF size, defined by the International Community and the Government of Islamic Republic of Afghanistan, envisages a force of 228,500 with an estimated annual budget of US $4.1 billion, and will be reviewed regularly against the developing security environment." This means that the size of the ANSF would be pruned 2015 onwards from 350,000 to nearly 228,500 as stated above. Interestingly, nothing was said or plans were put forth for nearly 120,000 trained ANSF personnel who would have to be retrenched after 2014. It was further stated that, "As the Afghan economy and the revenues of the Afghan government grow, Afghanistan's yearly share will increase progressively from at least US$500 m in 2015, with the aim that it can assume, no later than 2024, full financial responsibility for its own security forces."[1]

On the eve of the Chicago Summit, it was reported that as per a US-backed plan, the Afghan Government is expected to contribute $500 million, the NATO countries $1.3 billion, and the remaining shortfall in the total amount required will be taken care of by the US and other countries. More than $1.1 billion was pledged at the summit's end, including $110 million from Canada, and contributions from Australia, Denmark, Italy, Germany and others.[2] According to another report, the "Afghan funding commitments so far include $100 million annually from Britain, $120 million from Italy, $110 million from Canada, $100 million from Australia and $20 million from Turkey."[3]

Though the prospect of a complete US and NATO withdrawal from the region is ruled out, but the nature and level of their engagement post-2014 is far from clear. The US administration has already signed an *Enduring Strategic Partnership Agreement* with Kabul in May 2012, wherein it is committed to remain engaged in Afghanistan until 2024. However, serious differences have emerged between Kabul and Washington on the terms and conditions of the BSA, which was supposed to have been concluded by May 2013, within a year of the signing of the Partnership Agreement.[4] The negotiations are stuck on the issue of legal immunity for American forces from Afghan laws and jurisdiction over military operations. Until the agreement comes through, the ambiguity over the nature and level of US engagement after 2014 would remain. However, as of now, it is sufficiently clear that the US would be maintaining some military presence and would continue to assist the Afghan army well after 2014. Interestingly, within two days of the NATO Summit, Gen. John Allen, commander of the US forces in Afghanistan, during an interview made it clear that his troops will be requiring "significant power" in 2013-14 and that he owes the US president "some real analysis on this."[5]

In recent years, the West has explicitly staked its exit strategy on two processes: development of the ANSF, comprising both the ANA[6] and the ANP; and reconciliation with key Pakistan-backed Afghan insurgent groups, particularly the Taliban leadership. It is a foregone conclusion now that both the processes will not be delivering the desired results by 2014-15. Despite several attempts, no tangible progress has been made or is likely to be made on the reconciliation front in the near-term. A strong sense of pessimism is reported to have set in within the US establishment over the idea of direct talks and reconciliation with the Taliban leadership. The focus is said to be shifting from the current policy of finding ways to directly engage the Pakistan-based top Taliban leadership to working towards an intra-Afghan dialogue after 2014.[7] However, it is still too early to conclude that the US would be completely backing off from the idea of negotiating deals with the Taliban leadership. As of now, there is no reason to believe that the Haqqani-Taliban network would agree for a negotiated political settlement or the ANSF would be able to manage the combined Haqqani-Taliban onslaught without massive long-term external aid and assistance.

Given the rising cost of the Afghan war, both in terms of funding and casualties, building up a capable national army and police is seen as a more economical option. In the above context, it is worth pondering if ANA at all has the potential to emerge as an effective unifying and a sustainable national force after 2014.

Origin/Evolution of the New National Army

On December 02, 2002, during a meeting with representatives from the UN and the donor countries at Petersberg in Bonn, Germany, Hamid Karzai, then chairman of the ATA, had issued a decree for the establishment of the ANA. The *Petersberg Decree* declared that the US will be 'the designated lead nation for ANA restructuring' under the overall command of the 'legitimate Afghan civilian authorities.' It also designated the UN with Japan as the lead donor nation for preparing a comprehensive programme for the Disarmament, Demobilisation, and Reintegration (DDR) of various militia groups to augment the process of establishing the ANA. The decree initially envisaged a multi-ethnic and an all-volunteer national army of 70,000.[8] However, US Green Berets had already started training the first batch of Afghan soldiers in May 2002. The US soon partnered with the UK, France, Canada, Germany, New Zealand, Romania, Bulgaria and Mongolia to build a functional national army for Afghanistan.

Training and Mentoring

Following the decree, various camps and coalition/combined task forces were established by the Western countries and the partners in and around Kabul to train the new Afghan Army and to provide necessary logistics with regard to it. Camp Phoenix, established in early 2003 on the outskirts of Kabul and led by the Combined Joint Task Force (CJTF) Phoenix of the US coalition, soon began conducting broad-based training, mentoring, and assistance programmes for the ANA. The CJTF Phoenix has since undergone various rotations and has played a key role in establishing the ANA's five corps. The CJTF Phoenix VI later took up the additional responsibility of assisting in the training of the Afghan police.[9] Similarly, Camp Black Horse, located on the outskirts of Kabul, which hosts the Canadian Afghan National Training Centre Detachment, too has been providing training and mentorship to the ANA.[10] The US Special Forces are said to be training the ANA commando battalions at Camp Morehead in the south of Kabul.

The CJTF-82, headquartered at Bagram Airfield, has also played an important role in the training of the ANA, even though its main mission was 'to conduct operations to destroy remaining Al-Qaeda/hostile Taliban command and control and other hostile anti-Islamic elements'.[11] It operated directly under the US Central Command (CENTCOM), and functions as Regional Command-East or RC-E of the NATO-led ISAF in Afghanistan.

All programmes relating to training and mentoring of the ANA since 2002 were initially co-ordinated by the Office of Military Cooperation - Afghanistan (OMC-A) under overall US command. Later, the OMC-A came under the command of Combined Forces Command-Afghanistan (CFC-A) which was established in November 2003. Satisfied with the progress made on the development of the ANA, the US expanded the OMCA's role to include the entire Afghan security sector. On July 12, 2005, the OMC-A was re-designated as the Office of Security Cooperation-Afghanistan (OSC-A). On April 04, 2006, the OSC-A was in turn re-designated as Combined Security Transition Command – Afghanistan (CSTC-A) under the US CENTCOM.

However, in April 2009, the US and NATO agreed to establish NATO Training Mission-Afghanistan (NTM-A) to oversee institutional training for the ANSF. This shifted the responsibility for ANA's development from the US to the ISAF. NTM-A/CSTC-A's headquarter elements were fully operational by February 2010 and it now operates as an integrated NATO and US command with the mission of developing the ANSF.[12] While NTM-A/CSTC-A focuses on training recruits and building institutional training capacity, the ISAF Joint Command (IJC) now takes responsibility for training Afghan soldiers in the field as well as for conducting combat operations. Having achieved full operational capacity in November 2009, the IJC provides training to ANA units in the field through training teams and partner units. Both NTM-A/CSTC-A and IJC report to the commander of the ISAF and the US Forces in Afghanistan.[13]

On the ANA side, all training and education is managed and implemented by the newly formed ANA Training Command (ANATC). The Kabul Military Training Centre (KMTC) also comes under ANATC-HQ. Formal education and professional development courses for the senior ANA officers are conducted by US and Turkish military instructors at the newly established National Military Academy of Afghanistan (NMAA). Along with the NMAA, which is based on the American West Point model and conducts a four-year course for ANA officers, the newly established Afghan National Army Officer Academy (ANAOA) funded by the United Kingdom (UK) also conducts a one-year course to train officers as platoon commanders. Apart from Afghan military instructors, there are instructors from NATO countries as well at the Academy.

The Command and General Staff College (CGSC), built by France in early

2004, prepares mid-level ANA officers to serve on brigade and corps staffs. A team of French army instructors oversees operations at the school. The basic infantry training course for ANA troops was initially for ten weeks, which later varied from eight to 14 weeks.

Headquartered at Camp Eggers, the CSTC-A, established in April 2006 and operating directly under US CENTCOM, coordinates all programmes relating to training and mentoring of the ANA. It is "a joint service, coalition organisation with military personnel from the US, UK, Canada, Poland, Albania, Germany, France and Romania, as well as contracted civilian advisors, mentors and trainers."[14]

To boost the ANA's regional commands, an Afghan Regional Security Integration Command (ARSIC) has been attached to it. The objective is to carry forward the mission of the CSTC-A at the regional command level, "to plan, programme and implement structural, organisational, institutional and management reforms of the Afghanistan National Security Forces." Each ARSIC comprises a Regional Corps Advisory Command (RCAC) responsible for planning, training, and mentoring at the level of regional corps and below. Within each RCAC are a number of US-led Embedded Training Teams (ETTs) whose functions range from "daily mission planning and preparation to safety, unit training and moral and ethical training" for the ANA.[15] Then there are ISAF-led Operational Mentoring Liaison Teams (OMLTs) attached to regional commands in support of ARSIC.

In due course of time, the British forces were tasked with the training of Non-Commissioned Officers (NCOs) of the ANA; the Canadians began conducting a two-week training programme in squad and platoon level tactics; the French forces assisted in training the ANA officers; the German forces provided trainers and mentors for the ANA armour (tanks); the Romanian forces were responsible for the ANA Advanced Individual Training (AIT); Mongolia provided instructors for the ANA field artillery; and Croatian, Italian, Dutch, Norwegian, Slovenian, Swedish, and Polish forces provided OMLTs. The US forces, however, remain responsible for the overall mentoring and training of the ANA from the Afghan Ministry of Defence (MoD) to the company level.[16]

At first, the ANA soldiers were given a brisk two-month course and then sent out to battle the Taliban insurgents. But now, the training at KMTC is for 15 weeks, including six weeks of basic training, and nine weeks of AIT, during which soldiers are given specialised training, from rifleman to artillery to more elite commando duties. The NTM-A/CSTC-A reportedly follows a three-step approach: training Afghan recruits, training Afghans to be trainers, and training Afghans to assume control of their systems and institutions. It is said to be currently in the process of moving from the first step to the second and third steps.

According to the US Government Accountability Office (GAO):

> The ANA personnel are counted toward the force size after they have successfully passed vetting procedures. In order to pass vetting procedures, recruits must validate that they are Afghan citizens between 18 and 35 years old; present two vouchers of recommendation (often written by village elders); and pass a physical and mental examination and a drug test. Recruits also undergo biometric testing to verify that they are not assigned to any other armed forces unit and have not been involved in previous attacks against US, NATO, or Afghan forces.[17]

The Afghan Army is said to be growing despite all uncertainty, but it is difficult to assess its doctrinal focus. The ANA slogan of *Khuda*, *Watan* and *Wazifa* is still to characterise the new army. The senior officers are said to be a mix of veterans of the old pro-Soviet Afghan Army of the 1970s and 80s including the deserters and defectors from the old national army, elements from the anti-Soviet resistance, and more recently veterans of the anti-Taliban resistance. The diversity of the multi-national entities involved in the training and mentoring process has, to an extent, led to a complex mix of doctrines and approaches within the ANA. There are US/NATO/Soviet trained officers and instructors working with the ANA and their over all impact on the orientation of the new Afghan Army as well as at operational and coordination levels is yet to be assessed. The expansion of the ISAF and its role in training the ANSF further diversified the military doctrines and policy approaches to the development of the ANA.

Equally important is the training of officers and NCOs. The only veteran NCOs available are ones who had served in the old Soviet-trained Afghan Army. NATO has different standards for NCOs, with sergeants expected to lead, supervise and take responsibility. The training of the officer corps also presents similar challenges. The Soviet style varied from the NATO style of officer training, position and orientation. Since many of the mid-level and senior officers have been recruited from among old factional commanders and officers trained by the Russians, they are often at variance with the younger officers being trained on West Point or Sandhurst model.

Structure/Formation of ANA[18]

The ANA is said to comprise six ground manoeuvre corps and one air corps. The ANA is suppose to comprise '76 battalions or *Kandak*[19] organised into 13 light infantry brigades, a mechanised brigade, a commando brigade, enabling units and the initial operation of an air corps by the end of fiscal year 2009.'[20] The ANA is said to be 'primarily a light infantry based army equipped with towed artillery and mortars.'[21] The ANA, as of now, has a Capital Division and six regional corps commands:

- 111th Capital Division (Kabul)
- 201st *Selab* or Flood Corps based in Kabul (Central Command);
- 203rd *Tandar* or Thunder in Gardez (Eastern Command);
- 205th *Atal* or Hero in Kandahar (Southern Command);
- 207th *Zafar* or Victory in Herat (Western Command); and
- 209th *Shaheen* or Falcon in Mazar-e-Sharif (Northern Command); and
- 215th *Maiwand* in Lashkar Gah, Helmand.

The first regional corps command headquarters outside Kabul was established in Kandahar on September 19, 2004. The other three regional commands were soon established in late 2004 and early 2005. The 215th sixth corps command was formally established in April 2010. A new division, the 111th Capital Division, was created from the 201st Kabul Corps and it became operational in April 2009.

Afghan National Army Air Corps (ANAAC)

The ANAAC was re-established in January 2005 and at that time comprised of few ageing Russian helicopters and transport planes. The Russians had helped in overhauling 11 of them in 2004. It was also reported that the Afghan defence ministry had sought the return of 26 aircrafts including nine helicopters, five bombers, eight fighters, two trainer jets and two transporters - 19 of which are in Pakistan and seven in Uzbekistan.[22] In October 2005, there were reports suggesting that Russia will be supplying four helicopters and military equipments worth $30 million to the ANA.[23] The Czech Republic had also committed to supply six helicopters to the Air Corps.[24] Since then, efforts have been on to re-equip the ANAAC.

According to *The Long War Journal*, as of April 2010, the ANAAC had an estimated 3,000 personnel and a total of 46 aircrafts. The total cost of building the ANAAC, from its start in May 2007 to the completed organisation of 130-140 aircrafts, and nearly 8,000 personnel by the end of FY2015 is expected to be approximately $5 billion (for details, see Appendix IV).

According to a US Department of Defense report, the Afghan Air Force (AAF) would not be fully operational before 2018. The report stated that about 86 Mi-17 helicopters are planned for the post-2014 AAF fleet. The Mi-35s are likely to be phased out in 2016. As of March 31, 2013, there were 38 Mi-17 helicopters in the inventory of the AAF, 29 of which were operational. Another 12 Mi-17s are expected to be delivered between August and October 2013, bringing the total number of Mi-17s to 60. The AAF also has some 26 C-208s. About 20 Light Air Support (LAS) aircrafts are expected to be inducted beginning from August 2014. The C-130Hs too are expected to be introduced in the FY

2013. The strength of the AAF, as of early 2013, was stated to be around 6,277 personnel.[25]

The ANAAC is organised into three air wings and four regional support detachments (for details, see Appendix IV):

- **Kabul Air Wing**—Houses ANAAC headquarter, Supports National Commando Brigade, Fixed wing transport, VIP transport, attack, ISR.
- **Kandahar Air Wing**—Supports Regional Command (RC)—South/205th Corps, Fixed wing transport, attack, ISR.
- **Shindand Air Wing**—Supports RC—West / 207th Corps. Center for pilot training.
- **Jalalabad Regional Support Detachment**—Support RC—Central/201st Corps.
- **Mazar-e-Sharif Regional Support Detachment**—Supports RC—North/ 209th Corps.
- **Gardez Regional Support Detachment**—Supports RC—East / 203rd Corps.
- **Herat Regional Support Detachment**—Supports RC—West / 207th Corps.

Ethnic Representation

The ethnic composition of the ANA remains a tricky issue. Striking the right ethnic balance at various levels in the army remains a continuing challenge. It is a key factor in determining people's perception and trust in the ANA as a national institution. Though the ANA is said to be multi-ethnic in nature, imbalance at certain levels, especially the officer corps which is often stated to be dominated by the Tajiks, seems unavoidable for the time being given the prevalent socio-political equations within the country (see Table 6.1).

Table 6.1: Afghan National Army and Afghan National Police Ethnicity

	Pashtun		*Tajik*		*Hazara*		*Uzbek*		*Others*	
	ANA	*ANP*	*ANA*	*ANP*	*ANA*	*ANP*	*ANA*	*ANP*	*ANA*	*ANP*
Officer	42.4%	40%	39.1%	49%	7.9%	5%	4.5%	3%	6.1%	3%
NCO	51.8%	32%	38.2%	55%	9.6%	5%	3.2%	4%	1.5%	4%
Soldier/ Patrolman	43.0%	47%	29.2%	35%	11.0%	4%	8.5%	7%	8.2%	7%
Total Force	45.7%	42%	33.3%	42%	10.2%	5%	6.3%	6%	5.8%	6%
National Average	44%		25%		10%		8%		13%	

Note: ANA numbers as of March 2013, ANP as of December 2011.

Source: Ian S. Livingston and Michael O'Hanlon, *Afghanistan Index*, Figure 1.8, Brookings, September 30, 2013, p. 7, at http://www.brookings.edu/~/media/Programs/foreign%20 policy/afghanistan%20index/index20130930.pdf

Moreover, in the absence of proper census figures, the demographic composition of the country itself has been a controversial issue. In order to address the above issue and to lend a national character to the ANA, the Afghan defence ministry is reported to have set targets for the ethnic composition of the ANA. Ethnic quotas have been introduced especially at the level of officers—about 40-45 per cent for Pashtuns, 30-35 per cent Tajiks, 10-12 per cent Hazaras, and 8-10 per cent for Uzbek and other groups.[26]

The implementation of ethnic quota in the army may have invariably ended the dilemma over what is more urgent to its survival—ethnic balancing or professionalism. The Afghan view seems to be divided on this issue. Some are of the view that the priority should be given to first developing a highly professional national army. The issue of ethnic balance though important can be taken care of later. The other viewpoint is more in favour of first ensuring proportionate ethnic representation without which it would not be possible to build a legitimate national army.[27]

Despite efforts made from time to time to augment Pashtun representation, getting recruits from the south and east has been a major challenge. According to an estimate, only about three per cent of recruits are actually Pashtuns from southern provinces.[28] However, some success has been achieved in augmenting Pashtun representation at the officer level in recent years. Apart from the ethnic imbalance, the imbalance in regional representation too has the potential to trigger centrifugal tendencies within the Army in times to come. Much would, however, depend on the political configuration post-2014.

Funding

The US Central Command (CENTCOM) has the primary responsibility for managing the Afghan Security Forces Fund (ASFF). CSTC-A, under CENTCOM uses the ASFF to fund its mission. The ASFF provides for the equipment, supplies, services, training, facility, and infrastructure repair, renovation and construction. The ASFF is divided into Budget Activity Groups (BAG), both for the ANA, ANP, and for related activities, including detainee operations. The ANA Budget Activity Group is further divided into Sub-Budget Activity Groups (SAG). Both the BAG and SAG are monitored through the Army's Programme Budget Accounting System (PBAS) and a separate Afghan-run database. The international donor support for the ANA includes over 40 donor nations and international organisations, contributing approximately $470 million (as of October 2010) worth of equipment to the ANA. In addition, as of October 2010, the other donor countries had reportedly provided about $210 million in funding in support of ANA development, with nearly another $200 million pledged. The donor nations have provided funding for the army through the NATO-ANA Trust Fund which was established in 2007 "to support activities such as ANA training, equipment purchases, and transportation of donated equipment."[29] As of May 2012, contributions and pledges made to the Trust Fund totalled Euros 489,088,425.[30]

Between 2003 and 2009, the US is said to have spent $20 billion to finance the Afghan Army and Police. During 2010-11, the amount spent was $9 billion. Of the approximately $20 billion provided by the US, about $17.9 billion, or nearly 90 per cent, came from the DOD-managed ASFF. Of the $17.9 billion, the largest amount—about $7.0 billion, or 39 per cent—has been directed toward equipment purchases.[31] According to a recent US Department of Defense report, the US Congress had appropriated $11.2 billion for ASFF for the FY 2012. For the FY2013, the US Congress is stated to have appropriated $5.1 billion.[32] The international community provides funding for ANSF through NATO-ANA Trust Fund as well as the Law and Order Trust Fund for Afghanistan (LOTFA). As of now, nearly 23 nations are said to have contributed more than $700 million for the ANA Trust Fund. The LOTFA, which is administered by United Nations Development Program (UNDP), largely provides fund for police salaries and to build the capacity of the Afghan Ministry of Interior (MoI). Between 2002 and 2012, the US is stated to have donated roughly $1.0 billion to LOTFA, while the rest of the international community has committed more than $1.75 billion.[33]

In January 2011, Gen. William B. Caldwell, commander of NATO's training mission in Afghanistan, had announced that the US and its NATO allies plan to spend $11.6 billion during 2011-12 on building Afghanistan's security forces. This is said to be the largest yearly sum to date as the Western forces begin transferring security responsibility to the ANA in certain parts of the country this year. The new funding pushes the total for 2010-11 to nearly $20 billion, as much as in the seven previous years combined. It was also reported that, among other things, 24,000 Ford Rangers, 108,000 9mm pistols, 74,000 handheld radios, 44 helicopters and four bomb-sniffing robots have already been purchased from the funds available for the year.[34]

Interestingly, a large chunk of the ANA funding goes towards salaries. In 2002, recruits were offered $50 per month after they completed their basic training, while NCOs and officers were paid $50-70 and $150, respectively. The following year witnessed high levels of desertion and attrition, understandably linked with soldiers' dissatisfaction with poor pay. In 2003, a recruit's salary was increased to $70 per month while a battalion commander's salary was increased to $300 per month. As an added bonus, soldiers received two dollars for each day spent on field operations.[35]

The idea has also been to discourage defections in the ANSF as the Taliban part-time fighters were said to be better paid. In the summer of 2006, the Taliban were reportedly offering three times the daily pay of the ANA, approximately $300 a month for the equivalent of a first-year ANA soldier. Additionally, the Taliban reportedly offered "$10 to $20 per day for joining attacks on Western forces, $15 to launch a single mortar round into nearby coalition military bases, and US $1,000 for the head of a government worker or a foreigner."[36] Since then pay for Afghan army and police have been revised from time to time with the objective of checking the rising desertion rate. As of 2010, Afghan police officers and soldiers make on an average $165 a month; forces serving in the Helmand province and other such places get an additional $75 as hostile environment pay[37] (see Table 6.2).

Rushing for Numbers

Interestingly, there are no definitive figures on the current as well as future potential strength of the ANA. Initially the strength of the ANA was projected at 70,000 but the targeted strength has since been revised several times. Later, as the US began shifting its focus back from Iraq to Afghanistan in 2008-09, the targeted strength of the ANA was revised from 70,000 to 134,000. In January 2010, it was decided during the London Conference on Afghanistan to further augment its strength to 171,000 by October 2011. A further revision in the targeted strength of the ANA from 171,000 to 240,000 is already under consideration. As per the US plan announced earlier, about 10,000 Afghan troops were to be trained each year for four years beginning in 2010. In August 2010, it was said that the West has increased the capacity to train about 75,600 recruits from 27,000 annually, a nearly three-fold increase since January 2008.

It is difficult to ascertain the exact numerical strength of the ANA at any given point of time as different official sources provide different figures. According to the ISAF, the strength of ANA as of October 2012 stood at 184,676 or almost 99 per cent of the 187,000 to be inducted by December 2012 and fielded by December 2013.[38] The November 2013 biennial report of the US DoD stated that the strength of ANSF, as of August 2013, stood at 344,602, which is 98 per cent of its 352,000 authorised end strength.[39] For increase in the size of the ANA and ANP since 2003, see Table 6.3 given below, drawn from the *Afghanistan Index* published by the Brookings Institution.

The sustainability of the projected strength of the ANA has been the subject of debate in recent years. Though senior Afghan Army officials have been of the view that an army of at least 150,000-200,000 and a maximum of 300,000-400,000 would be needed to stabilise the country, the West had its reservation, fearing that it might undermine the authority of the nascent civilian government in Kabul. Arranging and sustaining necessary levels of external funding and direct assistance for a large Afghan army and police for at least a decade after 2014 is

Table 6.2: Pay Charts for Afghan National Security Forces

ANA Rank	*ANP Rank*	*Grade*	*<1to3*	*>3*	*>6*	*>9*	*>12*	*>15*	*>18*	*>21*	*>24*
GEN	GEN	0-10	945	990	1,005	1,020	1,035	1,050	1,065	1,080	1,095
LTG	LTG	0-9	845	890	905	920	935	950	965	980	995
MG	MG	0-8	745	800	815	830	845	860	875	890	905
BG	BG	0-7	645	700	715	730	745	760	775	790	805
COL	COL	0-6	495	530	545	560	575	590	605	620	635
LTC	LTC	0-5	445	480	495	510	525	540	555	570	585
MAJ	MAJ	0-4	395	430	445	460	475	490	505	520	535
CPT	CPT	0-3	345	345	350	365	380	395	410	425	
1LT	1LT	0-2	295	310	325	340	355	370			
2LT	2LT	0-1	275	290	305	320	335				
Sergeant Maj	Chief NCO	E-9	275	310	325	340	355	370	385	400	415
Master Sgt	1st Sergeant	E-8	255	270	285	300	315	330	345	360	375
Sgt First Class	2nd Sergeant	E-7	235	245	260	275	290	305	320	335	350
Staff Sergeant	3rd Sergeant	E-6	210	230	245	260	275	290	305		
Sergeant	1st Patrolman	E-5	180	215	230	245	260	275			
Soldier	2nd Partolman	E-4	165	200	215	230	245				

Note: All salary numbers above are in U.S. $ per month. Figures as of May 2010.

Combat Plans Division (CPD) Forces

Rank	*Current Salary*	*Numbers of Soldiers*
Lieutenant General	800	1
Major General	700	3
Brigadier General	600	6
Colonel	450	60
Lieutenant Colonel	400	193
Major	350	509
Captain	300	693
Ist Lieutenant	250	169
2nd Lieutenant	230	20
Senior Sergeant/1st Sergeant	210	1237
2nd Sergeant	190	Not Available
3rd Sergeant	165	Not Available
Soldier	120	2164

Note: All salary numbers above are in U.S. $ per month. Figures as of May 2010.
Source: Ian S. Livingston and Michael O'Hanlon, *Afghanistan Index*, Figure 3.3, Brookings, September 30, 2013, p. 22, at http://www.brookings.edu/~/media/Programs/foreign%20policy/afghanistan%20index/index20130930.pdf

considered a huge challenge. It was stated in the NATO Summit in Chicago that the over all size of the ANSF would have to be reduced three years after 2014 depending on the ground situation and, more importantly, availability of funds.

The Weaponry

The nature of weaponry available with the ANA has been largely of Soviet origin. However, attempts to make the ANA adapt to Western/American weaponry have

Table 6.3: Size of Afghan Security Forces on Duty, 2003-2013

Month	*MoD Forces (ANA)*	*Ministry of Interior Forces (ANP)*	*Total ANSF*
End 2003	6,000	—	6,000
End 2004	24,000	33,000	57,000
End 2005	26,000	40,000	66,000
End 2006	36,000	49,700	86,000
End 2007	50,000	75,000	125,000
October 2008	68,000	79,910	147,910
December 2009	100,131	94,958	195,089
December 2010	149,533	116,856	266,389
December 2011	179,610	143,800	323,410
March 2012	194,466	149,642	344,108
October 2012	178,501	148,536	327,037
January 2013	177,579	149,775	327,354
March 2013	177,725	151,766	329,491

The goal for ANSF levels is currently 352,000. As of October 2012 the breakdown was as follows: ANA, 146,339; ANP, 146,339; Afghan Air Force, 6,172. ANP figures do include border police and civil order police but do not include the Afghan Local Police.

Source: Ian S. Livingston and Michael O'Hanlon, *Afghanistan Index*, Figure 1.4, Brookings Institution, September 30, 2013, p. 6, at http://www.brookings.edu/~/media/Programs/foreign%20policy/afghanistan%20index/index20130930.pdf

met with several hurdles. It has been a contentious issue as most of the veteran commanders and militia fighters integrated into the army prefer Soviet weaponry. The US has in recent years acquiesced to the idea of buying Russian-made weapons and helicopters for the ANA. Equipping the rapidly expanding army and the need to ramp up maintenance services has raised several issues critical to the sustainability and orientation of the new Afghan Army.

In 2006, the NATO Equipment Donation Programme was introduced. The Programme 'provides a mechanism through which Allies donate essential equipment, from uniforms and medical equipment to ammunition and helicopters.' Similarly, the NATO-Russia Council (NRC) Helicopter Maintenance Trust Fund was launched in March 2011. The NRC Trust Fund "provides vitally-needed maintenance and repair capacity, including the provision of spare parts and technician training, to the Afghan Air Force helicopter fleet."[40] However, there have been serious differences between the NATO and the Afghan Army officials on what constitutes the right weaponry for the army. The ANA officials have often complained about supply of poor equipments, lack of maintenance facilities and critical spare parts, shortage of fuel and inadequate or incompatible weaponry. As the Haqqani-Taliban network are likely to intensify and expand their operations in the years to come, lack of functional equipments and shortage of necessary supplies could seriously hamper the ANA's operational capabilities and may even lead to unsustainable casualty levels.

Multiple Challenges

A number of limitations are inhibiting the development and growth of an effective national army in Afghanistan. These can be broadly categorised as: (i) logistical in terms of training and mentoring, weaponry and support structures, (ii) lack of internal cohesion and often motivation due to ethnic factionalism and under-representation, (iii) high attrition rate, desertions, absenteeism and low enlistment, (iv) rampant drug abuse and illiteracy, (v) occasional friction between the recruits and their foreign trainers and mentors, and (vi) infiltration by Taliban-Haqqani network and their allies and sympathisers.

The last of the two has emerged as a major challenge in recent times. There has been a phenomenal spurt in what is generally referred to as 'green-on-blue' or 'insider' attacks, which as of now seems to be making a devastating impact on the very core of the post-2014 Western strategy. The idea of Western troops moving into a supportive role and focussing on training and mentoring of the ANSF after 2014 could be jeopardised if such attacks do not abate. This could lead to mutual distrust, perpetuate negative perceptions and weaken the coordination between Afghan and Western forces.

According to the data provided by *The Long War Journal*, the 'green-on-blue' attacks accounted for nearly 15 per cent Coalition casualties in the year 2012, six per cent casualties in 2011, two per cent in 2010, two percent in 2009, and less than a per cent in 2008. Since January 2008, a total of 84 such attacks (12 until early October in 2013, 44 in 2012, 16 in 2011, five in 2010, five in 2009 and two in 2008) have taken place, with maximum number of casualties from such attacks mainly reported from Helmand (34), Kandahar (17), Kabul (12), Nangarhar (8), Kapisa (8), Wardak (8) & Laghman (8). They have resulted in total 140 coalition casualties (61 in 2012, 35 in 2011, 16 in 2010, 12 in 2009 and two in 2008), with 157 wounded (as of early October 2013).[41] According to the July 2013 biennial report of the US DoD on Afghan security, covering the period from October 2012 to March 2013, approximately 80 per cent of the total insider attacks occurred at military bases, and the remaining 20 per cent attacks were carried out during joint patrols. The majority of attackers were Pashtuns in the age group of 17-25 years.[42] The report also stated that the largest number of insider attacks, about 28, was reported from ISAF's Regional Command (East) headquartered in Bagram, followed by 26 from Regional Command (South) in Kandahar, 22 from Regional Command (South West) in Lashkar Gah, 12 from Regional Command (West) in Herat and 07 from Regional Command (North) in Mazar-e Sharif as well as Regional Command (Capital) in Kabul. According to the report, there was a 120 per cent increase in insider attacks from 2011 to 2012, rising from 22 to 48 incidents. Additionally, 29 percent (14) of the insider attacks in 2012 were executed by more than one person. Prior to 2012, only two attacks had been executed by more than one individual.[43]

Various reasons have been cited for the sudden spurt in what is now being more commonly referred to as 'insider' attacks during 2011-12. Initially, it was believed to be due to cultural differences and personal grievances within the ANA, but now given the emerging patterns and rising frequency of attacks, the Haqqani-Taliban network is understood to be behind most of these attacks. According to a recent *Associated Press* report, based on internal US military analyses, "a number of shooters were recruited into the Afghan army or police forces from Pashtun areas in eastern Afghanistan—including the provinces of Paktika, Paktia and Khost—where the Haqqanis wield great influence." The report adds, "In some cases these Afghans—most of whom had served in uniform for six months or less—returned to those areas on leave from their army or police duties, or briefly crossed into Pakistan, shortly before turning their guns on American or allied soldiers."[44]

Another notable aspect is the lack of credible data and detailed information on casualties among the ANSF and its impact on the morale of both army and police. Figures provided by the US or the ISAF are often at variance with each other or with the assessments of the Afghan ministries of defence and interior. The ISAF recently indicated that in 2012, the casualty among the ANA personnel averaged 243 killed and wounded per month, and among the ANP averaged 292 killed and wounded per month.[45] According to the latest biennial report of the US DoD on Afghan security, covering the period from April to September 2013, the ANSF casualties have increased by 79 per cent compared to the same period last year, while the ISAF casualties have dropped by 59 percent.[46] The figures released by the DoD were however contested and immediately rejected by the Afghan officials. Acoording to the Afghan Defence Ministry spokesperson, Gen. Zahir Azimi, the casualty among the Afghan army has only increased by 14.24 per cent since 2012. Similarly, the Afghan Ministry of Interior spokesperson, Sediq Sediqi, stated that the casualty among Afghan police has increased only by 15 per cent since 2012.[47] Yet another missing aspect is the 'green-on-green' or 'ANSF-on-ANSF' attacks that too have increased within the army and police. In September 2012, the *Associated Press* reported, quoting US military statistics, about 135 Afghan policemen and soldiers have been killed in insider attacks since 2007, which is much more than the number of Western troops killed in such attacks.[48] Such attacks where Afghan security personnel attack their compatriots could in the long run add to the general distrust and weaken the ANSF from within. However, vetting procedures and counter intelligence capabilities have since been strengthened within the ANSF.

There are also several reports suggesting that the ANA is largely incapable of conducting operations against insurgents on its own. Apart from severe logistical deficiencies, rampant ethnic factionalism, illiteracy, drug addiction and desertion are also regarded as key limiting factors. In the words of a senior ANA official from the national recruiting centre, "There are drug traffickers who want to use our units for their business, enemy infiltrators who want to raise problems, jailbirds who can't find any other job." He also candidly observed that, "The news of the American withdrawal has weakened our morale and boosted the morale of the enemy" and "if the international community abandons us again, we won't be able to last."[49] Lack of motivation and disoriented loyalties have also impacted the performance levels. It has been aptly observed that, "the rank and file soldiers are confused about what kind of culture they should follow. The US and NATO (too) are learning. The training has improved in recent months. But they have not created a message or an idea that the soldiers can believe in. What is it that they must be loyal to? What do they defend?"[50]

Desertion and absenteeism has been a particularly worrying feature. For instance, from November 2009 to October 2010, the ANA is reported to have lost over 30,000 soldiers due to desertion. In September 2010, it was reported that only 69 per cent of soldiers were present for duty. An analysis of data provided by IJC indicates that, from January to September 2010, on average, over a quarter of the ANA was absent during any given month.[51] In October 2012, it was reported that, "a third of the Afghan Army perpetually consists of first-year recruits fresh off a 10- to 12-week training course. And in the meantime, tens of thousands of men with military training are put at loose ends each year, albeit without their army weapons, in a country rife with militants who are always looking for help." In fact, a four-year programme has been proposed to order the recall of nearly 22,000 deserters.[52]

Illiteracy too is widely prevalent in the ANA. General Rahmatullah Raufi, the former corps commander in Kandahar, was on record having stated that 80 per cent of the soldiers in his corps are illiterate, 50 per cent of the officers are illiterate, and only 20 per cent of his soldiers have a professional knowledge of how to serve in an army; the rest are former militia fighters or young recruits.[53] At the more critical field level, there is a tremendous shortage of NCOs. As of October 2010, about one-quarter of NCO positions in ANA combat units were said to be lying vacant.

Future Prospects

The ANA is believed to enjoy a positive reputation. It is generally regarded as relatively less corrupt and an institution that often evokes cautious optimism and pride among the Afghan people in general. However, despite greater focus on developing the ANSF, the growing confusion over the Western commitment and Kabul's renewed efforts for reconciliation with the Taliban is invariably giving way to growing scepticism over the future prospects of the ANA.

The idea of creating Afghan Public Protection Force (APPF) or Afghan Local Police (ALP) to address the shortfall in the ANP or the gap in local policing by way of arming the tribes, especially in south-eastern parts of the country, has wider implications for the development and future prospects of the ANSF. Both are supposed to have been formed on the basis of lessons learnt from the earlier experience with the Afghan National Auxiliary Police (ANAP). The ANAP was created in 2006 and had to be disbanded within two years of it as it largely comprised of local militia, criminals and elements involved in drug trade. Such parallel informal structures may in the long run further strengthen the culture of private militias and undermine the credibility of both ANA and ANP in people's perception.

Though the Obama Administration has prioritised and accelerated the process of building up the ANSF, it still is decades away from being an effective and a professional national institution. It is clear that the ANA will not be in a position to either fully take on the security responsibilities from the Western forces or carry out counter-insurgency/terrorism operations on its own in a sustained manner. It is said that the Afghan Government currently spends almost $450 million out of approximately $1 billion annual revenue on security, which is a small fraction of the total cost.[54] According to a projection by the *International Monetary Fund* (IMF) released in January 2010, it will not be possible for Afghanistan—before 2023—to be able to cover all expenses relating to the army.[55] As the army grows, so is the need for infrastructure to sustain such a huge army across the country. In January 2011, it was pointed out by the US inspector general overseeing American contracts in the country that hundreds of new Afghan outposts, barracks and garrisons are "seriously behind schedule, making it doubtful that the construction efforts would keep pace with recruitment and training." He stated that "of 884 projects for completion over the next two years, only 133 are finished. Another 78 are under way, but 673 have not begun."[56]

Much would also depend on how the politics of Afghanistan shapes up; and the nature and level of Western role and commitment beyond 2014, which will be determined by BSA. The strength of the Afghan state institutions, including the ANSF, will be subjected to test once the Western forces end their combat mission in December 2014. The internal cohesion of the ANA is likely to remain fragile on account of competing agendas of various domestic and external actors involved in the Afghan war. Despite greater Western focus and investment, the ANA is still logistically speaking a chronically deficient force. The NATO training mission have for long been short of hundreds of trainers and mentors. The Western endeavour to train and mentor Afghan military and police instructors has a long way to go before ANSF evolves into a relatively self sufficient force. Some of the neighbouring countries who could have immensely contributed towards the rebuilding of the ANA were deliberately kept out of the whole process.

The challenges before ANA are thus immense in proportion and diverse in nature. A range of internal and external factors are arrayed against it. Pakistan, a critical element in the West's Afghan policy, has been strongly averse to the idea of a huge and a powerful Afghan Army on its western frontiers. The process of building institutions of governance in Afghanistan is today far more constrained than in the early years of the war on terror. The failure of the UN-led and externally-sponsored disarmament and demobilisation programmes, such as DDR and Disbandment of Illegal Armed Groups (DIAG) aimed at various private militias across the country; the prevalent socio-ethnic polarisation in the Afghan polity; fragmented Western efforts and failure to rein in Pakistan for supporting Haqqani-Taliban network, are some of the key factors directly impacting the development of ANSF.

At the domestic level, the future prospects of the ANA will to an extent also depend on the perceptions of the war-weary population, and the capacity of the national police to effectively respond to local security needs and sensitivities of the Afghan people across the country. The development of an efficient and well-resourced national police too is critical to the emergence of a strong ANA. In fact, both ANA and ANP will have to partner and compliment their efforts to be able to tackle the various challenges that are likely to emerge as the Western forces retreat.

The rush to increase the numerical strength of the army within a short span of time and without any emphasis on quality soldiering or developing a strong professional core too does not bode well for the future of the ANA. The centrifugal tendencies within the ANA coupled with subversive activities sponsored from outside, have the potential to wreck the army from within if the conflict intensifies and the West fails to neutralise the Haqqani-Taliban network and their numerous allies operating from Pakistan. The continuing short-termism in the Western approach towards 'stabilising' the Af-Pak region could lead to the undoing of the ANA as 'stakeholders' of various shades and hue could be preparing for the next round of war in Afghanistan.

NOTES

1. "Chicago Summit Declaration on Afghanistan," *Issued by the Heads of State and Government of Afghanistan and Nations contributing to the NATO-led International Security Assistance Force (ISAF)*, May 21, 2012, at http://www.nato.int/cps/en/SID-C2334E22-719429FC/natolive/official_texts_87595.htm.
2. Carol E. Lee, Adam Entous and Stephen Fidler, "NATO Leaders Seal Afghan Exit Plan," *The Wall Street Journal*, May 21, 2012, at http://online.wsj.com/article/SB1000142405270230479170457741827122825 5322.html?mod=world_newsreel
3. Matt Spetalnick and Missy Ryan, "NATO sets 'irreversible' but risky course to end Afghan war," *Reuters*, May 21, 2012, at http://www.reuters.com/article/2012/05/21/us-nato-summit-idUSBRE84J02C20120521

4. "Enduring Strategic Partnership Agreement between the United States of America and the Islamic Republic of Afghanistan," *The White House*, May 02, 2012, at http://www.whitehouse.gov/sites/default/files/2012.06.01u.s.-afghanistanspasignedtext.pdf.
5. "General says Afghanistan will need 'combat power,'" *Reuters*, May 23, 2012, at http://www.reuters.com/article/2012/05/23/us-usa-afghanistan-idUSBRE84M1DH20120523
6. The national army is known as *Ordou-e Melli* in the local Dari language.
7. Matthew Rosenberg and Rod Nordland, "U.S. Abandoning Hopes for Taliban Peace Deal," *The New York Times*, October 01, 2012, at http://www.nytimes.com/2012/10/02/world/asia/us-scales-back-plans-for-afghan-peace.html?_r=1&pagewanted=all
8. "Rebuilding Afghanistan: Peace and Stability," Petersberg (Bonn, Germany), *United Nations Assistance Mission in Afghanistan*, December 02, 2002, at http://www.unama-afg.org/docs/_nonUN%20Docs/_Internation-Conferences&Forums/Bonn-Talks/decree%20on%20army.pdf.
9. See the official website of the Combined Joint Task Force Phoenix VI, at http://www.taskforcephoenix.com/.
10. For details, see http://www.globalsecurity.org/military/world/afghanistan/kabul.htm.
11. See "Combined Joint Task Force-82," September 07, 2007, at http://cjtf-a.com/index.php/About/About.html.
12. NTM-A was established on November 21, 2009, bringing together NATO and national training efforts under one umbrella. It works in close partnership with the Afghan Ministry of Defence and Ministry of Interior, as well as in collaboration with the European Police Mission in Afghanistan (EUPOL) and the European Gendarmerie Force. There are currently 38 nations contributing to NTM-A. Training and mentoring of ANSF is carried out by NATO's Military Advisory Teams (MATs) and Police Advisory Teams (PATs). Additional ISAF advisor teams are provided to the Afghan Operation Coordination Centres (OCCs), which support the ANSF commanders in coordinating the employment of forces in their areas. As of May 11, 2012, nations contributing full MATs are—Albania 1, Australia 6, Belgium: 1, Bulgaria 3, Croatia 3, Czech Republic 1, Denmark 1, France 7, Germany 8, Greece 1, Hungary1, Italy 9, Latvia 1, Lithuania 1, Norway 1, Poland 3, Portugal 1, Romania 3, Slovakia 1, Slovenia 1, Spain 4, Sweden 1, Turkey 6, United Kingdom 7, United States 75, and Multinational 5. See "Afghan National Security Forces (ANSF): Training and Development," *North Atlantic Treaty Organization (NATO)*, at http://www.nato.int/nato_static/assets/pdf/pdf_topics/20120516_media_backgrounder_ANSF_en.pdf.
13. "Afghanistan Security: Afghan Army Growing, but Additional Trainers Needed; Long-term Costs Not Determined," *Report to Congressional Addressees, United States Government Accountability Office*, January 2011, p. 5.
14. "CSTC-A Fact Sheet," December 01, 2007, at http://www.cstc-a.com/mission/CSTCAFactSheet.Html.
15. "Fact Sheet on Afghan Regional Security Integration Command," September 2007, at http://www.cstc-a.com/mission/ARSIC.html.
16. "Coalition Forces Information," March 04, 2008, at http://www.taskforcephoenix.com/cofor.htm.
17. United States Government Accountability Office, no. 13, p. 3.
18. For detailed information on ANA structures, logistics & equipment, see C.J. Radin, "Afghan National Army," Afghan National Security Forces Order of Battle, *The Long War Journal*, at http://www.longwarjournal.org/multimedia/ANSF%20OOBpage4-ANA.pdf.
19. The *Kandak* or battalion comprising 600 troops is the basic unit of the ANA. Most of the present Kandaks are infantry units.

20. The strength and composition of some of the ANA units/sub units have been revised and accurate figures are not available in this regard.
21. "Fact Sheet Afghan National Army," September 2007, at http://www.cstc-a.com/mission/AfghanistanArmyFacts.htm
22. "Afghan military seeks return of fugitive planes," *Associated Press*, January 11, 2005, at http://msnbc.msn.com/id/6814109/.
23. "Russia to Supply Afghan Army," *The Washington Post*, October 10, 2005, at http://www.washingtonpost.com/wp-dyn/content/article/2005/10/09/AR2005100900985.html
24. "Afghan National Army gets three attack helicopters," *Pajhwok Afghan News*, December 02, 2008, at http://www.pajhwok.com/viewstory.asp?lng=eng&id=66215
25. See "Report on Progress Towards Stability & Security in Afghanistan", *Department of Defense, United States of America*, July 2013, pp. 75-76, at http://www.defense.gov/pubs/Section_1230_Report_July_2013.pdf
26. "Afghan army struggles with ethnic divisions," *CBS News*, July 27, 2010, at http://www.cbsnews.com/2100-202_162-6717786.html.
27. Based on author's personal observations during his research trips to Afghanistan.
28. US Government Accountability Office, no. 13, p. 1.
29. Ibid., no. 13, pp. 9-10.
30. "Afghan National Security Forces (ANSF): Training and Development," *North Atlantic Treaty Organization (NATO)*, at http://www.nato.int/nato_static/assets/pdf/pdf_topics/20120516_media_backgrounder_ANSF_en.pdf.
31. US Government Accountability Office, no. 13, p. 7.
32. Report on Progress Towards Stability & Security in Afghanistan, no. 25, p. 110.
33. Ibid.
34. Joshua Partlow, "U.S. and NATO allies plan to spend $11.6 billion this year for Afghan security," *The Washington Post*, January 05, 2011, at http://www.washingtonpost.com/wp-dyn/content/article/2011/01/05/AR2011010503337.html.
35. Antonio Giustozzi, "Auxiliary Force or National Army? Afghanistan's 'ANA' and the Counter-Insurgency Effort, 2002-2006," *Small Wars and Insurgencies*, 18 (1), March 2007, pp. 45-67.
36. Samuel Chan, "Sentinels of Afghan Democracy: The Afghan National Army," *Military Review*, January-February 2009, at http://usacac.army.mil/CAC2/MilitaryReview/Archives/English/MilitaryReview_20090228_art006.pdf
37. Ray Rivera, "Support Expected for Plan to Beef Up Afghan Forces," *The New York Times*, January 16, 2011, at http://www.nytimes.com/2011/01/17/world/asia/17afghanistan.html
38. "ISAF Factsheet on Current ANSF Status," *International Security Assistance Force (ISAF)*, October 2012, at http://www.isaf.nato.int/article/isaf-releases/isaf-factsheet-on-current-ansf-status.html
39. See "Report on Progress Toward Security and Stability in Afghanistan," *Department of Defense, United States of America*, November 2013, p. 3, at http://www.defense.gov/pubs/October_1230_Report_Master_Nov7.pdf
40. Afghan National Security Forces (ANSF): Training and Development, no. 30.
41. Bill Roggio and Lisa Lundquist, "Green-on-blue attacks in Afghanistan: the data," *The Long War Journal*, at http://www.longwarjournal.org/archives/2012/08/green-on-blue_attack.php
42. Report on Progress Towards Stability & Security in Afghanistan, no. 25, p. 34.
43. Ibid. pp. 34-35.
44. Robert Burns, "US: Haqqani tie to Afghan insider attacks possible," *Stars and Stripes*, October 06, 2012, at http://ap.stripes.com/dynamic/stories/A/AS_AFGHANISTAN_

INSIDER_ATTACKS?SITE=DCSAS&SECTION=HOME&TEMPLATE= DEFAULT &CTIME=2012-10-05-14-58-51

45. "Over 500 Afghan security forces killed or injured per month," *Khaama Press*, October 16, 2012, at http://www.khaama.com/over-500-afghan-security-forces-killed-or-injured-per-month-349/?utm_source=feedburner&utm_medium=email&utm_campaign=Feed%3A+khaama+%28KHAAMA+PRESS+%7C+Afghan+Online+Newspaper+%26+Magazine%29
46. Report on Progress Toward Security and Stability in Afghanistan, no. 39, p. 1.
47. Sharif Amiry, "Afghan, Foreign Officials Differ on ANSF Casualties," *TOLO News*, November 10, 2013, at http://www.tolonews.com/en/afghanistan/12544-afghan-forces-causalities-higher-than-last-year-officials
48. Deb Riechmann, "Afghan forces also suffer from insider attacks," *Associated Press*, September 30, 2012, at http://bigstory.ap.org/article/afghan-forces-also-suffer-insider-attacks
49. Rod Nordland, "Afghan Army's Turnover Threatens U.S. Strategy," *The New York Times*, October 15, 2012, at http://www.nytimes.com/2012/10/16/world/asia/afghan-armys-high-turnover-clouds-us-exit-plan.html?_r=1&nl=todaysheadlines&emc=edit_th_20121016&pagewanted=all
50. Simon Tisdall, "Behind the politics, Afghan army has a mountain to climb," *The Guardian*, December 03, 2009, at http://www.guardian.co.uk/world/2009/dec/03/training-afghan-army-kabul
51. US Government Accountability Office, no. 13, p. 19.
52. Rod Nordland, no. 49.
53. Scott Baldauf, "A 'half full' Afghan army," *The Christian Science Monitor*, February 10, 2006, at http://www.csmonitor.com/2006/0210/p06s02-wosc.html?s=hns.
54. "Costly coalition plan to recruit thousands more Afghan forces draws concerns," *The Washington Post,* January 17, 2011, at http://www.washingtonpost.com/wp-dyn/content/article/2011/01/17/AR2011011702058.html?sub=AR.
55. "Islamic Republic of Afghanistan: Sixth Review Under the Arrangement Under the Poverty Reduction and Growth Facility, Request for Waiver of Non Observance of a Performance Criterion, Modification and Performance Criteria, and Rephasing and Extension of the Arrangement," *International Monetary Fund*, Country Report No. 10/22, January 2010.
56. Ben Farmer, "Plans for Nato withdrawal could be hit by base construction delays," *The Daily Telegraph* (London), January 25, 2011, at http://www.telegraph.co.uk/news/worldnews/asia/afghanistan/8281330/Plans-for-Nato-withdrawal-could-be-hit-by-base-construction-delays.html.

"There is a popular perception in the United States that in the aftermath of 9/11, the United States formed a coalition and overthrew the Taliban. That is wrong. In the aftermath of 9/11, the United States joined an existing coalition, which had been trying to overthrow the Taliban for most of a decade. That coalition consisted of India, Russia, Iran, and the Northern Alliance. It was with the additional assistance of American air power that coalition succeeded in ousting the Taliban.

That coalition, along with Pakistan, was also very important to the success that the United States enjoyed in replacing the Taliban within a matter of weeks with a moderate, broadly representative government in Kabul, which relieved the United States of the necessity of itself occupying and trying to govern Afghanistan."*

—Ambassador James Dobbins, US House of Representatives, November 2007

"You'll be brought down to your knees if Pakistan doesn't cooperate with you *(the West)*. That is all that I would like to say. Pakistan is the main ally. If we were not with you, you won't manage anything. Let that be clear. And if ISI is not with you, you will fail."**

— Gen. Pervez Musharraf, former Pakistan President, to BBC Radio 4, September 2006

---

* Statement of Ambassador James Dobbins, "Iran: Reality, Options and Consequences, Part 2—Negotiating with the Iranians: Missed Opportunities and Paths Forward," *Hearing/Testimony Before the Subcommittee on National Security and Foreign Affairs, Committee on Oversight and Government Reform, House of Representatives*, US Government Printing Office, November 07, 2007, at http://www.gpo.gov/fdsys/pkg/CHRG-110hhrg50111/html/CHRG-110hhrg50111.htm

** "West 'will fail' without Pakistan," *BBC Radio 4*, September 30, 2006, at http://news.bbc.co.uk/2/hi/south_asia/5394278.stm

CHAPTER VII

The 'Other' Key Neighbours – Iran, India, China and Russia

The response of the regional countries to the Afghan challenge has been largely determined by their individual relations with the US, and their perceptions about huge Western presence and engagement in Afghanistan right across or in close proximity to their borders. It is a well acknowledged fact that in the immediate aftermath of the tragic events of 9/11, the US under Bush Administration had received tremendous support and cooperation from nearly all of Afghanistan's immediate and extended neighbours. There was enough space and scope for the US to have worked towards a broader regional approach to deal with complex processes of state-building in post-Taliban Afghanistan. But the US-led war on terror was conceived, launched and, more importantly, directed over a decade without fully taking into account the historically competing and ideologically conflicting dynamics of the Af-Pak region. America, perhaps, had no clear idea of what Afghanistan-Pakistan tribal frontier had turned into, a decade since the end of the Cold War.

The initial enthusiasm amongst Afghanistan's neighbours, except for Pakistan, over the overthrow of the Taliban regime and the subsequent signing of the Bonn Agreement quickly dissipated as the US declared Iran part of the "axis of evil" in January 2002 and walked away from Afghanistan into Iraq. The internationally-supported Western intervention thereafter tapered into what was to later become a US-Pakistan maze, with hardly any space for effective cooperation, based on necessary political consensus at the wider regional level, on the issue of counter-terrorism as well as stabilisation and rebuilding of Afghanistan in a sustainable manner. The Western mission, perhaps, was never meant to be this long and engaging. Even as it went through various phases of expansion and extension in later years, it could not fully comprehend and cope with the complex nuances of politics within the Af-Pak region. As a result, despite committing billions of dollars over a decade in Afghanistan and Pakistan put together, and sacrifices of thousands of its soldiers, the process of reviving or rebuilding Afghan state structures remain fragile and vulnerable, and now, even reversible.

As regional countries other than Pakistan too are expected to play a relatively greater role in Afghanistan post-2014, this chapter focuses specifically on the role and response of Afghanistan's supposedly 'other' key neighbours—Iran, India, China & Russia—since the overthrow of the Taliban regime. All the four hardly have had any effective role in the US' Af-Pak strategy. The dominant discourse on Afghanistan, which has thus far been dominated by the Western and Pakistani perspectives despite fundamental divergence in their objectives and policy approaches, perhaps, need to be balanced with a more nuanced understanding of the prevalent perceptions and resultant policy approaches of Iran, India, China and Russia towards developments in Afghanistan.

The deliberate idea here is not to understate or neglect the significance of Pakistan's role, but to take into account a more balanced and a broader regional view as Afghanistan undergoes yet another major transition in its over three-decade-old conflict. The overbearing US-Pakistan calculus, an extension of American unilateralism, has partly been both a cause and a factor for Afghanistan's 'other' key neighbours taking recourse to a more bilateral rather than regional approach, despite tremendous convergence of interest on the Afghan issue. The above-mentioned four countries also happen to be key regional and Asian powers with significant interest and stakes in developments taking place in the Af-Pak region. As the Western forces drawdown, the outcome of the ongoing security and political transition in Afghanistan, and Pakistan's role and response to it, is being closely watched in Tehran, New Delhi, Beijing and Moscow. The role and position of Central Asian neighbours, particularly Tajikistan, Uzbekistan and Kyrgyzstan, which remain wary of possible spill over of the Afghan conflict, has not been discussed here separately. Though they have a huge geo-strategic value in the Afghan context, but relatively limited scope and potential to directly influence and impact the situation in the Af-Pak region.

With the US-led Western coalition playing a lead role in shaping the security and political architecture of post-Taliban Afghanistan, most of Afghanistan's 'other' key neighbours preferred to have a rather cautious wait-and-watch approach, openly sceptical of the American unilateralism or unsure of Western objectives, strategy and level of commitment in Afghanistan. The US invasion of Iraq; the externally-sponsored 'colour revolutions' in parts of post-Soviet space; rising tension with Iran over its nuclear programme; divisions within the Western coalition; and limited or narrow scope of Western counter-terrorism efforts that remained singularly focussed on al Qaeda in the region, further raised concerns and apprehensions over the US' long-term objectives in the region as years passed by.

Even as the West reluctantly came to acknowledge the resurgence of the Taliban 2005-06 onwards, and the numerous challenges it posed for the nascent Afghan Government in years to come, the US Administration hardly showed any inclination for exploring prospects of a wider regional approach to deal with the deteriorating situation in the Af-Pak region. Meanwhile, Pakistan's military-intelligence apparatus having seized on the space and opportunity made available had reactivated and unleashed its old terror infrastructure against the Afghan Government and the Western forces. As the Western coalition and the Haqqani-Taliban network both sought to expand their foot prints and entered into a protracted conflict inside Afghanistan, Rawalpindi quietly pulled itself into a bargaining position *vis-à-vis* Kabul and the West. For the Pakistan Army, it was almost redemption when from a nuclear-armed 'epicentre of global terrorism' it turned into 'major non-NATO ally' of the US. As the ISAF expanded its military operations within Afghanistan, Western dependence on Pakistan increased as much of the supplies for burgeoning Western military presence came through Pakistan. Ironically, despite West committing huge military aid and civil assistance to Pakistan for over a decade, various armed militant groups openly sponsored and backed by the Pakistan Army and intelligence have throughout targeted and inflicted heavy casualties upon the Western coalition troops in Afghanistan. From 2006-07 onwards, the coalition troops as well the Afghan people in general were caught in a vicious war where it was hard to clearly distinguish allies from the enemies.

However, as the ISAF expanded its operations in 2006 and came in direct confrontation with the Taliban guerrillas in their southern strongholds, the idea of finding a political solution to the Afghan war began to be discussed informally and at track II levels. Along with it came up the idea of opening negotiations with the Pakistan-based Afghan Taliban leadership and seeking greater participation of the regional countries in stabilising Afghanistan. The former French President Jacques Chirac had proposed in December 2006 that a 'contact group' on Afghanistan be formed in consultation with Kabul, which would also include Afghanistan's neighbouring countries. The proposal was backed by the then NATO Secretary General Jaap de Hoop Scheffer and EU High Representative for the Common Foreign and Security Policy Javier Solana.[1] Thereafter, German Chancellor Angela Merkel's Christian Democratic Union (CDU) and the NATO Secretary General Jaap de Hoop Scheffer came out with somewhat similar proposals in January 2009, coinciding with the inauguration of Barack Obama as the US President. Merkel's party CDU in its policy paper, 'For a Closer Transatlantic Partnership,' had proposed the establishment of UN-mandated international 'contact group' on Afghanistan as an alternative to committing more troops to the ISAF.[2] At the same time, Scheffer, while speaking in Brussels, too had argued in favour of a broader regional approach in order to succeed in Afghanistan:

> "...we need to stop looking at Afghanistan as if it were an island. Afghanistan's problems cannot be solved by, or within, Afghanistan alone, because they are not Afghanistan's problems alone....If we are going to succeed in this game, we need to be playing on the right field. And that means a more regional approach. To my mind, we need a discussion that brings in all the relevant regional players: Afghanistan, Pakistan, India, China, Russia, and yes, Iran. We need a pragmatic approach to solve this very real challenge."[3]

Similarly, the *Atlantic Council of the United States (ACUS)* in an issue brief released in January 2008, had pointed to the need for a regional approach and solutions to the Afghan crisis as one of its four strategic recommendations. The brief stated, "Bringing in interested parties and neighbors could be done through a meeting or conference that could include the Shanghai Cooperation Organization (of which Russia and China are key members); India; Iran and, of course, Pakistan."[4] Again, the *Afghanistan Study Group Report*, released in January 2008 by the Washington-based *Centre for the Study of the Presidency*, recommended the need to "initiate a regional process to engage Afghanistan's neighbors and potential regional partners in future sustainable development of Afghanistan," which "can begin with relatively minor confidence building measures and the establishment of a regional forum for discussion of common challenges." The report envisages "a multilateral accord involving Afghanistan, all its neighbors, relevant major powers, and the UN" which would eventually enhance stability and the international standing of Afghanistan.[5]

As far as collective efforts at the regional level to deal with the Afghan challenge are concerned, especially since 2009, they have been largely symbolic and declaratory in nature and politically fragmented on account of politics of exclusion and lack of operational capabilities. Some such broad initiatives at the regional level, particularly the Istanbul Process or the "Heart of Asia" Conference and the Regional Economic Cooperation Conference on Afghanistan (RECCA), thus far have had very limited or virtually no success when it comes to coordinating and implementing their key agendas on the ground. Similarly, when it comes to political cooperation to collectively deal with the Afghan challenge, old politics and perceptions tend to come to the fore. Bilateral mechanisms have worked better thus far compared to multilateral ones which remain part of broader diplomacy at the regional level. India and China, two of the most prominent neighbours of Afghanistan, have already entered into long-term partnerships with Kabul. Iran too is working towards it. These bilateral understandings and mechanisms assume greater significance if one looks at Afghanistan together with Pakistan (Af-Pak) as posing a common challenge to the region and beyond. There has been a lot of emphasis on, though not full understanding of, Pakistan's interests and its role in Afghanistan, but not enough on Afghanistan's 'other' key neighbours who largely remain marginal in the Western narrative on Af-Pak. Their significance and position in the broader Af-Pak context, is generally a subject of wide speculation.

Conversely, even as the US decided to work closely with 'military dictatorship' in Pakistan to establish 'democracy' and 'rule of law' in Afghanistan, there was hardly any collective initiative on the part of other regional countries too to deal with the Afghan challenge. Though several bilateral and trilateral consultative mechanisms emerged in due course of time, but they remained largely symbolic and part of ongoing counter moves in the region, often working at cross purposes. Some initiatives though were taken in later years at the regional level, for instance, the SCO Special Conference on Afghanistan held in Moscow the day President Obama announced for the first time his Af-Pak strategy on March 27, 2009, but old geo-political equations and often Cold War mindsets continued to prevent regional countries from forging a common front against rapidly proliferating militant Islamist or pro-*jehadi* forces threatening the entire region. In the above context, it is not clear whether or to what extent most of the regional countries would be amenable to working with the US and NATO after 2014, particularly if the situation in Afghanistan rapidly deteriorates. Of the four 'other' key neighbours, India and Russia have already been cooperating in their own ways with the West in Afghanistan. Though both Iran and China remain opposed to the Western presence, but Beijing is not as vociferous as Tehran in calling for complete withdrawal of Western forces. Chinese response has been relatively nuanced keeping in view the rising threat to its own security, particularly in its south-western borderlands, from al Qaeda-linked militant Islamist and terrorist entities operating in tandem with Uighur militants from within Pakistan.

To begin with, the chapter briefly highlights Pakistan's growing paradoxes and dilemmas as it struggles with terrorism and religious extremism ravaging the country, prior to examining in detail the respective role and response of Afghanistan's 'other' key neighbours since the overthrow of the Taliban regime. The chapter also attempts to interpret their respective evolving strategies in response to Afghanistan's in-transition and post-transition challenges.

Pakistan: Terrorism without Terrorists!

Pakistan's quest for control over the national politics of Afghanistan through its various proxies and their affiliates is an old and continuing phenomenon. It has been a constant feature since before the 1979 Soviet invasion. The source of conflict between the two countries, in fact, has a long and complex history. Pakistan, as part of its struggle to manufacture and construct, and thereafter in its effort to justify and consolidate, a distinct national and cultural identity, has constantly perpetuated enemy images and conflicting perceptions about its immediate neighbours rather than making assets out of them. Seeking parity instead of partnership dictated its policy approaches. Successive governments in Pakistan, particularly the military regimes, have institutionalised and perpetuated negative constructs of existential threat perceptions from outside, disseminated systematically through formal school curriculum and educational text books based on tailored unscientific interpretations of history and culture of the region.

Though Islamabad keeps reiterating how Pakistan itself has been a victim of terrorism and how Pakistani soldiers and civilians have lost their lives either in acts of terrorism or in the fight against terrorism; nevertheless, the terror infrastructure and machinery built and nurtured by successive Pakistani regimes over the decades, remains largely intact and assertive. Though there is a growing realisation within a section of the Pakistani establishment that using terrorism and religious extremism as instruments of state policy against its immediate neighbours is hitting at the very foundation of the Pakistani state and society, but that has not deterred Pakistan's military leadership from sponsoring various militant extremist groups which continue to proliferate in the entire south-central Asia region and beyond, even as it comes at the very expense of the much-needed social and economic development of the people of Pakistan. Today's Pakistan is far more vulnerable to various ideological and security challenges arising from within, rather than from any imagined or projected sources of external threat. The brazen politicisation and instrumentalisation of religion on various pretext by successive Pakistani regimes, has rapidly transformed the socio-political landscape of the country in the last over three decades.

Various local and foreign militant Islamist outfits with abiding links to the al Qaeda-led international network have broadened their social support base and political influence within Pakistan. They have made a serious dent into the traditionally eclectic Sufi traditions of the region and have broadened the sectarian divide to further consolidate their hold over the society. Pakistan's struggle against seeping religious radicalisation, mindless sectarian violence, frequent suicide bombings, unravelling of ethnic fault lines, and a growing culture of socio-religious intolerance, which it had so assiduously tried to export to both Afghanistan and India, is likely to further destabilise the country unless the military and political elite is willing to undertake certain structural reforms within. In its quest to attain parity with India and control over Afghanistan, also as part of its quest to sustain its strategic value for the West, Pakistan is most likely to lose more of itself in the years and decades to come.

Perhaps, Pakistan is the only state in the world which acknowledges the threat from terrorism and also claims to be fighting against it, all of it without ever clearly identifying or stating as to who actually is a terrorist. More interestingly, a cursory glance through regular reporting in Pakistani vernacular media, often regarded as close to the country's military establishment, suggests how instead of acknowledging the role of successive Pakistani regimes and several madrassas patronised by them in mainstreaming religious extremism, intolerance and sectarianism, they have always blamed and sought recourse to ever conspiring outside forces. All ills inside the country are largely projected and constantly propagated as the result of an ever conspiring combine of *yahud-o-hunud-o-nasara* (Jews-Hindus-Christians) or alternatively their respective intelligence agencies. The influence of Pakistan's English media, which is relatively balanced and independent in its reporting and analysis, certainly more critical of the establishment, is confined to the country's progressive and still emerging middle class. The fight against terrorism in Pakistan, thus, remains very selective, narrow and limited. Who is a terrorist in Pakistan or whom the Pakistan state regards as terrorist is still a confusing issue. Pakistan's current struggle against terrorism would not make any sense, until it remains ambivalent or selective in defining and identifying the terrorists.

The biggest dichotomy that Pakistan state faces in its struggle against terrorism is best reflected in the debate over who should be regarded as 'martyr' and 'terrorist' in the conflict between jehadis and the army. How could a Muslim state treat a 'jehadi' as a 'terrorist' and if they cannot be terrorists then against whom are Pakistani forces fighting. Furthermore, a 'jehadi' killed in action has to be a 'martyr,' but then both jehadis and military personnel killed in action against each other cannot be treated as 'martyr' at the same time. Despite the fact that there is a growing acknowledgement of the threat from terrorism and sectarianism within the country, there is still no clarity on who is to be seen and fought as 'terrorist.' Often a 'terrorist' is a 'jehadi' as well. It is equally difficult to ascertain as to who is seen as 'martyr' by Islamabad and Rawalpindi in the ongoing battle between the Pakistan Army and various *jehadi* groups who are no more confined to parts of the Khyber Pakhtunkhwa region. Today they have expanded their reach across the country, from Waziristan to Punjab to Karachi. It is not clear whether the Pakistan Army and intelligence value the sacrifices of its own soldiers more or the *jehadi* groups which while supporting the Afghan insurgents against Western forces in Afghanistan are also targeting the government, the military and the society inside Pakistan.

The Pakistan Army may have over the decades strengthened and reinforced its position within the country by conjuring perceptions of a variety of existential threat from its immediate neighbours, but the dichotomy arising out of its direct conflict of interest with *jehadi* groups earlier sponsored by it, certainly presents a major ideological dilemma and more immediate existential threat for the Pakistan state and society from within. Pakistan is unlikely to overcome its various structural problems, be it civil-military or federal relations, or protracted internal struggle for identity formation and state consolidation, anytime soon. Pakistani leadership is caught in a complex web of *jehadi* politics reworked by al Qaeda after 9/11 within its tribal frontiers, of which the TTP and its various factions and affiliates are a direct by product, and has yet to fully comprehend the long-term challenge it poses for the Pakistani state and society. Until then, Pakistan, particularly the military and intelligence apparatus combined, will continue to be driven by its Cold War mindset of making distinctions between various *jehadi* groups and will remain largely averse to the idea of a stable and a progressive Afghanistan. The Afghan leadership, including President Karzai, has been constantly alluding to it and time and again emphasised on the need for the West to re-strategise the war on terror to address the institutionalised sources of terrorism and Islamist extremism enjoying sustained support from Pakistan.

The US' *aid-and-raid* approach towards Pakistan though has been quite effective in dealing with al Qaeda in the region, it has largely failed in enlisting Rawalpindi's support against the Haqqani group and the Afghan Taliban operating from within Pakistan. The US has also avoided targeting the Afghan Taliban leadership inside Pakistan. The US drone strikes have largely targeted al Qaeda and those Pakistani affiliated militant groups which are considered adversarial by the military establishment in Pakistan. Both Pakistan and the West continue to draw distinction among and between various armed Islamist groups active in the region. While militant Islamist groups which are either considered as dispensable or have turned against the Pakistan military, such as the al Qaeda and certain factions of the TTP, continue to be targeted, several other terrorist entities operating from within Pakistan remain largely intact and active with rather overt support from the country's military and intelligence.

It is no surprise that even when the US 'discovered' Osama bin Laden deep inside Pakistan, where he remained 'hidden' for almost a decade, it failed to bring about any major transformation in its policy approaches towards Pakistan's military and intelligence. The fact that Osama bin Laden was apprehended and eliminated in Abbottabad, which has a very strategic location as one of Pakistan's key military centres closer to the capital Islamabad, the north-western tribal areas where al Qaeda and TTP and their various affiliates have been active since long, and even close to the border with the eastern Kunar Province of Afghanistan where too al Qaeda and its affiliates have a strong presence, was rather a 'defeat' than 'victory' for the Obama Administration. The whole episode speaks of a much larger and a complex game that Pakistan has long been involved in as part of its struggle to retain its salience for both the Western world and the wider global Islamist network, something which evolved or was reinforced with anti-Soviet *jihad* in Afghanistan.

The idea is apparently to retain leverages with both and which could be manoeuvred and played up at various levels, often one against the other, or in whichever way it augments Pakistan's position in the region as well as its strategic value for the West. This perhaps explains as to why Pakistan handed over or allowed the US to carry out drone strikes against low or mid-level al Qaeda operatives in its tribal areas, on one hand, and sheltered Osama bin Laden and his close associates to the extent possible, on the other. This goes way beyond the usual explanation or justification for Pakistan's continuing support to various militant Islamist groups invariably made in the context of its traditional rivalry with India.

Despite conflicting interest with the US and NATO on the Afghan issue, Pakistan remains resentful of possible abandonment by the West as was the case after the Soviet withdrawal from Afghanistan. As the war weary US-led Western coalition prepares to drawdown in Afghanistan, there is not much hope of any structural transformation within Pakistan or change in its policy towards its neighbourhood in the near future. Due to the narrow scope and agenda of the war on terror and short-termism in its approach towards the region, the West largely failed in prioritising and gradually effecting necessary structural transformation in terms of civil military relations within Pakistan.

Degrading al Qaeda while strengthening Pakistan's military may have paid dividends for the US in the short run, but such an approach utterly failed in enlisting Pakistan's full support against growing threat from terrorism and religious extremism to the regional as well as international security. US' long-standing relationship with Pakistan's military establishment has also over the decades undermined democratic and civilian institutions in the country. When Pakistan under former military dictator, General Zia-ul Haq, emerged as the frontline state in the US-led war against Soviet intervention in Afghanistan, Pakistan Army gained tremendously from the huge flow of financial assistance and military hardware of various kinds, further reinforcing its dominant position within the country and its hold over both domestic and international affairs of the state.

However, even after the end of the Cold War, Washington continued to provide arms and strengthen the Pakistan Army and the intelligence. It subsequently emboldened the Pakistan Army to seek direct influence and control over its western neighbour Afghanistan, on one hand, and to sponsor and support a wide range of terrorist networks to inflict maximum damage on its eastern neighbour India, on the other. In the process, however, Pakistan itself turned into an international reservoir, a melting pot, of militant Islamists of various nationalities and persuasions. Almost two generation of militant Islamists of both local and foreign origin have flourished and multiplied several times over inside Pakistan. Their impact on the social structures particular in the north-western tribal areas, and the religious worldview of a generation of youth including in the rural areas of Punjab, has been immense. Looking at the rapid pace of religious radicalisation, proliferation of militant ideologies and groups, relentless sectarian violence and endless suicide bombings across the country, one wonders which particular ideology the military and political elite of the country want the people of Pakistan to identify with, and what exactly is their *vision* of 21st century Pakistan.

All is surely not lost in Pakistan. There are multiple political and social currents within the country, jostling for space and in the process colliding as well as blending into each other, making Pakistan a huge paradox that it is. The resilience of the struggling civil society and relatively bold media in the face of existential threat from various regressive forces from within, and the periodic activism displayed by its judiciary and the resurgence of political parties in recent years, does offer a ray of hope. Though the country has just been through its first ever democratic transfer of power and the current civilian government led by Nawaz Sharif is struggling to frame a comprehensive 'National Counter-Terrorism & Extremism Policy,' the country has a long way to go if it has to evolve into a normal progressive state with strong paradigms of socio-economic development and modern governance. Until then, Pakistan state will remain at conflict at various levels with itself and its immediate neighbours; and, at a more ideological level, with essentially pluralistic and tolerant religious and cultural traditions of the wider south-central Asia region.

IRAN: A DOMINANT FACTOR

Apart from sharing a long border and a longer history with Afghanistan, Iran has been a dominant political factor and a major cultural force in and around Afghanistan. This is where Iran completely stands out in relation to Afghanistan's other immediate neighbours. Also, Iran, unlike Pakistan, has a well settled border with Afghanistan, though, like Pakistan, it too is host to millions of Afghan refugees. Iranian role and involvement in the Afghan conflict has been conspicuously complex and multi-layered, often influenced and complicated by changing regional dynamics. On the one hand, if Iran's strong civilisational heritage, which spreads far and deep in the region, helps it to connect and communicate with diverse nationalities in its neighbourhood with relative ease; its pronounced Shiite identity with a confrontationist political legacy of an Islamic revolution, on the other, limits its ability to redefine its relationships within the region and the wider Western world.

For a landlocked and multi-ethnic Afghanistan, Iran holds immense strategic value and is considered a key factor in the country's over all security and economic calculus. As for Iran, it has invariably been more concerned about the larger objectives of the American presence than the possible implications of total Western withdrawal from Afghanistan. Though the US invasion of Afghanistan and subsequently in Iraq benefited Iran, but at the same time it also complicated the regional environment for Iran given its known scepticism about American unilateralism in the region. In view of its long standing adversarial relationship with the US, the incremental presence of the Western military right across its borders, raised Tehran's threat perceptions and dictated its response strategies. Iran has consistently called for total withdrawal of the Western forces from the region. Thus, America remains a notably huge factor in Iran's Afghanistan policy. In fact, Iran's role and presence in Afghanistan is to a large extent shaped by its own perceptions and assessments about American objectives in the region. According to Barnett R. Rubin, a leading authority on Afghanistan, "The overall Iranian role has been to work closely with us to bring Karzai into power. However, the Iranians believe the No. 1 threat is an American attack to overthrow their government. They may do anything it takes to make the United States and its allies uncomfortable there."[6] However, as the Western forces drawdown and as several transitions take place in Afghanistan, it is particularly important to examine Iran's supposedly complex political role in Afghanistan.

Context to Iran's Alleged Support to the Taliban

The US and NATO commanders have often accused Iran of supporting the Taliban elements as part of its continuing effort to counter and undermine the American endeavour in Afghanistan. Iran's alleged support for the Taliban also coincided with growing violence in some of the relatively peaceful south-western parts of Afghanistan, as well as forced repatriation of Afghan refugees from Iran. This brought in a new element into the complex equation between the US and Iran at the wider regional level. It was reflective of the evolving regional dynamics particularly since the US invasion of Iraq in March 2003 and labelling of Tehran as part of the "axis of evil" earlier in January 2002.

Whether Iran is supporting the Taliban or not has been a subject of wide speculation, but that Iran has been raising its profile in the region in view of the strong US presence in its immediate western and eastern neighbourhood, Iraq and Afghanistan, is a matter of fact. Though the US forces have completely pulled out of Iraq, nevertheless, Iran's continuing insecurity due to the US unilateralism and regime changes in the region and, more importantly, stand off with the West over its nuclear programme, continue to determine Iranian policy and response strategies towards both Afghanistan and Iraq. It is, therefore, pertinent to examine the role and position of Iran in Afghanistan and the sort of balancing act the Afghan Government has been trying to do in view of the ongoing US-Iranian stand-off.

It is generally believed that Shiite Iran and strictly Sunni Afghan factions particularly the Taliban make natural enemies, and that their mutual perceptions and respective ideological nuances mark a great divide in the regional polity. However, contrary to the above, there have been numerous precedents of linkages/ interactions between the two in the past as well as in the present. What is often clearly missed out is the strong element of shifting loyalties and changing alignments prevalent in the Afghan politics which would often throw bizarre alliances and combinations among various actors jockeying for leverage and influence within Afghanistan. In the context of Iranian involvement, the most notable instance was that of the Hezb-e Islami leader, Gulbuddin Hekmatyar, known for his militant Sunni Islamist leaning, who had shifted to Tehran after he was forced to flee under Taliban pressure from his base in Charasayab in eastern Afghanistan in 1995. In 1999, Hekmatyar had reportedly joined the Iranian-backed Cyprus Process which largely comprised of Afghan exiles based in Cyprus. Pakistan had already forsaken him in favour of the rising Taliban. Until then, it was unthinkable that a radical Sunni Islamist like Hekmatyar, who was known for his anti-Shiia stance, would find shelter in Shiite Iran of all the countries in the region.

Hekmatyar ran his Hezb office from Tehran from 1995 until his expulsion in February 2002.[7] Interestingly, while still exiled in Iran, he had announced his support for Osama bin Laden and the Taliban immediately after 9/11 on September 18, 2001. By October 26, 2001, he was reported to be in talks with the Taliban who too were known for their anti-Shiite bias. Later, in February 2003, reports appeared suggesting Hezb-e Islami's alliance with the al Qaeda and the Taliban. Perhaps, Hekmatyar's presence in Iran could be seen as latter's first major attempt to cultivate a Sunni Pashtun leader, either with the objective of further expanding its leverages within Afghanistan, including among the Pashtuns, or at least initially as counter to the Pakistan-backed Taliban, an equally radical and predominantly Sunni Pashtun group.

The Iranian-Taliban relations were said to be generally far from cordial, especially after the killing of 11 Iranian diplomats at its consulate in Mazar-e Sharif in 1998 allegedly by the Taliban.[8] However, the possibility of a section of Taliban leadership wanting to improve relations with a huge and influential neighbour like Iran cannot be completely ruled out. It was said that some of the senior members of the Taliban regime in Kabul, especially the then Foreign Minister Mullah Muttawakil, and his deputy, Sher Mohammad Abbas Stanakzai, were in favour of improving relations with Iran, though the same cannot be said about the Kandahar Shura headed by Mullah Omar. Possibly, there were strong differences of opinion within the Taliban leadership on the issue of engaging Iran.[9] Interestingly, later in July 2009, a report based on several hearings and testimonies of the former Taliban Governor of Herat, Mullah Khairullah Khairkhwa, who has been a detainee at Guantanamo Bay since 2002, informs about at least two visits made by Taliban officials from Kandahar to Iran, whom Khairkhwa had accompanied, in January 2000 and November 2001.[10]

However, the events of 9/11 were to soon change the regional dynamics as the US launched the *Operation Enduring Freedom* (OEF) in Afghanistan in October 2001 and later *Operation Iraqi Freedom* in March 2003. After the overthrow of the Taliban regime, Iran along with other neighbouring countries like India and Russia had played a significant role in building consensus among disparate Afghan groups on some very critical issues during the first Bonn Conference held in Germany from November 27-December 05, 2001. Given Iran's old leverage over the Northern Alliance, the Bonn Conference provided an opportunity for Iran and the US to briefly work together on the Afghan issue. This was later attested by the US special representative to the Bonn Conference, James F. Dobbins, currently the US special representative for Afghanistan and Pakistan, when he stated, "I was told I could deal with them (Iran) any time, any where under any circumstances as long as we were talking about Afghanistan." Dobbins acknowledged the crucial role played by the Iranians in persuading the Northern Alliance leaders when there was a deadlock on the issue of allocation of portfolios in the new Afghan Government.[11] However, within few months of it, any prospect of a thaw in relations between the two countries was completely blocked when the Bush Administration labelled Iran as member of the "axis of evil" along with Iraq and North Korea in January 2002.

It is worth noting what Dobbins, who was President Bush's first special representative to Afghanistan after 9/11, had stated later in November 2007 in relation to Iran in his testimony before the US House of Representatives:

> In January 2002, the President in his inaugural address included Iran in what he characterized as an axis of evil. Despite that, the Iranians persisted for a number of months in offering significant cooperation to the United States. For instance, in March 2002, the Iranian delegation asked to meet with me on the fringes of an international meeting in Geneva that I was chairing on assistance to Afghanistan. They introduced me to an Iranian general in full uniform who had been the commander of their security assistance efforts to the Northern Alliance throughout the war. The general said that Iran was willing to contribute to an American-led program to build the new Afghan national army. "We are prepared to house and train up to 20,000 troops in a broader program under American leadership," the general offered. "Well, if you train some Afghan troops and we train some, might they not end up having incompatible doctrines?" I responded somewhat skeptically. The general just laughed. He said, "Don't worry, we are still using the manuals you left behind in 1979."[12]

During the same hearing, Hillary Mann Leverett, a career foreign service officer who had directly participated in negotiations with Iran on behalf of the U.S. Government from 2001 to 2003 and shortly after 9/11 was called to serve as the Iran expert on the National Security Council, too while elaborating on Iranian assistance and willingness for broad engagement with the US had stated in her testimony:

> With regard to post 9/11 cooperation over Afghanistan, Iran hoped and anticipated that tactical cooperation with the United States would led to a genuine strategic opening between our two countries. In most cases, however, it was the United States that was unwilling to sustain and buildupon tactical cooperation to pursue true strategic rapprochement.
>
> In late spring 2001, I was a U.S. Foreign Service officer at the U.S. mission to the U.N. in New York responsible for dealing with Afghanistan. In that capacity, I was authorized to work with my Iranian counterpart as part of the Six Plus Two diplomatic process that had been set up by the United States to deal with the threats Afghanistan posed to the international community, even before 9/11. My Iranian counterpart and I worked openly and constructively on a wide range of Afghan-related issues, including the enforcement of an arms embargo on the Taliban regime, counter-narcotics initiatives and humanitarian relief for Afghan refugees, 2 million of whom were in Iran.
>
> For the first 2 months after 9/11, I worked openly and intensively with my Iranian counterpart to establish a framework for U.S.-Iranian cooperation in Afghanistan. My Iranian counterpart said that Iran was prepared to offer unconditional cooperation to the United States. Iran would not ask the United States for anything up front in return for its cooperation with Afghanistan. As I document in my written testimony, in the months after 9/11, Iran provided tangible support to United States and Coalition military operations in Afghanistan and robust support to U.S. efforts to stand up a post-Taliban political order, culminating in the Bonn Conference.
>
> Following the Bonn Conference...the Iranians provided considerable assistance to bolster the pro-American Karzai government in Afghanistan and on counter-terrorism, including deporting hundreds of al Qaeda and Taliban figures seeking to flee Afghanistan to or through Iran. The Iranians skipped one monthly meeting to protest President Bush's public condemnation of Iran as part of the axis of evil in January 2002, but otherwise they came to every monthly meeting over the 17 month course of the talks.
>
> It is important to emphasize that in the monthly meetings, my Iranian counterparts repeatedly raised the prospect of broadening our common agenda, both to achieve a strategic rapprochement between the United States and Iran, as well as to provide tactical support to a prospective U.S. attack on Saddam's Iraq. The prospect of rapprochement with Iraq had been explicitly rejected by the President and his senior national security team.[13]

With the US invasion of Iraq in March 2003, a sceptical Iran found itself encircled by the US. Though, on one hand, the US invasion of Afghanistan and Iraq helped destroy Iran's two biggest rival regimes, Taliban and Saddam Hussein, but, on the other hand, it led to a strong US presence close to its eastern and western borders. Increasingly wary of the continuing US adventurism in its immediate neighbourhood, coupled with Bush Administration refusing to further engage Iran, Tehran soon sought to assert its influence by way of leveraging its position in both Iraq and Afghanistan. Meanwhile, as was revealed later in May-June 2006, Iran had tried to reach out to the Bush Administration after the overthrow of the Saddam Hussain regime in Iraq in early 2003. The Swiss Government had reportedly forwarded a two-page document from the Iranian Government proposing dialogue between the two countries on a wide range of issues. It was reported by *The Washington Post* that:

> The document lists a series of Iranian aims for the talks, such as ending sanctions, full access to peaceful nuclear technology and a recognition of its "legitimate security interests." Iran agreed to put a series of U.S. aims on the agenda, including full cooperation on nuclear safeguards, "decisive action" against terrorists, coordination in Iraq, ending "material support" for Palestinian militias and accepting the Saudi initiative for a two-state solution in the Israeli-Palestinian conflict. The document also laid out an agenda for negotiations, with possible steps to be achieved at a first meeting and the development of negotiating road maps on disarmament, terrorism and economic cooperation.[14]

The same was acknowledged later by Leverett too in her November 2007 testimony before the US House of Representatives:

> By the spring of 2003, the dialog was at an impasse. It is in this context that one should evaluate the Iranian offer to negotiate a comprehensive resolution of differences with the United States. With the bilateral channel at an impasse, Tehran sent this offer in early May 2003 through Switzerland, the U.S.-protecting power in Iran, as Secretary Rice and former administration officials have acknowledged. In the offer, everything would be on the table, including Iran's material support for Hamas, for PIJ, for Hizballah as well as its nuclear ambitions and role in Iraq. But the Bush administration rejected this proposal out of hand and cutoff the bilateral channel with the Iranians less than 2 weeks later.[15]

The Bush Administration, thus, did not acknowledge the Iranian initiative and instead continued with sanctions regime on Iran along with the IAEA. The letter diplomacy between the two countries had started in July 1999 with former American President Bill Clinton sending a letter to then Iranian President Mohammad Khatami, through Omani foreign minister, seeking Tehran's support in the investigation of Khobar Towers Bombing of June 1996 in Saudi Arabia in which 19 American servicemen were killed.[16] In its response to President Clinton's letter in early September 1999, the Iranian Government rubbished the allegations made against Iran, calling it "inaccurate" and "unfounded."[17] In November 2000, it was reported quoting *Tehran Times* that President Clinton has written another letter to the Iranian Government, which was delivered on October 20 by the Swiss Embassy officials based in Tehran, expressing desire for opening talks on various issues of concern.[18]

Later, in 2006, it was reported that President Mahmoud Ahmedinejad too had written a letter to the Bush Administration. The reported letter in a way brought out the long list of historical grievances and resentment that has shaped the Iranian leadership's perception of the US: "the coup d'etat of 1953 and the subsequent toppling of the legal government of the day, opposition to the Islamic revolution, transformation of an Embassy into a headquarters supporting the activities of those opposing the Islamic Republic, support for Saddam in the war waged against Iran, the shooting down of the Iranian passenger plane, freezing the assets of the Iranian nation, increasing threats, anger and displeasure vis-a-vis the scientific and nuclear progress of the Iranian nation."[19]

Though the letter diplomacy failed to bring about any major breakthrough in the US-Iran relations frozen since 1979-80, but it did bring out the sense of urgency felt from time to time by both the American and the Iranian establishment to engage each other. Both the countries, however, have had phases of limited cooperation in Iraq and on the Afghan issue. Bush Administration missed a huge opportunity that came with the unprecedented support Iran extended to Washington in the immediate aftermath of 9/11, to redefine America's relations with Tehran. In fact, Washington completely failed to comprehend the various nuances of the regional dynamics while waging wars in Afghanistan and Iraq.

Within days of the tragedy that struck America on 9/11, Iran, in contrast to Washington's 'most allied ally,' Pakistan, had offered its full assistance and cooperation against al Qaeda and the Taliban regime in Afghanistan. The Iranian view at the time was, perhaps, best summed up by an anonymous high ranking Iranian diplomat, quoted in an article published in *The National Interest* in 2007:

> The general impression was that [9/11] was a national tragedy for the United States and that success in addressing that national tragedy was extremely important for the U.S. public in general and the administration in particular.... There was not another moment in U.S. history when there was more of a psychological need for success on the U.S. part. That is why we consciously decided not to qualify our cooperation on Afghanistan or make it contingent upon a change in U.S. policy, believing, erroneously, that the impact would be of such magnitude that it would automatically have altered the nature of Iran-U.S. relations.[20]

Sadat and Hughes in their article published in *Middle East Council*, quoting a former CIA intelligence analyst on the Middle East, Kenneth Pollack, inform that:

> While members of the six-plus-two group, such as Russia and Pakistan, opposed a U.S. invasion of Afghanistan, Iran supported the plan. Officials from the United States and Iran began meeting outside the six-plus-two forum to develop a plan to topple the Taliban. These meetings became known as the Geneva Contact Group, and although the Germans, Italians and the United Nations provided some political cover for these discussions, the group's focus was U.S.-Iran cooperation on Afghanistan.[21] Iran not (only) provided reliable intelligence regarding the Taliban, it arrested and deported hundreds of Al-Qaeda and Taliban fighters who had crossed into the country for sanctuary.[22]
>
> Pollack adds that the Iranian government also provided search and rescue for downed U.S. aircrew members. Iran permitted the offloading of humanitarian supplies at its port of Chah Bahar for transport into Afghanistan, and offered access to airfields near the Afghan border for use by U.S. transport aircraft. Iran also supported the initial discussions between the United States and the Northern Alliance, which enabled subsequent military success against the Taliban.[23] After the fall of the Taliban regime in late 2001, Iran played a critical role in international efforts to establish a new Afghan government and pledged and honored commitments toward Afghanistan's reconstruction. Through interaction with Iranian diplomats in this forum, U.S. officials succeeded in curbing the anti-U.S. activities of Iran's security and intelligence services inside Afghanistan.[24] Whether motivated by national interest or international goodwill, Tehran's participation in the Geneva Contact Group demonstrates a pragmatic foreign-policy approach indicating that U.S. engagement with Iran on common areas of interest in Afghanistan is achievable, despite disagreements on unrelated issues.[25]

The year 2003-04, however, saw escalating tensions between Iran and the IAEA and the US on the former's nuclear programme, which has since lingered on though a somewhat fragile interim deal was reached much later in November 2013 with P5+1. By 2005-06, fearing possible US invasion in view of rising tension between the two countries, Iran began to leverage its role in the Iraqi as well as the Afghan politics. The US commanders in Afghanistan soon began reporting about the influx of large quantities of Iranian-made weapons in Taliban-infested areas in western and southern parts of the country. On April 17, 2007, for the first time a senior American official, General Peter Pace, then Chairman of the Joint Chiefs of Staff, stated that, "we know that there are munitions that were made in Iran that are in Iraq and in Afghanistan. And we know that the Quds Force works for the I.R.G.C. We then surmise from that one or two things.

Either the leadership of the country knows what their armed forces are doing, or that they don't know. And in either case that's a problem." But at the same time, he had remarked that it is not clear as to which "Iranian entity" is responsible for it.[26] It was further reported that the said shipment which was intercepted in the Kandahar region by the Western coalition force involved mortars and C-4 type plastic explosives, similar to ones found in Iraq. In fact, the US commanders in Iraq too were accusing Iran of supplying components of roadside bombs to the shiite militants. They remained suspicious about the role of Quds Force, an elite unit of the Islamic Revolutionary Guards Corps (IRGC), in arming shiite insurgents in Iraq.[27]

However, while American and ISAF commanders continued to allege from time to time the Iranian complicity in arming the Taliban, but there assessments were generally incoherent and vague in the absence of any credible evidence. Initially, at least, the allegations were largely based on the recovery of Iranian-made weapons or components of commonly available weaponry within Iraq. Even before there were some anonymous US military briefs talking about Iranian involvement "at highest levels." But such claims were promptly rubbished by the former top US commander in Afghanistan, Lt. Gen. Karl Eikenberry, saying that there were no concrete evidences of Taliban guerrillas receiving Iranian weapons. It is noteworthy that Eikenberry at the same time maintained that Iranian security organisations were maintaining contacts with the Taliban.[28]

In early May 2007, the ISAF commanders too began reporting about Iranian-made weapons being seized in parts of Afghanistan during counter-insurgency operations. However, like General Peter Pace, the then ISAF Spokesperson Lt. Col. Maria Carl also stopped short of directly accusing the Iranian Government of providing weapons to the Taliban insurgents in the absence of concrete evidence, though she stated that the weapons seized including RPG-7 launchers, light guns and explosive devices "bore the distinct hallmarks of Iran."[29]

On June 01, 2007, for the first time a senior Afghan security official, Maj. Gen. Kiramuddin Yawar, border police chief for the western zone, claimed having seized six Iranian-made bombs in the relatively peaceful Ghorian District of the western Herat Province.[30] On June 04, 2007, the then US Defence Secretary Robert Gates in a joint press briefing with President Karzai during his visit to Kabul had stated that, "There have been indications over the past few months of weapons coming in from Iran," but was quick to add "we do not have any information about whether the government of Iran is supporting this, is behind it, or whether it's smuggling or exactly what's behind this."[31] In his statement, President Karzai categorically denied having any evidence so far in this regard and instead strongly defended Kabul's ties with Tehran stating, "We have a very good relationship with the Iranian government. Iran and Afghanistan have never been as friendly as they are today. In the past five years, Iran has been contributing to Afghanistan reconstruction. And in the past five years, Afghanistan has been Iran's very close friend."[32]

It is noteworthy that Kabul at no point of time joined the US and Britain in accusing Iran of supporting the Taliban by way of supplying weapons to them. Even when thousands of Afghan refugees were being forcibly pushed from across the border into western Afghanistan, Kabul maintained a tremendous semblance of calm and diplomatic goodwill *vis-à-vis* Tehran. The strategy adopted by Kabul was to steer clear of the long-standing animosity between the two countries which has been further exacerbated by a strong US presence in the Persian Gulf, Iraq and Afghanistan. However, given the influence of Iran in the regional politics Kabul decided to strike a balance between its strategic partnership with both the US and Iran.

During President Hamid Karzai's visit to Camp David for a two-day summit meeting with President George W. Bush on August 06-07, 2007, their differences of opinion on the issue of Iranian role in Afghanistan clearly came to the fore. Karzai had reportedly characterised Iran as "a helper and a solution" in an interview to the *CNN television* on August 05.[33] He added, "Iran has been a supporter of Afghanistan, in the peace process that we have and the fight against terror, and the fight against narcotics in Afghanistan." He went on to say that Afghanistan and Iran had "very, very good, very, very close relations. ... We will continue to have good relations with Iran. We will continue to resolve issues, if there are any, to arise."[34] But when he met Bush, the latter pointedly expressed his disagreement with Karzai's assessment and said, "I would be very cautious about whether the Iranian influence in Afghanistan is a positive force." He further added that it is "up to Iran to prove to the world that they are a stabilizing force as opposed to a destabilizing force."[35]

Again, during Iranian president's maiden visit to Kabul on August 14, 2007, Karzai had paid glowing tributes to the Afghan-Iranian relations, and, quite significantly, offered to help bring about a thaw in relations between Washington and Tehran. In his welcome address, he described relations between the two nations as "friendly and historic," and added, "Iran in the past five years since the Bonn Agreement has been helping people of Afghanistan in their efforts for security, counterterrorism, reconstruction and improving people's life." Describing Iran and Afghanistan as "two brother nations with common interests, cultures and histories," President Ahmadinejad further observed that, "we are neighbors whose relationship can not be bound by any restrictions; neighbors are the natural allies."[36] Iran and Afghanistan later signed six bilateral cooperation agreements.

Apparently, in an effort to strike balance in Kabul's ties with both Washington and Tehran, Karzai ascribed the success of Afghan-Iranian relations to the support and understanding of the international community and especially the US, and success of Kabul's ties with Washington, to the Iranian support and understanding.[37] Interestingly, within days Gates changes his statement when he openly stated on June 13, 2007 during his visit to Germany that, "Given the quantities that were seeing, it is difficult to believe that it's associated with smuggling or the drug business or that it's taking place without the knowledge of the Iranian government."[38] A day earlier, on June 12, 2007, the then US Undersecretary of State Nicholas Burns had told to the *CNN* that the US has "irrefutable evidence" that IRGC is arming Taliban fighters in Afghanistan.[39] Again, within days of statements from Pace, Burns and Gates, it was reported that Colonel Rahmatullah Safi, an Afghan border guard commander for three provinces bordering Iran, in his interview to the German news agency, *dpa*, on June 19 claimed that around 20 armed men had crossed over from Iran into the western province of Farah, where the Taliban activity was said to be on rise since early 2007. However, Rafi too, within days of his statement, denied having any evidence of Iranian Government's involvement in supplying arms to groups inside Afghanistan. On June 21, 2007, reacting to several such reports and statements, the Iranian Deputy Foreign Minister Mehdi Safari was quoted by the Iranian state news agency, *Islamic Republic News Agency* (IRNA), as stating that the allegations are "so unfounded and irrational" that independent officials in both the US and the UK have termed the claims as "unsubstantiated and unreal."[40]

On July 17, 2007, the then US Ambassador to Afghanistan, William Wood, had also remarked that "there are clearly some munitions coming out of Iran going into the hands of the Taliban. We believe that the quantity and quality of those munitions are such that the Iranian government must know about it."[41] On July 21, 2007, a member of the *Wolesi Jirga* or the lower house of the Afghan Parliament from the western Herat Province reportedly claimed that Iran has converted former *mujahideen* camps like Turbat Jam, Birjand, Taibat and Hajiabad areas into training camps for the anti-government elements. He said people who have returned from these camps to Herat and Farah Province have claimed that some high ranking Taliban commanders have also been visiting those training camps. He further said that Yahya Khurdturk, a former commander of the Islamic Movement of Shiekh Asif Mohsini and currently a member of the Islamic United Front of Ustad Akbari, a leader of the Shia community, had also received training along with his fighters at those camps. Yahya was said to be directly linked to the Revolutionary Guards known as *Sipah-i-Pasdaran*, which is said to have built a base called Muhammad Rasullullah in Pul-e Band area, located between Turbat Jam and Taibat on the border region. Another base was said to be located in Birjand area, bordering Farah Province of Afghanistan. Ahmad Behzad, another MP from Herat province, also accused *Sepah-i Qudus* (sacred force), a wing of the *Pasdaran*, of organising and equipping opposition forces inside Afghanistan as well as training them at the centres in Iran. He added that, "We have information that such centres are existing not only in the border areas, but also in remote provinces."[42]

General Rahmatullah Safi, border commander of the three western provinces (Herat, Farah and Badghis), also confirmed of intelligence reports suggesting presence of training camps and movement of militants from across the Iranian border, especially by Yahya Khurdturk's group. He claimed to have arrested a member of Yahya group who had confessed to smuggling narcotics to the other side of the border. He was of the opinion that Yahya group comprised of some 45 men, who were trained in terrorist activities and smuggling.[43] The very next day on July 18, the ISAF reported the discovery of several Iranian-made armour piercing explosives similar to ones used by Shiite insurgents in Iraq and Hezbollah in Lebanon in the western Afghan province of Herat bordering Iran and also in Kabul. These were said to be "something called explosively-formed projectiles (EFPs)" which are "designed to penetrate armored vehicles." But, at the same time, the senior spokeswoman for the ISAF, US Lt. Col. Claudia Foss, stressed that "we have no evidence of any formal supply of weapons from Iran."[44]

On August 14, 2007, on the eve of the then Iranian President Mahmoud Ahmadinejad's visit to Kabul, Balkh intelligence officials claimed having recovered a hundred Iranian-made improvised explosive devices (IED) in the northern border town of Hairatan. This was for the first time that Iranian-made weapons were seized from northern Afghanistan.[45] In January 2008, the police chief of Farah Province claimed to have discovered a large cache of various kinds of Iranian-made mines in the house of a Taliban commander, Abdul Ghani, in the Anaradara District of the province.[46]

As expected, the Iranian Government all through rejected the above allegations as baseless and illogical. President Ahmedinejad during his visit to Kabul on August 14, 2007, while expressing his "serious doubts" over the US charges on his country of covertly supplying weapons to the Taliban, had remarked that, "We support the political process in Afghanistan with all our strength and power." He added, "The security of Afghanistan has a [direct] impact on Iran because we [share] the longest borders and, for us, a secure and powerful Afghanistan is what is best."[47] In fact, Iran regarded the US accusations as part of a larger anti-Iranian campaign and has often argued that it makes no sense for a Shiite country like Iran to help strengthen the fundamentalist Sunni Taliban. Between September 2007 and March 2008 there was relative lull in the US tirade against Iran's alleged role in arming the Afghan Taliban.

Interestingly, while allegations were being made against Iran for strengthening the Taliban, Iran was forcibly repatriating thousands of Afghan refugees back into Afghanistan. It was in November 2006 when the Iranian Government had declared that Afghan workers illegally residing in Iran will be deported and that their Iranian employers will face fines if they fail to lay off illegal Afghan workers. According to Iranian officials, besides the 960,000 Afghans registered as refugees in Iran, around one to two million Afghan refugees are residing illegally in that country.[48] According to the United Nations High Commissioner for Refugees (UNHCR), there are 920,000 registered Afghan refugees in Iran and perhaps a million more illegal Afghan refugees.

However, Iran finally started evicting Afghan refugees on April 21, 2007. By the first week of May, Iran was reported to have forcibly expelled about 50, 000 Afghan refugees.[49] Both Presidential Spokesman Karim Rahimi and Foreign Minister Rangin Dadfar Spanta had expressed their resentment over the forced expulsion of the Afghan refugees in such large numbers by Iran, especially given the Afghan Government's lack of resources and means to manage such a massive influx of refugees.[50] As Iran tried to force Afghan migrants back into Afghanistan, there were later instances of clashes taking place between Iranian guards and Afghan police along the borders. For instance, in April 2008, it was reported by *Reuters* that about a dozen Afghan refugees have been killed allegedly by Iranian guards inside the Afghan border with Iran in the western Herat Province.[51] In the same month, the *Associated Press* reported about a clash between Iranian and Afghan border guards in south-western Nimroz Province bordering Iran.[52] The then Afghan Foreign Minister Spanta, however, again ruled out alleged Iranian interference. Calling Iran a "brotherly" and "friendly" country, he stated: "There are rumors about Iran's interference in Afghan domestic affairs, but I once again emphasize that there is no document to that effect. What the Iranian foreign minister and president say is important for us not what others claim."[53]

The refugee crisis generated a heated debate in and outside the Afghan Parliament. Apart from Afghan Foreign Minister Spanta speaking to his Iranian counterpart Manouchehr Mottaki, the then *Wolesi Jirga* Speaker Yunus Qanuni also reportedly spoke to his Iranian counterpart on the issue. There were many opinions with regard to the timing of the Iranian decision to expel a large number of Afghan refugees. However, it is generally believed that Iran fearing a possible attack by the US wanted to destabilise western Afghanistan by funnelling weapons to the Taliban and flooding the region with thousands of refugees as the US was said to be building a strategic airfield at Shindand in Herat Province close to the Iranian border since 2003. According to Ian Kemp, an independent defence analyst in London, "the presence of US forces at Shindand is seen by Tehran as a threat because Shindand could serve as a launching point if the United States decided to attack Iran's nuclear facilities from the air."[54]

Whereas, according to Ahmed Rashid, though convinced of the argument that Iran wants to make things difficult for the US, it still need not force Afghan refugees into Afghanistan as Iran has had "long-running relations with many of the commanders and small-time warlords in western Afghanistan—both Pashtun and non-Pashtun." Rashid added, "I have no doubt that Iran has been involved in channeling money and arms to various elements in Afghanistan, including the Taliban, for the last few years. I think Iran is playing all sides in the Afghan conflict. There are Pashtuns and non-Pashtuns who are being funded by Iran who are active in western Afghanistan. If the Iranians are convinced that the Americans are undermining them through western Afghanistan, then it is very likely that these agents of theirs have been activated."[55]

According to another opinion, there is no need to give too much of credence to reports about Iranian weapons interdicted in Afghanistan as old weaponry from many neighbouring and other countries have been afloat in Afghanistan since 1980s. Apart from this, al Qaeda or drug mafias active on the Afghan-Iranian border could have also brought Iranian weapons to Afghanistan. Peter Lehr, an expert on South Asia at St. Andrews University in Scotland, is of the opinion that, "If you take a look at the weapons smuggling, well that's been going on for decades. That is part of this drug route where heroin is shipped from Afghanistan via Iran and other countries and Russia to Europe. The best way of paying for drugs is either, of course, with money—or with weapons. And there is not even circumstantial evidence that the Iranian state, itself, is involved with that. That is organized-crime groups."[56]

There is an economic explanation to the Iranian decision to expel Afghan refugees as well. It was said that Iran has been facing serious internal economic difficulties owing to sanctions which have contributed to inflation and unemployment. By expelling thousands of Afghans, Tehran could have thought of generating employment for its own citizens.[57] Whatever may have been the reasons for the Iranian decision, the western regions of Afghanistan as a result were flooded with helpless Afghan refugees. It generated a huge debate in the Afghan Parliament which ultimately led to the removal of the then Minister of Refugees Muhammad Akbar Akbar on May 10, 2007. It also led to an impasse between President Karzai's office and the Parliament which had passed a vote of no confidence against Spanta as well on May 12, 2007. The treatment meted out to Afghan refugees in Iran has since been a cause of major concern for Kabul.

As the tension with Iran over its nuclear programme and its alleged role in arming Shiite militias in Iraq intensified in 2008, senior US officials and military commanders became more critical of the Iranian role in both Iraq and Afghanistan and the wider West Asian region. On April 24, 2008, former Principal Deputy Assistant Secretary, International Security and Nonproliferation, Patricia McNerney, in her testimony before the Senate Homeland Security and Governmental Affairs Committee, had clearly stated:

> "Iran presents a profound threat to U.S. national security interests. The radical regime in Tehran threatens regional and international security through its pursuit of technologies that could give it the capability to produce nuclear weapons, its support for terrorist groups and militants in Iraq, Afghanistan, Syria, Lebanon, and the Palestinian territories, its destabilizing regional activities, and its lack of respect for human rights and civil society." According to McNerney, "a nuclear-armed Iran would threaten countries on three continents, and potentially even the U.S. homeland directly sometime late next decade. A nuclear-armed Iran would also intimidate moderate states in the region and embolden Iran's support for Hizballah, certain Iraqi Shia militants, the Taliban, and Palestinian terrorist and rejectionist groups." Calling Iran "the world's most active state sponsor of terrorism", McNerney alleged that it "provides financial and lethal support to Hizballah, HAMAS, Palestinian Islamic Jihad, as well as to certain Iraqi militant groups and the Taliban."
>
> McNerney in her testimony further stated, "To respond to the range of challenges presented by Iran, the Administration has stressed the use of all tools and options available, including multilateral and bilateral diplomacy, financial and economic measures, counterproliferation actions such as interdictions, and, as a final resort, the threat and use of military force," and reminded how since May 2006 the US "have presented Iran with an increasingly stark choice between two paths: confrontation and isolation; or, cooperation and reward." Terming the role of the Qods Force of the IRGC in supporting foreign militants as "extremely problematic", McNerney claimed that it "provides lethal assistance to the Taliban, threatening Afghan, Coalition, and NATO forces operating under UN mandate in Afghanistan" and "has arranged a number of shipments of small arms and associated ammunition, rocket propelled grenades, mortar rounds, 107mm rockets, and explosives—including armor piercing explosively formed projectiles."
>
> McNerney further stated, "Recoveries of interdicted weaponry, ordnance, and EFPs in Afghanistan indicate the Taliban has Iranian weaponry. Weapons transfers to these groups violate Iran's Chapter VII obligation under UN Security Council Resolution 1747 not to export arms. Iran has also violated UNSCR 1267 and successor resolutions by failing to impose sanctions on al-Qaida and continues to refuse to bring to justice or confirm the whereabouts of senior al Qaida members it detained in 2003."[58]

On April 30, 2008, the then US Chief of Operations Lt. Gen. Carter Ham was quoted as stating that, "There is indication that the Iranian support of the Taliban has continued." Ham added, "We don't believe it to be at the same level which they have provided fighters and weapons into Iraq, but there is some clear evidence."[59] By now there was apparently greater clarity in the American assessment about Iran's complex role in Afghanistan. On May 06, 2008, the US Assistant Secretary of State for South and Central Asia, Richard Boucher, during a press conference in Paris, stated that Iran "interfere in a variety of different ways, perhaps not as violently as they do sometimes in Iraq." He added, "what we see is Iranian interference politically, Iranian interference in terms of the money that they channel into the political process, Iranian interference in terms of playing off local officials against central government, trying to undermine the state in that way. In many ways they (Tehran) do support the work of the government, but they also work with the political opposition." Boucher also alleged that, "They have funnelled some weapons to the Taliban, they seem kind of working with everybody to be hedging their bets, or just looking...like they want weakness or instability in Afghanistan more than anything else." Referring to the interception of "several shipments" of weapons from Iran to the Taliban, he stated that "I'm not sure they (Tehran) want to see the Taliban win, but I don't think they want the government to establish good control either. I think they are just trying to hedge their bets and keep everything fluid."[60]

In July 2008, after three foreign militants, two from Middle East and one from Turkey, were reportedly captured inside Afghanistan, an Afghan daily, *Anis*, for the first time alleged that Iran has become a "tunnel for terrorists" travelling from Middle East to the Waziristan tribal region of Pakistan to fight against the Western forces in Afghanistan.[61] In September 2008, however, a *BBC* report indicated how weaponry of Iranian and Russian origin were making their way to the Taliban also through the old networks of arms dealers from northern Afghanistan.[62]

Interestingly, while the US continued to accuse Iran of providing arms to the Taliban, the European member-states of the ISAF called for engaging Iran as part of a more regional approach to deal with Afghanistan. After French President Chirac had proposed the formation of a 'contact group' on Afghanistan involving the regional countries in December 2006, it was the turn of German Chancellor Angela Merkel to call for a new political approach to the Afghan mission. In January 2009, coinciding with the inauguration of Barack Obama as the US president, as stated earlier in the chapter, Merkel's Christian Democratic Union (CDU) had come out with a policy paper proposing the establishment of an international 'contact group' on Afghanistan. Though the paper did not specifically mentioned Iran as part of the proposed 'contact group,' the German media reportedly quoted Andreas Schockenhoff, vice chairman of CDU, as stating that his party would welcome Iran's participation.[63] Thereafter, NATO Secretary General Jaap de Hoop Scheffer too had argued in favour of a broader regional approach in Afghanistan in January 2009.[64]

On January 27, 2009, Adm. Mike Mullen, Chairman of the US Joint Chiefs of Staff, during a press briefing in Washington, too acknowledged the importance of engaging Iran as part of a regional approach to deal with Afghanistan.[65] In

March 2009, US President Obama, who had already expressed his willingness to directly engage Tehran, in his message to the Iranian people and the government on the occasion of *Nowroz*, had clearly stated:

> My administration is now committed to diplomacy that addresses the full range of issues before us, and to pursuing constructive ties among the United States, Iran, and the international community. This process will not be advanced by threats. We seek instead engagement that is honest and grounded in mutual respect. The United States wants the Islamic Republic of Iran to take its rightful place in the community of nations. You have that right—but it comes with real responsibilities, and that place cannot be reached through terror or arms, but rather through peaceful actions that demonstrate the true greatness of the Iranian people and civilization.[66]

The same month, the then US Secretary of State Hillary Clinton also announced that Iran would be invited to participate in the international conference on Afghanistan to be held at Hague on March 31. Finally, sometime in early March 2009, a senior NATO negotiator, Martin Erdmann, met Iranian Ambassador to the EU, Ali-Asghar Khaji for "informal" talks on Afghanistan.[67] NATO had for sometime been exploring prospects of having an alternate supply lines *via* Iran for its troops deployed in Afghanistan. Later, on March 27, President Obama in his new Afghanistan-Pakistan strategy referred to "creating new diplomatic mechanisms, including establishing a 'Contact Group' and a regional security and economic cooperation forum."[68] Though Iran participated in the international conference in The Hague on March 31 as well, but nothing eventually emerged in terms of possible cooperation on Afghanistan. On April 13, 2009, the National Security and Foreign Policy Deputy Chairman of the Iranian Parliament, Esmaeil Kosari, categorically ruled out any possibility of Iran allowing the NATO to ship military or non-military supplies via its territory as Iran basically does not accept the presence of NATO in Afghanistan.[69] In June 2009, President Obama while speaking at Cairo University in Egypt again expressed his willingness to redefine America's relations with Iran:

> For many years, Iran has defined itself in part by its opposition to my country, and there is in fact a tumultuous history between us. In the middle of the Cold War, the United States played a role in the overthrow of a democratically elected Iranian government. Since the Islamic Revolution, Iran has played a role in acts of hostage-taking and violence against U.S. troops and civilians. This history is well known. Rather than remain trapped in the past, I've made it clear to Iran's leaders and people that my country is prepared to move forward. The question now is not what Iran is against, but rather what future it wants to build.
>
> I recognize it will be hard to overcome decades of mistrust, but we will proceed with courage, rectitude, and resolve. There will be many issues to

> discuss between our two countries, and we are willing to move forward without preconditions on the basis of mutual respect. But it is clear to all concerned that when it comes to nuclear weapons, we have reached a decisive point. This is not simply about America's interests. It's about preventing a nuclear arms race in the Middle East that could lead this region and the world down a hugely dangerous path.[70]

If the Bush Administration earlier failed to realise the long term value of sustaining its engagement with Iran, the latter too failed to respond to the several Western initiatives in recent years. On the Afghan front, Iran since 2003 has been intensely critical of the Western coalition which in its perception remains a key destabilising factor in the entire region.

In June 2009, for the first time, American military commanders in Afghanistan claimed that they have killed a senior Taliban commander, Mullah Mustafa, who was linked to the Qods Force of the IRGC. Mustafa, who reportedly commanded a group of 100 Taliban fighters, was killed along with 16 of his fighters in the western Ghor Province.[71] In early September 2009, two years after first cache of Iranian-made weapons were found in parts of Afghanistan, it was reported that the Afghan police has discovered a cache of Iranian-made weapons including EFPs from Herat.[72]

An exclusive report published in December 2009 by the Saudi newspaper *Asharq Al-Awsat* on a member of Osama bin Laden's family held inside Iran seeking refuge in the Saudi Embassy in the country, once again turned the attention to Iran's role in sheltering members of al Qaeda and several Arab families who had slipped into Iran after the 9/11 attacks.[73] As brought out earlier in the chapter, though Iran did initially handover several of the al Qaeda operatives as part of its effort to engage Washington, but at the same time the above report highlighted prospects of several al Qaeda members still being in the country.

As tempers between Washington and Tehran continued to rise, American Defence Secretary Robert Gates and Iranian President Ahmadinejad, both visiting Kabul back-to-back in early March 2010, accused each other of playing a 'double game' in Afghanistan. Gates during his visit to Kabul pointed out that while Iran on one hand supported the Afghan Government, on the other hand, it was also undermining the stability of Afghanistan by extending support to the Taliban. Similarly, Ahmadinejad during his visit to Kabul immediately thereafter alleged that it is the US which is playing a double game as they are fighting terrorists whom they had once created and supported.[74]

In March 2010, it was reported by *The Sunday Times* that Taliban fighters are being trained by the Iranian security officials in camps located along the border with Afghanistan. The report was based on interviews conducted with two Taliban commanders, one from Ghazni and the other from Wardak, who were said to have been trained in Iranian camps. One of the Taliban commanders is even quoted as stating: "Our religions and our histories are different, but our target is the same—we both want to kill Americans." The report also elaborated on the three month course offered to the Taliban fighters in the Iranian training camps and the way weapons are being smuggled into Afghanistan.[75] Later, on May 30, 2010, while responding to a query during a press conference, General Stanley McChrystal, commander of the US and NATO forces in Afghanistan, accused Iran of providing training and weapons to the Taliban. McChrystal stated, "The training that we have seen occurs inside Iran with fighters moving inside Iran. The weapons that we have received come from Iran into Afghanistan."[76] Immediately thereafter, on June 05, 2010, the ISAF announced the killing of a Taliban commander, Mullah Akhtar, during a military operation in the Gulistan District of southwestern Farah Province bordering Iran. Mullah Akhtar was stated to have been responsible for coordinating the training of Taliban fighters in Iran.[77] Within two months, on August 03, the US Treasury Department added General Hossein Musavi, Commander of the IRGC-QF Ansar Corps based in Mashhad, and Colonel Hasan Mortezavi, a senior Qods Force commander, both charged with directly providing financial and material support to the Taliban, to its list of specially designated global terrorists.[78]

Couple of months later, in September 2010, in another report published by *The Sunday Times*, it was stated that there are Iranian companies based in Kabul which are covertly providing funds to the Taliban operating in the neighbouring provinces close to the capital. Quoting a Taliban treasurer, the report further stated that "Iran is paying bonuses of $1,000 (£647) for killing an American soldier and $6,000 (£3,882) for destroying a US military vehicle."[79] Thereafter, on October 07, 2010, it was reported that explosives weighing 19 tonne were recovered from Zaranj, capital of the southwestern province of Nimroz bordering Iran. Interestingly, the Afghan foreign ministry spokesperson immediately announced in a press conference that Iranian authorities have acknowledged that explosives seized in Zaranj were smuggled from Iran.[80] Within five days, Afghan border police claimed to have confiscated another weapons cache, including some Iranian-made, again from the same province, this time from the Char Brujak and Kang districts.[81]

The narrative on Iran's complex role and objectives inside Afghanistan further gained traction when an article published in *The New York Times* on October 23, 2010 reported about Iran making cash payments directly to President Karzai's office with his Chief of Staff Umar Daudzai acting as conduit between the two. The article alleged that Iranian money was also being used for winning the support and loyalty of Afghan lawmakers, tribal elders and even Taliban commanders. According to the report:

> Current and former Afghan officials say the Iranian government began financing Mr. Karzai before Mr. Daudzai became his chief of staff in 2003. It is not clear when Mr. Daudzai became a conduit for Iranian cash. In 2005, he was named ambassador to Iran. It was then, one Afghan official said, that Mr. Daudzai became acquainted with Iranian intelligence officials and grew close to senior Iranian leaders like Mr. Ahmadinejad.
>
> Mr. Daudzai returned to Kabul in 2007 to resume his job as chief of staff. Since then, officials said, Mr. Daudzai has maintained a close relationship with the Iranian ambassador. Iranian officials have nearly unfettered access to Mr. Karzai's palace, bypassing the normal rules of protocol.
>
> Accounts vary as to how much Iranian money flow into the presidential palace. An Afghan political leader said he believed that Mr. Daudzai received between $1 million and $2 million every other month. A former diplomat who served in Afghanistan said sometimes single payments totaled as much as $6 million.[82]

The above report, which was rejected by the spokesperson of the Iranian ambassador in Kabul as "devilish gossip by the West and foreign media,"[83] was largely interpreted by Western officials as part of Iran's continuing effort to undermine the Western endeavour in Afghanistan. In their perception, Iran has long been trying to drive a wedge between Kabul and the West. According to Iran's *Fars News Agency*, the Iranian Embassy in Kabul in a statement issued on October 25 had stated: "Such baseless rumors by certain western media are raised to create anxiety in the public opinion and impair the expanding relations between the two friendly and neighboring countries. The historical and cultural bonds between the Iranian and Afghan nations (are) too strong to be affected by media mischief and the false news fabricated by the western media."[84] Later, Abdullah, foreign minister in Karzai-led interim and transitional government, in an interview in April 2011, also confirmed that it was in 2003-04 that President Khatami's office had started providing cash in assistance to the Afghan president's office.[85]

The timing of the report was also significant as it came at a time when Karzai was under severe criticism from the West for his allegedly controversial role in the 2009 presidential election. Afghan officials considered close to President Karzai and those openly endorsing Karzai's views and perceptions about the Western strategy in Afghanistan, began to be seen as stridently anti-West by the American establishment. Aware of the several limitations with the ISAF, and rising levels of civilian casualty and collateral damage which was undermining government's credibility particularly in the volatile rural areas in the south and east, Karzai wanted the US and NATO to re-strategise the war on terror. By 2009-10, three years after ISAF had expanded its operations to the south and east of the country, Karzai and some of his senior officials including his chief of staff Umar Daudzai were apparently convinced that the Western coalition would not succeed against the Taliban and their allies until they change their military strategy and approach to the war on terror. The government in Kabul must be seen as independent and in control of affairs and the Western forces should not be seen as interfering in the daily lives of the Afghan people.

The above report had also appeared a month before the November 2010 NATO Summit in Lisbon where a time line for security transition and withdrawal of ISAF was to be laid out. It was also reported that the US special representative to Afghanistan and Pakistan, Richard Holbrooke, had expressed his concern over Daudzai's role and Iran's influence in the presidential palace to the Afghan Finance Minister Omar Zakhliwal in his meeting the week before. Interestingly, couple of months back in August 2010, there were similar reports in the media alleging that many of President Karzai's close aides have long been secretly paid by the CIA. Umar Daudzai, in an interview given to *The Washington Post* on August 28, 2010 denied that the presidential staff is receiving money from the CIA and instead remarked that "the whole government is paid, one way or the other, by the United States. That's different." During the same interview, Daudzai had also criticised the West for its public criticism and condemnation of the Karzai Government which he argued was working to the advantage of the Taliban and its propaganda machinery.[86]

However, shortly afterwards, President Karzai, during a joint press conference on October 24, 2010 with the visiting Tajikistan President Imomali Rakhmon, acknowledged that he receives cash in assistance from several "friendly countries" and specifically mentioned the US along with Iran. To put it in his words:

> The government of Iran assists (my) office with five or six or seven hundred thousand euros once or twice a year which is official aid. This is transparent, this is something that I have discussed even with (former) President George (W.) Bush, nothing is hidden, the United States is doing the same thing...it does give bags of money, yes, it's all the same. Cash payments are done by various friendly countries to help the presidential office to help expenses in various ways to help the employees around here, and people outside. We will continue to ask for cash from Iran.[87]

On President Karzai stating that his office receives cash from the US as well, the US State Department spokesperson, P.J. Crowley, responded stating, "Going back a number of years, because of the nature of the Afghan financial system, there have been times where assistance has come into Afghanistan in the form of cash. That's not the form that our assistance takes today."[88] Two months later, in December 2010, again news reports appeared, this time based on a leaked American diplomatic cable, alleging that Iran has secretly poured huge sums of cash in the Afghan parliamentary election in September to ensure the victory of their favoured candidates.[89]

Iran's sudden blockade of fuel supplies to Afghanistan beginning December 2010 led to tension between the two countries. About 2,500 fuel tankers including tankers from other countries but transiting via Iran too were reportedly stranded on the Iranian side of the border. It is said that though Iran supplies only 30 per cent of Afghanistan's refined fuel, but the remaining 70 per cent which is supplied by Iraq, Turkmenistan and Russia is also transited through Iran. Shortage of fuel during approaching winters led to sharp rise in price levels in large parts of Afghanistan. Though Iranians initially cited technical reasons for stalling the fuel exports, but later conveyed their concern to Kabul over Iranian fuel possibly being used by the Western forces in view of the military surge announced by the Obama Administration.[90] To some, it was part of a pressure tactic by Tehran to force the Afghan Government to accept the results of the September 2010 parliamentary election since several candidates allegedly funded by Iran were being investigated for electoral fraud.[91] Later, there were also statements from Iranian officials suggesting that the two countries have reached an agreement whereby Afghanistan will source all its fuel supplies from Iran.[92] The Afghan Government promptly denied having entered into any such agreement with Iran.[93] Though the matter was quietly settled towards the end of January with Iran resuming the supplies, the whole incident once again highlighted the fact that Tehran's hostility towards the Western coalition takes precedence over its traditional ties with neighbouring Afghanistan.

The dispute over sharing of river waters and construction of dam by Afghanistan on rivers flowing into Iran has been a lingering issue between the two countries. In February 2011, Afghan officials protested against repeated attacks on its personnel engaged in Bakhshabad hydropower facility in Farah Province bordering Iran, where cache of Iranian-made weapons were earlier reported to have been found. It was stated that two project engineers were abducted from the Khak-e Safed District of the province on November 26, 2010. One of the engineers was killed and the other was released after a ransom of US$ 100,000 was paid. The deputy provincial governor had reportedly blamed Iran for trying to stall the construction of the hydropower plant. He also referred to the killing of 12 Afghan policemen in March 2009 by militants at a check point close to the project site.[94]

In March 2011, it was again reported that NATO forces had seized about 50 Iranian-made 122-millimeter rockets on February 05, ahead of the Taliban spring offensive, from the southern Nimroz Province bordering both Iran and Pakistan.[95] It was suspected by Western officials that as tough sanctions are brought on Iran, the political and military establishment in Iran is more likely to ramp up its support for Afghan insurgents opposed to Western presence in the country. Given Iran's known opposition to the presence of Western forces in Afghanistan, Tehran was bound raise its protestations at the prospect of Kabul entering into a long-term strategic partnership with the US. When Kabul and Washington finally entered into a strategic partnership in May 2012, Iranian foreign ministry openly expressed its serious concerns over the prospect of an extended Western presence in bases across Afghanistan and reiterated that there can be no peace and security in the country until all foreign forces leave. Immediately thereafter, the Kabul correspondent of the semi-official Iranian *Fars News Agency* was detained by the Afghan intelligence claiming that he was spying for Tehran, bringing to fore the simmering tension between the two countries on the issue of Kabul entering into strategic partnership with Washington.[96]

Later, a *Pajhwok Afghan News* report, published on May 24, 2012, two days before Afghan Parliament was to vote on the US-Afghanistan strategic partnership agreement, alleged that Iran has earmarked $25 million to be paid to the Afghan lawmakers for blocking the approval of the strategic partnership agreement with the US in the parliament. According to the report, a "colossal amount of money" was paid to Hazrat Ali, a *Wolesi Jirga* (Lower House) member from Nangarhar, who was supposed to have persuaded and paid other lawmakers to oppose the agreement. The report added that on International Mother's Day, which was celebrated on May 13, Pakistani and Iranian spy services had paid $10,000 to each of the six female members of the lower house of the Afghan Parliament.[97] Interestingly, there were also reports of Taliban setting up an office in the eastern Iranian city of Zahedan in May 2012.[98]

The Afghan intelligence has often alleged that there are Iranian-funded media outlets operating in the country, such as the Afghan weekly *Insaaf* and TV channels like *Tamadon* and *Noor*.[99] According to the English translation of a report published in the Afghan daily *Hasht-e Sobh* in August 2012, certain Afghan media officials were invited on August 03 at the Iranian Embassy in Kabul to discuss the idea of establishing a "union of journalists" to coordinate the work of pro-Iranian media in Afghanistan. In the meeting, there were representatives from *Tamadon TV*, *Noor TV* and *Aina TV* and from dailies like *Insaaf* and *Roshd*. Iranian cultural attaché Naser Jahan-Shahi was said to have chaired the meeting and reportedly pledged that the embassy would fund the project. The meeting selected Hussein Rezvani Bamyani, Director of the Cultural Committee of Afghanistan's Shia Ulema Council, as the head of the union. Jawad Mohseni, director of *Tamadon TV*, and Zakaria Rahel, a prominent journalist, were appointed the first and second deputies respectively.[100]

The Iranian position on the role and presence of the US and its allies in Afghanistan, and its own response to the evolving scenario within Afghanistan, has thus far been guided by the nature of its over all relationship, or lack of it, with the US. Interestingly, *despite all*, the two countries apparently have managed to have somewhat regular trade relations. According to a the *US Census Bureau* data, released in early October 2012, the American exports to Iran rose by a third in 2012 mainly due to rise in sales of grain. The export reportedly jumped to $199.5 million in the first eight months of 2012 from $150.8 million a year earlier. The *Reuters* further reported:

> The largest category of U.S. exports to Iran through August, 2012 was $89.2 million in sales of wheat and other grains. During the same 2011 period, the United States exported no wheat or such grains to Iran, though it sold $21 million of maize. Without the wheat sales, U.S. exports to Iran would have declined through August overall, sharply in some cases.
>
> Medicinal and pharmaceutical products, including those sold in bulk and those for animals, fell to $14.9 million from $26.7 million. Pulp and waste paper, a category that includes the raw material for diapers, sank to $17.4 million from $40.9 million. However, exports rose in several other categories. Sales of milk products including cream, butter and other fats and oils derived from dairy more than doubled to $20.3 million from $7.8 million. Medical, dental, surgical and other "electro-diagnostic apparatus" rose to $8 million from $4.7 million.[101]

With Hassan Rouhani, who is considered to be a moderate, taking over as the president of Iran in 2013, it was expected that the relations with the US might improve. Though some positive steps have been taken from both sides, nevertheless, the two countries still have a long way to go before they could establish a working relationship. After 2014, post the Western drawdown, and after the formation of the new government in Kabul, Tehran is more likely to strengthen the various complex networks it has assiduously nurtured over the last one decade to further its economic and political interests within Afghanistan.

Since the overthrow of the Taliban regime, Iran has extensively invested in reviving and creating new infrastructure particularly in western Afghanistan. Iran's huge economic investments in western Afghanistan was not merely to reassert its traditional political influence over the region. By developing the bordering Afghan provinces to its east, Iran also wanted to check the inflow of drugs and refugees. Iran is stated to have announced assistance worth $1 billion for Afghanistan since 2002. By 2008, Iran had reportedly paved half of Herat's streets and about 40 miles of highway leading to the north, and had built schools, health clinics and partnered with Afghan companies in building an industrial park. Iran had also built the highway linking Mashhad in its northeast to Herat by 2006. Iran had also laid down power transmission lines providing electricity to the city of Herat.[102] It was reported in January 2011 that Iran exported goods worth $900 million to Afghanistan in the first nine months of the year 2010 as per the Iranian calendar, a 25 per cent increase in exports compared to previous year's figure. Iranian export was expected to surpass $1.2 billion in 2011.[103]

The Iranian port of Chahbahar, which provides Afghanistan a much shorter route to the Persian Gulf and an alternative to the Pakistani ports, is operational now. Iran has already completely the construction of road including the bridge over river Helmand in Milak connecting the port to the Afghan border town of Zaranj in Nimroz Province. On the Afghan side of the border, India in January 2009 handed over to the Afghan Government the newly constructed 218-km long road connecting Zaranj to the Afghan national highway at Delaram.

Later, in December 2011, the Iranian Industry, Trade and Mines Minister Mehdi Ghazanfari, during a meeting with the visiting Afghan Commerce and Industry Minister Anwar-ul Haq Ahady, stated that the value of trade between Iran and Afghanistan stood at around $2 billion in the first 11 months of 2011, of which $1.5 billion was Iran's exports to Afghanistan. Ahady in turn stated that Iranian companies are carrying out 110 technical-engineering projects worth $360 million inside Afghanistan. It was also decided that Afghanistan will open a trading hub in the upcoming Iranian port at Chahbahar.[104]

Though Tehran's influence in the south, among the Pashtuns, is relatively limited, but its leverages among the non-Pashtuns in western and parts of northern and central Afghanistan, including in Kabul, remains strong. Its several economic and political leverages have earned it both acknowledgement and criticism within Afghanistan. Iran is seen as both a stabilising and interfering force inside Afghanistan. Apart from Pashtuns in general, there are groups within Tajiks and Hazaras as well which remain highly sceptical as well as suspicious about the Iranian objectives. Iran's support for various media outlets and Shiite groups in Afghanistan is generally not seen as benign. The Iran-Afghanistan relations have had their share of bilateral irritants which would often complicate things for both countries from time to time. Iranian consulates in Afghanistan have often faced public protests and have even been attacked, the most recent being in February 2013 when an official of the Iranian consulate in Mazar-e Sharif was attacked by unknown gunmen.[105]

Afghanistan's former intelligence chief, Amrullah Saleh, in his article published by *BBC Pashto* in January 2013, identifies three key Iranian entities—the clerical establishment in Qom, the Ministry of Intelligence, and the IRGC, especially its secretive Qods Force—which are operating at different levels to further the Iranian interest inside Afghanistan. An English summary of his article, published by the *American Enterprise Institute*,[106] elaborates on the above three entities and their role:

> **Clerical establishment in Qom:** Saleh says the clergy in Iran's holy city of Qom is responsible for "expanding Iran's soft power and political influence through support for Shia minorities—not just in Afghanistan but in the entire region." He adds, "The establishment funds Shia mosques; provides

higher education for Shia clerics; holds public ceremonies for Ashura; and helps to foster harmony and religious unity between influential Shia figures. They [clergy in Qom] are said to possess a list of Afghan Shia clerics and maintain contact with each of them in one way or another. Religious leaders who do not agree with Qom...are deprived of Iranian assistance."

Ministry of Intelligence: According to Saleh, Iran's Ministry of Intelligence has assigned its external branch to collect intelligence in Afghanistan by cultivating close ties with Afghan officials, particularly in the ministries of foreign affairs, interior, defense and water and energy, as well as in western Afghan provinces bordering Iran.

Iran's Revolutionary Guards Corps (IRGC): Saleh alleges that the IRGC has assigned two branches of its secretive Quds Force—the Ansar Headquarters based in Mashhad and the 23rd Headquarters in Birjand—to carry out "sabotage" and other subversive activities in Afghanistan. Afghanistan and Iran have a reciprocal visa waiver program for diplomats, and Saleh believes this allows IRGC officers to enter Afghanistan as diplomats without any scrutiny and supervision by Afghan authorities. He adds that Iranian spies also disguise as businessmen, aid workers, journalists and civilians.

On June 01, 2013, it was reported by Iranian *Fars News Agency* that a Taliban political delegation had visited Tehran to hold talks with Iranian security officials. According to the report, the delegation comprised members of the Taliban office in Qatar and was headed by Tayyeb Agha. Interestingly, the report also referred to an earlier visit by former Taliban Higher Education Minister Mohammad Allah Namani and Governor of Maidan Wardak Province to attend the Islamic Awakening Conference in Tehran.[107] Though no details of the talks were provided in the report, but the very fact that a Taliban delegation had visited Tehran raised suspicions in Kabul about the Iranian objectives. Interestingly, though the Iranian foreign ministry spokesperson had dismissed the above report the very next day,[108] the Taliban spokesperson, Qari Yousuf Ahmadi, in his statement of June 04 fully acknowledged the *Fars* report regarding the visit of Taliban delegation to Iran at least on two occasions. In his statement posted on the *Voice of Jihad* website, he confirmed that:

> A delegation headed by the chief of political office of Islamic Emirate of Afghanistan went on a three day visit to the capital of Islamic Republic of Iran, Tehran, a while ago where issues of mutual interests were discussed by both sides after which the delegation returned.
>
> Similarly, high ranking officials of Islamic Emirate also made another visit in the recent past to the Islamic Republic of Iran after a formal invitation by the said country where the delegation of Islamic Emirate participated in an international Islamic conference which was convened in the capital Tehran. The delegation delivered a speech in which it furnished all the participants

> with general information about the legitimate demands of Islamic Emirate and made clear its policy concerning key Afghan and international issues.
>
> The Islamic Emirate has also previously made heard its policy to the world by participating in conferences in Japan and France, the outcomes of which have been positive.[109]

Interestingly, Taliban, immediately thereafter, again posted an article on the same website commenting on the coverage given to the Tehran visit of the Taliban representatives from Qatar by the *BBC* and various Afghan dailies. It is noteworthy that Tehran never dismissed the claims made by the Taliban on the issue. The comments were apparently made in the backdrop of Karzai Government's refusal to talk to the Taliban representatives based in Doha in 2012. The article emphasised that Taliban delegation had repeatedly visited Tehran at the formal invitation of the Iranian Government and have held official negotiations with them on issues of regional concern. The article clearly observed:

> Some political analysts called the abrupt announcement of this declaration as a diplomatic coup d'état against the Kabul Government which have made the foreign ministry of the Karzai Government very lax. While the internal and regional media are warmly commenting this diplomatic progress of Taliban, the Karzai regime is unable to identify her stance and proclaim it.
>
> The Taliban's visit to Iran by her invitation, their formal negotiations and then publicizing these diplomatic relations are considered a significant achievement for Taliban from political point of view because the nature of this visit and the language of the Taliban's declaration prove that Taliban have not visited Iran as an insignificant party or group, rather they have been invited by the Iranian side as an independent political system and crucial issues have been brought under discussion.[110]

Post-2014: Stronger Role and Presence

Iran is most likely to strengthen its ties with the new coalition in Kabul while continuing to make its way up through various political and cultural networks inside Afghanistan to secure its perceived interests and to retain its influence within the country. Both countries might upgrade the MoU on Strategic Cooperation Agreement signed by Afghan National Security Advisor Rangin Dadfar Spanta and Secretary of the Iranian National Security Council Saeed Jalili during President Karzai's Tehran visit to attend the inaugural ceremony of President Rouhani in August 2013. Interestingly, the document was termed as MoU and was not signed by the two heads of state as was the case with similar partnership agreements that Kabul had signed with India, US and China. It is noteworthy that the MoU while calling for enhanced security and economic cooperation between the two countries also called for cooperation with the national security councils of India and Russia.[111] This MoU was signed in the backdrop of President Karzai's growing differences with the Obama Administration particularly on the issue of terms and conditions of the BSA, which Tehran had long opposed. Certain traditional extraneous factors, such as the Saudi dynamics, too will continue to impinge on Iran's response strategies in Afghanistan. Iran's tenuous relation with Pakistan, which has had close relations with Saudi Arabia and also receives massive aid and assistance from the US, too is bound to impact on Tehran's regional strategy.

Iran has for long suffered from a perpetually hostile environment since the Islamic revolution of 1979. It has emerged from the two devastating Gulf Wars, effects of the collapse of the Soviet Union; frequent political alienation due to its antagonistic relations with the US/West, and after 9/11, despite supporting the US-led war on terror, was labelled as part of "axis of evil" by the Bush Administration; and thereafter has been coping with strict sanctions imposed due to its nuclear programme. The US-led unilateral interventionism and regime change in its immediate neighbourhood raised suspicions of Washington attempting a similar regime change in Tehran. In the absence of a broad understanding between Washington and Tehran, old resentments and distrust between the two countries continued to define their relationship and their respective approaches to the evolving conflict in both Iraq and Afghanistan.

In case of Afghanistan, Iran has been the traditional backer of Shia factions and the Northern Alliance since the days of anti-Soviet *Jihad* of the 1980s. However, Iran has been at the same time making an attempt to expand its support base among the Sunni Pashtuns in south-western and southern Afghanistan since the Northern Alliance (NA) had its own ethno-territorial limitations. Though Iran had earlier sheltered Hezb-e Islami chief, Gulbuddin Hekmatyar, it is difficult to assess whether it still has any influence over him. In all these years, since Iran has cultivated various factions and networks within Afghanistan, the possibility of Tehran having a political understanding with some pro-Taliban factions or a section of Taliban operating in south-western Afghanistan cannot be ruled out. The twin purpose here could be to expand its area of influence and at the same time to keep the Western forces tied down within Afghanistan, quite similar to its strategy in Iraq. For Iran, the US-led Western coalition remains a larger threat. However, at the same time, it would not like Taliban to gain in strength and influence beyond a point, which is why it also continues to leverage its influence over the Afghan Government and various factions of the former Northern Alliance.

Thus, Iran clearly appears to be operating at different levels within Afghanistan. At the international level, it has openly supported the internationally-recognised democratically-elected government in Kabul and is actively involved in the reconstruction process of Afghanistan. At the local level, it could be supporting certain Taliban guerrilla groups as well as the elements of the former

Northern Alliance in order to retain and further enhance its leverage within Afghanistan. At the same time, it has initiated a trilateral with Tajikistan and Afghanistan and another one with Afghanistan and Pakistan. These initiatives could be part of Tehran's countermeasure to the US-led trilaterals. It could also be part of its pro-active diplomacy at the regional level in anticipation of a post-West scenario. Given the complex nature of Pakistan's involvement in the Afghan politics and its close relationship with the US, Iran has enough reasons to augment its stakes in the Afghan polity by way of supporting groups hitherto considered anti-Iran. A section of Taliban, who are said to be a more factionalised lot now, too could be seeking to expand their political role by endearing to Iran in a limited way. Western military presence beyond 2014 would thus continue to provide an opportunity for the rival ideologies to merge their differences and enter into tactical and vague alliances.

Being a landlocked country with millions of its citizen still living as refugees or migrant workers inside Iran, Kabul at times might have to face intense pressure from the Iranian leadership particularly after the signing of the BSA with the US. Constant threat from entrenched drug mafia and organised criminal networks active along its borders with Afghanistan and Pakistan, including militant groups such as Jundullah, too would continue to impact on Iran's policy approaches in coming years. However, compared to Pakistan, Iran could be regarded as a huge moderating force inside Afghanistan, and its positive role will be all the more critical for the economic and political stability of Afghanistan in view of declining Western aid and assistance after 2014.

INDIA: PARTNER IN DEVELOPMENT

India has emerged as a major 'development partner' of the Afghan people since the overthrow of the Taliban regime in November 2001. Today, India is the fifth largest bilateral donor, certainly the largest from the region, to Afghan reconstruction. It has successfully carried out several large and small development projects across Afghanistan. However, when it comes to securing its core interests in an increasingly adversarial security environment in Afghanistan, India is often found lacking in terms of having necessary leverages to sustain and broaden its engagement beyond a point. Be it regional initiatives or the US' Af-Pak strategy, there is hardly enough recognition of India's discernible role and assistance in rebuilding the Afghan state over the last one decade. It is also often stated that it might be increasingly difficult for India to sustain the momentum of its engagement with Afghanistan after 2014.

Except for a brief period of relative peace and stability after the overthrow of the Taliban regime in 2001, India's presence and involvement in Afghan reconstruction has been increasingly contested and confronted by militant networks based inside Pakistan. The attack on the Indian Embassy in Kabul in July 2008 that left 58 people dead, including two senior embassy officials; on a guest house in Kabul in February 2010 that left nine Indians dead; and repeated attacks on its consulates and the killing of Indian and several Afghan personnel assigned to the road construction project in south-western Afghanistan, had brought to fore the nature and scale of threat that India faced in Afghanistan. It was reflective of the rising levels of frustration among forces inimical to India's growing contribution to the Afghan reconstruction.

As the West retreats and a range of Afghan and Pakistani militant groups threaten Kabul, India's security concerns are bound to grow. Even if one were to conclude that India needs to think its Afghan policy afresh, the situation in the Af-Pak region is currently so fluid and uncertain that it would be difficult for New Delhi to bring about a drastic change in its policy anytime soon. India's Afghan policy, however, has shown notable resilience in the face of rising threat to its presence and interests in Afghanistan. There are two very defining statements, one made immediately after the overthrow of the Taliban regime in 2002 and another as the country approached multiple transitions in 2014, that best reflect and sum up India's engagement policy towards Afghanistan for over a decade.

In March 2002, during the discussion on the situation in Afghanistan at the UN Security Council, India's then Permanent Representative Kamlesh Sharma had stated: "For its developmental efforts to be productive and lasting, the international community must match generosity with wisdom. It is, therefore, important to listen carefully to what the Afghans need and respect their priorities and preferences, as no one knows better than the Afghans what is good for them and how best to do it. Temptation to foist solutions or structures not suitable or responsive to the local environment should be resisted as these will neither serve the cause of the donors nor of the Afghans. In determining what will work, sustainability should be the touchstone."[112] This is very much reflected in India's economic and political approach towards Afghanistan. More than a decade later, in January 2014, Indian Foreign Minister Salman Khurshid while speaking at a meeting of the International Contact Group on Afghanistan held in New Delhi, remarked that "Clearly people may have many strategies and we will need to work on strategies but one strategy that we reject here in India is an exit strategy from Afghanistan."[113] In fact, both the above statements have aptly brought out the guiding principles of India's Afghan engagement.

A Development Partner

Indian was among the last of the countries to vacate its embassy in Kabul as the Taliban forces marched into the city in September 1996. Next five years, for the first time since the establishment of diplomatic ties between the two countries in January 1950, India was not to have any diplomatic presence in Afghanistan. It was finally on November 21, 2001, a week after the Taliban forces had retreated from Kabul on November 12-13, that India despatched a diplomatic mission to establish a liaison office in Kabul. Interestingly, the liaison office was upgraded as a full-fledged Indian Embassy the day Afghan Interim Administration (AIA) was inaugurated with Hamid Karzai as its chairman in Kabul on December 22, 2001. Both were indicators of the strong Indian support for the new political process in Afghanistan, particularly in the light of the hijacking of an Indian Airline flight to Kandahar by Pakistan-backed terrorists in December 1999 and blowing up of Bamiyan Buddhas by the Taliban in March 2001.

The tragic events of 9/11 had in a way validated India's position on the Pakistan-backed Taliban regime in Afghanistan. India had long argued for a global effort to deal with the rapidly spreading menace of terrorism and extremism. In February 2002, then Indian National Security Advisor Brajesh K. Mishra in his address at the 38th Munich Security Conference had stated:

> "It gives me no pleasure to say that we in India have experienced this reality for the past many years, but it took September 11 to dramatically bring the global reach of terrorism into the collective consciousness of the world. The world now accepts that terrorism can be tackled effectively only with a global and comprehensive approach. UN Security Council Resolution 1373 shows the right direction. However, the world's democracies have to co-operate effectively in its implementation and ensure compliance of other countries. This requires collective political will, undiluted by short-term political or economic calculations. Whatever our political predilections or strategic calculations, we cannot condone terrorism somewhere, while condemning it elsewhere, because this lenience will boomerang on all of us. We have to systematically choke off the three crucial lifelines of terrorist groups: refuge, finances and arms.
>
> It is also a fact, often ignored, that the sponsorship, bases and finances for terrorism come from totalitarian military or theocratic regimes. They nurture and support extremist terrorist groups to further their political agenda. In turn, these groups make themselves indispensable to these regimes by maintaining the focus on external campaigns and diverting attention from the inadequacies of their internal systems."[114]

Soon after the overthrow of the Taliban regime from Kabul, India promptly joined the international community in seeking ways to rebuild Afghanistan. India along with other regional countries played an important role at the UN-led Bonn Conference (November 27-December 05, 2001) that brought together four Afghan groups to decide on a future roadmap for post-Taliban Afghanistan. India also actively participated in the meeting of the UN-sponsored Group of 21 countries on Afghanistan held in New York in November and December 2001;

meeting on reconstruction and assistance to Afghanistan held in Washington on November 21, 2001; conference on "Preparing for Afghanistan's Reconstruction" in Islamabad from November 21-29, 2001; meeting of the steering group for assistance in the reconstruction of Afghanistan in Brussels on December 20-21, 2001; and in the meeting of the steering group on reconstruction assistance to Afghanistan held in Tokyo on January 21-22, 2002. Apart from the above, the Indian Government had announced a line of credit of US $100 million and pledged to provide one million tonne of wheat for the displaced Afghan people. Medical assistance was also promptly extended to the Afghan people in Kabul and Mazar-e Sharif.[115]

It was evident from the visit of various Afghan leaders immediately after the signing of the Bonn Agreement that Kabul was looking at New Delhi as a significant partner in its effort to re-build the country. Interior Minister Yunus Qanuni visited New Delhi on December 07, 2001; Minister of Labour and Communications Mirwais Sadiq on December 10, 2001; and Foreign Minister Abdullah from December 13-19, 2001. Later, after the appointment of interim administration in December 2001, Light Industries Minister Mohammad Arif Noorzai visited India in January 2002; Civil Aviation Minister visited New Delhi on January 25, 2002 in the first Afghan Airline flight. On January 31, 2002, Afghan Deputy Defence Minister Abdul Rashid Dostum arrived in New Delhi. Prior to him, Mohammad Mohaqiq, one of the Vice Chairmen of the AIA visited India on January 30, 2002.

As Chairman of AIA, Karzai made his first visit to New Delhi on February 26-27, 2002. During the luncheon meeting with Indian Prime Minister Vajpayee, Karzai stated that Afghanistan regards India as the "largest democracy and oldest culture."[116] Acknowledging that Afghanistan faces "complex economic and political challenges," Prime Minister Vajpayee extended India's "unflinching and unconditional cooperation" to the Afghan nation.[117] Recognising the urgent need for rehabilitation and reconstruction in Afghanistan, Prime Minister Vajpayee announced a grant of US $10 million to the Afghan Government. The two sides also agreed to enhance cooperation in the field of education, health, information technology, public transport, industry, energy, and training of Afghan officials.[118] Indian assistance to Afghanistan has since remained focussed on carrying out capacity-building and development programmes. In New Delhi's perception, rebuilding Afghan infrastructure and strengthening its institutional capacity was considered critical to sustaining the post-Taliban political process in the country.

In May 2002, Indian Foreign Minister Jaswant Singh stated that India's approach to Afghan reconstruction focuses on: (a) providing immediate humanitarian relief in the field of health, (b) building institutional strengths of the government machinery, (c) offering project and commodity assistance in priority sectors of health, education, civil aviation, information technology, industrial development, public transport, agriculture and training, and (d) synergising with international efforts to meet the requirements of the Afghan Interim Administration. He also suggested a ten-point programme as part of South-South cooperation on Afghan reconstruction: (i) Relevant capacities of developing countries can be easily and cost-effectively made available to the Afghan-led rebuilding effort. This could also apply to building democratic, transparent and responsive institutions—an important condition for reconstruction efforts, (ii) training of Afghan personnel in or by developing countries in accordance with Afghan requirements, (iii) regional and inter-regional cooperation, (iv) private sector partnership, (v) triangular cooperation between Afghanistan, developed and developing Countries, (vi) education, health, poverty alleviation, vocational training, public administration, inclusive of financial management, credit extension schemes and administrative reforms could be amongst areas, which can be identified for cooperation between Afghanistan and developing countries, (vii) Sharing experiences of developing countries in respect of their own citizens living abroad for utilizing the services and resources of Afghans living outside for the reconstruction effort in Afghanistan, (viii) share experiences of developing countries for encouraging role of women and their participation in political, social, economic and cultural life, (ix) practical application of S&T and IT technologies to address social and economic development based on the results in other developing countries, and (x) emphasis on implementation.[119]

India continued with its reconstruction and humanitarian assistance to the Afghan Transitional Administration (ATA) formed after the *Emergency Loya Jirga* held in June 2002. Indian External Affairs Minster Yashwant Sinha visited Afghanistan from August 10-12, 2002 aboard one of the three Air India Airbus gifted by India to Afghan Ariana Airlines. The fact that apart from Kabul, he also visited Mazar-e Sharif, Herat, and especially Kandahar (which few months before was a Taliban stronghold) had a huge symbolic value. Chairman Karzai made his second visit to India from March 05-08, 2003. During his visit, Indian Government announced an additional grant of US $70 million for the Zaranj-Delaram road project being carried out by India in Afghanistan's south-western Nimroz Province. The two countries also entered into a Preferential Trade Agreement on the occasion. The very next month, on April 27, 2003, Indian National Security Advisor Brajesh Mishra visited Kabul where he met both Chairman Karzai and his counterpart Zalmay Rassoul. Similarly, many of the Afghan ministers from the transitional administration visited New Delhi during 2003-04. India committed to provide 300 vehicles to the nascent Afghan National Army (ANA).[120] In August 2002, India announced that it would be training 250 Afghan police officers as part of its effort to strengthen the security institutions of the country.[121] India has also gifted 101 utility vehicles/equipments to the Kabul municipality.

Some of the large development projects that India undertook in Afghanistan beginning in 2003-04 were: Construction of 218-Km long Zaranj-Delaram Road linking Afghanistan's national highway to the Iranian border and thereafter to the Iranian port of Chabahar; reconstruction of Indira Gandhi Institute of Child Health and Habibia School in Kabul; construction of new parliament building in Kabul; Salma Dam hydro-electric project in the western Herat Province; a power sub-station at Chimtala as part of the transmission line from Pul-e Khumri to the capital city of Kabul; commenced emergency restoration of basic telecommunication networks in eleven provincial capitals; and has built a 5,000 tonne capacity cold storage in Kandahar. India has also announced the establishment of an agricultural university in Kandahar.

India is currently offering about 2,000 scholarships under various categories for Afghan students and young professionals. India has also been conducting various training programmes for Afghan civil and military officials. To help augment the capacity of Afghan bureaucracy, India has from time to time deputed Indian experts and government officials to the Afghan ministries and departments. India had also agreed to contribute US $ 200,000 per annum to the World Bank managed Afghan Reconstruction Trust Fund (ARTF).

Indian Prime Minister Manmohan Singh's first state visit to Kabul from August 28-29, 2005 was seen as India's growing commitment to Afghan reconstruction as several important MoUs were signed including on Small Development Projects (SDPs) between the two countries. Singh also became the first Indian head of state to visit the country since former Prime Minister Indira Gandhi's visit in 1976. President Karzai's visit to India in April and in November 2006; and India's strong support for Afghanistan's entry into the SAARC further consolidated the Indo-Afghan ties.

In consonance with India's growing reconstruction assistance to Afghanistan, India hosted the Second Regional Economic Cooperation Conference on Afghanistan during November 18-19, 2006 in New Delhi which led to President Karzai's fifth visit to India. Thereafter, the then Indian Foreign Minister visited Kabul in January 2007 to invite President Karzai for the 14th SAARC Summit at New Delhi and to reiterate India's continued reconstruction assistance to the Afghan Government. Afghanistan was finally made the 8th member of the SAARC during the summit meeting at New Delhi during April 3-4, 2007 which was attended by the Afghan President.

Amidst the growing uncertainty over the evolving situation in Afghanistan, the second Kabul visit of Prime Minister Singh on May 12-13, 2011 and the signing of the Strategic Partnership Agreement between the two countries subsequently on October 04 the same year was certainly a significant step forward in the Indo-Afghan ties. In many ways it had reinforced the continuity in India's traditional policy of working with the government in Kabul since the establishment of full diplomatic ties in January 1950 (the Taliban regime from 1996 to 2001 being an exception here); non-interference in Afghanistan's internal affairs; sustained commitment to Afghan reconstruction; and an adaptive approach in keeping with the socio-political dynamism and grass root realities of the Afghan polity. This was clearly evident when India supported the Kabul-led reconciliation initiative aimed at the Taliban leadership based in Pakistan. Former Indian Foreign Minister S.M. Krishna in an interview to *Wall Street Journal* in September 2009 had observed that "India doesn't believe that war could be a solution for solving any problem and it applies to Afghanistan also. I think there could be a political settlement. If there are internal differences within Afghanistan, I think the people of Afghanistan, the leaders of Afghanistan will sort it out by themselves."[122]

In October 2009, the then Indian Foreign Secretary Nirupama Rao had reportedly stated that India would support the process of "reintegrating individuals with the national mainstream;" that "the existing process under (Afghanistan's) National Committee for Peace for reintegrating individuals with the national mainstream must be both enlarged and accelerated." The foreign secretary, however, emphasised that "the Afghan government's determination to integrate those willing to abjure violence and live and work within the parameters of the Afghan constitution" should "go hand in hand with the shutting down of support and sanctuaries supported for terrorist groups across the (Afghanistan-Pakistan) border."[123] The shift in Indian position was part of its larger strategy to tactically strengthen the position of Kabul as it prepared to launch a major peace initiative after the January 2010 London Conference.

It is often argued that India's policy may have earned the goodwill of large sections of Afghan people but has failed to provide New Delhi with enough leverage to protect its interests as the West ends its combat mission by December 2014. There is an ongoing debate within the strategic community as to what should be India's approach and policy towards Afghanistan especially in a post-withdrawal scenario. The Indian view could be broadly categorised into following three sub-heads:

(a) A Neutral Afghanistan—A section of Indian analysts argue that India should pursue a policy of non-interference in Afghanistan's factional politics. India should avoid getting drawn into the proxy politics as India is more likely to be exploited at the expense of her own interest in Afghanistan. The only way to ensure a durable peace and stability in Afghanistan is to advocate and push for an internationally, basically the UN-guaranteed, neutrality of the Afghan state.

(b) A Balanced Approach—Some analysts are of the opinion that India's interests are better served by reaching out to all Afghan factions, including the Taliban. India should especially try to rebuild its traditional ties with the Pashtuns for

without their support it would not be possible for India to achieve any of its objectives. However, at the same time, it is important for India to retain and reinforce her old ties with the non-Pashtun factions as well. Apart from strengthening the position of the central government, India needs to further engage all the major ethnic groups of Afghanistan at a much broader level.

(c) Pre-emptive Militaristic Approach—Though a minority view, it calls for India to play a more direct, on the ground, and a pro-active role in Afghanistan. India must pre-empt, if need be by employing physical force, the return of the Taliban and the Pakistani influence. In this regard, India should train the ANSF and if required should deploy its armed forces either in assistance to the Western forces or later as part of the UN-led peace keeping force in the post-West scenario.

The above categorisation of the Indian view is not to be taken in absolute terms since there are overlaps on certain issues. However, there is a general consensus on the need for India to remain engaged and help Afghanistan evolve into a relatively moderate, independent and a democratic state. India's policy options remain limited as the Afghan situation deteriorates and presents India's policy-makers with challenges similar to that of the 1990s.

Policy Constraints

It is equally important here to state that India's Afghan policy is constrained by various factors: (i) Geographical limitations. Since Pakistan continues to deny overland transit facility, India takes a long circuitous route via Iranian ports to reach out to Afghanistan. (ii) Uncertainty in the US approach. The continuing paradox in the approach of the American administration on the issue of war against terrorism that has remained singularly obsessed with al Qaeda, and the centrality of Pakistan in its regional calculus, has often left India and other regional countries doubtful of America's over-all commitment to its stated objectives.

At least in the near-term, India may be far too constrained to adopt a relatively independent approach though it very much remains a debatable option as multilateral approaches remain ineffective and India stands relatively marginalised in regional as well as international diplomatic initiatives on the Afghan issue. A big challenge for India could be how to sustain the momentum of its engagement in post-ISAF Afghanistan, which is likely to depend on following factors: (i) Sustenance of the current political system (ii) composition and orientation of the next government (iii) nature and level of Western engagement in post-transition period, and (iv) strength of India's ties with various Afghan factions. Among these, Afghan perceptions about India's role and presence and the sensitivity of the next political set up in Kabul to India's concerns are of critical importance. It is still early to state if India is willing to adopt a more pro-active approach which would call for major policy alterations; massive resource commitment; re-prioritised objectives; and creating leverages and exercising options hitherto considered unthinkable.

India to Stay the Course

Being a close neighbour, India is expected to take a long-term view of the developments taking place in its north-western neighbourhood. Since the overthrow of the Taliban regime, India has emerged as a major 'development partner' of the Afghan people, cutting across social and political divides. Assuming that building Afghanistan's institutional capacities is in India's long-term interest and apparently is the only viable way forward, India is likely to continue with its capacity-building and training programmes even in the worst case scenario. As a neighbouring country, India cannot afford to either abandon Afghanistan or rush into mad action.

It is important to understand why and how India, unlike other regional or Western countries with far greater leverages and resources at their disposal, has done relatively well in implementing its aid and assistance programmes and, more importantly, in managing people's perceptions. India has been extremely innovative in diversifying its assistance programmes as per the changing situation and specific requirements of the Afghan people. India today is seen as a relatively neutral neighbour and a positive force by the Afghan people. This is, perhaps, where the strength of India's Afghan policy lies.

However, as the Afghan war enters a turning point, India will have to explore its future options especially keeping in view the Obama Administration's decision to pull out troops and the post-Karzai scenario.

(i) To Remain Engaged and Continue with Reconstruction Assistance

Given the several constraints and limitations, India will have to make do with its current policy of assisting in the socio-economic reconstruction of Afghanistan. Indian assistance must continue to focus on capacity building and human resource development assuming that building institutions of governance and strong state structures is the only way forward in Afghanistan. However, as India remains committed to Afghan reconstruction, the security of the Indian personnel must be integral to its Afghan policy given the heightened state of insecurity in the country. There might be a situation where India may have to do more to secure its missions and projects. It is imperative for India to sustain its presence and to protect its interests by diversifying its Afghan engagement in anticipation of reduced Western military presence in years and decade to follow. Sustenance of its presence and goodwill has to be the bedrock of India's long-term engagement in Afghanistan.

(ii) Need for Broader Engagement

Apart from strengthening the position of the central government in Kabul, India needs to further engage a broad spectrum of Afghan leadership comprising all the major ethnic groups and factions of Afghanistan at a much broader level. This would require a differentiated approach as relations with various Afghan groups have its own dynamics. Any over-identification with a particular Afghan group/faction is to be avoided to the extent possible in view of the intensely factionalised and polarised Afghan polity. Similarly, since the West-sponsored political process has failed to establish a strong centre-province relationship and an internal balance of power, India will have to do a certain balancing act and be cautious against making any direct intervention in the conflict.

While reinforcing its ties with elements of the former Northern Alliance, India must also explore ways of leveraging its engagement with the Pashtun factions, including the former Taliban. Today, Taliban are a key actor on the Afghan chessboard and cannot be simply wished away. Taking full advantage of the weaknesses in the US policy and divisions within the trans-Atlantic alliance, the Afghan Taliban with backing from the Pakistan establishment have transformed the US-led war to their advantage. Assuming that the Taliban are a much more decentralised entity than ever before, Kabul has been trying to reach out to the Taliban as part of its effort for reconciliation. India as a pro-active measure should back indigenous efforts for national reconciliation and must engage former Taliban elements working with Kabul. In fact, India can go a step forward and offer its assistance, given its vast experience in various aspects of counter-insurgency, in the rehabilitation of surrendered Afghan insurgents.

(iii) Strengthening the Afghan National Security Forces

India has so far largely kept out of Afghanistan's security sector except for conducting some training programmes for the Afghan police earlier in deference to the US' counter-terrorism cooperation with Pakistan. The growing unease in the US-Pakistan relations over the latter's continuing complicity in backing insurgent/terrorist groups killing Western & Afghan troops across the Durand Line, opportunities may open up for other neighbouring countries worried over the prospects of Taliban making a full comeback to invest in the training, mentoring, and equipping of the ANA and the ANP. Since long there has been shortage of trainers and mentors for the Afghan army and the police. The NATO countries have continuously failed to deliver the necessary resources in this regard. Countries like India and Russia have an edge over NATO countries in view of complementarities in weaponry, past experiences in military cooperation, and better understanding of Afghan culture. The new Afghan Army has the potential to evolve into a major unifying national institution provided it is adequately resourced and trained in a sustained manner.

The involvement of some of the neighbouring countries in the training of Afghan security forces can also create opportunities for greater regional cooperation as the West draws down troops. It may also help nurture an enduring partnership between Afghanistan's neighbours and the NATO as part of a long-term stabilisation programme for Afghanistan. It is clear that the US and NATO alone cannot defeat the forces of religious obscurantism and terrorism flourishing on either sides of the Durand Line without a broad-based regional approach in strengthening the Afghan state institutions.

(iv) Gauging Varied Afghan Perception

As a neighbour of Afghanistan, it is imperative to India's Afghan policy to constantly factor in the varying views and perceptions of the various Afghan factions and groupings. It is important to figure out as to what extent the Afghans are willing to go with India's interests; and to what extent India matters in their perceptions on national security and development. Having a good grasp of the thinking across the social and political spectrum of Afghanistan would help Indian policy-makers in shaping viable responses to the newer challenges emerging from the Afghanistan-Pakistan region.

In prospective, taking clue from the weaknesses in the Western strategy in Afghanistan and Pakistan—patience, information, innovation and sustained focus—would be critical to strengthening India's position within Afghanistan and the wider south-central Asia region.

CHINA: PRETENDING DISTANCE

China has long been part of the Afghan maze. Interestingly, China is often seen as a minor or distant player in the Afghan conflict, not only in the Western analyses but in Afghan perceptions as well. Though China may not have been directly involved in terms of aiding or siding with any particular faction during the Afghan civil war, it has had a significant role in the long-drawn Afghan conflict. Right from persuading Pakistan on supporting the anti-Soviet *jihad* in the late 1970s to engaging the Taliban regime in late 1990s; from being a member of the 'Six-plus-Two' Group to supporting the US' *Operation Enduring Freedom* (OEF) against the Taliban regime in October–November 2001; and thereafter in the post-Taliban period, from emerging as the largest foreign direct investor in the Afghan mining industry to finally concluding a *Strategic and Cooperative Partnership*[124] with Afghanistan in June 2012, China all through has been part of the larger politics on the Afghan war. In fact, China is the second regional country after India to have institutionalised a supposedly long-term strategic partnership with Afghanistan. Today, China has the strongest ever economic presence inside Afghanistan since the establishment of full diplomatic ties between the two countries in 1955.

China's notably limited bilateral engagement with Afghanistan has largely been governed by its wider geo-strategic interests and its regional security concerns. Chinese interest and involvement in Afghan affairs have in the past grown in times of external interventions or internationalisation of the Afghan conflict, i.e., in the years following the Soviet intervention in 1979; and, in more recent times, since the begining of the US-led war on terror in Afghanistan. Broadly, with the exception of the years of Soviet occupation, China has dealt with whosoever has been in power in Kabul, including the Taliban. There has also been a strong Pakistani influence on its Afghan policy, especially since the late 1990s. In fact, it could be debatable whether China at all has had an independent approach or policy towards Afghanistan particularly since the establishment of the Pakistan-backed Taliban regime in Kabul.

Unlike in the 1980s and early 1990s, China today is evidently worried about the post-2014 situation and the prospect of a fresh round of civil war in Afghanistan. Chinese concerns mainly stem from the rising Uighur secessionism in its western Xinjiang Uyghur Autonomous Region (XUAR) bordering Pakistan-occupied Kashmir (PoK) and Afghanistan, its increased economic stakes in the Afghan mining sector, its expanding investments in the Central Asian energy resources, the growing narco-menace, and the possibility of a prolonged US presence in Afghanistan. In recent years, Beijing has noted with concern the rise in Taliban activity in Afghanistan's north-eastern province of Badakhshan bordering its Xinajiang region. Rising religious extremism and sectarian violence in Pakistan is also of concern to Beijing. Uyghur secessionists have been known to be operating from Pakistan's tribal areas since long. Until the emergence of the Taliban regime in mid-1990s, China never felt threatened by the spectre of religious extremism and violence spilling over from Pakistan and Afghanistan into its predominantly Muslim Xinjiang region.

China's Earlier Engagement with the Taliban

As the Soviet forces withdrew from Afghanistan and subsequently the Soviet Union disintegrated, China's domestic and foreign policy priorities changed. At the domestic level, there were challenges in the form of pro-democracy movements in Beijing leading to the Tiananmen Square episode in 1989. At the external level, the emergence of resource-rich Central Asian Republics (CARs) close to its borders opened up an entirely new range of both opportunities and challenges to its foreign policy. China was no more interested in the faction-ridden domestic politics of post-Soviet Afghanistan, especially after the closure of its embassy in

Kabul in February 1993 as the capital city turned into a battleground for rival resistance groups. Like the West, China too forgot Afghanistan until its south-western frontiers were threatened by the emergence of a new radical force, the Taliban, in Afghanistan. China later joins the 'Six-plus-Two' Group, the UN-sponsored initiative comprising of Afghanistan's six neighbouring countries and Russia and the US that was formed to explore ways to resolve the Afghan conflict. Along with the sudden rise of the Pakistan-backed Taliban and the fall of Kabul in 1996, China must have also taken note of the growing involvement of Russia, Iran and India in consolidating and strengthening the anti-Taliban coalition. China initially followed a wait-and-watch policy, but later given its close ties with Pakistan and the growing unrest in its Xinjiang Province preferred to engage the Taliban regime.

It was in February 1999 when a Chinese delegation comprising five senior diplomats was said to have first visited Kabul to meet the Taliban officials. China could not have been completely unknown to the Taliban leadership who had their roots in the leading Pashtun militant groups that China had supported against the Soviet forces in the 1980s. China was also said to have announced the beginning of direct flights between Kabul and Urumqi, capital of its restive western Xinjiang Province, and opening of formal trade ties with Afghanistan.[125] While referring to the aforesaid visit of the Chinese delegation to Kabul, Surya Ganagadharan observes:

> "The visit was never commented upon publicly by Beijing. Unofficial reports suggested that that the visit was China's way of saying thank you to the Taliban, who, in October 1998, had allowed in Chinese missile experts to recover and examine the remains of the cruise missiles the US had fired on Afghan terrorist bases in August that year. The Taliban also allowed the Chinese to take back an unexploded cruise missile. But it is difficult to accept the argument that the Chinese had sent a top team of diplomats to Kabul merely to say thank you."[126]

In fact, there were also reports that China had agreed to train Taliban pilots at Jalalabad. Apart from all this, an agreement on military cooperation was also reportedly signed on December 10, 1998 between the senior commanders of the People's Liberation Army (PLA) and the Taliban military representatives.[127] The former Taliban Ambassador to Islamabad, Abdul Salaam Zaeef, describes in his book how the Chinese ambassador in Islamabad "was the only one to maintain a good relationship" with his embassy and with Afghanistan, and how he had facilitated his visit to Kabul and Kandahar. Zaeef also mentions that the Chinese ambassador was the "first foreign non-Islamic ambassador ever to see" Taliban chief Mohammad Omar.[128]

All these developments were taking place in the backdrop of rising incidents of violence in the Xinjiang region. There was a flurry of activity relating to Xinjiang before China initiated talks with the Taliban in February 1999. Ahmed Rashid reports that on January 29 the Chinese authorities had arrested some 29 Uighurs for allegedly masterminding the bloody anti-government riots in the city of Yining which went on for two days in February 1997 in Xinjiang before it was suppressed with great difficulty by the Chinese Government. Since then the region has witnessed a steady rise in violence. The situation in the Yining city was reportedly still volatile when the Chinese delegation went to meet the Taliban in February 1999.[129] Later, in August 2011, Chinese Ambassador to Kabul, Xu Feihong, informed that there were over 200 cases of militant attacks in Xinjiang between 1990 and 2001.[130] China's decision to engage the Taliban regime which was supposed to be internationally isolated was initially viewed with scepticism across much of the world, and especially among countries who were supporting the anti-Taliban coalition inside Afghanistan.

However, from China's point of view, it was the fear of Taliban-style radical Islam spreading among its Muslim Uighur population in the Xinjiang Province bordering Afghanistan, and threat from cheap Afghan heroin flooding its market, that necessitated its engagement with the Taliban. The Uighur militants were known to have fought along with the Afghan *mujahideen* at least since 1986 and later in 1990s were also known to have developed links with the Islamic Movement of Uzbekistan (IMU). China's use of the Karakoram Highway to transport assistance to the anti-Soviet *jihad* had also invariably opened the way for the Uighur militants to Afghanistan, and especially Pakistan, where they still have a presence in the Pashtun tribal areas which has been acknowledged by Islamabad from time to time. In fact, there have been instances when China had to close down the Karakoram Highway because of the tension with Islamabad over the issue of curbing the activities of the Uighur militants operating from Pakistan. Though the bilateral irritants in the Sino-Pakistan relations are rarely reported, but often issues pertaining safety of the Chinese personnel engaged in development projects and differences over terms and conditions of contracts with Chinese firms have weighed in on the bilateral ties. As recently as September 2013, there were reports of a Chinese firm, Panyn Chu King Steel Limited, pulling out of the proposed Iran-Pakistan gas pipeline project.[131]

In June 2008, President Karzai during his meeting with Chinese President Hu Jintao had proposed the opening up of a direct road link between the two countries through the Wakhan Corridor. The security risks and threats that came with the establishment of the Karakoram Highway, perhaps, could have been one of the reasons why Beijing did not show any enthusiasm for President Karzai's proposal. Later, Afghan Vice President Karim Khalili too had raised the same proposal in his talks with Chinese Premier Wen Jiabao during his visits to Beijing in 2009.[132] However, according to an article, quoting from Chinese media reports, there are three major infrastructure development projects that China had been carrying out since 2009 close to the Wakhjir Pass that connects Xinjiang region with Afghanistan: first, a 75 kilometre long road, which will extend up to 10 kilometres from the China-Afghanistan border. The road is reportedly intended for use by Chinese frontier patrols and for the transportation of supplies to border units; second, construction of a supply depot which will reportedly raise the food quality standard for the police forces guarding the volatile Afghan frontier; and third, a mobile communications centre was reportedly established along the Wakhan Corridor in 2009 that permits the operation of mobile devices along the border, unlike before when Chinese units only had one functioning satellite telephone. Moreover, a specialized optical cable for web connection and internet access has been laid, with plans to construct a special line for the frontier police force.[133] In view of the growing Taliban influence in parts of northern Afghanistan including the Badakhshan Province bordering Xinjiang region, China would rather strengthen its defences along its narrow border with Afghanistan and look for connectivity via Tajikistan than expose its own volatile south-western region to the Afghan militant Islamists.

The prospects of an abiding nexus between militant Uighur separatists and the Pakistani, Afghan and Uzbek militant Islamists, as well as the drug mafia, may have further propelled China into engaging the Afghan Taliban who in turn were desperate for international recognition and legitimacy. It was probably for the first time since the Soviet withdrawal in 1989 that Afghanistan had again appeared in China's security calculus. However, this time the Sino-Afghan or rather the Sino-Taliban relations do not seem to have been fashioned by any larger geo-strategic calculus or great power politics, but by a more domestic security consideration. China's concerns over the Xinjiang region also arises from the fact that it has its nuclear testing site at Lop Nor, and the region is also suppose to have about 30 billion tonnes of proven petroleum reserves, and more is expected to be found in the Tarim Basin.

There is no doubt that China's engagement with the Taliban was facilitated by the Pakistan, which had enormous influence over the Taliban and was one of the three countries to recognise the Taliban regime. Pakistan had reportedly been pursuing China and the US to adopt a more modest approach towards the Taliban. According to Ahmed Rashid, "Pakistan has been trying to convince Beijing that the Taliban, to which it gives substantial military and financial aid, are willing to clamp down on the drug trade and have no desire to fund or support Islamic Uighurs in their fight for independence."[134]

Whatever might have been the nature of relationship or the level of interaction between China and the Taliban, the most notable aspect of it was that China dealt with the Taliban regime without ever extending an official recognition to it. In fact, despite China having opened lines of communication with the Taliban since 1998-99, it had also at the same time endorsed the UNSC's partial as well as additional sanctions against the Taliban in 1999 and 2000 respectively. As it did not have any formal diplomatic relationship with Afghanistan during 1993-2001, China had also used the Shanghai Five (later Shanghai Six and then finally Shanghai Cooperation Organisation or SCO)[135] forum to evolve a detailed plan of action with Afghanistan to combat "terrorism, illicit drug trafficking and organised crime in the region."[136] With the international attention turning towards Afghanistan in the wake of Taliban regime destroying nearly 1,500 year old two giant statues of Buddha in Bamiyan Province in March 2001, it could not have been possible for China to keep up its informal engagement with the Taliban regime. China had reportedly turned down Pakistan's offer of convening a meeting with the Taliban foreign minister in July 2001. China was also opposed to any direct military action against the Taliban regime by external powers as it believed that there was no military solution to the Afghan problem. Instead, China advocated a more active role by the UN.[137] Perhaps, China's Afghan policy preferred accommodation to confrontation, and advocated non-militaristic means which included a combination of diplomatic coercion and engagement.

In this context, it was aptly observed by Swaran Singh that China had a two-fold policy of "overt acquiescence" and "covert engagement" with Afghanistan's Taliban regime. Singh attributed such a policy to "the rise of PRC as the major Asian power" that made its Afghan policy "both much more visible as also much more complicated exercise." He added that it "aptly reflects a fusion of China's traditional cautious approach towards its Muslim neighbours as also its current compulsion in dealing with this issue of Islamic fundamentalism which remains at the core of China's Afghan policy initiatives."[138] In fact, China's decision to engage the Taliban was apparently a part of its larger effort to delink the Uighur separatists from its external linkages and to deny them support bases in countries bordering Xinjiang.

China's Role in Afghanistan since 2001

China did not protest when US decided to wage *Operation Enduring Freedom* (OEF) in Afghanistan in response to the events of September 11, 2001. Neither, China reacted to the positioning of US forces in the neighbouring Central Asian countries. The Chinese Government, like governments of many other countries distraught with violent separatist movements, was rather busy building a case for its own 'war on terror' against the Uighur militants, especially those belonging to the Eastern Turkestan Islamic Movement (ETIM). China was perhaps looking for a possible rapprochement with the US and greater understanding on the issue of terrorism within its own borders. In the Chinese perception, apart from posing newer challenges, the US intervention in Afghanistan was also seen as an opportunity for the two countries to come closer and explore ways of future cooperation. In fact, it was reported that in October 2002 the Chinese Ambassador to Brussels had met the NATO Secretary General Lord Robertson "to discuss the potential for building a closer relationship between his country and the Alliance."[139]

In his message to President Bush on September 11, Chinese President Jiang Zemin had stated that "the Chinese government consistently condemns and opposes all manner of terrorist violence."[140] The next day, Jiang had called up President Bush and reportedly offered to cooperate with the US on the issue of terrorism. At the UN Security Council on the same day, China as a permanent member had voted in favour of Resolution 1368 (to combat terrorism). On September 20, Beijing offered "unconditional support" to the US in fighting terrorism. On September 20-21, visiting Chinese Foreign Minister Tang Jiaxuan reiterated China's cooperation, and the US Secretary of State Colin Powell indicated that their discussions covered intelligence-sharing but not military cooperation. Meanwhile, China's counter-terrorism experts attended a counter-terrorism meeting on September 25, 2001 in Washington. On September 28, 2001, China voted in favour of Resolution 1373, reaffirming the need to combat terrorism. However, Jiang in a phone call with British Prime Minister Tony Blair on September 18 said that war against terrorism required conclusive evidence, specific targets to avoid hurting innocent people, compliance with the UN Charter, and a role for the Security Council. China had also reportedly sent its vice minister of foreign affairs to convince Pakistani President Pervez Musharraf to support the US in its war in Afghanistan. Later, testifying to the US Congress in February 2002, Powell had acknowledged the Chinese assistance in the war against terrorism.[141] However, it is noteworthy that the Pentagon's June 2002 report on foreign contributions in the counter-terrorism war did not mention China among the 50 countries in the coalition.[142] This was very much in continuation of the Bush Administration's failure to engage the regional countries other than Pakistan after the overthrow of the Taliban regime.

Post 9/11, China was clearly articulating its position on the issue of terrorism and the need for a stronger UN role in Afghanistan. On November 12, 2001, Chinese Foreign Minister Tang Jiaxuan, in his speech during the meeting of the foreign ministers of the 'six-plus-two' countries at the UN, had observed that "China closely follows the situation in Afghanistan and stands for a political solution through negotiation and dialogue." He argued that certain principles should be followed while dealing with Afghanistan: (i) Maintain the national sovereignty, independence, and territorial integrity of Afghanistan; (ii) The Afghan people should choose their own solution; (iii) The future government in Afghanistan should be broadly based, represent all ethnic interests, and co-exist with all countries, neighbors in particular, in amity; (iv) Regional peace and stability should be maintained; and (v) The UN should play a more active and constructive role. He also stated that "the 6+2 mechanism is important and effective in discussing and promoting a political settlement of the Afghan Issue, and should be given full play."[143]

Further articulating the Chinese position, Foreign Minister Jiaxuan in an interview to the Italian daily *La Stampa* on November 24, 2001 stated:

> "China supports the war against all forms of terrorism and upholds the resolutions approved by the UN Security Council. We strongly believe that such actions must avoid harming innocents and shall be consistent with the principles of the UN Charter and other universally recognized norms of international law. This serves the interests of peace and long-term stability in the world and in the region. The war against terrorism is a delicate issue having long-term impact. In agreement with the European Union, China also thinks that the war against terrorism requires the strengthening of international cooperation and the full development of the role of the UN and of its Security Council.
>
> No double standard should be adopted in connection with anti-terrorism. No matter where and when terrorist acts occur or which form they take, what the target is, or who is involved or supports them, the international community should condemn them with equal severity and firmly counterstrike.
>
> It is worth noting that China is also a victim of terrorism. The terrorist forces of Eastern Turkestan have been trained by international terrorist organizations, which have supported and financed them. Such forces have staged many attacks both in China and abroad, causing innocent victims. The Eastern Turkestan group is certainly a terrorist organization and fighting against it is part of the international war against terrorism."[144]

On Afghanistan, while expressing his support to what he described as "positive" and "constructive proposals" by the special envoy of the UN secretary general, Jiaxuan stated that the resolution of the Afghan issue has to be consistent with the following principles:

1. Afghanistan's political independence and territorial integrity shall be guaranteed;
2. The Afghan people shall finally decide by themselves how to solve the problems of Afghanistan;
3. Afghanistan's future government shall have a broad base and represent

the interests of each ethnic group, it shall pursue a peaceful foreign policy and abandon extremism, it shall entertain friendly relationships with all countries and specifically with neighboring ones;

4. The UN shall intervene in a more intensive and active fashion;
5. The solution of the Afghan issue shall serve the interests of peace and stability in the region.[145]

Similarly, in a report issued by the Chinese Information Office of State Council in January 2002, it was stated:

> "The Chinese government opposes terrorism in any form; at the same time it opposes the application of double standards concerning the anti-terrorism issue. Any tolerance or indulgence toward the "East Turkistan" terrorist forces will not harm China and the Chinese people alone. Today, as the international community becomes more clearly and deeply aware of the harm brought about by terrorism, we hope that all peace-loving people throughout the world, regardless of ethnic status or religious belief, region or country, political or social system, will fully recognize the nature of the "East Turkistan" terrorist forces and the serious harm caused by them, see through all their disguises, and jointly crack down on their terrorist activities, leaving not a single opportunity for them to exploit to their advantage."[146]

Though China's cooperation with the US in the wake of September 11 did not transform the Sino-US relations, but it did help in tiding over the bilateral tension over the bombing of the Chinese Embassy in Belgrade in May 1999 and EP-3/F-8 aircraft collision crisis in April 2001. The visit by US President George Bush to Shanghai in October 2001 to attend the APEC Forum was seen as an opportunity to make advances in the Sino-US relations. Though the Sino-US relations did ease a bit after September 11, but fundamental problems between the two countries remained. China was well aware of the fact that Uighur militants were still in Afghanistan and in the north-western tribal areas of Pakistan. Initially, it appeared that the US invasion of Afghanistan had once again provided an opportunity for China and the US and NATO to come closer and explore ways of future cooperation as was the case in the wake of the Soviet invasion of Afghanistan in 1979, but that was not to happen.

China's approach towards the emerging Afghan reality was characteristically cautious. China endorsed the Bonn Agreement signed among diverse Afghan groups on December 05, 2001. In Tokyo, on January 21, 2002, at a conference on reconstruction aid to Afghanistan, China pledged $1 million, in addition to humanitarian goods worth $3.6 million. It is noteworthy that China was among the first countries that Hamid Karzai paid visit to in January 2002, days after his appointment as head of the Afghan interim administration on December 22, 2001. Chinese President Jiang Zemin had promised to the visiting Afghan interim leader an additional reconstruction aid of $150 million spread over four to five years.[147] Of the $150 million, China had offered $47 million by 2003 and $15 million in 2004. In March 2002, a Chinese delegation carrying the first batch of assistance arrived in Kabul as part of the urgent humanitarian assistance committed by Beijing during the January 2002 Tokyo Conference on Afghanistan. Under the exchange of letters signed by the visiting Chinese delegation with Afghan officials, it was said that China will provide Kabul with 20,000 sets of uniforms and boots for the police and 50,000 sets of uniforms and boots for the army, and stationery and office supplies for 80,000 civil servants.[148]

Thereafter, what was notable was a series of high-level visits between the two countries. Chinese Foreign Minister Tang Jiaxuan was the first senior Chinese official to visit Kabul on May 15, 2002. He met Chairman Hamid Karzai, his Afghan counterpart Abdullah and the former Afghan King Zahir Shah. Jiaxuan welcomed the idea of holding a *Loya Jirga* (assembly of tribal elders and chieftains) to elect the leader for the Afghan transitional government in June 2002. He remarked that "China hopes that the *Loya Jirga* could turn out to be a success and all parties in Afghanistan would bear in mind national and ethnic minorities, conscientiously abide by the Bonn Agreement and work for national reconciliation, peace and prosperity."[149] In his meeting with Afghan Foreign Minister Abdullah, Jiaxuan announced that China will send teams to study the rehabilitation of the Kabul Republic Hospital, the water conservancy project in Parwan and a hospital in Kandahar. He also assured his Afghan counterpart that "China will fulfill as soon as possible its pledges to provide Afghanistan with police uniforms and stationery and office supplies for 80 thousand people." He further stated that "Chinese businesses are ready for economic and technological cooperation with Afghanistan in various ways and at various levels." The two ministers also signed an agreement on economic and technological cooperation.[150] The next month, in June 2002, Chairman Karzai made his second visit to China just days ahead of the *Emergency Loya Jirga* which was called for deciding on the Afghan Transitional Administration.

When Afghan Vice-President Niamatullah Shahrani visited China on May 27, 2003, and met his Chinese counterpart Zeng Qinghong, the two leaders again reiterated their cooperation against East Turkistan terrorists. China also announced $15 million grant to Afghanistan; another $1 million in cash to support the Afghan Government budget; resumption of the China-Afghanistan Friendship Association; inter-college relations between Beijing University and Kabul University; and an economic and technical cooperation agreement.[151] Chairman Karzai made his second good-will visit to Beijing on June 05, 2002 and exchanged views with President Jiang Zemin.

On March 10, 2004, Chinese Foreign Minister met Afghan Foreign Minister Abdullah and remarked that "Afghanistan was now in a critical period and the international community should continue to offer their attention and support in addition to the efforts made by the Afghan government and its people."[152] The same month, Chinese Ambassador Sun Yuxi, in a joint press conference with the Afghan Finance Minister Ashraf Ghani Ahmadzai, announced that China has decided to write off about $18 million debt Afghanistan owed to China since 1965.[153] The debt was finally signed off during a meeting between Chinese Foreign Minister Li Zhaoxing and Afghan Foreign Minister Abdullah held on the sidelines of the Berlin Conference on March 31, 2004. On December 07, 2004, China had sent a special envoy to attend the inauguration of Hamid Karzai as elected President of Afghanistan. It is interesting to note that in most of the meetings between the senior leaders and officials of the two countries, China always emphasised on "good neighbourliness" and appreciated Afghanistan's support for its "one-China policy" *vis-à-vis* Taiwan and the issue of cooperation against the activities of the East Turkistan militants, which were of prime concern for the Chinese security.

On June 10, 2004, about 11 Chinese workers engaged in a World Bank-funded road construction project in northern Kunduz Province were killed.[154] Though not much was stated about the identity of perpetrators of this attack and their objectives, it is significant that it did not deter China from bidding for huge mining contracts in Afghanistan in times to come. Later, in December 2006, Chinese workers engaged in another road construction project in Badghis Province again come under attack but no casualty was reported.[155] In August 2005, Chinese Ambassador to Afghanistan Liu Jian, during an interview to the *Pajhwok Afghan News*, had stated that more than 100 Chinese businessman are involved in various reconstruction projects in Afghanistan. He stated that the Sino-Afghan trade volume which was about $25 million in 2002 has increased as per the Afghan statistics to $380 million in 2004. Jian further stated that about 5,000 Afghans, mostly businessmen, had visited China in 2004 and that the number was likely to reach 7,000 by the end of 2005. He had also called for establishing a banking credit system between the two countries to further boost the bilateral economic ties.[156] Thereafter, on November 04, 2005, a protocol on establishing *SCO-Afghanistan Contact Group* was signed in Beijing.

In October 2005, it was reported that an Afghan defence ministry delegation was on an eight-day official visit that began on October 12 to China. The delegation was led by Afghan Deputy Defence Minister General Hamayun Fauzi who was quoted as stating that China would be providing military equipment worth $2 million in accordance with a list handed over by the Afghan defence ministry to the Chinese Government. It was further stated that apart from supplying equipment, China has also agreed to impart training and education to the Afghan defence ministry personnel.[157] Later, on June 19, 2006, Afghan

Defence Minister General Abdul Rahim Wardak, who was accompanying President Karzai during his four-day state visit to China, met Chinese Defence Minister Cao Gangchuan. According to *Xinhua*, Chinese Defence Minister Gangchuan, who was also vice chairman of the Central Military Commission and State Councilor, in his meeting with General Wardak had stated that "China is committed to developing its military ties with Afghanistan, and will continue efforts to upgrade such relations."[158] Thereafter, on June 24, spokesperson of the Afghan defence ministry, General Zahir Azimi, announced that a MoU was signed according to which China would impart training to 30,000 Afghan soldiers during the next four years and that China would allocate $3 million for the training.[159] On October 31, 2006, during General Wardak's good-will visit to Beijing, Chinese Defence Minister Gangchuan again reiterated his commitment to strengthening cooperation between the armed forces of the two countries. General Wardak was also reported to have visited Xinjiang Province and Shanghai during his visit.[160] On November 12, 2007, Chief of the Afghan National Army, Bismillah Mohammadi, visited Beijing and met Chinese Defence Minister Cao Gangchuan and his Chinese counterpart Chen Bingde.

In December 2010, Afghan Deputy Defence Minister General Mohebullah Moheb was reported to have visited China. On July 23, 2012, General Wardak again visited Beijing and met Chinese Defence Minister and State Councilor Liang Guanglie who was quoted as having stated that "the military-to-military exchanges are increasing, the high-level interactions are going on and the pragmatic cooperation in terms of personnel training and military aid...are going ahead in a stable way." He added that "the Chinese side was willing to cement and enhance the current cooperation between the two militaries based on mutual respect and win-win reciprocity to advance the military ties in a sustainable way."[161] On April 15, 2013, Afghan Deputy Interior Minister Abdul Rahman Rahman was reported to have met China's Assistant Public Security Minister Li Wei.

President Karzai's third visit to China in June 2006, this time as an elected President, led to the signing of the *Treaty on Good Neighbourliness and Mutual Cooperation* between the two countries on June 19, 2006.[162] However, the Treaty was ratified later by the Standing Committee of China's National People's Congress and the Afghan Parliament on August 14, 2008.[163] President Karzai's June 2006 visit was particularly significant in view of the large number of agreements and MoUs, a total of 11 documents, which were signed between the two countries. The joint statement issued on the occasion was probably the most comprehensive one by the two countries. The joint statement clearly stated that "trade and economic relations are an important part of China-Afghanistan good-neighborliness and friendly cooperation," which was well reflected in the long list of agreements and MoUs envisaged in the document:

Agreement on Cooperation on Combating Trans-national Crime;
Agreement on Trade and Economic Cooperation;
Agreement on Economic and Technical Cooperation;
Exchange Letter for China Granting Zero Tariff Treatment to Certain Goods Originated in Afghanistan;
Agreement on Air Service;
Protocol on Institutionalizing Consultations between foreign ministries of the two countries;
MoU on Agricultural Cooperation;
MoU on Cooperation in the Maintenance and Preservation of Cultural Heritage;
Memorandum of Agreement between the Afghanistan Chamber of Commerce and Industry and the China Council for the Promotion of International Trade; and
Memorandum of Agreement between the Afghanistan Investment Support Agency and the China Council for the Promotion of International Trade.

The joint statement announced that China would grant zero-tariff treatment to 278 items of Afghan exports to China as of July 01, 2006; train 200 Afghan professionals in the coming two years and offer 30 government scholarships to Afghanistan annually starting from 2007. While welcoming Afghanistan's engagement with the SCO within the context of "Contact Group Protocol," the Chinese side also "expressed readiness to enter into cooperation in pragmatic terms with the Afghan side within the framework of regional cooperation." The Afghan side too welcomed China's entry as an observer state into the SAARC.[164] By now, China was Afghanistan's third major trading partner after Japan and Pakistan with its export volume to Afghanistan totalling US$ 317 million in the fiscal year 2005-2006.[165] In November 2006, China reportedly donated 20 jeeps, 20 pickup trucks, sets of security monitoring system and kitchenware worth $1 million to the Afghan Parliament.[166]

Chinese Foreign Minister Yang Jiechi in his speech at the Paris Conference on Afghanistan on June 12, 2008 articulated the Chinese position on future Afghanistan in very simple terms. While endorsing the newly formulated Afghanistan National Development Strategy (ANDS), he emphasised that: (i) We need a safe and secure Afghanistan; (ii) We need an Afghanistan that enjoys development; (iii) We need an Afghanistan that stays far away from drugs; and (iv) We need a sustainable Afghanistan.[167]

At a time when President Karzai was coming under intense criticism from the Western countries for his allegedly controversial role in the August 2009 presidential election, Chinese Foreign Minister Jiechi met President Karzai on the sidelines of the Istanbul Summit on January 26, 2010 and assured him of China's continued assistance to Afghanistan. He stated that:

> "Under the leadership of President Karzai, the Afghan government and people have made arduous efforts for post-war reconstruction and achieved positive progress, which China highly appreciates. China supports the international community to work closely with the Afghan government and offer positive aid to the country for its reconstruction. China fully respects the will and initiative of the Afghan government and people and supports the UN's leading role in coordinating international efforts. China will continue to offer assistance within its ability for Afghanistan's peaceful reconstruction..."[168]

Again, on January 28, 2010, Chinese Foreign Minister Jiechi in his address at the London Conference on Afghanistan remarked that "Afghanistan's reconstruction process has gone through twists and turns, yet its future holds great promise." In his opinion, "the successful elections held by the Afghan people have opened a new chapter in the history of Afghanistan" and that "the international community should give continued attention to Afghanistan and offer greater support and assistance" which "is of particular importance to help Afghanistan strengthen its sovereignty, ownership and development capacity, thus laying the groundwork for a full transition to governance of Afghanistan by the Afghan people." While emphasising on Afghan ownership, Jiechi argued that "it is up to the Afghan people to shape the future of Afghanistan, but the help and support of the international community is indispensable." On the role of the regional countries, he was of the view that, "the neighboring countries should take advantage of their geographical proximity and play a unique role in assisting with Afghan reconstruction, and the international community should take concrete actions to support such regional cooperation." He also emphasised on the UN role, a known Chinese position, and stated that "there are now quite a number of mechanisms in the world regarding the issue of Afghanistan, and we should make good use of these mechanisms. We should encourage them to enhance coordination and work together to play an active role under the leadership of the United Nations. The United Nations Assistance Mission in Afghanistan has done an outstanding job in performing its missions in extremely challenging circumstances. China highly commends its work."[169]

Karzai paid his fourth visit to China as second term elected president on March 23-25, 2010. During the visit, he had a meeting with the Chinese President Hu Jintao on March 24 in the Great Hall of the People, where Hu identified five priority areas for both the countries to build a "comprehensive cooperative partnership of good-neighbourliness, mutual trust and friendship for generations": (i) strengthen overall bilateral ties by engaging in more regular meetings and exchanges; (ii) promote further bilateral economic collaboration; (iii) deepen cooperation in the humanities in areas such as personnel training, education, culture and public health; (iv) enhance security and police collaboration by combating cross-border organized crimes and the three evil forces of terrorism, extremism and separatism; and (v) coordinate with each other in multilateral affairs. The two presidents oversaw the signing of three bilateral cooperation agreements on aid, tax reduction and personnel training. Hu emphasised that both the countries should work together against cross-border crimes and "the three evil forces of terrorism, extremism and separatism." Hu also expressed his concerns about security of Chinese citizens working in Afghanistan and urged Karzai to ensure a sound environment for bilateral cooperation.[170]

Later, President Jintao, in his address at the second Bonn Conference on Afghanistan held on December 05, 2011, again proposed a five-point proposal as the way forward: First, the international community should firmly support an "Afghan-led and Afghan-owned" process of peace and reconstruction; second, the international community should firmly support Afghanistan in capacity building so that it can take over the responsibility of safeguarding national peace and stability as early as possible; third, the international community should firmly support Afghanistan in advancing national reconciliation through its own efforts and help create a favorable environment for reconciliation; fourth, the international community should firmly support Afghanistan in developing the economy. During the transition period and beyond 2014, the international community should continue to honor its commitments and provide support and assistance with no strings attached to bolster Afghanistan's capacity for sustainable development; fifth, the international community should firmly support Afghanistan in developing external relations. The international community should fully respect and accommodate the legitimate concerns of countries in the region. We should support the United Nations in continuing to play a leading role in coordinating international assistance to Afghanistan. The role of the Shanghai Cooperation Organization and other existing international organizations and cooperation mechanisms should be brought into full play.[171]

In 2011, according to the Chinese customs data, the total bilateral trade stood at $234.4 million, a rise of 31 per cent on the previous year, and Chinese imports from Afghanistan were worth just $4.4 million. However, more than trade, it is China's direct investments which could be facing grave security risks as is evident from the local media reports suggesting that the Chinese workers had to withdraw from the Aynak site in September 2012 due to security reasons.

On June 08, 2012, during Karzai's fifth visit to Beijing to attend the SCO summit, Hu Jintao, the then President of China, met Karzai in the Great Hall of the People (like in March 2010) and came out with his five-point suggestions for both sides: (i) to deepen political mutual trust and maintain close high level contacts; (ii) to expand cooperation in areas including economy and trade, contracted projects, resource and energy development, agriculture and infrastructure based on mutual benefit and common development; (iii) to expand cultural and people-to-people exchanges; (iv) to enhance security cooperation and jointly combat the "three forces" of terrorism, separatism and extremism as well as trans-national crimes, including drug trafficking and (v) expand multilateral coordination and cooperation within the framework of the SCO and the South Asian Association for Regional Cooperation (SAARC).[172]

Prior to the above meeting, the same day, China and Afghanistan upgraded their relationship by establishing a *Strategic and Cooperative Partnership*, building on the June 2006 *Treaty of Good-neighbourliness and Friendly Cooperation*. In the joint statement issued on the occasion, it was stated that the Strategic and Cooperative Partnership "will be an enduring and comprehensive relationship between the two nations which will serve the fundamental interests of two countries and peoples, facilitate the efforts to consolidate the traditional friendship of the two countries, expand cooperation in various fields, including political, economic, cultural and security." It was also stated that "cooperation in the political, economic, cultural and security fields, as well as on regional and international affairs, are the five pillars" of the China-Afghanistan Strategic and Cooperative Partnership.[173]

Growing violence in Xinjiang, particularly the riots of July 2009, had heightened the Chinese concerns regarding the impact of an unstable Afghanistan on security situation in Xinjiang. In retrospect, it is quite clear that China was accelerating its process of diplomatic engagement on the Afghan issue both at the bilateral and multilateral levels. As the process of security transition entered into its final phase and the distance and difference between Kabul and Washington continued to grow on a wide range of issues—from the US role in opening negotiations with the Taliban representatives based in Qatar to the terms and conditions of the BSA—China further raised its diplomatic support for Kabul and its initiatives.

At the SCO Summit held in Beijing from June 06-07, 2012, China also backed Afghanistan's observer status and discussed the evolving situation in Afghanistan. Chinese President Hu laid emphasis on strengthening cooperation through SCO to turn it into "a fortress of regional security and stability" and urged the members to fully implement the Shanghai Pact on fighting the "three evil forces" of terrorism, separatism and extremism, establish and perfect the security cooperative mechanism and take consistent actions to strike on the "three evil forces." In November 2012, at the Vice Foreign Ministerial Level Consultation on Regional Security of the SCO in Moscow, which was also attended by Jan Kubis, the Special Representative of the UN Secretary General for Afghanistan, China pushed for greater role of the SCO in the Afghanistan issue and held that China "support[ed] the international community's efforts in Afghanistan's peaceful reconstruction, and [was] willing to contribute to maintaining security and stability in Afghanistan and promoting its economic growth."[174]

On September 22, 2012, Zhou Yongkang, a senior member of the Standing Committee of the Politburo of the Communist Party of China (CPC), and former minister of public security (responsible for counter-terrorism, counter-insurgency, intelligence and internal security), went to Kabul in an unannounced four-hour-long visit. The media reported it as the most important visit by a senior Chinese leader since 1966 when the then Chinese President Liu Shaoqi had visited Afghanistan. It was reported in the media that the two sides signed a formal security liaison agreement which provided for Chinese support for Afghan efforts "to counter terrorism and maintain national security" and expressed Chinese willingness "to provide help within its ability to improve Afghanistan's security capacity-building."[175] It was also stated that China will be training 300 Afghan police officers over the next four years.[176]

After June 2012, President Karzai visited China in September 2013 to attend the Euro-Asia Economic Forum. Chinese President Xi Jinping met President Karzai on September 27, 2013 in the Great Hall of the People. Jinping described China and Afghanistan as "traditionally friendly neighbours" and pointed out that with the signing of the Strategic and Cooperative Partnership in 2012 relations between the two countries "have entered a new stage" and that China "firmly adheres to the policy of friendship towards Afghanistan and is ready to deepen strategic cooperative partnership with the Afghan side." Jinping thereafter proposed the following for developing China-Afghanistan relations:

> "First, to maintain high-level exchanges as well as contacts between the governments, legislative bodies and political parties, to strengthen strategic communication on major issues, to enhance political mutual trust. Second, to boost cooperation in the fields of economy, trade, project contracting, resources and energy development, infrastructure construction. China supports competent Chinese companies to invest in Afghanistan and will continue to offer help within its ability for peace and reconstruction as well as economic and social development in Afghanistan. Third, to strengthen security cooperation, to join hands (in) combating the 'three evil forces', drug trafficking and transnational crime. Hope the Afghan side will take effective measures to create a safe environment for bilateral cooperation. Fourth, to expand people-to-people and cultural exchanges. China is ready to continue to train all kinds of talented people for Afghanistan. Fifth, to enhance communication and coordination within the UN and other frameworks, to support the SCO for playing a greater role on the Afghanistan issue."[177]

Chinese President Jinping also stressed that the year 2014 is a "critical one for Afghanistan to achieve transition" and reiterated China's support for "the development path chosen by the Afghan people in accordance with their own national conditions, supports Afghanistan for achieving smooth transition and for improving and developing relations with other countries in the region." Jinping also reiterated Beijing's support for an "Afghan-led, Afghan-owned" reconciliation process. During this visit, extradition treaty was also signed between the two countries.[178] The signing of the extradition treaty clearly indicates China's growing concern about security in its volatile Xinjiang region after 2014. A MoU on cooperation between Shanxi Normal University and Kabul University too was signed.

On September 27, 2013, President Karzai also met Chinese Premier Li Keqiang who on the occasion stated, "China and Afghanistan are traditionally friendly neighbours and there are neither historical grievances nor realistic contradictions between both sides, only friendship and cooperation." Keqiang also stated that China is "ready to deepen bilateral strategic cooperative partnership with Afghanistan, to strengthen trade and investment cooperation, to promote the construction of energy resources and other major projects." Premier Keqiang further stated that "security and stability as well as improvement of people's livelihood in Afghanistan are two "wheels". China is ready to work with the international community to push for balanced turning of the two "wheels" in order to promote peace, stability and development of the region."[179]

Just before President Karzai's visit to Beijing, the Chinese Foreign Minister Wang Yi had met the then Afghan Foreign Minister Zalmai Rassoul on September 25, 2013 at the UN headquarters in New York. During the meeting, he too had reiterated China's firm support to the "Afghan-led and Afghan-owned" reconciliation process and stated that "China is ready to play a constructive role" in this regard.[180]

On February 22, 2014, Chinese Foreign Minister Wang Yi led a Chinese delegation to Kabul. During his one-day visit, he met a plethora of Afghan leaders and senior government officials. Apart from meeting his Afghan counterpart, Zarar Ahmad Osmani, he met Afghan President Hamid Karzai, then Afghan National Security Advisor Rangin Dadfar Spanta and the UN Secretary General's Special Representative for Afghanistan Jan Kubis. Interestingly, he also interacted with Zalmay Rassoul, Abdullah, Ashraf Ghani Ahmadzai and Abdul Qayum Karzai, all four leading candidates for the April 2014 presidential election.

In his press conference with Afghan Foreign Minister Osmani, he particularly focused on the upcoming Fourth Ministerial Conference of the Istanbul Process which China is hosting in Tianjin on August 29, 2014. He stated that China "expects to work closely with all parties including Afghanistan to make sure that practical outcomes will be achieved" from the conference. He described the Istanbul Process as "the only international mechanism on the Afghan issue led by the countries in the region" and added that the "member countries, adjacent or close to Afghanistan, all have connections with Afghanistan in both historical exchanges and realistic interests." Commenting on the Afghan transition, he stated that "with the accelerated withdrawal of the US and NATO troops and the upcoming of Afghan presidential election, Afghanistan is now experiencing a triple transition in politics, security and economy, which brings about both challenges and opportunities. At this point, the holding of the fourth Foreign Ministers' Conference of the Istanbul Process on the Afghan issue is of great practical significance." He also stated that the Chinese side "hopes to pool consensus from all parties by holding this conference and make concerted efforts to assist Afghanistan in realizing the triple transition."[181]

Calling Afghanistan "an important neighbouring country of China" and also "a country exerting unique and important influence in this region," Wang Yi clearly acknowledged that "Afghanistan's peace and stability has a bearing on the security of western China, and more importantly, bears on the peace and development of the entire region." Hinting at the urgency of political reconciliation as Western forces drawdown, Wang Yi pointed out that as "harmony boosts everything," it is "only by allowing all factions to participate in the reconciliation process can Afghanistan realize its lasting peace and stability." He stated that "the Chinese side expects that Afghanistan can achieve broad and inclusive political reconciliation as soon as possible, and is willing to continue to play a constructive role in this regard."[182]

While supporting sustained international engagement in Afghanistan, Chinese Foreign Minister Yi pointed out that, "The aid of the Chinese side, though limited, is very sincere with no political conditions attached." Probably emphasising on the need for Afghanistan and Pakistan to mend their ties, Yi noted that "The Chinese side supports Afghanistan in improving its relations with all countries, especially with neighboring countries; supports Afghanistan in actively participating in regional cooperation, including conducting cooperation with the Shanghai Cooperation Organization (SCO)." Yi also invited Afghanistan to join the "Economic Belt along the Silk Road."[183] In his meeting with President Karzai, Yi stated that 2014 is "a crucial year of Afghanistan's transition", and that "his visit to Afghanistan this time is to deliver a clear message that China attaches great importance to China-Afghanistan relations, and will continue to stick to the friendly policies towards Afghanistan and firmly support the domestic political reconciliation and reconstruction process in Afghanistan."[184]

Reports quoting diplomatic cables exposed by *Wikileaks*, show how the US efforts to gain Chinese cooperation for opening up alternate overland transit supply routes for the Western troops and delivery of non-lethal aid to Afghanistan were earlier rebuffed by China.[185] It is pertinent to mention here that in May 2010, Robert Blake, the US Assistant Secretary of State for South and Central

Asian Affairs, had visited Beijing and expressed the hope that China would contribute more to the ongoing process of reconstruction in Afghanistan. In his meeting with Hu Jintao, the Chinese media reported, Blake "suggested that Beijing provide more aid in agriculture, education and training of officials." Though Hu agreed that China should "actively contribute to helping Afghanistan with people's livelihood, economic growth and social stability,"[186] but nothing substantive in terms of bilateral cooperation on Afghan issue emerged from the initiative. However, it appears that the two countries have been discussing the Afghan situation at some level. Later, on May 17, 2012, the Joint China-US Training Programme for Afghan diplomats was launched at the China Foreign Affairs University in Beijing.[187]

China's Economic Engagement with Afghanistan

The Karzai Government opened up Afghanistan's energy, mineral and raw materials to foreign investment in 2006-07. China' interests in Afghanistan grew subsequently. In 2007, China followed Pakistan, European Union (EU), the US and India (in that order) as the fifth largest trading partner of Afghanistan. Chinese telecom companies like Huawei Technology Company Ltd. and Zhong Xing Telecommunication Equipment Company Limited (ZTE) have provided equipments to Afghan Ministry of Communications and Information Technology (MCIT),[188] and in November 2012, Afghan Telecom and ZTE signed a contract for $32 million dollars to implement part of MCIT plans to apply GSM and 3G services with 100 million dollars investment during 2012-2014. Afghan Telecom will receive 700 telecommunication towers from ZTE. Many development projects sponsored by the EU and even USAID are being executed through Chinese companies and workers.

China provided Afghanistan aid worth 1.3 billion Yuan (US$ 203 million) and waived debt worth US$ 19.5 million during 2002-2010. While signing Strategic and Cooperative Partnership with Afghanistan in June 2012, China pledged an additional assistance of 150 million Yuan (US$ 23.7 million). Altogether, Chinese assistance is a small fraction (about 0.60 per cent) of the total global assistance that Afghanistan has received since 2002. On an average, Chinese assistance to Afghanistan amounts to approximately US$ 22-23 million per year which is about 1.1-1.47 per cent of the total assistance China commits annually around the world. [189]

China is engaged in reconstruction and developmental work as well. It has built the Republic Hospital in Kabul, renovated the Parwan irrigation project, established a Confucius Institute in Kabul University[190] and provided training to Afghan officials and technicians. In August 2011, the Chinese Ambassador to Kabul, Xu Feihong, stated that about 600 Afghan officials & technical personnel and 140 anti-narcotics police officers had reportedly received training in China.[191] Apart from the above, China is also building multi-purpose centre in the presidential palace, and a National Education Centre of Science and Technology as well as a teaching building and a guest house for Kabul University. In 2011, China had donated 100 ambulances to the Afghan ministry of public health. Chinese media agencies, such as *Xinhua News Agency*, *China Central Television* (CCTV) and *China Radio International* (CRI) have set up offices in Afghanistan. To encourage trade from Afghanistan, it has progressively withdrawn tariff from about 278 items and signed off old Afghan debts as stated earlier in the chapter. Despite this, the volume of trade between the two countries remains very modest.

In late 2007, China emerged as the largest source of foreign direct investment (FDI) when state-owned China Metallurgical Group (MCC) in collaboration with two other Chinese mining groups, Jiangxi Copper, the biggest copper producer in the country, and Zijin Mining Group, China's leading gold mining company, won the contract bid for exploring Aynak copper mines in the Logar Province south of Kabul. The Aynak mine is projected to have some of the largest untapped reserves of copper in the world. The $3.5 billion copper mining contract was the first largest ever Chinese investment in Afghanistan.[192] This project is likely to be expanded to include building railways, investment in coal mines and a coal-fired power plant (400 MW), which could lead to potential Chinese investment up to US$ 10 billion.[193] In late 2008 and early 2009, through additional agreements, China secured a commitment from the Afghan Government to secure the project area, agreed to develop an ancillary 400-MW thermal power plant, and in return the Afghan Government agreed to provide water supply, and other minerals, including coal and limestone, required as inputs for copper production. Subsequently, in mid-2010, an agreement for a proposed regional shared-use railroad was finalised.[194] According to some estimates, this will enable the Afghan Government to earn about $808 million from the Chinese as payment for the rights for exploitation of its resources, and about $70 million per year as taxes over a period of about ten years.[195]

In 2010, total Sino-Afghan bilateral trade stood at $715.7 million, a rise of about 94 per cent from the previous year, and Chinese imports from Afghanistan were worth just $7.9 million.[196] However, more than trade, it is China's direct investments which could be in danger as evident from local media reports suggesting that the Chinese workers had to withdraw from the Aynak site in September 2012 due to security reasons.[197] Taliban influence and activity has been rising in Logar Province since 2011. The project has still not picked up and remains vulnerable to growing insecurity in the region.[198]

In December 2011, the state-owned China National Petroleum Corporation (CNPC) became the first foreign firm to sign the deal to jointly explore oil blocks with Afghanistan's Watan Group in the Amu Darya Basin in the north-western provinces of Sar-e Pul and Faryab.[199] Under this deal Afghan government will earn 70 per cent from sales apart from CNPC's commitment to pay 15 per cent royalty and other corporate taxes and land-rents. CNPC has also offered to build an oil refinery which will be a money spinner and may help Afghanistan to earn about US$ 7 billion over next 25 years.[200] All this seem very assuring from Afghanistan's point of view which regards such projects as critical to its economic revival and growth. However, some analysts suggest that Chinese bids are sometimes unrealistically generous and often re-negotiated with national governments. In case of Aynak Copper Mine, there are reports about Chinese firm wanting to re-negotiate the contract. Chinese deals are also characterised by "a lack of transparency," "miscommunication of partnership terms," "lax environmental standards," and "disputes with local communities over working conditions, biased hiring and procurement practices and inadequate assistance for villages displaced by mining."[201] Chinese companies engaged in Afghanistan have often come under criticism for lack of respect for Afghan laws. In November 2007, it was reported that the Afghan finance ministry had alleged that the ZTE had not paid taxes since three years and was operating without obtaining proper license. The allegation came immediately after the ZTE had signed a $64.5 million contract with the Afghan ministry of communications for extending the fibre optic cable network in the country.[202]

Chinese Perspectives

China regards Afghanistan as a regional hotspot and aims at an end-state where Afghan people would govern Afghanistan. China, as evident from the statements made by Chinese Ambassador Wang Yi during his visit to Kabul on February 2014, now fully acknowledges the direct linkage between its Xinjiang concerns and Afghan instability. Since 2013-14, there has been a relatively greater clarity in the Chinese articulation on the evolving scenario in Afghanistan. The prospect of a direct and long-term threat emerging from Afghanistan and Pakistan is too serious for China to ignore. As a Chinese scholar argues, China maintains an independent but low key policy *vis-à-vis* Afghanistan which reflects "the peculiarities of its interests, concerns and priorities," however, "domestic concerns about the security and stability of the largely Muslim region of Xinjiang, overwhelm all others"[203] and China views Afghanistan as "an inseparable part of building Xinjiang's security."[204]

In its position paper presented at the UN General Assembly in September 2012, without directly establishing the linkage between terrorism and insurgency in Xinjiang and the situation in Afghanistan, China in the section on "counter terrorism" stated that despite the efforts of the international community "the breeding ground of terrorism has not been removed," and China has been a victim of terrorist plots instigated by "Eastern Turkestan" terrorist forces, to fight against whom "is an important part of the international anti-terrorism campaign." It then goes on to state that the "situation in Afghanistan concerns peace and stability in the region and the world at large and affects the progress of the international counter-terrorism effort."[205]

However, China has taken absolute care not to mention the Taliban as a source of concern. It is, therefore, no surprise that China has not issued any official reaction on the issue of Taliban resurgence, despite having "friendly" relations with the Karzai Government in Kabul. Perhaps, that is to be expressed through a multilateral forum like the SCO. China has also effectively used the SCO to further reinforce the fundamental aspects of its own approach on the Afghan issue. For instance, in his speech at the Special Conference on Afghanistan held in Moscow on March 27, 2009, the then SCO Secretary General Bolat Nurgaliev had stated:

> The difference in assessments of the situation in Afghanistan seen from the statements of the participants is quite wide. Nonetheless, almost everyone acknowledges the fact that despite certain reinforcement of the capabilities of the central government, the gravity of the threat from the resurgent Talib militants and continuing instability in southeastern regions of the IRA remains on the rise. 98 % of opium poppy is harvested in 7 provinces of Afghanistan, where the positions of Talibs and organised criminal groups are quite strong, which shows cause and effect connection between the drug trafficking and never-ending conflict. The ability of drug dealers and their terrorist supporters to sell more than 600 cubic tons of pure heroin per annum is generating profits, which exceed the expenditure part of Afghanistan's whole annual budget.
>
> Effective settlement of existing problems can be possible only with due regard for the interests of all parties, through their involvement in the ongoing process, not through isolation. I am confident that this conclusion of the SCO states vis-à-vis general principles of maintaining international security is fair as regards the assessment of the potential role of Afghanistan's neighbours.
>
> The staging in Moscow of the Special Conference reaffirms the unconditional solidarity of the SCO states with the efforts of the international community to restore law and order in every part of Afghanistan, put this long-suffering country on the road to steady progress, ensure due regard for the state sovereignty of the IRA and the right of the Afghan people to choose their own way of development.
>
> It is stability, not transformation imposed from outside, it is long-term and steady international aid, not interference aimed to achieve unilateral interests, which Afghanistan needs the most. Once all the states involved in the Afghan

settlement adhere to such position, the current alarming situation in Afghanistan will surely change for the better.[206]

There have been reports suggesting that China has established indirect contact with the *Quetta Shura* through Pakistan.[207] Taliban too may not mind having limited engagement with Beijing, a powerful neighbour and a permanent member of the UN Security Council. Moreover, given China's long-standing strategic relationship with Islamabad and latter's control over the Taliban, China may consider pushing for a Taliban-inclusive dispensation in Kabul that is favourable to its interests. Driven by its wider economic interests in the south-central Asia region, including its investments in the Afghan resources, China may not be averse to the idea of Taliban being part of a broad coalition in Kabul, as the latter has re-emerged as a force to reckon with. But the fundamental question remains: whether the *Quetta Shura* and its various allies are at all willing for a negotiated political settlement of the conflict with Kabul and, more importantly, whether the Taliban are willing to accept the known social and political diversity of the country which remains at the heart of the long-standing conflict within the country?

Though it is more than a decade since Beijing established its first contact with the Taliban in 1998-99, and has also since consciously avoided directly criticising the Haqqani-Taliban network or the Pakistani military-intelligence apparatus for sustaining them, but the Uighur militancy and incidents of violent attack in China have only been increasing with time. As for the Taliban leadership, they continue to fight for establishing an "Islamic Emirate" and have not yet shown any willingness to accept the inclusive political system currently in place in Kabul and a constitution that recognises and acknowledges the inherent diversity of the country. China has all through emphasised on the need for a broad-based inclusive politics in Afghanistan, but at the same time has failed to articulate its position on how the *Quetta Shura* and the various Pakistan-based militant Islamist groups which owe their allegiance to Mohammad Omar, whom they regard as their *Amir-ul Momineen*, and who remain committed to the idea of establishing an 'Emirate,' could be reconciled with a vast majority of Afghan people who have constantly rejected the notion of an 'Islamic Emirate.' It is noteworthy that in none of the several Chinese statements quoted in this chapter one would find any reference to the three pre-conditions or the red lines that were spelt out and endorsed during the January 2010 London Conference on Afghanistan for the Taliban to join an "Afghan-led" and "Afghan-owned" reconciliation process. The paradox in the Chinese approach towards Afghanistan is at times too compelling and often conveys a serious lack of understanding or rather willingness to recognise the ultimate ideological objectives and socio-political agendas of the various trans-national Islamist networks now well embedded in the south-central Asia region.

China is more likely to continue to work closely with the Pakistani military establishment in the hope that it would rein in the Uighur militants. It is not understood as to how threat from Uighur militants to China or TTP to Pakistan could be eliminated without destroying several other local or foreign affiliate groups based inside Pakistan which continue to sustain and motivate each other. The evolving security situation in Afghanistan and the unprecedented levels of violence and sectarian divide inside Pakistan has only brought out the futility of a narrow and selective approach towards fighting forces of militant extremism and terrorism that continue to multiply and proliferate in the region.

China apparently continues to look at Afghan conflict within the context of old competing geo-political rivalries in the region. The opinion piece published in the state-owned *People's Daily Online* in February 2009, perhaps the first clear articulation of Chinese position on the evolving situation in Afghanistan, had stated that the "Afghan problem," the "Pakistani problem" and the "Indian-Pakistani problem" are all related. Questioning the Obama Administration's decision to send additional troops to Afghanistan, the opinion piece argued that first the US "must stabilize South Asia, especially Pakistan and the India Pakistan relationship" and added that:

> "...without Pakistan's cooperation, the US cannot win the war on terror. Therefore, to safeguard its own interests in the fight against terrorism in South Asia, the US must ensure a stable domestic and international environment for Pakistan and ease the tension between Pakistan and India."[208]

As stated above, there is no denying the fact that Pakistan has a critical role but then what does "Pakistan's cooperation" mean? Despite its efforts to upscale inter-state cooperation through the SCO to ensure regional security in post-withdrawal Afghanistan, China has been extremely wary of committing either itself or the SCO to any active role inside Afghanistan. In February 2014, the SCO Secretary General had clearly stated that "The SCO is not supposed to shoulder the responsibilities and duties of NATO" but added that "this does not mean an evasion of the issue as the organization has actively participated in international efforts to seek desirable solutions to Afghanistan's security issues."[209] The Chinese offer to train Afghan security forces has been pretty minimal though some reports in the Afghan media referred to earlier in the chapter indicate Kabul's growing desire for Chinese assistance in strengthening the capabilities of the Afghan security forces.

While China remains sceptical about the American presence and its long-term objectives, it is at the same time mindful of its own limitations to engage militarily in the Afghan theatre. China, therefore, understands the necessity of international policing of some sort, including greater UN role, to ensure long-term Afghan stability. In view of the persisting threat to the government in Kabul,

Beijing as of now seems to have acquiesced to a prolonged but reduced Western presence in the region.

Otherwise, Beijing remains reflexively allergic to a strong US presence across its borders. While China continues to support the larger international and multilateral endeavours in Afghan reconstruction, it has hardly evinced any serious interest in making common cause with the West's Af-Pak strategy, partly because of Pakistan factor and partly due to its competitive relationship and conflicting interests with the US at the wider regional and global levels. Perhaps, the dynamics of the US-Pakistan, China-Pakistan and US-China relations are too intricate and complex to cause any strategic shift in their respective regional strategies. The same remains the case with the various trilateral initiatives in the region, including the US-Pakistan-Afghanistan and the Pakistan-Afghanistan-China Trilateral Dialogue which was launched in 2012.

Post-2014: Increased Diplomatic Engagement

It remains to be seen as to what extent Pakistan would be central to China's policy towards post-2014 Afghanistan. Though, as of now, there are no discernible trends indicating any strategic shift in China's thinking as far as its relationship with Pakistan or its response to Afghan uncertainty is concerned, the prospect of China re-strategising or re-aligning its Asia policy in the long-term cannot be ruled out. A combination of several factors that directly impact Chinese interests in its geographical proximity, are discussed below:

(i) The prolonged, though reduced, US presence in Afghanistan beyond 2014 as sufficiently indicated in the US-Afghanistan strategic partnership agreement and the ongoing negotiations for a bilateral security agreement, coupled with the planned shift in the US strategy in the Asia-Pacific region, could present an altogether new regional context for China. It has direct implications for the wider Asian geo-politics. Though it is too early to project possible Chinese responses, but as the balance of power changes, China may try to re-align and re-adjust its regional strategies by increased cooperation, competition, and if needed, even confrontation, to further its perceived interests.

(ii) Where would Afghanistan figure in China's long-term regional and overall security calculus, and whether Pakistan would continue to be an asset or prove to be a growing liability in China's own re-balancing of foreign policy priorities, is difficult to envision. Nevertheless, continued Western presence amidst the rising threat of religious extremism and narcotics from Afghanistan-Pakistan will, in all likelihood, necessitate a greater Chinese interest in developments close to its south western frontiers. China would not like the Afghan conflict to spill over into its restive western borderlands and would expect Pakistan not to destabilise the government in Kabul.

Based on the past trends, it may be said that China would continue to remain engaged in Afghanistan, irrespective of the ideological orientation and the political composition of the leadership in Kabul. In fact, depending on the success or the failure of the ongoing security and political transition, Beijing may like to upscale its assistance to Afghanistan including reinforcing the capabilities of the ANSF.

(iii) Although China has expectedly avoided articulating its anxieties about Pakistan's inability to control the extremist and terrorist groups operating out of its tribal borderlands, it understands quite well that it would be difficult for China to insulate itself from the continued turbulence along and across the Durand Line. The sheer range of extremist and terrorist groupings active along the Pakistan-Afghanistan frontiers with continued support from sections of the Pakistani establishment, and their proven ability to mount offensives, both physical and ideological, is likely to pose a more serious ideological and political threat for the region including China after 2014. Never before did China face a direct security threat of this scale and scope from both Pakistan and Afghanistan. The prospects of militant Islamists conducting attacks outside Xinjiang region in mainland China is growing.

It is expected that given its security concerns in Xinjiang, its growing economic interests and investments in Afghanistan and its inclination to enhance its stature in the southern-central Asian region, China may play a relatively more active diplomatic role in Afghanistan in the coming years. China hopes to contain the negative influence of possible Afghan instability beyond 2014 by engaging various Afghan factions, including the Taliban, and also by continuing to work closely with the Pakistani security establishment. Though China has cordial relations with Kabul and more than cordial ties with Islamabad, it is not clear to what extent Beijing would be keen on mediating between the two countries in the post-2014 scenario. Similarly, whether Beijing is in a position to exert enough pressure on Rawalpindi to help bring about political reconciliation between the Quetta Shura and the next Afghan Government too is a matter of conjecture. Beijing has thus far cautiously avoided giving Kabul any impression of a Sino-Pakistan axis seeking to influence the politics of Afghanistan.

Interestingly, Kabul seems to have been keen on Beijing playing an active role in facilitating the reconciliation process with the Pakistan-backed Afghan Taliban leadership. This could also be part of Kabul's ongoing effort to diversify its foreign policy in view of the soaring differences with the West. In September 2013, the chief of staff of the Afghan presidential office, Abdul Karim Khurram, was quoted by *Xinhua* as stating that "This is our desire and we have wished it many times that China should play a role in the peace process of Afghanistan.

We certainly would welcome it."[210] China's decision to upgrade the Karakoram Highway as part of the planned China-Pakistan Economic Corridor and to undertake the management of Gwadar Port in Pakistan is, however, likely to reinforce China's strategic presence in the region.

(iv) China is unlikely to assume any direct military role inside Afghanistan in foreseeable future. Instead, China may assert its position through declarations and joint statements in multilateral forums like the SCO. It seems to prefer a broader security approach towards Afghanistan, perhaps, under the UN aegis. In the long run, much would depend on China's own threat perceptions, evolving security situation within Pakistan, the level of future US presence and the nature of its engagement in Afghanistan and Pakistan, the evolving trajectory of the US-China relations, and changes in the wider regional power politics.

RUSSIA: HESITANT BUT CONCERNED

Russia has increased its engagement with Afghanistan since the West decided to militarily drawdown and handover the security to the Afghan forces beginning in 2011. Kabul too had been keen on engaging Moscow as part of its effort to diversify its foreign policy in view of rising tension with the West. Russia has long been weighing its options, wary of what may unfold in Afghanistan after 2014. In fact, contrary to general assumption, Russia has very much been a part of the post-Soviet Afghan matrix. In the 1990s, Russia had played a key role in building the anti-Taliban Afghan coalition that later proved to be an asset for the US in its war on terror in Afghanistan.

Russia was also part of the 'six-plus-two' group on Afghanistan and has long been concerned about potential threat from the Afghan conflict to the security and stability of its southern periphery, particularly its highly volatile Northern Caucasus region. Russia has also actively contributed to strengthening the security structures in Kyrgyzstan and along the Afghanistan-Tajikistan border since the outbreak of the Afghan civil war in the 1990s. Aware of the security vacuum in the post-Soviet space and potential threat to regional stability, Russia had established the Collective Security Treaty Organisation (CSTO).[211]

Since the US invasion of Afghanistan, Russia had been trying to strengthen the regional security alliance and has often called for coordination between the CSTO and the NATO on jointly dealing with the menace of international terrorism and drug trafficking. In 2007, during an informal NATO-Russia Council meeting at Seville in Spain, the then Russian Defence Minister and also a Deputy Prime Minister, Sergei Ivanov, while deriding the "inertia of old approaches," had stated that "Russia, along with the [anti-terrorism] alliance, is seriously concerned by the continuously deteriorating military and political situation in Afghanistan. Combining the potentials of the CSTO and NATO working on both sides of the Afghan border, we believe, could yield better results. Therefore, the invitation to NATO to take part in the CSTO's annual anti-drug operation, Channel, remains in force."[212] However, owing to the old distrust, competing geo-political interests and Cold War mindsets, the two largely failed to engage each other in a mutually beneficial and concrete manner.

Russia and Post-Taliban Afghanistan

On October 02, 2001, even before the overthrow of the Taliban regime in Kabul, the Russian emergency situations ministry had announced that it will deliver humanitarian aid to the people of north Afghanistan via Dushanbe in three stages. The Russian aid included food, medicines, field hospitals, ambulances, diesel power plants, tents, stoves and kitchen wares.[213]

With the American invasion of Afghanistan becoming imminent, Moscow saw an opportunity to redefine its troubled relations with the NATO. On October 03, 2001, Russian President Vladimir Putin met the then NATO Secretary General George Robertson at Brussels. While addressing a press conference after the meeting, President Putin stated that the discussions covered "full range of relations between Russia and NATO." Describing the talks as "very frank" and "substantive," Putin informed that the NATO Secretary General Robertson has proposed "an initiative to create a working body that would consider the possibility of expanding, deepening and qualitatively changing the relations between Russia and NATO." In response to a query whether the Western leadership is heeding to Moscow's desire for closer cooperation with the NATO, President Putin had stated:

> "We'll have to see how this becomes realized on a practical plane. But the position of the President of the United States is known to me, which he has quite explicitly stated, and we feel a change of the approaches of the Western community and of the United States after the clear signals from the US President about a necessity to alter the character of relations between Russia, and the States and the Western community as a whole. We feel that practical changes are beginning to occur in the quality of our relations. Approximately the same I can state after the meeting with the European Union leadership. And the practical proposal which was today formulated by the NATO Secretary General, confirms the same very fact, indicating that they in NATO too are willing to expand and change the quality of relations with the Russian Federation."[214]

Despite efforts by Moscow, no substantive change occurred in the quality of relations between Russia and the West. Moscow was sidelined as the Bush

Administration having overthrown the Taliban regime in Kabul decided to destroy the Saddam Hussein regime in Iraq. Meanwhile, a year after the overthrow of the Taliban regime, Moscow had signed a contract with the Afghan Transitional Administration (ATA) in December 2002 to provide military–technical assistance. Between 2002 and 2005, Russia's military–technical assistance to Afghanistan reportedly totalled more than $200 million. Russia had "delivered airport maintenance equipment, a missile defence system to protect the Kabul airport, communication equipment, trucks, repair equipment, spare parts and manuals." However, after 2005, Russia had to suspend its military assistance in view of the alleged 'duplication' of the US military assistance to the ANA.[215] It was not until 2008–09 that Russia was able to resume its humanitarian and military assistance to Kabul. Meanwhile, Moscow was getting increasingly restless about the US role in the 2004 Ukrainian presidential election. In December 2004, Moscow had announced its decision to hold the first ever joint military exercise with China later in 2005.[216] At the same time, Moscow was also pushing for a trilateral with China and India.

However, Moscow probably remained hopeful of working together with the US on the issue of counter-terrorism despite growing differences with the Bush Administration on developments in Ukraine and also over the war in Iraq. The Beslan school hostage crisis in North Ossetia in September 2004 reinforced the urgency in Moscow to continue to engage the West on the issue of global terrorism. It is noteworthy that in his annual Christmas news conference in December 2004, President Putin had described American President Bush as Russia's "priority partner" and "ally" in the war against terrorism.[217] At the same time, then CSTO General Secretary Nikolai Bordyuzha too announced that the CSTO has invited NATO to join in the *Channel 2005* annual anti-drug operation.[218] Later, on April 21, 2005, during an informal NATO-Russia Council meeting in Lithuania, Russia signed the Status of Forces Agreement with NATO that paved the way for military cooperation between the two including joint training and exercises and reciprocal transit facilities. According to then NATO Secretary-General Jaap de Hoop Scheffer, "The SOFA will allow us to organize better a rich menu of cooperative activities. It will save us time by providing a legal basis for movement of people and equipment agreed in advance, and it will allow us to act together in new areas, such as strategic airlift." Later, the above agreement provided the basis for the establishment of the Northern Distribution Network (NDN), an alternative supply route running through Russian and Central Asian territories for the NATO-led force in Afghanistan. It is noteworthy that the Russian foreign ministry at the same time had reportedly cautioned the NATO against inviting members of the CIS to the alliance.[219]

Later, it was in the 16th Session of the US-Russia Counter Terrorism Working Group (CTWG) held on June 19-20, 2008 in Moscow that Russia was allowed to resume its military supplies to the Afghan army. As per the joint statement issued on the occasion: "Through the CTWG, the United States and Russia are working together to combat terrorism and other international threats by focusing on several important areas including Afghanistan, counter narcotics, United Nations designations of terrorists and terrorist financiers, terrorism finance, intelligence sharing, law enforcement, weapons of mass destruction (WMD), Man Portable Air Defense Systems (MANPADS), and transportation security." With regard to cooperation specifically on Afghanistan, it was stated that 'liaison connections between Russian Federal Drug Control Service (FSKN) and the U.S. Drug Enforcement Administration (DEA) have been established in Washington and Kabul; made permanent the NATO-Russia Council (NRC) counter narcotics project on joint training in Domodedovo for Afghanistan and Central Asia; and continued support for Organization for Security and Cooperation in Europe (OSCE) projects to build Afghanistan and Central Asia border security capacity by providing training and mentoring of customs and borders officials, as well as adequate training facilities.'[220]

Despite some progress in NATO-Russia relations, Moscow remained sceptical of the Western intentions in the post-Soviet space. The tension between Russia and the West was to grow in the coming years particularly over the course of events in Ukraine, Georgia and even Belarus. With Baltic States joining the EU and NATO in 2004, Moscow had been extremely wary of the growing Western forays in what it regarded as its "near abroad." Added to it was the NATO's plan to establish ballistic missile defence in Eastern Europe close to the Russian borders. The perception in Moscow with regard to the Western strategy could perhaps be gauged from the observations made by Natalia Narochnitskaya, then Vice Chairman of the International Affairs Committee in the State Duma, the Lower House of the Russian Parliament, and a member of the nationalist Rodina Party:

> "We are gradually being pushed to the northeast of the Eurasian continent away from the seas...to the place where the depths of freezing is more than two meters.
>
> The messianism of American foreign policy is a remarkable thing. When Secretary of State Condoleezza Rice speaks, it seems like Khrushchev reporting to the party congress: 'The whole world is marching triumphantly toward democracy but some rogue states prefer to stay aside from that road, etc. etc.'"[221]

As opposed to the American unilateralism, Russia was clearly calling for a much broader and a multilateral approach to deal with the rising challenge of international terrorism. Since the collapse of the Soviet Union and the end of the Cold War, Moscow had been concerned about the various processes of transition from a bipolar to a multi-polar international system. In his article published in 2005, former Russian Foreign Minister Sergey Lavrov had stated:

> Like an overwhelming majority of other countries, Russia believes that the future world order must be based on collective mechanisms for addressing global problems. Whether this will be named a multipolar system or otherwise does not really matter. More important, this system must contain as many fulcrum points as possible in order to guarantee its stability. The international community must discover a platform for broad accord and interaction between the main actors on the global arena, including the G-8, the European Union, China, India, Japan, and the key countries of Southeast Asia, the Middle East, Latin America, and Africa. This platform must rest on mutual confidence and respect for each other's interests in addressing international problems, as opposed to a group of countries invited to join a single nation that has already decided everything unilaterally.
>
> Another aspect of more reliable international governance is improving mechanisms of multilateral cooperation; of these, the United Nations is undoubtedly the most universal. This organization, which has unique legitimacy and an extensive record of global and regional activities, must be made more effective in crisis management and acquire better-defined criteria for using coercive measures, including force, by a Security Council decision.
>
> Russia maintains that the UN Security Council must avoid applying mechanical approaches when advancing criteria for giving the green light to the use of force. Each individual situation must be considered taking into account its specificity. There can be no universal recipe or simple arithmetic solutions, such as "99 people killed are not quite genocide, but 100 people killed are, so the Security Council must automatically make a respective decision." It is also important for the international community to make decisions on its interference in a crisis, especially on "preventive interference," on the basis of verified and irrefutable facts rather than conjecture and unsubstantiated accusations, as was the case, for example, with assertions about weapons of mass destruction in Iraq.[222]

The NATO, however, in its new strategic concept released in May 2010 had acknowledged the need to engage Russia on various issues of common concern. It was stated:

> "NATO should pursue a policy of engagement with Russia while reassuring all Allies that their security and interests will be defended. To this end, the Alliance should demonstrate its commitment to the NRC (and invite Russia to do the same) by focusing on opportunities for pragmatic collaboration in pursuit of such shared interests as nuclear non-proliferation, arms control, counter-terrorism, missile defence, effective crisis management, peace operations, maritime security, and the fight against trafficking in illegal drugs."[223]

Describing the NATO's relations with Russia as "a combination of shared interests and strained feelings," the new strategic concept called for "a policy of active and constructive engagement both on NATO's part and Russia's." The document acknowledged that Russia because of its size and stature "will inevitably play a prominent role in shaping the Euro-Atlantic security environment." Further elaborating on the relationship, the strategic concept stated:

> "On the positive side, Russia has shown an increased willingness to support the air and land transport of supplies to NATO forces in Afghanistan, has engaged in productive strategic arms control negotiations with the United States, and has expressed strong opposition to terrorism, piracy, and the further proliferation of nuclear weapons states. Experience teaches, however, that Russian and NATO leaders do not always view the same set of facts in the same way. Leaders in Moscow have expressed concerns about past and prospective NATO enlargement, while Allies have voiced concerns about possible attempts by Russia to engage in acts of political or economic intimidation."[224]

Though the new strategic concept recommended forging "more formal ties" with regional organisations including the CSTO as "preferable alternative" to exploring the "possibility of new regional subgroups," the NATO countries remain sceptical of the idea of formally acknowledging the CSTO. The wider distrust between Russia and the West regarding each other's geo-political intentions continue to restrain the two from effectively cooperating on various issues of common concern and interest including international terrorism. The new NATO strategic concept clearly acknowledged that the NATO-Russia Council (NRC) "has not always been adequately employed......to provide the means for preventing crises, analyzing events, broaching ideas, and agreeing on joint actions to deal with mutual concerns. Although the Alliance neither poses a military threat to Russia, nor considers Russia a military threat to the Alliance, doubts persist on both sides about the intentions and policies of the other." At the same time, the strategic concept specifically recommended "constructive re-engagement" with Russia, underscoring "NATO's desire for a qualitatively better relationship with Russia based on shared interests, mutual confidence, transparency and predictability."[225]

Amidst contradictory and diverse perceptions of each other, Russia and the NATO were, nevertheless, able to find some common ground on the Afghan issue by 2010-11. Moscow along with CARs agreed to provide the Western coalition with a network of alternative transit routes, formally known as the Northern Distribution Network (NDN), extending right till the northern borders of Afghanistan. With this also increased Moscow's quest for reinforcing its military presence particularly in Tajikistan and Kyrgyzstan and further seeing to it that the Western alliance is expelled from the Central Asian bases leased out earlier.

It is noteworthy that despite persisting tension with the West including the ongoing Ukrainian crisis, Moscow owing to its own security concerns has welcomed the proposed Western presence in Afghanistan after 2014 and has thus far not closed down the NDN. The cooperation between Russia and the West in Afghanistan, however, remains far below its potential. Though Moscow has been reluctant to play an active role inside Afghanistan, it has kept a close watch on developments taking place in Afghanistan as well as in the tribal areas of Pakistan. Though seriously concerned about potential threat to its own security and in its 'near abroad,' Moscow is still to define its bilateral relationship with Kabul. President Karzai's state-visit to Moscow in January 2011, however, signalled the growing willingness of the two nations to re-engage each other.

Karzai's First State Visit to Russia

Though President Karzai had visited Russia earlier but his first state visit to the country finally took place on January 20-21, 2011. President Karzai's visit was seen as a major step towards reviving the Russo-Afghan relations. During his visit, while acknowledging that "Russia is a great political, economic and military power," President Karzai stated that "In the past years our bilateral relations have significantly strengthened. We see Russia as a neighbour and important partner and want to develop good ties with this partner."[226] Interestingly, despite lingering differences and competing interests, both Russia and the West too were acquiescing to each other's position and role in Afghanistan.

The significance of Karzai's January 2011 Moscow visit lay in the fact that it came immediately after the November 2010 NATO Summit in Lisbon where Western alliance agreed on a time frame for a phased withdrawal of its forces from Afghanistan. The likelihood of a security vacuum and growing uncertainty about the future of Afghanistan, have since raised concerns in many neighbouring countries, including Russia. The phenomenal growth in Afghan opium production and relentless drug-trafficking via Eurasian countries; the growing instability in hitherto peaceful northern Afghanistan; and the re-coalescing of highly motivated extremist forces of various hues in the Af-Pak tribal frontier south of the Pamirs, were bound to draw increased Russian attention. The geo-strategic rationale of checking, if not directly confronting, the trans-national threats away from the Russian borders was gaining traction in Kremlin. Moscow has for long been wary of Afghan conflict spilling over into its 'near abroad' where socio-political stability remains fragile.

During the joint press conference on January 21, 2011, Russian President Dmitry Medvedev termed Karzai's visit as "a very important event" that "should open a new page" in Russo-Afghan relations. He referred to Afghanistan as "a close neighbour" that Russia would like to evolve into "an independent, prosperous nation with effective state institutions."[227] Describing his discussions with Medvedev as "in depth" and "comprehensive," Karzai expressed Kabul's willingness for greater economic, political and security cooperation with Russia. Importantly, Karzai sought Russian assistance in the ongoing process of transfer of security responsibilities by the NATO-led force to the Afghan army.[228] Kabul wanted Russia to go beyond reviving old Soviet-era projects and make investments in Afghanistan in view of the challenges emerging from the Western drawdown.

Medvedev's statements suggested that Russia was picking up from where the former USSR had left in terms of resuming economic and military assistance to Afghanistan. He talked of reviving some of the old Soviet-era projects, rather than initiating new ones, and that too mainly in the northern parts of the country. During the London Conference on Afghanistan in January 2010, Russia had, for the first time, offered to restore or modernise about 142 Soviet-era projects (primarily taken up between 1952–88) in Afghanistan if the West was willing to provide security guarantees and fund them.[229] Russia had time and again expressed its desire to partner with the West in Afghan reconstruction.

Arguing for greater Russo-Afghan economic cooperation, it was pointed out that trade between the two countries had quadrupled in previous years and stood at $500 million in 2010. Medvedev stated that Russian companies are already involved in the modernisation of the Naglu Hydro Power Plant (built by the Soviet Union in the 1960s) in the Kabul Province, and in building small-scale power generation facilities in other provinces. Medvedev also referred to ongoing talks with the Afghan Government regarding the Salang Tunnel, a nitrogen fertiliser plant, a thermal power plant in Mazar-e Sharif, and other facilities, such as an integrated home-building factory. An agreement for institutionalising trade and economic cooperation between the two countries was also signed.[230] Importantly, back in August 2007, Russia had written off about 90 per cent of the Soviet-era debt totalling $11.1 billion, with the remaining $723 million to be repaid by Afghanistan over a period of 23 years.[231] Interestingly, Zamir Kabulov, who had served in the Soviet Embassy in Kabul earlier and again as Russian Ambassador after 2001, had noted:

> "After the fall of the Taliban, the new Afghan government and some Western sponsors wanted to bring some of the most modern Western techniques and top notch companies to the country. And we tried to persuade our Western partners that restarting some of the old Russian factories in Afghanistan could be a good idea. Afghans remember how to work at them and most of these factories specialized in producing construction materials, foodstuffs and other things which Afghans need most now. So, this could allow us to solve the problems of employment, housing and hunger, the three main problems of Afghanistan."[232]

Medvedev also expressed Russia's desire to revive training and assistance programmes for the Afghan civil and military personnel as was the case during the days of former USSR. He also proposed increased scholarships for Afghan students and professionals in Russian institutions. Medvedev cited how Afghan professionals were earlier trained in Russia and how projects were implemented in Afghanistan with the help of Russian expertise. Afghan technocrats and intellectuals educated and trained in the former Soviet Union had gradually made a comeback in the post-Taliban Afghanistan. Their familiarity with Russian language remains an important link between the two countries.

The Russian Ambassador to Kabul, Andrey Avetisyan, in his interview to *Eurasianet* during Karzai's visit, reportedly stated that 225 Afghan police officers were taken to Russia for training and special courses were conducted for several hundred Afghan counter-narcotics officials in 2010. Russia has also supplied the Afghan Ministry of Interior with 20,000 AK-47 rifles. He also said that Russia is discussing the possibility of providing the Afghan Army and Police with transport helicopters. Avetisyan further stated that during the November 2010 NATO summit in Lisbon, NATO and Russia agreed to set up a trust fund for the service and maintenance of Soviet-era Afghan helicopters and to train Afghan technicians.[233] Later, in February 2001, Avetisyan stated that "Russia and Afghanistan may not share a common border these days but we are still neighbours, very close to each other, and I dare say, understanding each other better now, like the two old friends who may part, come through difficult times but keep thinking about each other and eventually get together again."[234]

Zamir Kabulov, former Russian ambassador to Kabul and head of Russian foreign ministry's Asia department, told *RIA Novosti* on January 21, 2011 that experts from the foreign ministry and Russia's state arms exporter, Rosoboronexport, would be meeting with the US officials in Washington to discuss the issue of supply of Russian helicopters to the Afghan Army. Russia reportedly plans to deliver about 21 new Mi-17 multi-purpose helicopters to Afghanistan under a NATO contract or as part of a US-run tender worth about $400 million.[235]

At the political level, in continuation of its policy of supporting the post-Taliban political process, Medvedev welcomed the 2010 Afghan parliamentary elections and said that Russia "very much [counted] on the new parliament to become an integral political body," which will "contribute to national reconciliation, consolidating all vital, responsible patriotic forces (emphasis added) in Afghanistan," and is also expected to help rebuild "full-fledged Afghan statehood." Medvedev also hoped that Afghanistan "will integrate itself into regional associations more actively with every year."[236] It was not clear as to which regional association was Medvedev referring to. Afghanistan until then did not have observer status either in the CSTO or the SCO. Though the SCO-

Afghanistan Contact Group was established in November 2005, the observer status was finally granted in June 2012. Similarly, Afghanistan was accorded an observer status in the CSTO Parliamentary Assembly in April 2013.

As for the Kabul-led reconciliation process, Moscow though remains sceptical but has avoided opposing or criticising the several initiatives taken in this regard. The Russian Deputy Foreign Minister Alexei Borodavkin, in an interview to *Interfax* in March 2009, had stated: "If the Afghan leadership sees fit to establish contact with the moderate wing of the Taliban, Russia will not object to this on condition that they lay down their arms, recognise the Afghan constitution and government, and denounce any ties with Al Qaeda. We are categorically against any agreements with them."[237] Similarly, Victor Korgun, head of the Afghanistan Department at the Russian Academy of Sciences, was quoted by *Reuters* in February 2009 as saying that "Taliban is not a single entity" and "there are elements within it with which we can communicate and negotiate. Russia is in favour of dialogue. But that said, we will not have dialogue with terrorists or those with Afghan blood on their hands."[238] It is notable that in January 2010 Russia did not block the UN Security Council's decision to de-list five Taliban members.[239] Russia's insistence on certain pre-conditions for opening formal negotiations with the Taliban was in stark contrast to that of China which like other regional countries too supported the reconciliation process but remain opposed to setting pre-conditions for talks with the Taliban.

On the energy front, Medvedev and Karzai had expressed their willingness to cooperate on a range of energy projects, including the construction of the 1,700 km long Turkmenistan, Afghanistan, Pakistan and India (TAPI) pipeline and the Central Asia–South Asia (CASA 1000) project involving construction of power transmission lines from Kyrgyzstan and Tajikistan to Afghanistan and onwards to Pakistan. In October 2010, the Russian Deputy Prime Minister Igor Sechin is reported to have stated that the Russian gas giant Gazprom might participate in a consortium to build the pipeline.[240] Similarly, the Russian Prime Minister Vladimir Putin in his meeting with the visiting Afghan president had expressed Russia's willingness to invest $500 million in the CASA 1000 project.[241]

Later, in November 2011, the commercial attaché of the Afghan Embassy in Moscow, Mohammad Qasim, stated during an interview that the Russia-Afghanistan bilateral trade which stood at $510 million in 2010 is expected to reach $1 billion in 2011. Russia mainly exported oil products, wheat, building materials, automobile and aviation spare parts to Afghanistan. By 2011, Russia had also emerged as one of the key suppliers of oil products to Afghanistan, which mainly supplied dry fruits and carpets to Russia. Due to the energy blockade by Iran in 2011, Kabul had to turn to other sources of energy particularly in view of approaching winters. Qasim also informed that in August 2011 a MoU on energy cooperation was signed, and in November 2011, a contract was signed between Afghan Ministry of Commerce and Industries and Russia's state-run Gazprom-Neft Company to supply 10,000 tonnes of oil products to Afghanistan. Among the several Soviet-era projects including the Salang Tunnel that were discussed during President Karzai's January 2011 visit to Moscow, Qasim stated that priority is being given to reviving the integrated house-building factory and the grain elevator in Kabul, the cement factory at Jabal-us Saraj in Parwan Province, a fertilizer plant in Mazar-e Sharif, an irrigation canal in Nangarhar and the hydropower station in Sarobi-2.[242]

During the first meeting of the Russia-Afghanistan Inter-Governmental Commission on Trade and Economic Cooperation held in Moscow on March 02, 2012, the Russian Energy Minister Sergei Shmatko stated that the volume of bilateral trade in 2011 grew by 72.5 per cent compared to 2010, and 12 times compared to 2004. In 2010, the turnover was stated to be $571.3 million, while in 2011, it was $984.96.[243]

Wider Context

Russia's growing Afghan engagement has a wider geo-political context and is not propelled by mere bilateral interests. It partly flows from long-term security concerns arising out of the known demonstrative and motivating influence of the Taliban resurgence on the aspiring Islamists in Central Asia and the Northern Caucasus, and partly from the challenge to preserving Russia's political and economic influence in what it regards as its 'near abroad.'

The 9/11 attacks were, in many ways, a game changer in the Eurasian geo-politics. The US, for the first time in history, had acquired a direct foothold in Central Asia, which had been under Russian influence or control since the 19th century. Russia's position and influence in the vast Eurasian space has since been directly contested by the US and the NATO, especially in the early years of the war on terror. The ongoing Ukranian crisis is a manifestation of several old factors including the competitive relationship between Russia and the West.

An increased American presence in Afghanistan with bases in Central Asia; the supposedly West-sponsored 'colour revolutions' in some of the former Soviet countries; the Georgian conflict; NATO's push into Russia's 'near abroad;' and the US missile defence plan for Europe, have compounded Moscow's suspicions regarding Western intent and strategy in the region. However, in recent years, Moscow has increasingly been supportive of the West in view of the rising threat from the Taliban and a multinational assortment of militant Islamist groups converging along and across the Durand Line.

The remaking of the Russo-Afghan ties is especially significant in view of the West's zest for 'transition' and 'Afghanisation' as critical components of its exit strategy. Both Karzai and Medvedev, quite notably, avoided making any criticism of the Western strategy and approach on the occasion. The worsening Afghan situation to an extent was redefining the relations between Russia and the West. The joint US–Russia anti-drugs operation, first of its kind, in the Achin District of the eastern Afghan province of Nangarhar bordering Pakistan in October 2010 was a case in point.[244] However, it is not known if more of such coordinated counter narcotic operations have since been conducted or why the above joint effort which was successfully conducted could not be institutionalised and taken to the next level. In recent years, the US has also allowed Russia to resume its military assistance to the Afghan Army and especially its air corps, which was suspended in 2005. However, it is still to be seen to what extent the US would seek to diversify its regional partnership as it drawdown its troops without stabilising Afghanistan.

Meanwhile, growing attacks on NATO supply lines coming via Pakistani territory, and the US-Iranian standoff, had further intensified NATO-Russia cooperation on the Afghan front. Russia provided NATO with an alternative supply route—the Northern Distribution Network. In years to come, prospects of closer NATO-Russia or US-Russia cooperation in Afghan war, especially in strengthening the Afghan Army, cannot be ruled out. As the Afghan situation worsens, and as attacks on NATO supply lines continue in Pakistan, the Russian position is likely to strengthen within Afghanistan in year to follow.

Anticipating worst case scenarios, Russia has been positioning itself in the Af-Pak region using both bilateral mechanisms and regional instruments:

(1) **The NATO-Russia Council** (NRC)—Moscow has been leveraging its engagement with the US/NATO despite known trust deficit and competitive geo-strategic interests. In July 2009, Russia extended transit facilities for supply of critical logistics through the NDN. During the 2010 Lisbon Summit, Russia also approved a reverse transit agreement that allows NATO to ship armoured vehicles and other military equipment back from Afghanistan to Europe by the same route.

(2) **The SCO**—Russia has been seeking to advance its interests through the SCO, especially to deal with the narco threat emanating from Afghanistan. According to *RIA Novosti*, an estimated 90 per cent of heroin consumed in the country is trafficked from Afghanistan via Tajikistan and Uzbekistan. In May 2009, the head of Russia's Federal Drug Control Service (FDCS), Viktor Ivanov, had stated that about 180 Afghan drug cartels are engaged in heroin trafficking to Russia.[245] For the first time, a regional conference on Afghanistan under the

SCO auspices was held in Moscow on March 27, 2009, the day President Obama announced his Af-Pak strategy. Notably, it had brought Americans and Iranians together on the same forum over the Afghan issue.

(3) **Engaging Pakistan**—Russia has been engaging Pakistan as part of trilateral/ quadrilateral arrangements involving Afghanistan and Tajikistan as well. Until now, three rounds of meetings have been held in 2009, 2010 and 2012 respectively. Besides this, Russia has been improving its ties with Islamabad on the bilateral level as well.

(4) **Emphasis on CSTO**—Russia has been pushing for greater coordination between NATO and the CSTO but without much success. Nevertheless, the CSTO remains part of the wider Russian strategy to reinforce its position in what it regards as its traditional sphere of influence. As the Taliban began to re-emerge in 2004-05 and the Bush Administration continued to rebuff Moscow, the then Russian Foreign Minister Sergei Lavrov announced the establishment of a CSTO Working Group on Afghanistan in November 2005.[246] Later, from March 09-13, 2007, a delegation of the CSTO Working Group visited Kabul and held meetings with senior Afghan officials of the defence, interior and foreign ministries. According to a statement issued by the CSTO press office on March 14, the meeting led to the opening of "direct contacts" between the CSTO and the Afghan Government. It further stated that, "The Afghan side is most interested in having their military and law enforcement officers trained in Russia and other CSTO member states, as well as in purchasing Russian weaponry." The statement also revealed that the group intends to transform the *Channel 2006* annual anti-drug operation, which is designed to curb trafficking of drugs from Afghanistan, into a permanent regional operation.[247]

The Sino-Russian ties have undergone significant transformation over the last decade, but the geo-economic competition for control over Central Asian energy resources remain, as evident from Moscow's effort to strengthen the Russian-led Customs Union. Moreover, the Chinese response to the current cooperation between Russia and US/NATO on the Afghan front is not quite clear. It is difficult at this point in time to comment on the prospects of US–Russia and Sino-Russian cooperation or competition over the Afghan issue in the years beyond 2014. As of now, Chinese and Russian perceptions of the Western role in the Af-Pak region remain complicated and ambiguous. The Chinese and to an extent Russian engagement with Afghanistan has so far been majorly driven by their respective security concerns and commercial interests, but that may not remain the case in view of their growing stakes in Afghanistan. Despite the developing Afghan uncertainty, Russia's involvement in Afghanistan—infrastructure development, training of security and civilian personnel, and military assistance to Afghan forces—is set to increase in years to come. In October 2013, it was announced that a delegation from the CSTO Parliamentary Assembly would visit Afghanistan in December to familiarise themselves with the situation in the country and to deepen contacts with the Afghan parliamentarians.[248]

As for the regional groupings such as the SCO and CSTO, they are unlikely to play any direct role in the stabilisation of Afghanistan. They suffer from varying limitations, internal contradictions and competition, and policy incoherence. Their relevance would greatly depend on how Eurasian geo-politics plays out in coming years. Prospects of limited cooperation or engagement between Kabul and both CSTO and SCO on issues pertaining to counter-narcotics or counter-terrorism is very much there. However, the role of Central Asian countries assumes significance as they try to balance their engagement given the increased Russian, American and the Chinese interests in the region. The Afghan war in a way could mean re-scripting of the Eurasian geopolitics particularly in view of the US' Asia "pivot" strategy.

Given the prevailing uncertainty and dynamism in the politics of Afghanistan, it is difficult at present to gauge what shape and direction the Russo-Afghan relationship would acquire in the longer run. Countries opposed to the Western role in the region have already reconciled with an extended though limited US and NATO presence in the region. The nature and extent of Russia's future role would, thus, broadly depend on six factors: (1) US/NATO strategy beyond 2014; (2) Moscow's leverages with the US/NATO; (3) post-Karzai developments and Moscow's leverages within Afghanistan; (4) response/reactions of other regional countries; (5) Russia's economic health; and (6) perceptions and levels of consensus within Kremlin on the Afghan issue.

Awaiting 'Post-2014' Afghanistan

Interestingly, even as the US and NATO are likely to remain lead external players irrespective of their smaller and far more restricted military presence post-2014, the neighbouring countries other than Pakistan are still expected to play a greater role. On the other hand, most of Afghanistan's 'other' neighbours remain cautious and in a wait-and-watch mode as Washington and Kabul negotiate a Bilateral Security Agreement and various Afghan factions prepare for the next round of presidential and parliamentary elections in 2014-15. The outcomes of the security and political transitions in Afghanistan; level of Western commitment post-2014; and finally, Pakistan's likely response to the extended US-NATO mission in Afghanistan, thus, is being closely watched in Afghanistan's immediate as well as extended neighbourhood. These may well be regarded as decisive or rather determining factors as far as response from Afghanistan's 'other' neighbours are concerned.

Though it is still early for any definitive assessment of the likely role of 'other' neighbours as it would depend on the outcome of host of developments expected to take place during 2014-15; nevertheless, there are some continuing trends and emerging indicators available that suggest possible conflict or cooperation among them in years to come. Apart from continuing prospects of deepening of prevalent geo-political fault lines, there are also possibilities of new regional equations emerging in the longer run. The regional responses to post-transition Afghanistan—whether it would be a repeat of 1990s or else—is more likely to be reactive in the short-term based on immediate direct threat from instability in the Af-Pak region; and could be transformatory in the long run keeping in view the prospects of incremental economic benefit by cooperating in the stabilisation and development of Afghanistan. The nature and scale and the effectiveness or ineffectiveness of Western presence in the region after 2014-15 will be closely watched by Afghanistan's 'other' neighbours as they ponder over their respective response strategies to deal with possible security vacuum and factional conflict within Afghanistan, as well as threat from various armed terrorist and religious extremist groups operating from Pakistan.

Interestingly, the most commonly and a long held perception in the region that the West would not be able to hold on for too long and that it will withdraw sooner than later, has been completely proved wrong. Both the US and NATO expanded and extended their military deployments for almost a decade before deciding on a phased security transition and withdrawal of troops beginning 2011. Currently, even as member states of the Western coalition/alliance continue to drawdown troops, Washington is negotiating a long-term security agreement with Kabul and NATO has already approved "concept of operations" for its "Resolute Support" mission in post-transition Afghanistan. However, it remains to be seen as to how in future the Western coalition intends to deal with growing uncertainty and insecurity in the Af-Pak region, and more importantly, Pakistan's continued support to various extremist militant groups most of which are also affiliated with al Qaeda and its regional/international networks.

Afghanistan's 'other' neighbours will rather wait for the post-2014 Western strategy to unfold than rush into any strong action or make any dramatic shift in their policy approaches. Apart from developments in the internal politics of Afghanistan, Pakistan's role and salience in the future Western strategy too is being closely watched. Interestingly, some of them who were hitherto opposed to a strong Western military presence are now rather opposed to a complete or swift Western withdrawal from Afghanistan. They have acquiesced to a smaller but effective Western military presence well after 2014 for fear of Afghan conflict spilling over into their territory. The spectre of Pakistan-based and sponsored radical militant groups expanding their ideological base and influence and thereby deepening the sectarian divides in theirs respective societies has raised serious security concerns among neighbouring countries as was the case in late 1990s.

Ironically, despite enough convergence of interest, the region is apparently not prepared to deal in a collective manner with a scenario where there might be total chaos and anarchy in Afghanistan. It is also equally pertinent to observe here that an unstable Afghanistan after a point too does not leave its neighbours with many options and choices. Most of the 'other' neighbours at best continue to focus on Afghanistan without ever sufficiently acknowledging and addressing the key external dimension to the Afghan conflict. Pakistan's continuing role in reinforcing terrorism and militant Islamist extremism in the entire south-central Asia region, and the need to address the same while dealing with the Afghan challenge, is hardly acknowledged and taken into account by most of Afghanistan's 'other' key neighbours which makes their approach somewhat similar to that of the West. Without dealing with state-sponsored terrorism and religious extremism emanating from Pakistan, it would be difficult to stabilise Afghanistan particularly in view of near absence of effective state structures in much of the country. The resource base of current state institutions in Afghanistan is limited and their survival itself is far from assured in coming years.

The Cold War mindsets remain a major stumbling block when it comes to working towards a regional approach to tackle the menace of religious extremism and terrorism plaguing the south-central Asia region. Most of the regional countries remain indifferent or are simply averse to acknowledging Pakistan's central role in sponsoring and building up a sustainable terror infrastructure that threatens the entire region. For instance, the Chinese position throughout has been ambiguous on the issue of Pakistan's direct support for various militant extremist organisations. The Cold War mindset continues to dictate China's relations with Pakistan as it remains consciously unmindful of the rapid proliferation of extremist groups and ideologies within Pakistan and its potential implications for stability and security in the wider south-central Asia region. In fact, China's tunnelled view about Pakistan's direct support and sponsorship of several terrorist and extremist groupings in the region has emboldened the Pakistani establishment. While China regards Uighur Islamist militants as terrorists and an entity that poses a serious threat to its national unity, it prefers to look the other way when it comes to Pakistan's support for terrorist and extremist ideologies posing similar threat to both Afghanistan and India and other neighbouring states in Central Asia. Similarly, while Beijing supports initiatives for political reconciliation with militant Islamists in Pakistan and Afghanistan, but prefers a heavy handed approach when it comes to Islamist militancy and insurgency in its own western Xinjiang region. China is yet to take full cognisance of the transformed nature of terrorism and religious radicalisation in the 21st century and the kind of long-term ideological and physical threat it poses both to the new states that have emerged next to its borders and which are still in a state of complex transition, as well as old and established civilisational states, which remain increasingly vulnerable to terrorist strikes and protracted insurgencies.

NOTES

1. "NATO to Start Consultation on Formation of Afghan Contact Group," *IRNA*, December 04, 2006, at http://www.irna.ir/en/news/view/menu-234/0612042566170752.htm
2. See "Merkel's Party Calls for New Political Approach to Afghanistan," *Deutsche Welle*, January 21, 2009, at http://www.dw.de/merkels-party-calls-for-new-political-approach-to-afghanistan/a-3966013
3. "Transatlantic Leadership For A New Era," *North Atlantic Treaty Organization*, January 26, 2009, at http://www.nato.int/cps/en/natolive/opinions_50116.htm
4. "Saving Afghanistan: An Appeal and Plan for Urgent Action," *Issue Brief*, The Atlantic Council of the United States, January 2008, at http://www.acus.org/docs/012808-AfghanistanbriefwoSAG.pdf
5. Gen. (Retd.) James L. Jones and Ambassador Thomas R. Pickering, "Afghanistan Study Group Report," *Center for the Study of the Presidency*, Washington D.C., January 30, 2008, at http://www.thepresidency.org/pubs/Afghan_Study_Group_final.pdf
6. Michael R. Gordon, "U.S. Says Iranian Arms Seized in Afghanistan," *The New York Times*, April 18, 2007, at http://www.nytimes.com/2007/04/18/world/middleeast/18military.html
7. The Iranian Government ordered the closure of all offices of the Hezb-e Islami on February 10, 2002.
8. There was also an opinion that the Iranian diplomats were killed by the Pakistani intelligence or the Lashkar-e Taiba cadres and not by the Taliban. This came to the author's notice in his discussion with Afghan academics during his visit to Afghanistan in 2007.
9. This view came to the notice of the author in his personal interactions with a former Taliban official based in Kabul during his visit to Afghanistan in 2007.
10. Thomas Joscelyn, "Iran and the Taliban, allies against America," *The Long War Journal*, July 28, 2009, at http://www.longwarjournal.org/archives/2009/07/iran_and_the_taliban.php. Mullah Khairullah was considered as a senior member of the Taliban regime who had served as Taliban spokesperson (1995-96), interior minister (1996-99) and governor of Herat (1999-2001) prior to being captured from Pakistan in January 2002.
11. See "US, Iran have history of contact since cutting ties," March 10, 2007, at http://www.iranmania.com/News/ArticleView/Default.asp?NewsCode=50238&NewsKind=Current%20Affairs
12. Statement of Ambassador James Dobbins, "Iran: Reality, Options and Consequences, Part 2—Negotiating with the Iranians: Missed Opportunities and Paths Forward," *Hearing/Testimony Before the Subcommittee on National Security and Foreign Affairs, Committee on Oversight and Government Reform, House of Representatives*, US Government Printing Office, November 07, 2007, at http://www.gpo.gov/fdsys/pkg/CHRG-110hhrg50111/html/CHRG-110hhrg50111.htm
13. Statement of Hillary Mann Leverett, "Iran: Reality, Options and Consequences, Part 2—Negotiating with the Iranians: Missed Opportunities and Paths Forward," *Hearing/Testimony Before the Subcommittee on National Security and Foreign Affairs, Committee on Oversight and Government Reform, House of Representatives*, US Government Printing Office, November 07, 2007, at http://www.gpo.gov/fdsys/pkg/CHRG-110hhrg50111/html/CHRG-110hhrg50111.htm
14. Glenn Kessler, "In 2003, U.S. Spurned Iran's Offer of Dialogue," *The Washington Post*, June 18, 2006, at http://www.washingtonpost.com/wp-dyn/content/article/2006/06/17/AR2006061700727.html
15. Statement of Hillary Mann Leverett, no 13.
16. Jane Perlez, "U.S. to Deport Saudi Suspect In a 1996 Terror Bombing," *The New York Times*, October 05, 1999, at http://www.nytimes.com/1999/10/05/world/us-to-deport-

saudi-suspect-in-a-1996-terror-bombing.html. For more details, see Malcolm Byrne, "Secret U.S. Overture to Iran in 1999 Broke Down Over Terrorism Allegations," *The National Security Archive*, May 30, 2010, at http://www2.gwu.edu/~nsarchiv/NSAEBB/NSAEBB318/

17. *The National Security Archive*, May 18, 2010, at http://www2.gwu.edu/~nsarchiv/NSAEBB/NSAEBB318/doc03.pdf
18. "Clinton Sends Letter to Khatami to Seek Dialog," *People's Daily Online*, November 07, 2000, at http://english.peopledaily.com.cn/english/200011/07/eng20001107_54525.html
19. "Ahmadinejad's Letter to Bush," *The Washington Post*, May 09, 2006, at http://www.washingtonpost.com/wp-dyn/content/article/2006/05/09/AR2006050900878.html
20. Barbara Slavin, "A Broken Engagement," *The National Interest*, November-December 2007, at http://nationalinterest.org/article/a-broken-engagement-1849
21. Kenneth Pollack, *The Persian Puzzle: The Conflict between Iran and America*, Random House, 2005, p. 346, as quoted in Mir H. Sadat, and James P. Hughes, "U.S.-Iran Engagement Through Afghanistan," *Middle East Policy*, 17 (1), Spring 2010, at http://mepc.org/journal/middle-east-policy-archives/us-iran-engagement-through-afghanistan
22. Flynt Leverett and Hillary Mann Leverett, "Have We Already Lost Iran?," *The New York Times*, May 23, 2009, at http://www.nytimes.com/2009/05/24/opinion/24leverett.html (as quoted in Mir H. Sadat, and James P. Hughes, "U.S.-Iran Engagement Through Afghanistan")
23. Kenneth Pollack, no. 21.
24. Ibid.
25. Mir H. Sadat, and James P. Hughes, no. 21.
26. Michael R. Gordon, "U.S. Says Iranian Arms Seized in Afghanistan," *The New York Times*, April 18, 2007, at http://www.nytimes.com/2007/04/18/world/middleeast/18military.html
27. Ibid.
28. Jim Mannion, "Iranian-Made Weapons Intercepted in Afghanistan: U.S. General," *Defense News*, April 17, 2007, at http://defensenews.com/story.php?F=2692237&C=landwar
29. Ahmad Khalid Mohid, "Iran-made weapons recovered in operations: ISAF," *Pajhwok Afghan News*, May 09, 2007, at http://www.pajhwak.com/viewstory.asp?lng=eng&id=36075
30. Zubair Babakarkhel, "Karzai, Gates see no proof of Iran moving arms to Taliban," *Pajhwok Afghan News*, June 04, 2007, at http://www.pajhwak.com/viewstory.asp?lng=eng&id=37324
31. "Transcript: DoD Press Briefing with Secretary Gates And President Hamid Karzai from Kabul, Afghanistan," *US Department of Defense*, June 05, 2007, at http://www.defense.gov/transcripts/transcript.aspx?transcriptid=3978
32. Ibid.
33. See "CNN Late Night Edition With Wolf Blitzer. Interviews With Robert Gates, Benazir Bhutto, Hamid Karzai," August 05, 2007, at http://transcripts.cnn.com/TRANSCRIPTS/0708/05/le.01.html
34. See "Bush challenges Karzai on Iran," August 07, 2007, at http://www.iranmania.com/News/ArticleView/Default.asp?NewsCode=53373&NewsKind=Current%20Affairs
35. See "Bush and Karzai differ over Iran," *International Herald Tribune*, August 06, 2007, at http://www.iht.com/articles/2007/08/06/asia/afghan.php
36. See "President Karzai meets President Ahmadinejad of Islamic Republic of Iran," *Office of the President, Islamic Republic of Afghanistan*, at http://www.president.gov.af/english/news/190807_prekarzaimeetsahmadinej.mspx
37. Transcript: DoD Press Briefing with Secretary Gates And President Hamid Karzai from Kabul, Afghanistan, no. 31. Also, see Zubair Babakarkhel, "Karzai, Gates see no proof of Iran moving arms to Taliban," *Pajhwok Afghan News*, June 04, 2007, at http://www.pajhwak.com/viewstory.asp?lng=eng&id=37324

38. See "Gates shifts stance on Iranian arms flows to Taliban," *Pajhwok Afghan News*, June 14, 2007, at http://www.pajhwak.com/viewstory.asp?lng=eng&id=37839
39. "Iran arming Taliban, U.S. claims," *CNN*, June 13, 2007, at http://edition.cnn.com/2007/WORLD/asiapcf/06/13/iran.taliban/index.html?eref=rss_latest
40. Ron Synovitz, "Afghanistan: Kabul Investigates Reported Militant Movement From Iran," *Radio Free Europe/Radio Liberty*, June 22, 2007, at http://www.rferl.org/featuresarticle/2007/06/a2c93f15-f2be-49f5-8371-4a2441001bf2.html
41. Jon Hemming, "U.S. says Iran knows its weapons reaching Taliban," *Reuters*, July 17, 2007, at http://www.reuters.com/article/worldNews/idUSISL6933820070717
42. Makia Monir, "Taliban being trained on Iranian soil: MPs," *Pajhwok Afghan News*, July 21, 2007, at http://www.pajhwak.com/viewstory.asp?lng=eng&id=39807
43. Ibid.
44. See "Copy of Hezbollah explosives found in Afghanistan by Nato," *Ya Libnan*, July 19, 2007, at http://yalibnan.com/site/archives/2007/07/copy_of_hezboll.php
45. See "100 Iran-made bombs seized, claim Afghan officials," *Pajhwok Afghan News*, August 14, 2007, at http://www.pajhwak.com/viewstory.asp?lng=eng&id=41102
46. Ron Synovitz, "Afghanistan: Official Says Iranian Mines Found In Taliban Commander's House," *RFE/RL*, January 25, 2008, at http://www.rferl.org/featuresarticle/2008/01/d4846c20-8760-4d23-a2a9-fd23d07a0df3.html
47. President Karzai meets President Ahmadinejad of Islamic Republic of Iran, no. 36.
48. "Iran mulls harsh measures to expel illegal Afghan workers," *Pajhwok Afghan News*, November 07, 2006, at http://www.pajhwak.com/viewstory.asp?lng=eng&id=27091
49. Iran had planned to remove all the estimated one million illegal Afghan refugees by the end of March 2008. The UNHCR says more than 52,000 were forced out between April 21 and May 08, 2007. The IWPR gave a figure of 54,600 in Herat and Nimroz provinces by local Afghan officials. However, by May 13, 2007, the Iranian authorities were saying they had expelled 85,000 illegal Afghan refugees in the past three weeks. See Hafizullah Gardesh, "Forcible Expulsions From Iran Put Pressure on Kabul," *Institute of War & Peace Reporting*, May 17, 2007, at http://www.iwpr.net/?p=arr&s=f&o=335650&apc_state=henparr
50. Zubair Babakarkhel & Najib Khilwatgar, "Kabul resents wave of refugees evicted by Iran," *Pajhwok Afghan News*, May 08, 2007, at http://www.pajhwak.com/viewstory.asp?lng=eng&id=36010
51. Sayed Salahuddin, "Iranians kill 13 Afghan refugees - Afghan police," *Reuters*, April 09, 2008, at http://www.alertnet.org/thenews/newsdesk/ISL51154.htm
52. "Iranian, Afghan forces clash at southwestern border," *The New York Times*, April 20, 2008, at http://www.nytimes.com/aponline/world/AP-Afghanistan.html
53. "Kabul Rules out Alleged Iran's Support for Afghan Opposition," *Fars News Agency*, April 08, 2008, at http://english.farsnews.com/newstext.php?nn=8701200709
54. Ron Synovitz, "Iran/Afghanistan: Repatriations Spark Debate On Tehran's Aims," *RFE/RL*, May 10, 2007, at http://www.rferl.org/featuresarticle/2007/05/26def642-c098-4e1f-a93e-96c3a5858e9f.html
55. Ibid.
56. Ibid.
57. Ibid.
58. See "Iran's Nuclear Ambitions," Patricia McNerney, Principal Deputy Assistant Secretary, International Security and Nonproliferation, Testimony before the Senate Homeland Security and Governmental Affairs Committee; Subcommittee on Federal Financial Management, Government Information, Federal Services, and International Security, Washington, D.C., April 24, 2008, at http://2001-2009.state.gov/t/isn/rls/rm/104482.htm

59. Al Pessin, "US Cites New Evidence of Iranian Support for Taliban," *Voice of America*, April 30, 2008, at http://voanews.com/english/2008-04-30-voa73.cfm; and Kristin Roberts, "U.S. military criticizes Iran but says no strike plan," *Reuters*, May 01, 2008, at http://in.reuters.com/article/2008/04/30/idINIndia-33333920080430
60. "Iran seeking to keep Afghanistan unstable: US official," *Agence France-Presse*, May 06, 2008, at http://afp.google.com/article/ALeqM5ifzcvOwE0ZMFYCy84gwNgytPIi1g
61. "Iran becoming main route for militants: Afghan daily," *Dawn*, July 28, 2008, at http://www.dawn.com/2008/07/28/top7.htm
62. Kate Clark, "Arming the Taliban," *BBC News*, September 18, 2008, at http://news.bbc.co.uk/2/hi/south_asia/7623496.stm
63. See "Merkel's Party Calls for New Political Approach to Afghanistan," *Deutsche Welle*, January 21, 2009, at http://www.dw.de/merkels-party-calls-for-new-political-approach-to-afghanistan/a-3966013
64. "Transatlantic Leadership For A New Era," *North Atlantic Treaty Organization*, January 26, 2009, at http://www.nato.int/cps/en/natolive/opinions_50116.htm
65. "U.S. National Security Strategy Update," *FPC Briefing*, Admiral Mike Mullen, Chairman, Joint Chiefs of Staff, US Department of State, Washington DC, January 27, 2009, at http://fpc.state.gov/115471.htm
66. "Videotaped Remarks By The President In Celebration Of Nowruz," *Office of the Press Secretary, The White House*, March 20, 2009, at http://www.whitehouse.gov/the_press_office/VIDEOTAPED-REMARKS-BY-THE-PRESIDENT-IN-CELEBRATION-OF-NOWRUZ
67. "Iran and Nato end 30-year impasse," *BBC News*, March 27, 2009, at http://news.bbc.co.uk/2/hi/middle_east/7966263.stm
68. "White Paper of the Interagency Policy Group's Report on U.S. Policy toward Afghanistan and Pakistan," *The White House*, March 27, 2009, at http://www.whitehouse.gov/assets/documents/afghanistan_pakistan_white_paper_final.pdf
69. "MP dismisses possible Iran-NATO cooperation on Afghanistan," *Tehran Times*, April 14, 2009, at http://www.tehrantimes.com/Index_view.asp?code=192204
70. "Remarks By The President On A New Beginning," Cairo University, Cairo, Egypt, *Office of the Press Secretary, The White House*, June 04, 2009, at http://www.whitehouse.gov/the_press_office/Remarks-by-the-President-at-Cairo-University-6-04-09
71. Bill Roggio, "US strike kills Iranian-backed Taliban commander in western Afghanistan," *The Long War Journal*, June 10, 2009, at http://www.longwarjournal.org/archives/2009/06/us_strike_kills_iran.php
72. Barbara Starr, "Afghan police find Iranian-made weapons, source says," *CNN News*, September 10, 2009, at http://edition.cnn.com/2009/WORLD/asiapcf/09/10/afghan.iran.weapons/
73. "Bin Laden's Family Under House Arrest in Iran," *Asharq Al-Awsat*, December 23, 2009, at http://www.aawsat.net/2009/12/article55252427
74. "Iran Leader: US Playing 'Game' in Afghanistan," *The New York Times*, March 10, 2010, at http://www.nytimes.com/aponline/2010/03/10/world/AP-AS-Afghan-Iran.html?ref=world
75. Miles Amoore, "Taliban fighters being taught at secret camps in Iran," *The Sunday Times*, March 21, 2010, at http://www.timesonline.co.uk/tol/news/world/middle_east/article7069817.ece
76. Sanjeev Miglani, "General McChrystal says Afghan insurgents trained in Iran," *Reuters*, May 30, 2010, at http://www.reuters.com/article/2010/05/30/us-afghanistan-iran-idUSTRE64T0U920100530
77. Bill Roggio, "Al Qaeda-linked Taliban commander killed in western Afghanistan," *The*

Long War Journal, June 06, 2010, at http://www.longwarjournal.org/archives/2010/06/al_qaedalinked_talib.php#

78. "Fact Sheet: U.S. Treasury Department Targets Iran's Support for Terrorism. Treasury Announces New Sanctions Against Iran's Islamic Revolutionary Guard Corps-Qods Force Leadership," *US Department of the Treasury*, August 03, 2010, at http://www.treasury.gov/press-center/press-releases/Pages/tg810.aspx
79. Miles Amoore, "Iran pays the Taliban to kill US soldiers," *The Sunday Times*, September 05, 2010, at http://www.thesundaytimes.co.uk/sto/news/world_news/Afghanistan/article387113.ece
80. Abasin Zaheer, "Explosives smuggled into Nimroz from Iran," *Pajhwok Afghan News*, October 07, 2010, at http://www.pajhwok.com/en/2010/10/07/explosives-smuggled-nimroz-iran
81. Ramin, "Weapons, including Iranian-made, seized in Nimroz," *Pajhwok Afghan News*, October 12, 2010, at http://www.pajhwok.com/en/2010/10/12/weapons-including-iranian-made-seized-nimroz
82. Dexter Filkins, "Iran Is Said to Give Top Karzai Aide Cash by the Bagful," *The New York Times*, October 23, 2010, at http://www.nytimes.com/2010/10/24/world/asia/24afghan.html?pagewanted=all&_r=0
83. Ibid.
84. "Iran's Embassy in Kabul Dismisses Bribery Claims by US Media," *Fars News Agency*, October 25, 2010, at http://english2.farsnews.com/newstext.php?nn=8908031057
85. Ben Birnbaum, "Iran's cash for Karzai buys years of loyalty," *The Washington Post*, April 14, 2011, at http://www.washingtontimes.com/news/2011/apr/14/ex-afghan-minister-iran-paid-karzai-early-2003/?page=all
86. David Nakamura and Joshua Partlow, "Taliban fighters, some disguised as American soldiers, attack two U.S. bases," *The Washington Post*, August 28, 2010, at http://www.washingtonpost.com/wp-dyn/content/article/2010/08/28/AR2010082801152.html?sid=ST2010082606494
87. "Karzai Says His Office Gets "Bags Of Money" From Iran," *The New York Times*, October 25, 2010, at http://www.nytimes.com/reuters/2010/10/25/world/international-uk-afghanistan-karzai.html?ref=world
88. Hamid Shalizi, "Karzai says his office gets "bags of money" from Iran," *Reuters*, October 26, 2010, at http://in.reuters.com/article/2010/10/25/idINIndia-52430020101025
89. Ben Farmer, "Iran 'spent millions' on influencing Afghan elections," *The Irish Times*, December 08, 2010, at http://www.irishtimes.com/newspaper/world/2010/1208/1224285025061.html
90. Ray Rivera and Ruhullah Khapalwak, "Afghans Strained by Shortages as Iran Tightens Flow of Fuel," *The New York Times*, January 09, 2011, at http://www.nytimes.com/2011/01/10/world/asia/10afghan.html?ref=world&pagewanted=all
91. Ashraf Hanifi, "Iran's Fuel Tankers Blockade Seen a 'Pressure Tool,'" *Pajhwok Afghan News*, January 06, 2011, at http://www.pajhwok.com/en/2011/01/06/irans-fuel-tankers-blockade-seen-pressure-tool
92. "Afghanistan to Purchase All Fuel Needs from Iran," *Fars News Agency*, February 07, 2011, at http://english.farsnews.com/newstext.php?nn=8911180637
93. "Kabul denies agreeing to buy all fuel from Iran," *AFP*, February 07, 2011, at http://www.google.com/hostednews/afp/article/ALeqM5jdhhty6DkJrXJs54uDaOGt4Wsv0w?docId=CNG.30a945d880fb0c467a82e584423dac3f.141
94. Jawid Tabish, "Iran Faces Renewed Afghan Dam Sabotage Claims," *IWPR*, ARR Issue 389, February 01, 2011, at http://iwpr.net/report-news/iran-faces-renewed-afghan-dam-sabotage-claims

95. "Intel Official: Iran Sends Taliban Deadly Rockets," *The Associated Press*, March 09, 2011, at http://www.nytimes.com/aponline/2011/03/09/world/asia/AP-AS-Afghanistan-Iran.html?ref=world
96. "FNA Correspondent Arrested in Kabul," *Fars News Agency*, May 06, 2012, at http://english2.farsnews.com/newstext.php?nn=9102110905; also, see Ghanizada, "Iranian Fars News Agency reporter detained in Kabul," *Khaama Press*, May 06, 2012, at http://www.khaama.com/iranian-fars-news-agency-reporter-detained-in-kabul-227
97. "Iran sets aside $25m to derail Afghan-US deal," *Pajhwok Afghan News*, May 24, 2012, at http://www.pajhwok.com/en/2012/05/24/iran-sets-aside-25m-derail-afghan-us-deal
98. Ben Farmer, "Taliban Opens Office in Iran," *The Telegraph*, August 01, 2012, at http://www.telegraph.co.uk/news/worldnews/middleeast/iran/9444402/Taliban-opens-office-in-Iran.html
99. Amie Ferris-Rotman, "Insight: Iran's "Great Game" in Afghanistan," *Reuters*, May 24, 2012, at http://www.reuters.com/article/2012/05/24/us-afghanistan-iran-media-idUSBRE84N0CB20120524; Also, see Jawed Roostapur, "Concerns over Iran's influence in Afghan media agencies," *Khaama Press*, January 09, 2013, at http://www.khaama.com/concerns-over-irans-influence-in-afghan-media-agencies-1225?utm_source=feedburner&utm_medium=email&utm_campaign=Feed%3A+khaama+%28KHAAMA+PRESS+%7C+Afghan+Online+Newspaper+%26+Magazine%29
100. Ahmad K. Majidyar, "Iran's hard and soft power in Afghanistan," *American Enterprise Institute*, August 27, 2012, at http://www.aei.org/article/foreign-and-defense-policy/regional/india-pakistan-afghanistan/irans-hard-and-soft-power-in-afghanistan/
101. Arshad Mohammed, "U.S. exports to Iran rise nearly one-third despite sanctions," *Reuters*, October 15, 2012, at http://www.reuters.com/article/2012/10/15/iran-usa-exports-idUSL1E8LF03820121015
102. Bill Varner, "Iran Pours Cash Into Afghanistan, Seeking Leverage Against US," *Bloomberg*, July 17, 2008, at http://www.bloomberg.com/apps/news?pid=20601087&sid=aNaIqaODpvrU&refer=worldwide
103. "Iran exports to Afghanistan up 25%, hit $900m," *Tehran Times*, January 18, 2011, at http://www.tehrantimes.com/index_View.asp?code=234327
104. "Tehran-Kabul Trade Close to $2billion," *Tehran Times*, December 25, 2011, at http://www.tehrantimes.com/economy-and-business/93886-tehran-kabul-trade-close-to-2-billion
105. Sajad, "Gunmen attack Iranian consulate staff in Mazar-e-Sharif city," *Khaama Press*, February 13, 2013, at http://www.khaama.com/gunmen-attack-iranian-consulate-staff-in-mazar-e-sharif-city-2190?utm_source=feedburner&utm_medium=email&utm_campaign=Feed%3A+khaama+%28KHAAMA+PRESS+%7C+Afghan+Online+ Newspaper +%26+Magazine%29
106. Ahmad Majidyar, "Iran wields soft power in Afghanistan," *American Enterprise Institute*, January 25, 2013, at http://www.aei-ideas.org/2013/01/iran-wields-soft-power-in-afghanistan/
107. "Taliban Political Office Sends Delegation to Iran," *Fars News Agency*, June 01, 2013, at http://english2.farsnews.com/newstext.php?nn=9202246158
108. "No Taliban delegation visiting Iran: Araqchi," *Press TV*, June 02, 2013, at http://www.presstv.com/detail/2013/06/02/306799/iran-rejects-taliban-teams-visit/
109. "Remarks of Qari Yousuf Ahmadi regarding visits to the Islamic Republic of Iran by delegations of Islamic Emirate," *Voice of Jihad*, June 04, 2013, at http://shahamat-english.com/index.php/paighamoona/32277-remarks-of-qari-yousuf-ahmadi-regarding-visits-to-the-islamic-republic-of-iran-by-delegations-of-islamic-emirate
110. "The official visit of Taliban to Iran in the eyes of the analysts," *Voice of Jihad*, June 10, 2013, at http://shahamat-english.com/index.php/articles/32565-the-official-visit-of-taliban-

to-iran-in-the-eyes-of-the-analysts

111. Jawed Stanakzai, "Afghanistan Signs Strategic Cooperation Agreement With Iran," *TOLO News*, August 05, 2013, at http://www.tolonews.com/en/afghanistan/11462-afghanistan-signs-strategic-cooperation-agreement-with-iran
112. "Statement by Mr. Kamalesh Sharma, Permanent Representative, on the Situation in Afghanistan in the Security Council on March 26, 2002," *Permanent Mission of India to the UN*, at https://www.pminewyork.org/adminpart/uploadpdf/16869ind591.pdf
113. "Speech by External Affairs Minister at the meeting of International Contact Group (ICG) on Afghanistan in New Delhi," *Indian Ministry of External Affairs*, January 16, 2014, at http://www.mea.gov.in/Speeches-Statements.htm?dtl/22755/Speech+by+External+Affairs+Minister+at+the+meeting+of+International+Contact+Group+ICG+on+Afghanistan+in+New+Delhi
114. "Statement by Mr. Brajesh Mishra Principal Secretary to the Prime Minister and National Security Advisor, Government of India '38th Munich Conference on Security Policy,'" Indian *Ministry of External Affairs*, February 02, 2002, at http://www.mea.gov.in/Speeches-Statements.htm?dtl/6310/Statement+by+Mr+Brajesh+Mishra+Principal+Secretary+to+the+Prime+ Minister+and+National+Security+Advisor+Government+of+India+quot38th+Munich+Conference+on+Security+Policyquot
115. "Annual Report 2001-02," *Indian Ministry of External Affairs*, at http://www.mea.gov.in/Uploads/PublicationDocs/164_Annual-Report-2001-2002.pdf
116. "Chairman Karzai's remarks at luncheon hosted by Honble Prime Minister of India, Shri Atal Bihari Vajpayee," *Indian Ministry of External Affairs*, February 27, 2002, at http://www.mea.gov.in/Speeches-Statements.htm?dtl/5756/Chairman+Karzais+remarks+at+luncheon+hosted+by+Honble+Prime+Minister+of+India+Shri+Atal+Bihari+Vajpayee
117. "Prime Minister Shri Atal Bihari Vajpayee's Speech at the Lunch hosted in the honour of H.E. Mr. Hamid Karzai, Chairman of the Afghan Interim Administration," *Indian Ministry of External Affairs*, February 27, 2002, at http://www.mea.gov.in/Speeches-Statements.htm?dtl/5766/Prime+Minister+ Shri+Atal+Bihari+Vajpayees+Speech+at+ the+Lunch+hosted+in+the+honour+of+HE+Mr+Hamid+Karzai+Chairman+of+the+Afghan+Interim+Administration
118. "Statement on Areas of Cooperation between India and Afghanistan on Reconstruction and Rehabilitation in post conflict Afghanistan," *Indian Ministry of External Affairs*, February 27, 2002, at http://www.mea.gov.in/Speeches-Statements.htm?dtl/5767/Statement+on+Areas+ of+Cooperation+between+India+and+Afghanistan+on+Reconstruction+and+Rehabilitation+in+post+conflict+Afghanistan
119. "Opening address by Shri Jaswant Singh, Minister of External Affairs, at the Government of India-UNDP Joint Conference on South-South Cooperation and the Reconstruction of Afghanistan," *Indian Ministry of External Affairs*, May 23, 2002, at http://www.mea.gov.in/Speeches-Statements.htm?dtl/7962/Opening+address+by+Shri+Jaswant+Singh+Minister+of+External+Affairs+at+the+Government+of+IndiaUNDP+Joint+Conference+ on+ SouthSouth+Cooperation+and+the+Reconstruction+of+Afghanistan
120. "Annual Report (1 January 2003-31 March 2004)," *Indian Ministry of External Affairs*, at http://www.mea.gov.in/Uploads/PublicationDocs/165_Annual-Report-2003-2004.pdf
121. "Text of External Affairs Minister Shri Yashwant Sinha's address at the reception hosted by EAM for Afghan Police Officers and Diplomats currently undergoing training in India," *Indian Ministry of External Affairs*, August 07, 2002, at http://www.mea.gov.in/Speeches-Statements.htm?dtl/8526/Text+of+External+Affairs+Minister+Shri+Yashwant+Sinhas+address+at+the+reception+hosted+by+EAM+for+Afghan+Police+Officers+and+Diplomats+currently+undergoing+training+in+india
122. Joe Lauria, "Indian Minister Urges Afghan Political Settlement," *The Wall Street Journal*, September 23, 2009, at http://online.wsj.com/article/SB125364105273431343.html

123. Ajai Shukla, "India supports reconciliation with Taliban," *Business Standard,* October 08, 2009, at http://www.business-standard.com/india/news/india-supports-reconciliationtaliban/372609/
124. "Joint Declaration between the People's Republic of China and the Islamic Republic of Afghanistan on Establishing Strategic and Cooperative Partnership," *Ministry of Foreign Affairs of the People's Republic of China*, June 08, 2012, at http://www.fmprc.gov.cn/eng/zxxx/t939517.htm
125. Hamid Wahed Alikuzai, *From Aryana-Khorasan to Afghanistan: Afghanistan History in 25 Volumes*, Trafford Publishing, United States of America, 2011, p. 345.
126. Surya Gangadharan, "The China–Taliban Equation," *Aakrosh*, 3 (6), January 2000, p. 58.
127. Ibid, pp. 67-68.
128. Abdul Salam Zaeef, *My Life with the Taliban*, Hachette India, 2010, p. 135.
129. Ahmed Rashid, "Taliban Temptation," *Far Eastern Economic Review* (Hong Kong), March 11, 1999, p. 22.
130. Xu Feihong, "A unique neighbor of Afghanistan: China's Xinjiang," *Embassy of the People's Republic of China in the Islamic Republic of Afghanistan*, August 27, 2011, at http://af.china-embassy.org/eng/dsxx/remarks/t852487.htm
131. "Chinese firm pulls out of IP pipeline project," *Pak Tribune*, September 05, 2013, at http://paktribune.com/business/news/Chinese-firm-pulls-out-of-IP-pipeline-project-11554.html
132. Zhang Xin, "Afghanistan re-opens request for corridor road," *China Daily*, October 16, 2009, at http://www.chinadaily.com.cn/china/2009-10/16/content_8800563.htm. Also, see Abbas Daiyar, "President Karzai at SCO," *Daily Outlook Afghanistan*, June 07, 2012, at http://outlookafghanistan.net/topics.php?post_id=4520
133. Russell Hsiao and Glen E. Howard, "China Builds Closer Ties to Afghanistan through Wakhan Corridor," *China Brief*, 10 (1), January 07, 2010, at http://www.jamestown.org/single/?tx_ttnews%5Btt_news%5D=35879
134. Ahmed Rashid, no. 129, p. 21.
135. The SCO member states are China, Kazakhstan, Kyrgyzstan, Russia, Tajikistan and Uzbekistan. Among observer states are Afghanistan, India, Iran, Mongolia and Pakistan. The SCO's dialogue partners are Belarus, Turkey and Sri Lanka.
136. The plan of action also spoke of "counter terrorist collaboration for comprehensive measures to jointly respond to terrorist threats" in the region. For details, see "Plan of Action of the Shanghai Cooperation Organization Member States and the Islamic Republic of Afghanistan on combating terrorism, illicit drug trafficking and organized crime," *SCO Summit*, Yekaterinburg, Russia, March 27, 2009, at http://www.sectsco.org/EN123/show.asp?id=99. Also, see "Declaration of the special Conference on Afghanistan convened under the auspices of the Shanghai Cooperation Organization" in the special conference during the same summit meeting, at http://www.sectsco.org/EN123/show.asp?id=98
137. Ibid., see the declaration cited above, where emphasis is on "importance of sustained international efforts to achieve a stable, peaceful, prosperous and democratic Afghanistan ...under the leadership of Afghanistan and the central role of the UN in coordinating international assistance and based on strict adherence of the UN Charter."
138. Swaran Singh, "China's Afghan Policy: Limitations versus Leverages" in K. Warikoo (ed.), *The Afghanistan Crisis: Issues and Perspectives*, Bhavana Books, New Delhi, 2002, p. 406.
139. Zuqian Zhang, "Beijing Calling," *NATO Review*, Autumn 2003, at http://www.nato.int/docu/review/2003/issue3/english/special.html
140. "China active in global counter-terrorism," *Ministry of Foreign Affair of the, People's Republic of China*, September 10, 2002, at http://www.fmprc.gov.cn/ce/cegv/eng/zt/zgfk/t89060.htm
141. Senate Foreign Relations Committee, hearing, Fiscal Year 2003 Foreign Affairs Budget,

February 05, 2002.

142. Department of Defense, "Fact Sheet: International Contributions to the War Against Terrorism," June 14, 2002.
143. "Foreign Minister Tang Jiaxuan Attended the Foreign Ministers' Meeting on the Afghan Issue," *Ministry of Foreign Affairs of the People's Republic of China*, November 14, 2001, at http://www.fmprc.gov.cn/mfa_eng/wjb_663304/zzjg_663340/yzs_663350/gjlb_663354/2676_663356/2678_663360/t15825.shtml
144. Francesco Sisci, "China breaks its silence," *Asia Times Online*, November 28, 2001, at http://www.atimes.com/china/CK28Ad01.html
145. Ibid.
146. "East Turkistan Terrorist Forces Cannot Get Away With Impunity," *Issued by the Chinese Information Office of State Council*, January 21, 2002, at http://www.china-un.ch/eng/xwdt/t88226.htm. It is interesting to note that exactly a year after 9/11, the ETIM was included in the list of global terrorist organisations by the UN on September 11, 2002.
147. "President Jiang Zemin Meets Chairman Hamid Karzai of the Afghan Interim Government," *Ministry of Foreign Affairs of the People's Republic of China* January 25, 2002, at http://www.fmprc.gov.cn/mfa_eng/wjb_663304/zzjg_663340/yzs_663350/gjlb_663354/2676_663356/2678_663360/t15827.shtml
148. "Afghanistan-China Relations Excellent: Karzai," *People's Daily Online*, March 27, 2002, at http://english.peopledaily.com.cn/200203/26/eng20020326_92826.shtml
149. "Former Afghan King Met with Foreign Minister Tang Jiaxuan," *Ministry of Foreign Affairs of the People's Republic of China*, May 21, 2002, at http://www.fmprc.gov.cn/eng/wjb/zzjg/yzs/gjlb/2676/2678/t15831.htm
150. "Foreign Minister Tang Jiaxuan Held Talks with His Afghan Counterpart," *Ministry of Foreign Affairs of the People's Republic of China*, May 21, 2002, at http://www.fmprc.gov.cn/mfa_eng/wjb_663304/zzjg_663340/yzs_663350/gjlb_663354/2676_663356/2678_663360/t15832.shtml
151. "Vice President Zeng Qinghong Holds Talks with Afghan Vice President Nimartullah Shaharani," *Ministry of Foreign Affairs of the People's Republic of China*, May 27, 2002, at http://gr.china-embassy.org/eng/xwdt/xw2003/xw200305/t145713.htm
152. "Li Zhaoxing Meets with Afghan Foreign Minister," *Ministry of Foreign Affairs of the People's Republic of China*, March 10, 2004, at http://www.fmprc.gov.cn/mfa_eng/wjb_663304/zzjg_663340/yzs_663350/gjlb_663354/2676_663356/2678_663360/t72653.shtml
153. "China to write off huge Afghan debt," *China Daily*, March 28, 2004, at http://www.chinadaily.com.cn/english/doc/2004-03/28/content_318619.htm
154. "Mystery Surrounds Attack on Road Workers," *China Daily*, June 13, 2004, at http://www.chinadaily.com.cn/english/doc/2004-06/13/content 338972.htm. Also, see Sayed Salahuddin, "Bodies of Chinese Workers Flown to Afghan Capital," *Reuters*, June 11, 2004, at http://www.afghanistannewscenter.com/news/2004/june/jun122004.html
155. "Unknown militants attack Chinese construction camp in Afghanistan," *Pak Tribune*, December 06, 2006, at http://www.paktribune.com/news/index.shtml?162239
156. "China suggests deepening friendship, trade with Afghanistan," *Pajhwok Afghan News*, August 18, 2005, at http://www.pajhwak.com/viewstory.asp?lng=eng&id=6593
157. Ahmad Khalid Mowahid, "Beijing to provide Kabul military equipment," *Pajhwok Afghan News*, October 23, 2005, at http://www.pajhwak.com/viewstory.asp?lng=eng&id=8023
158. "China pledges to strengthen military ties with Afghanistan," *Xinhua*, June 19, 2006, at http://news.xinhuanet.com/english/2006-06/19/content_4715712.htm
159. Ahmad Khalid Mowahid, "China to train Afghan soldiers on logistics," *Pajhwok Afghan News*, June 24, 2006, at http://www.pajhwak.com/viewstory.asp?lng=eng&id=20374
160. "China, Afghanistan vow to strengthen military co-op," *Xinhua*, October 31, 2006, at

http://news.xinhuanet.com/english/2006-10/31/content_5271908.htm

161. "Chinese DM holds talk with Afghan counterpart," *People's Daily Online*, July 24, 2012, at http://english.peopledaily.com.cn/90786/7885062.html; "Defense Minister Liang Guanglie Holds Talk with Afghan Defense Minister Wardak," *Embassy of the People's Republic of China in the Islamic Republic of Afghanistan* July 23, 2012, at http://af.china-embassy.org/eng/zagx/sbgx/t1099454.htm
162. "Treaty of Good-Neighbourly Friendship and Cooperation," *Ministry of Foreign Affairs, Islamic Republic of Afghanistan*, at http://www.mfa.gov.af/Documents/ImportantDoc/Afghanistan-China%20Frienship%20accord.pdf
163. "Treaty of China-Afghanistan Friendship, Cooperation and Good-neighbourly Relations Takes Effect," *Ministry of Foreign Affairs of the People's Republic of China*, August 14, 2008, at http://www.fmprc.gov.cn/eng/wjb/zzjg/yzs/gjlb/2676/2678/t484518.shtml
164. "Full text of Joint Statement Between China, Afghanistan," *People's Daily Online*, June 21, 2006, at http://english.people.com.cn/200606/21/eng20060621_275755.html
165. Qin Jize, "China, Afghanistan sign deals to fight terrorism," *China Daily*, June 20, 2006, at http://www.chinadaily.com.cn/china/2006-06/20/content_620943.htm
166. "China donates stuffs worth 1 mln USD to Afghanistan," *People's Daily Online*, November 10, 2006, at http://english.people.com.cn/200611/10/eng20061110_320066.html
167. "Foreign Minister Yang Jiechi Attends the International Conference in Support of Afghanistan," *Ministry of Foreign Affairs of the People's Republic of China*, June 13, 2008, at http://www.fmprc.gov.cn/mfa_eng/wjb_663304/zzjg_663340/yzs_663350/gjlb_663354/2676_663356/2678_663360/t465642.shtml
168. "Afghan President Karzai Meets with Yang Jiechi," *Ministry of Foreign Affairs of the People's Republic of China*, January 26, 2010, at http://www.fmprc.gov.cn/mfa_eng/wjb_663304/zzjg_663340/yzs_663350/gjlb_663354/2676_663356/2678_663360/t654227.shtml
169. "Yang Jiechi Attends the London Conference on Afghanistan and Delivers a Speech," *Ministry of Foreign Affairs of the People's Republic of China*, January 20, 2010, at http://www.fmprc.gov.cn/mfa_eng/wjb_663304/zzjg_663340/yzs_663350/gjlb_663354/2676_663356/2678_663360/t654971.shtml
170. Richard Weitz, "Karzai's State Visit Highlights Beijing's Afghan Priorities," *China Brief*, 10 (8), April 16, 2010, at http://www.jamestown.org/uploads/media/cb_010_41.pdf
171. "Remarks by H.E. Yang Jiechi Minister of Foreign Affairs of the People's Republic of China at the International Afghanistan Conference Bonn," *Ministry of Foreign Affairs of the People's Republic of China*, December 06, 2011, at http://www.fmprc.gov.cn/mfa_eng/wjb_663304/zzjg_663340/yzs_663350/gjlb_663354/2676_663356/2678_663360/t884443.shtml
172. "Hu Jintao Holds Talks with His Afghan Counterpart Karzai," *Ministry of Foreign Affairs of the People's Republic of China*, June 08, 2012, at http://www.fmprc.gov.cn/eng/wjb/zzjg/yzs/xwlb/t941392.htm
173. For details, see "Joint Declaration between The People's Republic of China and The Islamic Republic of Afghanistan on Establishing Strategic and Cooperative Partnership," *Ministry of Foreign Affairs of the People's Republic of China*, June 08, 2012, at http://www.fmprc.gov.cn/eng/wjb/zzjg/yzs/xwlb/t939517.htm
174. For details, see "Vice Foreign Minister Cheng Guoping Attends Vice Foreign Ministerial Level Consultation on Regional Security of SCO," *Ministry of Foreign Affairs of the People's Republic of China*, November 15, 2012, at http://www.fmprc.gov.cn/eng/zxxx/t991773.htm
175. See "Top Chinese security official makes surprise visit to Afghanistan," *Xinhua*, September 23, 2012, at http://news.xinhuanet.com/english/china/2012-09/23/c_131867386.htm; Also, see "Foreign Ministry Spokesperson Hong Lei's Regular Press Conference," *Ministry of Foreign Affairs of the People's Republic of China*, September 24, 2012, at http://

www.fmprc.gov.cn/eng/xwfw/s2510/2511/t973835.htm

176. "China and Afghanistan sign economic and security deals," *BBC News*, September 23, 2012, at http://www.bbc.com/news/world-asia-china-19693005
177. "Xi Jinping Holds Talks with President Hamid Karzai of Afghanistan Stressing to Deepen Bilateral Strategic Cooperative Partnership and to Support Peace and Reconstruction Process in Afghanistan," *Ministry of Foreign Affairs of the People's Republic of China*, September 27, 2013, at http://www.fmprc.gov.cn/eng/wjb/zzjg/yzs/gjlb/2676/2678/t1083933.shtml
178. Ibid.
179. "Li Keqiang Meets with President Hamid Karzai of Afghanistan, Stressing to Strengthen China-Afghanistan Traditional Friendship and to Promote Peace, Stability and Development of the Region," *Ministry of Foreign Affairs of the People's Republic of China*, September 27, 2013, at http://www.fmprc.gov.cn/eng/wjb/zzjg/yzs/gjlb/2676/2678/t1083929.shtml
180. "Wang Yi: China Is Ready to Play a Role in Achieving Smooth Transition in Afghanistan," *Ministry of Foreign Affairs of the People's Republic of China*, September 26, 2013, at http://www.fmprc.gov.cn/mfa_eng/wjb_663304/zzjg_663340/yzs_663350/gjlb_663354/2676_663356/2678_663360/t1082833.shtml
181. "Wang Yi: China Calls for Joint Efforts to Assist Afghanistan's Triple Transition," *Ministry of Foreign Affairs of the People's Republic of China*, February 22, 2014, at http://www.fmprc.gov.cn/mfa_eng/wjb_663304/zzjg_663340/yzs_663350/gjlb_663354/2676_663356/2678_663360/t1131886.shtml
182. "Wang Yi: China Hopes to See a United, Stable, Developing and Amicable Afghanistan," *Ministry of Foreign Affairs of the People's Republic of China*, February 22, 2014, at http://www.fmprc.gov.cn/mfa_eng/wjb_663304/zzjg_663340/yzs_663350/gjlb_663354/2676_663356/2678_663360/t1131887.shtml
183. Ibid.
184. "Afghan President Hamid Karzai Meets with Wang Yi," *Ministry of Foreign Affairs of the People's Republic of China*, February 23, 2014, at http://www.fmprc.gov.cn/mfa_eng/wjb_663304/zzjg_663340/yzs_663350/gjlb_663354/2676_663356/2678_663360/t1131896.shtml
185. Craig Whitlock, "China rebuffed U.S. request to open route for Afghanistan war supplies, cables show," *The Washington Post*, July 03, 2011, at http://www.washingtonpost.com/national/national-security/china-rebuffed-us-request-to-open-route-for-afghanistan-war-supplies-cablesshow/ 2011/06/30/AG8cdYvH_story.html
186. Zhang Haizhou, "US seeks bigger role for China in Afghanistan," *China Daily*, May 05, 2010, at http://www.chinadaily.com.cn/world/2010-05/05/content_9809311.htm
187. "Joint China-U.S. Training Program for Afghanistan Diplomats Holds Opening Ceremony," *Embassy of the People's Republic of China in the Islamic Republic of Afghanistan*, March 17, 2013, at http://af.china-embassy.org/eng/zagx/sbgx/t1099461.htm
188. ZTE is entrusted with the job of installing digital telephone switches and CDMA WLL equipments in 11 Provinces and the total subscriber lines in this project is 91,000 CDMA and fixed lines. Huawei is providing similar equipment in 12 provinces and the total subscriber lines in this project are 113,000 CDMA and fixed lines.
189. A detailed analysis is provided by Steven A. Zyck, "The Role of China in Afghanistan's Economic Development & Reconstruction," *Civil Military Fusion Centre*, March 2012, p. 2.
190. Chinese Ambassador Deng Xijun, while addressing the students of the Confucius Institute at the Kabul University on October 20, 2013, stated that the Institute has enrolled 174 Afghan students in 5 years and 50 of them have studied in China for two-year course with scholarship sponsored by the Chinese Government. Out of 33 graduates, some have been employed by local Chinese companies, some work for the Chinese Embassy in Kabul and

others became lecturers of the Chinese language in the Kabul University. The agreement to establish Confucius Institute was signed with the Kabul University on January 09, 2008. See "Remarks by H.E. Deng Xijun, Chinese Ambassador to Afghanistan at 'My Chinese Dream' Speech Competition, Kabul," *Embassy of the People's Republic of China in the Islamic Republic of Afghanistan*, October 21, 2013, at http://af.china-embassy.org/eng/dsxx/remarks/t1091235.htm

191. Xu Feihong, "China's Always with Afghanistan," *Embassy of the People's Republic of China in the Islamic Republic of Afghanistan*, August 27, 2011, at http://af.china-embassy.org/eng/dsxx/remarks/t852489.htm
192. The four other companies short listed for final bid were: Strikeforce, part of Russia's Basic Element Group; the London-based Kazakhmys Consortium; Hunter Dickinson of Canada; and the US copper mining firm, Phelps Dodge.
193. "Speech by Ambassador Yang Houlan at Reception for National Day," *Ministry of Foreign Affairs of the People's Republic of China*, September 29, 2008, at http://www.fmprc.gov.cn/eng/wjb/zwjg/zwbd/t515714.htm, accessed on January 12, 2013.
194. Michael Stanley and Ekaterina Mikhaylova, "Mineral Resource Tenders and Mining Infrastructure Projects Guiding Principles, Case Study: The Aynak Copper Deposit, Afghanistan," *Extractive Industries for Development Series 22*, The World Bank, September 2011, p. 64.
195. "Based on the long-term win-win—Hutchison MCC acquisition Aynak copper mine in Afghanistan," *Xinhua*, June 04, 2008, at http://news.xinhuanet.com/fortune/2008-06/04/content_8311160.htm,
196. Zhao Huasheng, "China and Afghanistan: China's Interests, Stances and Perspectives," A report of the CSIS Russia and Eurasia Programme, Centre for Strategic and International Studies, Washington, D.C., March 2012, p. 7.
197. "Chinese mine workers leave Afghanistan due to instability," *Khaama Press*, September 08, 2012, at http://www.khaama.com/chinese-mine-workers-leave-afghanistan-due-to-instability-766/?utm_source=feedburner&utm_medium=email&utm_campaign=Feed%3A+khaama+%28KHAAMA+PRESS+%7C+Afghan+Online+Newspaper+%26+Magazine%29
198. "Afghan mining deal with China facing failure," *Deutsche Welle*, July 31, 2013, at http://www.dw.de/afghan-mining-deal-with-china-facing-failure/a-16989797
199. According to the deal, the CNPC and Watan Group will explore for oil in three fields in the Amu Darya Basin – Kashkari, Bazarkhami and Zamarudsay, which are estimated to hold around 87 million barrels of oil. The CNPC will agree to pay a 15 per cent royalty on oil, a 20 per cent corporate tax and give up to 70 per cent of its profit from the project to the Afghan government. The Afghan Mines Ministry reportedly stated in October 2011 that the deal was likely to result in government revenues of US$5 billion over the next 10 years. See Mirwais Harooni, "Afghanistan signs oil development deal with China," *Reuters*, December 26, 2011, at http://business.financialpost.com/2011/12/26/afghanistan-signs-oil-development-deal-with-china/
200. "China, Afghanistan sign first oil contract," *Chinese Network Television (CNTV)*, December 29, 2011, at http://english.cntv.cn/program/newsupdate/20111229/107468.shtm
201. Steven A. Zyck, no. 189, pp. 5-6.
202. Mustafa Basharat, "Chinese enterprise faces tax evasion scam," *Pajhwok Afghan News*, November 02, 2007, at http://www.pajhwak.com/viewstory.asp?lng=eng&id=26865
203. Zhao Huasheng, "China and Afghanistan: China's Interests, Stances and Perspectives," *A report of the CSIS Russia and Eurasia Programme*, Centre for Strategic and International Studies, Washington, D.C., March 2012, p. 1.
204. Ibid., p. 5.

205. "Position Paper of the People's Republic of China at the 67th Session of the United Nations General Assembly," *Ministry of Foreign Affairs of the People's Republic of China*, September 19, 2012, at http://www.fmprc.gov.cn/eng/zxxx/t970926.htm
206. "Speech of the Secretary-General of the Shanghai Cooperation Organisation Bolat Nurgaliev at the Special Conference on Afghanistan," March 27, 2009, at http://www.sectsco.org/EN123/show.asp?id=55
207. Andrew Small, "China's Afghan Moment," *Foreign Policy*, October 03, 2012, at http://www.foreignpolicy.com/articles/2012/10/03/chinas_afghan_moment. Also, see Andrew Small, "Comment: Why is China talking to the Taliban?," *Foreign Policy*, June 21, 2013, at http://www.sbs.com.au/news/article/2013/06/21/comment-why-china-talking-taliban
208. "Will adjustments in US anti-terror strategy be successful?," *Opinion, People's Daily Online*, February 23, 2009, at http://english.people.com.cn/90001/90780/91343/6598630.html
209. Sun Xiaob, "SCO 'active' in seeking solution for Afghan security problems," *Global Times*, February 14, 2014, at http://www.globaltimes.cn/content/842415.shtml
210. "Interview: Afghanistan welcomes China's role in peace process," *Xinhua*, September 18, 2013, at http://news.xinhuanet.com/english/world/2013-09/18/c_132731879.htm
211. The Collective Security Treaty (CST) was first signed on May 15, 1992. The CST later in October 2002 was upgraded into a regional military alliance which came to be known as the Collective Security Treaty Organisation (CSTO). In December 2004, the organisation was granted an observer status in the UN General Assembly. In February 2009, member-states of the organisation decided to create Collective Rapid Reaction Force. The CSTO presently consists of Armenia, Belarus, Kazakhstan, Kyrgyzstan, Russia and Tajikistan. Afghanistan and Serbia became observer states in the CSTO Parliamentary Assembly in April 2013. Azerbaijan, Georgia and Uzbekistan were earlier members of the CSTO.
212. "Post-Soviet security group could help with Afghanistan – Ivanov," *RIA Novosti*, February 09, 2007, at http://en.rian.ru/russia/20070209/60476302.html
213. "On Rendering of Humanitarian Aid to Afghanistan," *Ministry of Foreign Affairs of the Russian Federation*, October 02, 2001, at http://www.mid.ru/bdomp/brp_4.nsf/e78a48070f128a7b43256999005bcbb3/a40ba243847864f843256adb003d1f5c!OpenDocument
214. "Russian President Vladimir Putin Remarks and Replies to Questions from Journalists During Joint Press Conference After End of Conversation with NATO Secretary General George Robertson, Brussels," *Ministry of Foreign Affairs of the Russian Federation*, October 03, 2001, at http://www.mid.ru/bdomp/brp_4.nsf/e78a48070f128a7b43256999005bcbb3/0c3788a5ccb0e42a43256adb003ce6e6!OpenDocument
215. "Russia ready to resume military aid to Afghanistan – diplomat," *RIA Novosti,* March 05, 2007, at http://en.rian.ru/russia/20070305/61570158.html
216. Tom Regan, "Russia and China forge new military ties," *The Christian Science Monitor*, December 28, 2004, at http://www.csmonitor.com/2004/1228/dailyUpdate.html
217. Claire Bigg, "Putin warns west against isolating Russia as Ukraine run-off looms," *The Guardian*, December 24, 2004, at http://www.guardian.co.uk/russia/article/0,2763,1379562,00.html
218. "CSTO to Cooperate with NATO in Central Asia," *RIA Novosti*, December 28, 2004, at http://en.rian.ru/rian/index.cfm?prd_id=160&msg_id=5261492&startrow=1&date=2004-12-28&do_alert=0
219. "Russia to join Partnership Status of Forces agreement," *NATO Update,* April 21, 2005, at http://www.nato.int/docu/update/2005/04-april/e0421a.htm. Also, see Bakir Rahmanovic, "Russia signs NATO status of forces pact," April 22, 2005, at http://www.isn.ethz.ch/news/sw/details.cfm?id=11153
220. "The United States-Russia Working Group on Counterterrorism Joint Press Statement

and Fact Sheet," *The Ministry of Foreign Affairs of the Russian Federation*, June 23, 2008, at http://www.mid.ru/brp_4.nsf/0/755BC0FCB70601F1C3257472003B7D5A

221. Peter Finn, "Russians Sense the Heat of Cold War," *The Washington Post*, April 03, 2006, at http://www.washingtonpost.com/wp-dyn/content/article/2006/04/02/AR2006040200749.html
222. Sergey Lavrov, "Democracy, International Governance, and the Future World Order," *Russia in Global Affairs*, No. 1, January-February 2005, at http://eng.globalaffairs.ru/number/n_4422
223. "NATO 2020: Assured Security; Dynamic Engagement," *Analysis and Recommendations of the Group of Experts on a New Strategic Concept for NATO*, May 17, 2010, p. 10.
224. Ibid., p. 15.
225. Ibid., p. 30, 10 & 27.
226. Afghan President Hamid Karzai addressing the Russian Diplomatic Academy, Moscow, January 2011. See "Afghan Leader Says Russia 'Important Partner', Seeks Closer Ties," *RIA Novosti*, January 21, 2011, at http://en.rian.ru/world/20110121/162233983.html
227. "Speech and answer to journalist's question at news conference following Russian-Afghan talks," The Kremlin, Moscow, *Official Website of the President of Russia*, January 21, 2011, at http://eng.news.kremlin.ru/transcripts/1663
228. "Speech and answer to journalist's question at news conference following Russian-Afghan talks," The Kremlin, Moscow, *Official Website of the President of Russia,* January 21, 2011, at http://eng.news.kremlin.ru/transcripts/1663
229. Dmitri Trenin and Alexei Malashenko, "Afghanistan: A View from Moscow," *Carnegie Moscow Centre*, 2010, p. 27.
230. "Speech and answer to journalist's question at news conference following Russian-Afghan talks," The Kremlin, Moscow, *Official Website of the President of Russia,* January 21, 2011, at http://eng.news.kremlin.ru/transcripts/1663
231. Dmitry Babich, "Afghanistan: Open For Russian Business," August 07, 2007, at http://www.russiaprofile.org/page.php?pageid=International&articleid=a1186493752
232. Ibid.
233. Aunohita Mojumdar, "Moscow Wants to Supply More Arms to Kabul – Russian Envoy," *EurasiaNet*, January 20, 2011, at http://www.eurasianet.org/node/62741
234. Russian Ambassador to Kabul, Andrey Avetisyan, "Are the Russians Coming Back?," *Daily Outlook Afghanistan* (Kabul), February 14, 2011.
235. "Russia, US to discuss Afghan helicopter deal in Washington," *RIA Novosti,* January 21, 2011, at http://en.rian.ru/russia/20110121/162241157.html
236. "Speech and answer to journalist's question at news conference following Russian–Afghan talks," *Kremlin, Moscow*, January 21, 2011, at http://eng.kremlin.ru/transcripts/1663
237. "Russian diplomat: Russia rules out its military presence in Afghanistan," *Interfax*, March 25, 2009, at http://www.interfax.com/17/482022/Interview.aspx
238. Luke Baker, "Time to talk to Taliban, says former Soviet general," *Reuters*, February 11, 2009, at http://in.reuters.com/article/southAsiaNews/idINIndia-37965820090211?sp=true
239. Colum Lynch, "Russia won't block removal of former Taliban members from UN terrorism List," *The Washington Post,* January 27, 2010, at http://www.washingtonpost.com/wp-dyn/content/article/2010/01/26/AR2010012602557.html
240. "Russia re-engages Afghanistan on Karzai visit," *Tehran Times*, January 24, 2011, at http://www.tehrantimes.com/index_View.asp?code=234687
241. "Russia ready to invest $500 million in Central Asian electricity project," *RIA Novosti,* January 21, 2011, at http://en.rian.ru/world/20110121/162243812.html
242. "Mohammad Qasim: "Afghanistan and SCO are coming closer," *Afghanistan.Ru*, November 18, 2011, at http://en.afghanistan.ru/doc/284.html. Also, see Ghanizada, "Russia exports

10,000 tons fuel to Afghanistan: Officials," *Khaama Press*, September 05, 2011, at http://www.khaama.com/russia-exports-10000-tons-fuel-to-afghanistan-officials

243. "Russian-Afghan trade and economic cooperation gaining momentum," *Afghanistan.Ru*, March 05, 2012, at http://en.afghanistan.ru/doc/326.html. Also, see Lyuba Lulko, "Russia to return to Afghanistan after US occupation," *Pravda*, November 20, 2012, at http://english.pravda.ru/world/asia/20-11-2012/122866-russia_afghanistan-0/

244 "Joint Counternarcotics Operation in Nangarhar Province," Press Release, *Embassy of the Russian Federation in the Islamic Republic of Afghanistan*, October 30, 2010, at http://www.afghanistan.mid.ru/en/

245. "Afghanistan seeks Russian help in anti-drug efforts," *RIA Novosti,* May 13, 2009, at http://en.rian.ru/world/20090513/155011410.html

246. "CSTO to set up working group on Afghanistan," *RIA Novosti*, November 30, 2005, at http://en.ria.ru/russia/20051130/42267027.html

247. Vladimir Socor, "Russia Returning to Afghanistan with Not-So-Soft Power," *The Jamestown Foundation*, March 16, 2007, at http://www.jamestown.org/edm/article.php?article_id=2372016

248. "CSTO Parliamentary Assembly delegation to visit Afghanistan," *Interfax*, October 08, 2013, at http://www.interfax.com/newsinf.asp?id=449491

"Eight years into the war in Afghanistan, the vast intelligence apparatus is unable to answer fundamental questions about the environment in which US and Allied forces operate and the people they seek to persuade."*

— *Maj. Gen. Michael Flynn, US Deputy Chief of Staff for Intelligence in Afghanistan, September 2010*

"Everything in Afghanistan seems very ambiguous now. There are a hundred questions to be answered, but nothing is clear, and we have no magic formula."**

— *Abdul Hakim Mujahid, a former Taliban diplomat and member of the government-appointed High Peace Council.*

---

* "Interview with ISAF Commander Petraeus: We're Not 'Going to Turn Afghanistan into Switzerland,'" *Der Spiegel,* September 19, 2010, at http://www.spiegel.de/international/world/interview-with-isaf-commander-petraeus-we-re-not-going-to-turn-afghanistan-into-switzerland-a-718285.html

** Pamela Constable, "Afghan Peace Lost in Transition Worries," *The Washington Post,* May 20, 2013, at http://www.washingtonpost.com//world/asia_pacific/afghan-peace-lost-in-transition-worries/2013/05/20/8af1780c-c09b-11e2-9aa6-fc21ae807a8a_story.html

CHAPTER VIII

The Unfinished War

With every passing year, one wonders where Afghanistan is headed. The post-Taliban political process is yet to take firm roots in the Afghan polity and remains vulnerable to potential threat from a range of internal and external forces. Though Afghanistan in many ways has benefited from increased international attention, investment and engagement over the past one decade, yet it remains wide at risk of succumbing under sustained pressure to destabilising forces. Violence is spreading and rising, calling into question all elements of the Western approach and strategy towards both Afghanistan and Pakistan since 2001. What led America back into Afghanistan a decade after the Soviet retreat, hardly finds sense in the American thinking today.

The politico-military stalemate in Afghanistan, effectively manoeuvred by the Haqqani-Taliban network with support from their numerous allies, state and non-state, local and global, operating mainly from within Pakistan, has over the years made the war increasingly unviable and unsustainable for the West. The Taliban guerrillas along with the Haqqani network have quietly succeeded in raising the rate of attrition among the Western forces. They have been constantly (re-)adjusting their response strategies both military and political, and adapting to the changing situation much faster than the political set up in Kabul and the Western coalition supporting it. All these years, Western forces have been winning the battles but not the war. The Afghan Taliban and their allies might not have been winning the battles, but they certainly do not appear to be loosing the war either. While the Western coalition constantly suffered from differing rules of engagement and perceptions about the war on terror, the Taliban and allies instead consolidated their influence and made common cause against a vastly superior Western military. In fact, the term 'war on terror' itself is history now and has been replaced by the Obama Administration with a more technical term, 'overseas contingency operation.' At another level, the fault lines within the post-Taliban political process too have also invariably worked to the advantage of the Taliban and their Pakistani sponsors.

Since the overthrow of the Taliban regime in the end of 2001, successive US administrations have constantly failed in breaking the decades-old link between Pakistan's military-intelligence apparatus and militant Islamist groups, which the US itself had patronised in the 1980s as part of *jihad* against the Soviet forces and the communist regime in Afghanistan. The discovery of al Qaeda chief, Osama bin Laden, deep inside Pakistan a decade after 9/11, was more a defeat of the long-standing American alliance with the Pakistan Army and particularly the ISI, than a victory for the Obama Administration. Time and again, the US Administration had failed to build on the momentum generated by its military successes against militant Islamist networks to devise a long-term political strategy to address the fundamental issue of Pakistan's continuing support to forces of extremism and terrorism in a sustained manner. Instead, the entire focus has shifted to 2014, the year when the world's largest military coalition would end its combat mission in Afghanistan. Today, the US-led 'war on terror' may be fast receding from the region but Afghanistan's struggle against the 'terror of war' continues.

The Haqqani-Taliban network centred inside Pakistan continues to execute well-coordinated high profile attacks on carefully chosen targets including Western forces and bases inside Afghanistan. This apparently is part of a continuing trend from the late 1970s when armed Afghan Islamists with support from Pakistan first began carrying out attacks against the government of President Daoud Khan and later the communist PDPA regime. Pakistan has since nurtured and sustained several generation of violent Islamists as a potent tool to constantly weaken and undermine Afghanistan both as a state and a nation. With the Soviet invasion in 1979, Pakistan's policy of sponsoring and unleashing militant Islamists against the central authority in Kabul evolved into a more organised and complex operation fully controlled and directed by its military-intelligence apparatus. Factionalising the Afghan unity and exacerbating divisions among the Pashtuns remains at the core of Pakistan's Afghan policy. It had not only destroyed the Afghan state and in the process militarised its polity, but also made the Afghan conflict one of the most intractable ones. It has had long lasting implications for Pakistan state and society too. The same forces of religious extremism and terrorism, which Pakistan's powerful military-intelligence apparatus had created and over the decades developed them into a lethal force as part of its proxy wars against its immediate neighbours, are now directly tearing into the social and political fabric of the Pakistan state itself. Whether the civilian leadership in Pakistan have the wherewithal and, more importantly, enough political will to transform Pakistan into a normal state, remains the big question.

Interestingly, with several transitions—political, security and economic—simultaneously underway, Afghans often are both cautiously optimistic and widely sceptical about the future of their country. A post-ISAF or post-West scenario invariably evokes a mixed sense of guarded euphoria and lingering fear within the country and also at the wider regional level. As the country's nascent institutions struggle to assume wider role and responsibility after 2014, various stakeholders in the Afghan conflict are consolidating their position in anticipation of possible re-alignment of power structures in the country. The fear of being again abandoned by the international community and the country subsequently relapsing into complete chaos and anarchy is rattling a vast section of the Afghan society. Several achievements of the past decade in Afghanistan are still considered fragile and reversible as forces of violent extremism and terrorism continue to adapt and multiply and transform and morph into more lethal networks, willing to expand their operations both within and beyond the Afghanistan-Pakistan region.

Interestingly, though the Western coalition is pressing ahead with its planned withdrawal, it is perhaps for the first time in the Afghan history, a country which is known to be a 'graveyard of empires,' that not a single organised internal rebellion could be noted in the last thirteen years against the presence of thousands of foreign troops across Afghanistan. The Haqqani-Taliban network is Pakistan-based and sponsored, and if they do have support base in parts of south and east of the country, it is more due to the weak presence of government and lack of alternatives and various other local factors. There never was any groundswell of political opposition or any organised mobilisation against the Western engagement within Afghanistan. While anti-Americanism remains rampant in Pakistan and several countries in the region have been sceptical of the huge Western military presence, but Afghans in general have widely supported the Western presence and want them to stay put well beyond 2014. All eight candidates, coming from diverse political backgrounds, for the presidential election in April 2014 have endorsed an extended Western military presence in the country. Prior to that, in November 2013, a *Loya Jira* which brought together about 2,500 representatives from across the country and was specially convened by President Karzai to discuss the prospects of BSA, had unanimously endorsed the extended presence of Western coalition in bases spread across the country for the next ten years. Despite severe criticism of the US and NATO-led military operations for causing civilian casualties and violating cultural norms of the Afghan society, which is supposed to have been particularly taken care of in the proposed text of the BSA, the Afghans have by and large embraced the idea of a limited Western military presence beyond 2014 to protect the current political system and avert any possibility of country sliding into a full scale civil war. As Afghanistan undergoes a major political transition in 2014 and awaits change of government, the nature and scale of future Western engagement in the region, however, still remains to be seen.

The third round of presidential election held in April 2014 marks the beginning of a long-drawn process which is supposed to conclude with parliamentary elections in 2015. The whole exercise is considered critical to the survival and sustenance of a 'post-Taliban' Afghanistan. The 2014 elections are not merely about change of leadership in Kabul, but also about ushering the country into a 'decade of transformation' (2015-24) as discussed and agreed upon during the second Bonn Conference in December 2011.[1] However, elections alone would not mean much to the future of the country if it fails to further strengthen the relatively inclusive political system and the new constitution that emerged after the overthrow of the Taliban regime. Unfortunately, the Western discourse today is more about the way out of what is perceived as an un-winnable war rather than the way forward in what the US President Obama had described in 2009 as a "war of necessity."

The threat of 'zero option' entailing near-complete withdrawal of the Western forces in the absence of BSA had inevitably raised several issues of long-term concern. The American over-emphasis on BSA, though critical to the future of Afghanistan, is undermining several other critical components of the *Enduring Strategic Partnership Agreement* which the two countries had signed in May 2012. After a decade-long direct intervention and engagement, and despite loss of thousands of its soldiers, the US/NATO strategy and approach towards both Afghanistan and Pakistan today clearly lacks clarity in its objectives and future trajectory. It is characterised by growing apathy and indifference towards the future of Afghanistan. To what extent Kabul is able to offer necessary hope and assurance against possible chaos and anarchy, would depend on the success of the electoral process in 2014-15. The outcome of the 2014 presidential election could prove to be a major turning point depending on how lead political actors tactfully position themselves for a broad-based coalition taking a long-term view of various challenges that lie ahead. If they opt for narrow identity based politics of exclusion of the 1990s, Afghanistan could again enter into a prolonged phase of instability and violence. Meanwhile, irrespective of the BSA, the conflict between that section of the Afghan society which has benefited from the international engagement and has developed stakes in the new political system and those which have suffered in terms of loss of political power and control over resources could further sharpen in times to come.

The politics of reconciliation with the Afghan Taliban, which has evolved into a highly competitive and an ambiguous process, is likely to gain traction after the new government assumes power in Kabul. In this context, whether the new political coalition that emerges from the elections would be able to temper the geo-political aspirations of the Pakistani establishment remains to be seen. However, Kabul still does not have the institutional strength to withstand the impact, foreseen and largely unforeseen, of any power-sharing arrangement particularly with the Taliban leadership. Of particular long-term concern is the sustenance of the Afghan army and police, both of which are far from being in a position to deal with direct threat to the Afghan political system, particularly the influence and control of the government in provinces, from an assortment of Pakistan-backed extremist forces in a sustained manner.

For now, the year 2014-15 could be regarded as another watershed in the making. By the end of 2014, President Karzai's second (and final as per the Afghan Constitution) presidential term would have come to an end, and the NATO is expected to have withdrawn bulk of its troops. However, Karzai's political innings could be far from over. Karzai as incumbent president retains certain political leverages, and given his vast understanding and experience of the politics of coalition building, might play a significant role should there be a constitutional crisis in the near future. The Afghan Constitution may have barred Karzai from seeking a third consecutive term, but not from contesting the next presidential election in 2019. At the age of 56, though twice elected president of his country, Karzai is unlikely to politically fade away in the coming years.

If the West decides to remain militarily engaged and maintains minimal force level in Afghanistan beyond 2014, it is still not clear as to how would it help in improving or transforming the situation on the ground. The hardline segment of the Taliban and their Pakistani allies are convinced of their impending 'victory.' They seek to establish strong centres of resistance in different parts of the country to be able to sustain their offensive against the Afghan army, and also to subsequently cut off key provincial centres and highways from Kabul. Even if in years to come, the remaining Western forces register big operational successes; maintain bases in parts of the country; and a section of middle or top Afghan Taliban elements defect from key shuras based in Pakistan, several of armed Islamist groups that remain active along and across the Durand Line will continue to pose both ideological and physical challenge to the new government in Kabul and countries of the south-central Asia region and even beyond.

Beyond 2014: Continuing Concerns and Challenges

The likely trajectory of politics and conflict beyond 2014 is obscured by several transitions simultaneously underway in Afghanistan. There are several ifs and buts to any potential future scenario that one could think of. As Afghanistan wades through yet another major transition in 2014-15, it is important to identify certain factors which despite over a decade of Western intervention remain germane to the nature of politics and conflict in the country. Following are key historical and contemporary factors as well as issues of concern that are likely to continue to impact developments in post-transition Afghanistan:

(i) Historical Conflict Dynamics

The missing power equilibrium

By the time monarchy was uprooted in 1973, a complex mix of mutually diverse and competing forces seeking to redefine the social and political values often at each other's expense had emerged. The Afghan communists as well as the Islamists, both inspired by the internationalist spirit of the respective movements in the post-World War II period, were struggling to shape the destiny of Afghanistan in their own ways. But political transitions in Afghanistan have since been abrupt, reactive and inconclusive. Be it King Zahir Shah's experiment with limited democracy in 1960s, the absolute presidentialism of Sardar Daoud Mohammad (1973-78), the radical modernisation drive of the early Afghan communist regimes (1978-92), the internecine power struggle among the Afghan Islamists (1992-96), or the Taliban endeavour for an Islamic emirate (1996-2001), Afghanistan could never see a sustainable socio-political transition.

The democratisation process that began with the framing of the 1964 constitution under Zahir Shah was disrupted by the 1973 coup which itself was a result of the political churning caused by the emergence of competitive forces, who were either opposed to the political reforms or were restless at the slow pace of its implementation. But the tectonic shifts taking place in the Afghan polity were unmistakable. There was no going back to a monarchical order. However, the process of socio-political modernisation that began a century ago under King Habibullah Khan (1901-1919) and assumed greater salience under King Amanullah Khan (1919-29) and Zahir Shah (1933-73), has had a lasting impact on the Afghan polity. A classic example is the 2004 constitution which is largely drawn from the 1964 constitution, and the current national flag of Afghanistan which is a slightly modified adaptation of the royal flag used between 1929 and 1973. After the achievement of full independence from Britain in 1919, Afghanistan embarked on redefining its foreign relations, particularly with the West. The Afghan monarchs were notably open to changing and modernising Afghan society and structures of governance. The influence of the post-renaissance Europe and the modernist policies of Kemal Ataturk of Turkey and Reza Shah in Iran on the reform-oriented approach of the Afghan monarchs of the 20th century were both tangible and palpable. It even extended to the personal attire of the members of the royal family and officials, and to the then royal flag of Afghanistan. Unfortunately, the notions of modernity as understood and endorsed by the Afghan royalty remained imitative rather than adaptive to the local traditional setting, which constantly proved to be a major drawback with successive efforts for modernisation.

As Afghanistan began to focus on economic development and military modernisation, it became a leading recipient of aid and assistance from various European powers, such as Germany and Italy, to begin with, and later from both the US and the USSR, and even Japan. Though Kabul professed a neutral foreign policy or *betarfi* towards the bloc politics of the Cold War era, nevertheless, Afghanistan saw constant engagement by various global and regional powers. However, the pace of implementation of reforms differed from sector to sector depending on the interests and priorities of the reigning monarch or the regime. Amanullah's reforms were far more intense, demonstrative and pro-active than Zahir Shah, who patiently crafted institutional reforms and more in reaction to the socio-political and ideological churning taking place in the 1950s and 60s, though with varying degrees of success and failure.

The 1923 constitution initiated under Amanullah Khan and the 1964 constitution under Zahir Shah were reflective of the changing realities in view of developments that had taken place in late 19th and early 20th centuries in and around Afghanistan. The emergence of an educated urban class with a Western outlook influenced the modernisation drive as well as suffered on account of it. Zahir Shah's limited democratisation with the framing of 1964 constitution that abolished absolute monarchy and established constitutional monarchy with a relatively independent parliament was quite a remarkable achievement. It was also an acknowledgement of the rising power of the educated elites who were fired with an internationalist zeal for transforming Afghanistan into a socialist, democratic and a relatively secular modern nation-state. In reaction to it emerged a parallel Islamist discourse that ruthlessly opposed the modernisation process.

Except for the Taliban movement, the communist as well as the older Islamist movements were never unified, neither ideologically or politically. They suffered from factionalism and internal power struggle often along socio-ethnic lines. Interestingly, none had pan-Afghan appeal, including the Taliban, which remains characteristic of the Afghan politics to this day. Such tectonic shifts in the Afghan politics last three decades have led to destruction of old and traditional state institutions; periodic political vacuum; and chronic instability, a perfect breeding ground for regressive ideologies and blatant foreign interference.

It is important to take into account the way ethnic and tribal dynamics have played out in the face of externalisation and militarisation of the Afghan civil war through the 1980s and the 90s. Until the overthrow of the monarchy in 1973 and the 1978 coup by the Afghan communists, the Afghan state was defined and dominated by the Pashtuns of a particular tribe or a clan from southern Afghanistan. The minority ethnic groups from the northern and central

Afghanistan—especially the Tajiks, the Hazaras, and the Uzbeks—had a notably limited role in the national/Kabul politics. The north-south or the Pashtun and non-Pashtun divide emerged as a significant determining factor after complete Soviet withdrawal in early 1989 and the collapse of the Najibullah's national unity initiatives and his government in April 1992. To this day, national reconciliation has eluded Afghanistan.

Historically, Kabul had been the seat of Pashtun power and authority since late 18th century, except for a brief interregnum in 1929. The traditional elites of the non-Pashtun groups were generally allowed to retain their autonomous status and in lieu they recognised the suzerainty, often nominal, of the Pashtun dynasties ruling from Kabul. They also paid revenue to the Kabul treasury, and provided men and resources in times of expeditionary wars. Until the overthrow of monarchy in 1973, the above traditional balance of power defined/institutionalised the relationship between Kabul and the provincial elites at the political level, and between Pashtuns and non-Pashtuns, at a more societal level.

The destruction of traditional institutions and structures during the civil war left Pashtuns further divided and politically fragmented and created conditions for the well-armed minority ethnic factions to become more assertive. It often led to a strong sense of political deprivation and alienation among the Pashtuns. The proxy politics of the neighbouring countries also deepened the ethnic polarisation in the country.

The other notable fallout of the civil war of the 1990s was the systematic destruction of Afghanistan as a state. The denudation of state authority and institutions led to the emergence of highly militarised informal power structures and authorities at the provincial or sub-national level, incessantly competing for political space and control over resources. The traditional ruling elite too was destroyed and replaced in the process. The old internal balance of power that had defined and institutionalised the relationship between the state and the people, and the centre and the provinces, and had kept the country stable under single authority for almost a century, finally withered away with the collapse of the Najibullah Government in early 1992. Thereafter, both the *mujahideen* governments and the Taliban regime either made no efforts or were simply incapable of re-building strong state institutions.

Even a decade after the overthrow of the Taliban regime, the position of government in Kabul remains severely constrained and vulnerable to centrifugal tendencies. In the absence of unifying national state structures and institutions, the government had to rely on multiple power centres that have come to dominate the political landscape of the country. The push and pull between a more centralised or federalised state structure that runs through the various political processes including the politics over reconciliation with the Taliban and the electoral politics since after 2001 is reflective of the emerging social and political realities of the country. The perception divide among various ethnicities and regions of the country has only widened over the decades. A 'New Afghanistan,' which has always been an urban phenomenon, continues to face resistance from the localised centres of power that had emerged stronger in the countryside since the destruction of monarchy. All these factors have made the process of rebuilding Afghanistan, its state institutions, and implementing the much-needed political and economic reforms, a daunting task.

Perhaps, answer to some of the continuing challenges to Afghan state-building lie in understanding what has kept the country together despite decades of war. For much of its modern history, Afghanistan was not a highly centralised state. Amir Abdur Rehman (1880-1901), however, did succeed at the turn of 19th century to bring Afghanistan under one centralised rule, but that was to an extent in response to drawing of the Durand Line by the British which had divided the Pashtun population and had weakened their position inside Afghanistan. Within few decades of his rule, the centralisation process was hardly a priority for the successive regimes in Kabul. In the given circumstances, political stability will continue to elude the country unless the political transition in 2014 succeeds in establishing a sustainable balance of power within the country, and strengthens governance at sub-national levels through decentralised or localised approaches to socio-economic development.

(ii) Post-Karzai Leadership

Old and familiar challenges

The leadership question assumes significance as the Western drawdown is stated to be 'irreversible' and the Haqqani-Taliban network continues to receive political and material support from the Pakistan Army and intelligence. The outcome of the third round of Afghan presidential and parliamentary elections may be difficult to assess at this point in time, it is clear that the lengthy election process will test the resilience of the nascent political and security institutions of the country. The 2014 presidential election is not just about transition of leadership, but also about ushering Afghanistan into a 'decade of transformation' (2015-24) where the international community continues to extend relevant support and assistance to further strengthen the capacities of the Afghan state. The issue of legitimacy and credibility is at the core of the ongoing political transition. Rising uncertainty is making domestic politics more competitive as alignments and re-alignments take place in an effort to cobble an alternative political arrangement. This could be both an opportunity for further cooperation as well as potential conflict.

Though Karzai has announced that he would remain neutral in the election process, but as an incumbent president and somebody who has been at the helm of his country's affairs for more than a decade might still have stakes in the formation of the next government. Given his vast experience and understanding of the complex nature of the Afghan politics and the regional dynamics, his role remains critical to the success of the transition process. Karzai's presidency might have been under severe criticism both from within and outside, but it has set certain political templates which the next elected president will find hard not to follow.

Afghanistan is a chaos of localised power structures jostling for political autonomy and space both within and outside the post-Taliban political setting. In the circumstances, managing diverse perceptions about state and its authority in the larger context of establishing functional centre-province and state-society relations are bound to pose a major challenge to the credibility and legitimacy of the next leadership in Kabul. In fact, the challenges before the next president will be similar to what Karzai has been confronted with: managing divergent perceptions and factional interests, patronage networks and informal power structures at the sub-national level and protracted armed resistance by militant Islamist groups operating from Pakistan.

In addition, the new president will also have to cater to the rising aspirations as well as scepticism among the Afghan people. It remains to be seen to what extent the ongoing political transition and the next dispensation in Kabul would succeed in institutionalising the relatively inclusive political culture that has emerged since the overthrow of the Taliban regime, in mainstreaming a political order which is in tune with the changing socio-political realities and, most importantly, in keeping the international community engaged after 2014.

(iii) US' Missing Future Strategy

No more a war of necessity

The *Enduring Strategic Partnership Agreement* signed between the US and Afghanistan in May 2012 is yet to be fully functional and implemented. Though it clearly states that the US would remain engaged until 2024, the effectiveness of the US presence in terms of transforming the conflict in Afghanistan remains doubtful. President Karzai's refusal to sign BSA until certain conditions put forth by his government are met could be seen as an attempt by Karzai to ensure that the American military presence in the years to come benefits Afghanistan in a more substantive manner. It is about changing the war scenario by addressing the root causes of the conflict rather than simply dragging it the same way for another decade. For Afghanistan, the nature and scale of threat from various armed Islamist groups operating from Pakistan remains the way it has been since decades before.

In Karzai's perception, perhaps, the idea of an extended Western military engagement would not make sense until it is geared to protect Afghanistan against constant threats from Pakistan. It is more about an American presence that is deterrent to Pakistan's proxy war in Afghanistan; and should there be direct threat to Kabul from Pakistan, the American military should be able to take the war to the sources of Islamist extremism and terrorism in the region. Karzai's emphasis on putting an end to civilian casualties and raiding of Afghan homes, and providing security guarantees and helping Kabul in bringing about a political reconciliation with the Afghan Taliban, could well be seen in continuation of his long-pending demand for the need to re-strategise the war on terror.

Karzai's perception about the US role has to be seen in the context of the protracted nature of threat to Kabul from across the Durand Line. It was about developing a counter-strategy to the Pakistan's continuing quest for control over Kabul. Karzai had been raising issues that were fundamental to the war against militant extremism and terrorism plaguing the region, but the West preferred to look at its future disengagement-engagement dilemma through the prism of 'Afghan good enough.' Karzai's exhortations might prove to be prophetic and the future elected government in Kabul too might be urging the West to re-strategise its approach towards the region. Nothing perhaps as puzzling as the Western strategy in Afghanistan.

Though the nature and level of future Western engagement may still not be clear, it is most unlikely that the US and NATO would withdraw lock, stock and barrel from Afghanistan after 2014-15. Even with minimal presence, the US would remain a key actor in the region well beyond 2014. The American military strategy too has been in a state of transition as forces drawdown and the Afghan Army assumes greater operational role. In fact, since 2011-12, both American and NATO-led forces have been withdrawing from smaller bases in far flung areas and concentrating more on population centres. The US forces have been gradually moving away from counter-insurgency to a more counter-terrorism intensive approach which could be managed with limited military assets and capabilities in the coming years. The emphasis is likely to remain on precision strikes, though in a more restricted manner, against militant hideouts in the tribal areas of Pakistan and on conducting special operations targeted at the Haqqani-Taliban commanders within Afghanistan. This will also help take the domestic pressure off the US Administration as the casualty levels among troops are likely to remain low in the coming years.

While keeping the pressure on al Qaeda and their affiliate groups active in the region, the West has also been pushing for reconciliation with the Afghan Taliban leadership based inside Pakistan. In recent years, some of the Taliban elements have been de-listed from the UN sanctions list. Much would, however, depend on how the US decides to deal with Pakistan as it continues to resist the American pressure to move against the Afghan Taliban and the Haqqani network. It is also understood that that the Afghan Army would not be in a position to take on the Haqqani-Taliban network on their own for many years to come. In such a scenario, future Western role and engagement in post-transition Afghanistan becomes a critical factor particularly as al Qaeda seeks to reassert its role and position in the region. Perhaps, certain lessons too need to be drawn from the evolving situation in Iraq and potential threat from the emergence of entities such as the Islamic State of Iraq and Syria (ISIS).

Differences over certain operational and authority issues pertaining BSA could persist with the next political dispensation as well in Kabul, even after it has been signed. However, BSA is still deemed necessary for the survival of the current political system and the sustenance of the ANSF in the years to come. The presence of American troops however small in number in bases across Afghanistan also has a huge psychological dimension to it. It is likely to assure the next government in Kabul of continued international engagement and financial support which Afghanistan would critically require after 2014. The US has given indications that the withdrawal of conventional forces and end of active combat operations by December 2014 would not mean the withdrawal of Special Forces or end of training and mentoring mission for the ANSF. However, it is the lack of consensus within the US Administration with regard to the size and scope of post-ISAF mission that is adding to the confusion and scepticism about future Western commitment in Afghanistan.

(iv) Survival of the National Army

Quantity or quality force

One of the vital components of the Western exit strategy is phased transition of security to the Afghan army and police by 2014. The process has been underway even as serious doubts persist over the preparedness of the ANSF. This is perhaps one of the most challenging aspects of the Afghan transition. The Western military officials involved in the training of the Afghan Army have time and again warned that the army will not be in a position to assume full security responsibilities by the end of 2014. The army, despite phenomenal growth in its numerical strength since the Obama Administration shifted the focus from Iraq to Afghanistan in 2009, is far from being an effective deterrent to a sustained onslaught from Pakistan-sponsored armed Islamist guerrillas. The army would need long-term external support in terms of funding, mentoring, and regular supply and maintenance of equipments, in order to transform into a cohesive national force. The doctrinal orientation and future prospect of the national army and police is closely entwined with the overall state-building process and the political trajectory of the country. A dysfunctional state with fragmented polity would have serious implications in terms of sustaining the motivation levels and raising the professional standards of the army and police. A rapidly withering trained force of 350,000 could severely undermine the stability of the country. Though any such scenario is ruled out in the short-term, but potential threat from Haqqani-Taliban infiltration and rise in subversive activities remain.

However, compared to other institutions, the Afghan Army despite continuing logistical deficiencies and socio-political challenges is said to be doing relatively well. If the army is able to survive the turbulence and uncertainties of the Afghan transition, it could play a significant role in building trust and confidence among the people of the country. However, in the immediate term, the biggest challenge before the army would be to hold itself together in the face of continuing political uncertainty, social polarisation and donor fatigue. There is already a view that the strength of the ANSF may have to be downsized depending on the level of Western assistance after 2014. There could be a situation where Kabul and its partners might have to make a strategic choice: whether the emphasis has to be on quality soldiering, on developing a comparatively sustainable and a highly professional force, or developing an ethnically balanced and a large force by simply adding numbers to it.

(v) Resilience of the Taliban

Surviving the Western invasion

The emergence of the Taliban movement with full backing from the Pakistani establishment in the mid-1990s had a strong Islamist and Pashtun derivative to it. They challenged the dominance of old Afghan Islamist groups which too had earlier been patronised by Pakistan and after the Soviet retreat had led the country towards a destructive civil war. The minority ethnic factions responded to the rapidly expanding Taliban influence by forming a loose alliance against it in the late 1990s.

Being new and relatively well organised, the establishment of a predominantly Sunni Pashtun Taliban regime was viewed as the return of a centralised Pashtun rule over Kabul, and an effective counterforce to the corrupted Pashtun commanders and the powerful Tajik militia from the north. However, the US invasion of Afghanistan after 9/11 proved to be yet another turning point in the Afghan civil war. It led to the ousting of the Taliban from power, re-establishment of Tajik dominance in Kabul, re-emergence of factional politics, and the return of the West to Afghanistan. Taliban soon re-emerged on the political landscape of Afghanistan and began challenging the West-sponsored political process. From a 'ragtag' force, they soon evolved into a strong guerrilla force for the Western military to reckon with. Today, Taliban along with their Pakistani patrons are central to the discourse on the Pakistan-Afghanistan region as the Western forces continue to drawdown.

Though not regarded as a monolith, Taliban have so far stood unified, defying all attempts to engineer defections within its rank-and-file. Kabul's effort for reconciliation with the Taliban leadership as the West prepares to drawdown its troops, however, is likely to assume an altogether different dimension after the new government is formed in Kabul in 2014. As of now, Taliban as a movement is most unlikely to come to power though it will strive hard to strengthen its control over key highways and cities in the south and east of the country to keep up the pressure on Kabul in the years to come. At the same time, a turf war among the Taliban commanders and groups within the Quetta Shura is likely to grow and could lead to splintering of the group in the longer run in view of possible differences over matters of political strategy as the Western forces drawdown. Meanwhile, the Pakistan Army would like to consolidate its hold over the tribal frontiers in anticipation of a post-West scenario. One would have to wait and see how the new political coalition in Kabul responds to the old dynamics of the Pakistan-Afghanistan tribal frontier.

NOTES

1. "The International Afghanistan Conference in Bonn. Conference Conclusions," *German Federal Foreign Office*, December 05, 2011, at http://www.auswaertiges-amt.de/cae/servlet/contentblob/603686/publicationFile/162762/Conference_Conclusions_-_International_Afghanistan_Conference_Bonn_2011_engl.pdf. For the author's analysis, see Vishal Chandra, "The Bonn II Conference on Afghanistan: A Step Forward Amidst Uncertainty," *IDSA Comment*, December 19, 2011, at http://www.idsa.in/idsacomments/TheBonnIIConferenceonAfghanistan_vchandra_191211

APPENDICES

Appendix I

Agreement on Provisional Arrangements in Afghanistan Pending the Re-establishment of Permanent Government Institutions

The participants in the UN Talks on Afghanistan,

In the presence of the Special Representative of the Secretary-General for Afghanistan,

Determined to end the tragic conflict in Afghanistan and promote national reconciliation, lasting peace, stability and respect for human rights in the country,

Reaffirming the independence, national sovereignty and territorial integrity of Afghanistan,

Acknowledging the right of the people of Afghanistan to freely determine their own political future in accordance with the principles of Islam, democracy, pluralism and social justice,

Expressing their appreciation to the Afghan mujahidin who, over the years, have defended the independence, territorial integrity and national unity of the country and have played a major role in the struggle against terrorism and oppression, and whose sacrifice has now made them both heroes of jihad and champions of peace, stability and reconstruction of their beloved homeland, Afghanistan,

Aware that the unstable situation in Afghanistan requires the implementation of emergency interim arrangements and expressing their deep appreciation to His Excellency Professor Burhanuddin Rabbani for his readiness to transfer power to an interim authority which is to be established pursuant to this agreement,

Recognizing the need to ensure broad representation in these interim arrangements of all segments of the Afghan population, including groups that have not been adequately represented at the UN Talks on Afghanistan,

Noting that these interim arrangements are intended as a first step toward the establishment of a broad-based, gender-sensitive, multi-ethnic and fully representative government, and are not intended to remain in place beyond the specified period of time,

Recognizing that some time may be required for a new Afghan security force to be fully constituted and functional and that therefore other security provisions detailed in Annex I to this agreement must meanwhile be put in place,

Considering that the United Nations, as the internationally recognized impartial institution, has a particularly important role to play, detailed in Annex II to this agreement, in the period prior to the establishment of permanent institutions in Afghanistan,

Have agreed as follows:

The Interim Authority

I. General Provisions

1) An Interim Authority shall be established upon the official transfer of power on 22 December 2001.
2) The Interim Authority shall consist of an Interim Administration presided over by a Chairman, a Special Independent Commission for the Convening of the Emergency Loya Jirga, and a Supreme Court of Afghanistan, as well as such other courts as may be established by the Interim Administration. The composition, functions and governing procedures for the Interim Administration and the Special Independent Commission are set forth in this agreement.
3) Upon the official transfer of power, the Interim Authority shall be the repository of Afghan sovereignty, with immediate effect. As such, it shall, throughout the interim period, represent Afghanistan in its external relations and shall occupy the seat of Afghanistan at the United Nations and in its specialized agencies, as well as in other international institutions and conferences.
4) An Emergency Loya Jirga shall be convened within six months of the establishment of the Interim Authority. The Emergency Loya Jirga will be opened by His Majesty Mohammed Zaher, the former King of Afghanistan. The Emergency Loya Jirga shall decide on a Transitional Authority, including a broad-based transitional administration, to lead Afghanistan until such time as a fully representative government can be elected through free and fair elections to be held no later than two years from the date of the convening of the Emergency Loya Jirga.

5) The Interim Authority shall cease to exist once the Transitional Authority has been established by the Emergency Loya Jirga.
6) A Constitutional Loya Jirga shall be convened within eighteen months of the establishment of the Transitional Authority, in order to adopt a new constitution for Afghanistan. In order to assist the Constitutional Loya Jirga prepare the proposed Constitution, the Transitional Administration shall, within two months of its commencement and with the assistance of the United Nations, establish a Constitutional Commission.

II. Legal Framework and Judicial System

1) The following legal framework shall be applicable on an interim basis until the adoption of the new Constitution referred to above:
   i) the Constitution of 1964, a/ to the extent that its provisions are not inconsistent with those contained in this agreement, and b/ with the exception of those provisions relating to the monarchy and to the executive and legislative bodies provided in the Constitution; and
   ii) existing laws and regulations, to the extent that they are not inconsistent with this agreement or with international legal obligations to which Afghanistan is a party, or with those applicable provisions contained in the Constitution of 1964, provided that the Interim Authority shall have the power to repeal or amend those laws and regulations.
2) The judicial power of Afghanistan shall be independent and shall be vested in a Supreme Court of Afghanistan, and such other courts as may be established by the Interim Administration. The Interim Administration shall establish, with the assistance of the United Nations, a Judicial Commission to rebuild the domestic justice system in accordance with Islamic principles, international standards, the rule of law and Afghan legal traditions.

III. Interim Administration

A. Composition

1) The Interim Administration shall be composed of a Chairman, five Vice Chairmen and 24 other members. Each member, except the Chairman, may head a department of the Interim Administration.
2) The participants in the UN Talks on Afghanistan have invited His Majesty Mohammed Zaher, the former King of Afghanistan, to chair the Interim Administration. His Majesty has indicated that he would prefer that a suitable candidate acceptable to the participants be selected as the Chair of the Interim Administration.
3) The Chairman, the Vice Chairmen and other members of the Interim Administration have been selected by the participants in the UN Talks on Afghanistan, as listed in Annex IV to this agreement. The selection has been

made on the basis of professional competence and personal integrity from lists submitted by the participants in the UN Talks, with due regard to the ethnic, geographic and religious composition of Afghanistan and to the importance of the participation of women.

4) No person serving as a member of the Interim Administration may simultaneously hold membership of the Special Independent Commission for the Convening of the Emergency Loya Jirga.

B. Procedures

1) The Chairman of the Interim Administration, or in his/her absence one of the Vice Chairmen, shall call and chair meetings and propose the agenda for these meetings.
2) The Interim Administration shall endeavour to reach its decisions by consensus. In order for any decision to be taken, at least 22 members must be in attendance. If a vote becomes necessary, decisions shall be taken by a majority of the members present and voting, unless otherwise stipulated in this agreement. The Chairman shall cast the deciding vote in the event that the members are divided equally.

C. Functions

1) The Interim Administration shall be entrusted with the day-to-day conduct of the affairs of state, and shall have the right to issue decrees for the peace, order and good government of Afghanistan.
2) The Chairman of the Interim Administration or, in his/her absence, one of the Vice Chairmen, shall represent the Interim Administration as appropriate.
3) Those members responsible for the administration of individual departments shall also be responsible for implementing the policies of the Interim Administration within their areas of responsibility.
4) Upon the official transfer of power, the Interim Administration shall have full jurisdiction over the printing and delivery of the national currency and special drawing rights from international financial institutions. The Interim Administration shall establish, with the assistance of the United Nations, a Central Bank of Afghanistan that will regulate the money supply of the country through transparent and accountable procedures.
5) The Interim Administration shall establish, with the assistance of the United Nations, an independent Civil Service Commission to provide the Interim Authority and the future Transitional Authority with shortlists of candidates for key posts in the administrative departments, as well as those of governors and uluswals, in order to ensure their competence and integrity.
6) The Interim Administration shall, with the assistance of the United Nations, establish an independent Human Rights Commission, whose responsibilities

will include human rights monitoring, investigation of violations of human rights, and development of domestic human rights institutions. The Interim Administration may, with the assistance of the United Nations, also establish any other commissions to review matters not covered in this agreement.

7) The members of the Interim Administration shall abide by a Code of Conduct elaborated in accordance with international standards.
8) Failure by a member of the Interim Administration to abide by the provisions of the Code of Conduct shall lead to his/her suspension from that body. The decision to suspend a member shall be taken by a two-thirds majority of the membership of the Interim Administration on the proposal of its Chairman or any of its Vice Chairmen.
9) The functions and powers of members of the Interim Administration will be further elaborated, as appropriate, with the assistance of the United Nations.

IV. The Special Independent Commission for the Convening of the Emergency Loya Jirga

1) The Special Independent Commission for the Convening of the Emergency Loya Jirga shall be established within one month of the establishment of the Interim Authority. The Special Independent Commission will consist of twenty-one members, a number of whom should have expertise in constitutional or customary law. The members will be selected from lists of candidates submitted by participants in the UN Talks on Afghanistan as well as Afghan professional and civil society groups. The United Nations will assist with the establishment and functioning of the commission and of a substantial secretariat.
2) The Special Independent Commission will have the final authority for determining the procedures for and the number of people who will participate in the Emergency Loya Jirga. The Special Independent Commission will draft rules and procedures specifying (i) criteria for allocation of seats to the settled and nomadic population residing in the country; (ii) criteria for allocation of seats to the Afghan refugees living in Iran, Pakistan, and elsewhere, and Afghans from the diaspora; (iii) criteria for inclusion of civil society organizations and prominent individuals, including Islamic scholars, intellectuals, and traders, both within the country and in the diaspora. The Special Independent Commission will ensure that due attention is paid to the representation in the Emergency Loya Jirga of a significant number of women as well as all other segments of the Afghan population.
3) The Special Independent Commission will publish and disseminate the rules and procedures for the convening of the Emergency Loya Jirga at least ten

weeks before the Emergency Loya Jirga convenes, together with the date for its commencement and its suggested location and duration.

4) The Special Independent Commission will adopt and implement procedures for monitoring the process of nomination of individuals to the Emergency Loya Jirga to ensure that the process of indirect election or selection is transparent and fair. To pre-empt conflict over nominations, the Special Independent Commission will specify mechanisms for filing of grievances and rules for arbitration of disputes.
5) The Emergency Loya Jirga will elect a Head of the State for the Transitional Administration and will approve proposals for the structure and key personnel of the Transitional Administration.

V. Final Provisions

1) Upon the official transfer of power, all mujahidin, Afghan armed forces and armed groups in the country shall come under the command and control of the Interim Authority, and be reorganized according to the requirements of the new Afghan security and armed forces.
2) The Interim Authority and the Emergency Loya Jirga shall act in accordance with basic principles and provisions contained in international instruments on human rights and international humanitarian law to which Afghanistan is a party.
3) The Interim Authority shall cooperate with the international community in the fight against terrorism, drugs and organized crime. It shall commit itself to respect international law and maintain peaceful and friendly relations with neighbouring countries and the rest of the international community.
4) The Interim Authority and the Special Independent Commission for the Convening of the Emergency Loya Jirga will ensure the participation of women as well as the equitable representation of all ethnic and religious communities in the Interim Administration and the Emergency Loya Jirga.
5) All actions taken by the Interim Authority shall be consistent with Security Council resolution 1378 (14 November 2001) and other relevant Security Council resolutions relating to Afghanistan.
6) Rules of procedure for the organs established under the Interim Authority will be elaborated as appropriate with the assistance of the United Nations.

This agreement, of which the annexes constitute an integral part, done in Bonn on this 5th day of December 2001 in the English language, shall be the authentic text, in a single copy which shall remain deposited in the archives of the United Nations. Official texts shall be provided in Dari and Pashto, and such other languages as the Special Representative of the Secretary-General may designate. The Special Representative of the Secretary-General shall send certified copies in English, Dari and Pashto to each of the participants.

For the Participants in the UN Talks on Afghanistan:
Ms. Amena Afzali
Mr. S. Hussain Anwari
Mr. Hedayat Amin Arsala
Mr. Sayed Hamed Gailani
Mr. Rahmatullah Mousa Ghazi
Eng. Abdul Hakim
Mr. Houmayoun Jareer
Mr. Abbas Karimi
Mr. Mustafa Kazimi
Dr. Azizullah Ludin
Mr. Ahmad Wali Massoud
Mr. Hafizullah Asif Mohseni
Prof. Mohammad Ishaq Nadiri
Mr. Mohammad Natiqi
Mr. Aref Noorzay
Mr. Yunus Qanooni
Dr. Zalmai Rassoul
Mr. H. Mirwais Sadeq
Dr. Mohammad Jalil Shams
Prof. Abdul Sattar Sirat
Mr. Humayun Tandar
Mrs. Sima Wali
General Abdul Rahim Wardak
Mr. Azizullah Wasefi
Mr. Pacha Khan Zadran

Witnessed for the United Nations by:
Mr. Lakhdar Brahimi
Special Representative of the Secretary-General for Afghanistan

ANNEX I
INTERNATIONAL SECURITY FORCE

1. The participants in the UN Talks on Afghanistan recognize that the responsibility for providing security and law and order throughout the country resides with the Afghans themselves. To this end, they pledge their commitment to do all within their means and influence to ensure such security, including for all United Nations and other personnel of international governmental and non-governmental organizations deployed in Afghanistan.

2. With this objective in mind, the participants request the assistance of the international community in helping the new Afghan authorities in the establishment and training of new Afghan security and armed forces.
3. Conscious that some time may be required for the new Afghan security and armed forces to be fully constituted and functioning, the participants in the UN Talks on Afghanistan request the United Nations Security Council to consider authorizing the early deployment to Afghanistan of a United Nations mandated force. This force will assist in the maintenance of security for Kabul and its surrounding areas. Such a force could, as appropriate, be progressively expanded to other urban centres and other areas.
4. The participants in the UN Talks on Afghanistan pledge to withdraw all military units from Kabul and other urban centers or other areas in which the UN mandated force is deployed. It would also be desirable if such a force were to assist in the rehabilitation of Afghanistan's infrastructure.

* * *

ANNEX II
ROLE OF THE UNITED NATIONS DURING THE INTERIM PERIOD

1. The Special Representative of the Secretary-General will be responsible for all aspects of the United Nations' work in Afghanistan.
2. The Special Representative shall monitor and assist in the implementation of all aspects of this agreement.
3. The United Nations shall advise the Interim Authority in establishing a politically neutral environment conducive to the holding of the Emergency Loya Jirga in free and fair conditions. The United Nations shall pay special attention to the conduct of those bodies and administrative departments which could directly influence the convening and outcome of the Emergency Loya Jirga.
4. The Special Representative of the Secretary-General or his/her delegate may be invited to attend the meetings of the Interim Administration and the Special Independent Commission on the Convening of the Emergency Loya Jirga.
5. If for whatever reason the Interim Administration or the Special Independent Commission were actively prevented from meeting or unable to reach a decision on a matter related to the convening of the Emergency Loya Jirga, the Special Representative of the Secretary-General shall, taking into account the views expressed in the Interim Administration or in the Special Independent Commission, use his/her good offices with a view to facilitating a resolution to the impasse or a decision.

6. The United Nations shall have the right to investigate human rights violations and, where necessary, recommend corrective action. It will also be responsible for the development and implementation of a programme of human rights education to promote respect for and understanding of human rights.

* * *

ANNEX III
REQUEST TO THE UNITED NATIONS BY THE PARTICIPANTS AT THE UN TALKS ON AFGHANISTAN

The participants in the UN Talks on Afghanistan hereby—

1. Request that the United Nations and the international community take the necessary measures to guarantee the national sovereignty, territorial integrity and unity of Afghanistan as well as the non-interference by foreign countries in Afghanistan's internal affairs;
2. Urge the United Nations, the international community, particularly donor countries and multilateral institutions, to reaffirm, strengthen and implement their commitment to assist with the rehabilitation, recovery and reconstruction of Afghanistan, in coordination with the Interim Authority;
3. Request the United Nations to conduct as soon as possible (i) a registration of voters in advance of the general elections that will be held upon the adoption of the new constitution by the constitutional Loya Jirga and (ii) a census of the population of Afghanistan.
4. Urge the United Nations and the international community, in recognition of the heroic role played by the mujahidin in protecting the independence of Afghanistan and the dignity of its people, to take the necessary measures, in coordination with the Interim Authority, to assist in the reintegration of the mujahidin into the new Afghan security and armed forces;
5. Invite the United Nations and the international community to create a fund to assist the families and other dependents of martyrs and victims of the war, as well as the war disabled;
6. Strongly urge that the United Nations, the international community and regional organizations cooperate with the Interim Authority to combat international terrorism, cultivation and trafficking of illicit drugs and provide Afghan farmers with financial, material and technical resources for alternative crop production.

* * *

ANNEX IV
COMPOSITION OF THE INTERIM ADMINISTRATION

Chairman: Mr. Hamid Karzai

Membership (of whom 5 will be Vice-Chairs)
Department of Defence:
Department of Finance:
Department of Foreign Affairs:
Department of the Interior:
Department of Planning:
Department of Commerce:
Department of Mines & Industries:
Department of Small Industries:
Department of Information & Culture:
Department of Communication:
Department of Labour & Social Affairs:
Department of Hajj & Auqaf:
Department of Martyrs & Disabled:
Department of Education:
Department of Higher Education:
Department of Public Health:
Department of Public Works:
Department of Rural Development:
Department of Urban Development:
Department of Reconstruction:
Department of Transport:
Department of Water and Electricity:
Department for the Return of Refugees:
Department of Agriculture:
Department of Irrigation:
Department of Justice:
Department of Air Transport & Tourism:
Department of Border Affairs:
Department of Women's Affairs

* * *

Source: http://www.un.org/News/dh/latest/afghan/afghan-agree.htm

Appendix II

North Waziristan Peace Pact

Here is the text of the September 2006 deal between the Pakistani government and local tribesmen in North Waziristan. The Pakistani Army agreed to dismantle checkpoints it had set up recently inside North Waziristan, release tribesmen it had arrested and return weapons it had confiscated. The army will keep some checkpoints on the border and retain the majority of its forces in the barracks. In return, the tribesmen agreed to stop attacking the military and cease cross-border infiltration into Afghanistan. Critics paint the agreement as a victory for Al Qaeda and the Taliban because it grants militants a safe haven from which to launch more cross-border attacks.

Peace Pact North Waziristan

Participant One: Political Agent North Waziristan representing Governor N.W.F.P Federal Government.
Participant Two: Tribal Representatives North Waziristan, Local Mujahideen N.W.F.P, Atmanzai Tribe

---

According to this pact, the participants will agree to the following conditions.

Students Scholars Atmanzai Tribes

Participant Two meaning Tribal Representatives of North Waziristan and Local Mujahideen Students and Scholars of Atmanzai will make it sure that—

1. Law Enforcement Agencies, installations and officers will not be attacked and there will be no Targeted Killing whatsoever.

2. There will be no Balanced Administration. Pakistan Government will be the working body. Political Administration will be contacted for resolving issues. Administration will resolve issues according to the laws implemented by Atmanzai Tribes and FCR.
3. There will be no cross border infiltration into the neighboring country Afghanistan for any type of Armed Activity. However, there will be no restriction on traveling according to the rules and regulations for the purpose of Business, Trade and meeting relatives.
4. There will be no incursions into districts adjacent to North Waziristan. Nor will there be a common government.
5. All foreigners would go outside of North Waziristan Agency. If any one who is not in a position, will be allowed to stay away in the area on surety or guarantee of the local tribesmen. Such type of foreigners would remain with peace and would honour all clauses of the agreement.
6. During the fights, whatever Government [illegible] in the form of weapons and wireless came into the hands of Participant two will be returned to the government.

Government

1. Every person arrested during the operation will be released. They will not be arrested again for what they have done in the past.
2. Government will lift all the public sanctions.
3. Government will remove all the new check posts from the roads and on the old check posts, soldiers and levis will be stationed just like in the past.
4. Government will return the vehicles and other stuff confiscated during the operation.
5. After the pact, government will continue the ground and air operation according to normal routine.
6. For the recovery of those who were innocently killed during the operation and as a compensation for the property that was damaged during the operation, government will provide grants.
7. There is no ban on (use of) weapons according to the Tribal Traditions and there is no ban (on weapons) from the government either; but the ban on large weapons will continue.
8. The implementation of pact will start with the removal of Army check posts.

All Sides

1. According to this pact, a 10-member committee will be formed with mutual consultation. In this committee, scholars, elders and representatives of political administration will perform the following duties;
   a. Constant communication between the government and Atmanzai tribes.

b. To review and ensure implementation of the pact

2. If a person or a group (local or foreigner) will not follow the peace pact and will try to sabotage peace in Waziristan, then action will be taken against him.

Source: http://www.pbs.org/wgbh/pages/frontline/taliban/etc/nwdeal.html (accessed October 05, 2006)

Appendix III

White Paper of the Interagency Policy Group's Report on U.S. Policy Toward Afghanistan and Pakistan

Published: March 27, 2009

The United States has a vital national security interest in addressing the current and potential security threats posed by extremists in Afghanistan and Pakistan. In Pakistan, al Qaeda and other groups of jihadist terrorists are planning new terror attacks. Their targets remain the U.S. homeland, Pakistan, Afghanistan, India, Europe, Australia, our allies in the Middle East, and other targets of opportunity. The growing size of the space in which they are operating is a direct result of the terrorist/insurgent activities of the Taliban and related organizations. At the same time, this group seeks to reestablish their old sanctuaries in Afghanistan.

Therefore, the core goal of the U.S. must be to disrupt, dismantle, and defeat al Qaeda and its safe havens in Pakistan, and to prevent their return to Pakistan or Afghanistan.

The ability of extremists in Pakistan to undermine Afghanistan is proven, while insurgency in Afghanistan feeds instability in Pakistan. The threat that al Qaeda poses to the United States and our allies in Pakistan—including the possibility of extremists obtaining fissile material—is all too real. Without more effective action against these groups in Pakistan, Afghanistan will face continuing instability.

Objectives

Achieving our core goal is vital to U.S. national security. It requires, first of all, realistic and achievable objectives. These include:

- Disrupting terrorist networks in Afghanistan and especially Pakistan to degrade any ability they have to plan and launch international terrorist attacks.
- Promoting a more capable, accountable, and effective government in Afghanistan that serves the Afghan people and can eventually function, especially regarding internal security, with limited international support.
- Developing increasingly self-reliant Afghan security forces that can lead the counterinsurgency and counterterrorism fight with reduced U.S. assistance.
- Assisting efforts to enhance civilian control and stable constitutional government in Pakistan and a vibrant economy that provides opportunity for the people of Pakistan.
- Involving the international community to actively assist in addressing these objectives for Afghanistan and Pakistan, with an important leadership role for the UN.

A New Way Forward

These are daunting tasks. They require a new way of thinking about the challenges, a wide ranging diplomatic strategy to build support for our efforts, enhanced engagement with the publics in the region and at home, and a realization that all elements of international power –diplomatic, informational, military and economic—must be brought to bear. They will also require a significant change in the management, resources, and focus of our foreign assistance.

Our diplomatic effort should be based on building a clear consensus behind the common core goal and supporting objectives. To this end, we will explore creating new diplomatic mechanisms, including establishing a "Contact Group" and a regional security and economic cooperation forum. The trilateral U.S.-Pakistan-Afghanistan effort of February 24-26, 2009 will be continued and broadened, into the next meeting planned for early May, in Washington.

The United States must overcome the 'trust deficit' it faces in Afghanistan and Pakistan, where many believe that we are not a reliable long-term partner. We must engage the Afghan people in ways that demonstrate our commitment to promoting a legitimate and capable Afghan government with economic progress. We must engage the Pakistani people based on our long-term commitment to helping them build a stable economy, a stronger democracy, and a vibrant civil society.

A strategic communications program must be created, made more effective, and resourced. This new strategy will have no chance of success without better civil-military coordination by U.S. agencies, a significant increase of civilian resources, and a new model of how we allocate and use these resources. For too long, U.S. and international assistance efforts in Afghanistan and Pakistan have suffered from being ill-organized and significantly under-resourced in some areas. A large portion of development assistance ends up being spent on international consultants and overhead, and virtually no impact assessments have yet been done on our assistance programs.

We must ensure that our assistance to both Afghanistan and Pakistan is aligned with our core goals and objectives. This will involve assistance that is geared to strengthening government capacity and the message that assistance will be limited without the achievement of results.

Additional assistance to Afghanistan must be accompanied by concrete mechanisms to ensure greater government accountability. In a country that is 70 percent rural, and where the Taliban recruiting base is primarily among under-employed youths, a complete overhaul of our civilian assistance strategy is necessary; agricultural sector job creation is an essential first step to undercutting the appeal of al Qaeda and its allies. Increased assistance to Pakistan will be limited without a greater willingness to cooperate with us to eliminate the sanctuary enjoyed by al Qaeda and other extremist groups, as well as a greater commitment to economic reforms that will raise the living standard of ordinary Pakistanis, including in the border regions of the Federally Administered Tribal Areas, the North West Frontier Province, and Baluchistan.

Summary of Recommendations for Afghanistan and Pakistan

The following steps must be done in concert to produce the desired end state: the removal of al-Qaeda's sanctuary, effective democratic government control in Pakistan, and a self-reliant Afghanistan that will enable a withdrawal of combat forces while sustaining our commitment to political and economic development.

- ***Executing and resourcing an integrated civilian-military counterinsurgency strategy in Afghanistan***

Our military forces in Afghanistan, including those recently approved by the President, should be utilized for two priority missions: 1) securing Afghanistan's south and east against a return of al Qaeda and its allies, to provide a space for the Afghani government to establish effective government control and 2) providing the Afghan security forces with the mentoring needed to expand rapidly, take the lead in effective counterinsurgency operations, and allow us and our partners to wind down our combat operations.

Our counter-insurgency strategy must integrate population security with building effective local governance and economic development. We will establish the security needed to provide space and time for stabilization and reconstruction activities.

To prevent future attacks on the U.S. and its allies—including the local populace—the development of a strategic communications strategy to counter the terror information campaign is urgent. This has proved successful in Iraq (where the U.S. military has made a significant effort in this area) and should be developed in Afghanistan as a top priority to improve the image of the United States and its allies. The strategic communications plan—including electronic media, telecom, and radio—shall include options on how best to counter the propaganda that is key to the enemy's terror campaign.

- ***Resourcing and prioritizing civilian assistance in Afghanistan***

By increasing civilian capacity we will strengthen the relationship between the Afghan people and their government. A dramatic increase in Afghan civilian expertise is needed to facilitate the development of systems and institutions particularly at the provincial and local levels, provide basic infrastructure, and create economic alternatives to the insurgency at all levels of Afghan society, particularly in agriculture. The United States should play an important part in providing that expertise, but responding effectively to Afghanistan's needs will require that allies, partners, the UN and other international organizations, and non-governmental organizations significantly increase their involvement in Afghanistan.

- ***Expanding the Afghan National Security Forces: Army and Police***

To be capable of assuming the security mission from U.S. forces in Afghanistan's south and east, the Afghan National Security Forces must substantially increase its size and capability. Initially this will require a more rapid build-up of the Afghan Army and police up to 134,000 and 82,000 over the next two years, with additional enlargements as circumstances and resources warrant.

The international community must assume responsibility for funding this significantly enhanced Afghan security force for an extended period. We will also have to provide support for other Afghan security forces such as the Afghan Public Protection Force. Salaries paid to Afghan National Army and Afghan National Police must become more competitive with those paid by the insurgents.

Over time, as security conditions change, we should continue to reassess Afghan National Security Forces size, as it will be affected by such factors as: the overall security situation, the capabilities of the Afghan National Security Forces, and the rate at which we can grow local security forces and integrate them into the overall ANSF structure.

• ***Engaging the Afghan government and bolstering its legitimacy***

International support for the election will be necessary for a successful outcome. We should do everything necessary to ensure the security and legitimacy of voter registration, elections, and vote counting. The international military presence should help the Afghan security forces provide security before, during and after the election. International monitoring will also be required to ensure legitimacy and oversee Afghanistan's polling sites.

The overall legitimacy of the Afghan government is also undermined by rampant corruption and a failure to provide basic services to much of the population over the past 7 years. Where Afghan systems and institutions have benefited from high quality technical assistance and mentoring, they have made great progress. Making such support more consistent with qualified mentors to advise and monitor officials, pushing such efforts to the provincial and district levels, and channeling more assistance through Afghan institutions benefiting from this high quality support will help restore and maintain the legitimacy of the Afghan government.

• ***Encouraging Afghan government efforts to integrate reconcilable insurgents***

While Mullah Omar and the Taliban's hard core that have aligned themselves with al Qaeda are not reconcilable and we cannot make a deal that includes them, the war in Afghanistan cannot be won without convincing non-ideologically committed insurgents to lay down their arms, reject al Qaeda, and accept the Afghan Constitution.

Practical integration must not become a mechanism for instituting medieval social policies that give up the quest for gender equality and human rights. We can help this process along by exploiting differences among the insurgents to divide the Taliban's true believers from less committed fighters.

Integration must be Afghan-led. An office should be created in every province and we should support efforts by the Independent Directorate of Local Governance to develop a reconciliation effort targeting mid-to-low level insurgents to be led by provincial governors. We should also explore ways to rehabilitate captured insurgents drawing on lessons learned from similar programs in Iraq and other countries.

• ***Including provincial and local governments in our capacity building efforts***

We need to work with the Afghan government to refocus civilian assistance and capacity-building programs on building up competent provincial and local governments where they can more directly serve the people and connect them to their government.

- ***Breaking the link between narcotics and the insurgency***

Besides the global consequences of the drug trade, the Afghan narcotics problem causes great concern due to its ties to the insurgency, the fact that it is the major driver of corruption in Afghanistan, and distorts the legal economy. The NATO/ International Security Assistance Forces and U.S. forces should use their authorities to directly support Afghan counternarcotics units during the interdiction of narco-traffickers. The new authorities permit the destruction of labs, drug storage facilities, drug processing equipment, and drug caches and should contribute to breaking the drug-insurgency funding nexus and the corruption associated with the opium/heroin trade. Crop substitution and alternative livelihood programs that are a key pillar of effectively countering narcotics have been disastrously underdeveloped and under-resourced, however, and the narcotics trade will persist until such programs allow Afghans to reclaim their land for licit agriculture. Targeting those who grow the poppy will continue, but the focus will shift to higher level drug lords.

- ***Mobilizing greater international political support of our objectives in Afghanistan***

We need to do more to build a shared understanding of what is at stake in Afghanistan, while engaging other actors and offering them the opportunity to advance our mutual interests by cooperating with us.

- ***Bolstering Afghanistan-Pakistan cooperation***

We need to institutionalize stronger mechanisms for bilateral and trilateral cooperation. During the process of this review, inter-agency teams from Afghanistan and Pakistan came to Washington, DC for trilateral meetings. This new forum should continue and serve as the basis for enhanced bilateral and trilateral cooperation.

- ***Engaging and focusing Islamabad on the common threat***

Successfully shutting down the Pakistani safe haven for extremists will also require consistent and intensive strategic engagement with Pakistani leadership in both the civilian and military spheres. The engagement must be conducted in a way that respects, and indeed enhances, democratic civilian authority.

- ***Assisting Pakistan's capability to fight extremists***

It is vital to strengthen our efforts to both develop and operationally enable Pakistani security forces so they are capable of succeeding in sustained counterterrorism and counterinsurgency operations. In part this will include increased U.S. military assistance for helicopters to provide air mobility, night vision equipment, and training and equipment specifically for Pakistani Special Operation Forces and their Frontier Corps.

- ***Increasing and broadening assistance in Pakistan***

Increasing economic assistance to Pakistan—to include direct budget support, development assistance, infrastructure investment, and technical advice on making sound economic policy adjustments—and strengthening trade relations will maximize support for our policy aims; it should also help to provide longer-term economic stability. Our assistance should focus on long-term capacity building, on agricultural sector job creation, education and training, and on infrastructure requirements. Assistance should also support Pakistani efforts to 'hold and build' in western Pakistan as a part of its counterinsurgency efforts.

- ***Exploring other areas of economic cooperation with Pakistan***

We need to enhance bilateral and regional trade possibilities, in part through implementing Reconstruction Opportunity Zones (which were recently re-introduced in Congress) and encouraging foreign investment in key sectors, such as energy. In addition, assisting Islamabad with developing a concrete strategy for utilizing donor aid would increase Islamabad's chances for garnering additional support from the international community.

- ***Strengthening Pakistani government capacity***

Strengthening the civilian, democratic government must be a centerpiece of our overall effort. Key efforts should include fostering the reform of provincial and local governance in the Federally Administered Tribal Areas and the North West Frontier Province. We need to help Islamabad enhance the services and support in areas cleared of insurgents so that they have a real chance in preventing insurgents from returning to those areas.

With international partners, we should also promote the development of regional organizations that focus on economic and security cooperation, as well as fostering productive political dialogue.

- ***Asking for assistance from allies for Afghanistan and Pakistan***

Our efforts are a struggle against forces that pose a direct threat to the entire international community. While reaching out to allies and partners for their political support, we should also ask them to provide the necessary resources to accomplish our shared objectives. They have the same interest in denying terrorists and extremists sanctuaries in Pakistan and Afghanistan that we do. In approaching allies we should emphasize that our new approach is integrated between civilian and military elements and in looking at Afghanistan and Pakistan as one theater for diplomacy.

For the mission in Afghanistan, we should continue to seek contributions for combat forces, trainers and mentors, strategic lift, and equipment from our friends and allies. The U.S. will also pursue major international funding and experts for civilian reconstruction and Afghan government capacity building at the national and especially the provincial and local levels.

The United Nations Assistance Mission in Afghanistan should take the lead in exploring ways that donors could systematically share the burden of building Afghan capacity and providing civilian expertise. As part of its coordination role for civilian assistance, the UN should consolidate requests and identify gaps.

In Pakistan, the U.S. will urge allies to work closely with us both bilaterally and through the 'Friends of Democratic Pakistan' to coordinate economic and development assistance, including additional direct budget support, development assistance, infrastructure investment and technical advice on making sound economic policy adjustments. Similarly, we should ask them to provide technical advice and assistance in strengthening government capacity, such as improving Pakistani institutions.

Conclusion

There are no quick fixes to achieve U.S. national security interests in Afghanistan and Pakistan. The danger of failure is real and the implications are grave. In 2009-2010 the Taliban's momentum must be reversed in Afghanistan and the international community must work with Pakistan to disrupt the threats to security along Pakistan's western border.

This new strategy of focusing on our core goal—to disrupt, dismantle, and eventually destroy extremists and their safe havens within both nations, although with different tactics—will require immediate action, sustained commitment, and substantial resources. The United States is committed to working with our partners in the region and the international community to address this challenging but essential security goal.

Source: http://www.nytimes.com/2009/03/27/us/politics/27text-whitepaper.html?_r=1&ref=politics&pagewanted=all (accessed March 28, 2009)

Appendix IV

Status of ANAAC (as of April 2010)

Personnel: 3000
Total aircraft: 46

Rotary wing aircraft:
22 × MI-17v5 transport
3 × MI-17DV VIP transport
9 × MI-35 attack
3 × C-27
5 × AN-32
1 × AN-26
3 × L-39

Operations for 2008: 6,754 sorties; 469,706 kilograms of cargo; 80,653 passengers.
End state goal (by end 2015)

Capabilities: VIP transport, CASEVAC, MEDEVAC, operational airlift, tactical battlefield mobility, training, intel/surveillance/reconnaissance, light ground attack, air superiority

Personnel: 8000
Total aircrafts: 130-140

Rotary wing:
58 MI-17v5 (battlefield mobility)
3 Mi-17 (VIP transport),
6 training helicopters

Mi-35 will be replaced by armed Mi-17 by FY14

Fixed wing:
20 C-27 (18 operational airlift, 2 VIP transport configurable)
4 propeller cargo aircraft based ISR
14 propeller light attack/ISR
20 light multi role attack/air superiority jets
8 propeller basic training aircraft,
6 propeller advanced training aircraft
AN32/AN-26 will be replaced by C-27 by FY12

Total cost ~$5billion

FY2009 to FY2011 goal: 100 aircraft, 4900 airmen.

- Build English skills, focus on air-mobility, develop logistics and sustainment, build initial infrastructure, and build training capability.
- Initiate training 48 pilots per year. Sent to US for 2 years.
- Acquire 20×C27 cargo aircraft. First four arriving end 2009 and two per quarter thereafter.
- Acquire 58 Mi-17v5

FY2012 goal:

- ANAAC takes full control of all airfields, except Bagram Air Base.
- Add more training capability. Add trainer aircraft

FY2013 to FY2015 goal: 130-140 aircraft, 8000 airmen.

- Add light attack capability (single-engine turboprop with precision attack capability)
- Add intelligence, surveillance, and reconnaissance capability.
- Add attack/air sovereignty

Source: C.J. Radin, "Afghan National Army Air Corps (ANAAC)", Afghan National Security Forces Order of Battle, *The Long War Journal*, at http://www.longwarjournal.org/multimedia/ANSF%20OOBpage5-ANAC.pdf

Index